Dear Nicole,

ROAD TO RECOVERY

Ben Wardle x

SURVIVING ANOREXIA, ACCEPTING MY SEXUALITY & TRANSFORMING MY LIFE.

BEN WARDLE

CONTENTS

THE PRAYER OF ST FRANCIS OF ASSISI 4
DEDICATION 5
PREFACE 6
1. STARVING TO DEATH 9
2. HOSPITALISED AT 13 19
3. TURNING 13 IN HOSPITAL 28
4. ROAD TO RECOVERY 36
5. BACK TO SCHOOL 48
6. PROGRESS MAKES PERFECT 52
7. THE G-WORD 61
8. PRIMARY SCHOOL PROBLEMS 66
9. IGNORANCE, REPRESSION & SELF-EXPRESSION 80
10. KNOWLEDGE IS POWER 93
11. YEAR 10 100
12. PARIS, NEW PEOPLE & PASSING EXAMS 109
13. THE LGBT+ CLUB DISASTER 121
14. THE ONE WHERE I SIT MY GCSEs… 130
15. SUMMER OF 2016 137
16. SIXTH FORM: NEW SUITS AND NEW STARTS 154
17. THE UNEXAMINED LIFE IS NOT WORTH LIVING 160
18. NEW FRIENDS, NEW AMBITIONS…AND MORE EXAMS 172
19. FIVE STAR SERVICE 187
20. THE ONE WHERE I BECAME HEAD BOY 204
21. THE RESULTS ARE IN… 214
22. LONDON'S CALLING 221
23. WORK HARD, PLAY HARDER 231
24. LECTURES, READING & RUSH HOUR IN LONDON 236
25. JUST CALL ME NIGELLA? 242
26. MY LONDON LIBERATION 248

27. MEN, MESH TOPS & MENTAL HEALTH 255
28. WALKING IN A (HYDE PARK) WINTER WONDERLAND 269
29. CHRISTMAS ON CANAL STREET 275
30. NEW YEAR, NEW ME? 283
31. ONE SUMMER IN SOHO… 293
32. BACK TO REALITY IN CHESHIRE 297
33. GETTING SERIOUS ABOUT SECOND YEAR 306
34. NEW YEAR, NEW CAREER 317
35. CHRISTMAS NIGHTS ON REGENTS STREET 323
36. ONE VIRAL VIDEO LATER… 328
37. THE STUDENT PRIDE SPECTACULAR 342
38. THE ONE WHERE LONDON GOES INTO LOCKDOWN 347
39. STAY AT HOME, FILM TIKTOKS….AND WRITE A BOOK 352
40. SAYING GOODBYE TO GRANDAD 361
41. A WHOLE NEW PERSPECTIVE 367
42. THIRD TIME LUCKY IN LONDON? 371
43. ASPIRING TO INSPIRE 385
AFTERWORD 390

THE PRAYER OF ST FRANCIS OF ASSISI

Lord, make me an instrument of your peace
Where there is hatred, let me sow love
Where there is injury, pardon
Where there is doubt, faith
Where there is despair, hope
Where there is darkness, light
And where there is sadness, joy

O Divine Master, grant that I may
Not so much seek to be consoled as to console
To be understood, as to understand
To be loved, as to love
For it is in giving that we receive
And it's in pardoning that we are pardoned
And it's in dying that we are born to Eternal Life

Amen

DEDICATION

To anyone suffering in silence – I promise you that things will get better. You've got this.

To Sarah (my therapist), Dana (my online counsellor), the team at CAMHS & the Macclesfield Hospital Children's Ward Staff. Thank you for saving my life – and changing my life - all of those years ago.

To the teachers who went above and beyond. You changed my life, and I wouldn't be here today without you. In particular, thank you, Mrs G Moulsdale, Mrs A M Connor, Mrs M Garvey, Mrs K Sutton, Mrs A Williams, Mrs B Stewart, Miss R Gerrard. And thank you to my gorgeous Pam Shatwell, a true angel in this world.

To the best friends, I could have ever imagined. You have all been there for me and given me more support than you will ever realise. In particular, Becky (Queen B), Freya (the FM), Kristina (the KM), Erin, Erin, Emma, Harriet, Morgan, Shadi, Farah, Emily, Megan, Alice, Darragh, Douglas, Jamie (TikTok manager), Alyce (AK), Abby, Natalia, Leah, Carl, Maisie, Nana, Nathan, Holly, Ella (EP), Jemma, Amy, Liddy, Nicola, Tegan, Hannah & everyone so kind to me over the years…

And most importantly, the world's biggest thank you to the best people in the universe – Mum (Queen P), Dad, Sam, Granny, Grumpy, Grandma & Grandad. You are the most incredible and loving family I could have ever dreamed of being blessed with. Thank you for everything.

To you, my wonderful reader. Be proud of who you are, be kind to yourself – and make sure that you enjoy every single step of your journey. You've got this x

PREFACE

It's an Autumnal Wednesday afternoon and, for once, the sun is shining down on Cheshire. My friend Erin and I are sat in Café Nero, catching up on our lives over festive-themed drinks and an unlimited supply of caramel waffles. We chat away and watch the world go by, reminiscing about Sixth form and looking forward to Christmas. I tell Erin all about my latest dramas at university in London, and she updates me on her life at university in London. As we talk, a man comes over to our table and hands us a leaflet advertising psychic readings. 'Oh thanks!', I say, taking the leaflet and discarding it on the table. 'Oh my God', I laugh after he has left, 'do these people think we're actually going to buy into that?'

'Oh I know' says a female voice to my side, 'these people can't be trusted'. I look to my right and see a glamorous, beaming lady who has a little dog sat on her knee. 'I'm Debbie', she continues, 'and – unlike whoever he is – I am a genuine psychic'.

Erin and I look at one another. Who on earth is Debbie? Is she being serious? Where on earth has she come from? 'Sorry for interrupting your conversation', Debbie beams, 'but I just have to say that you have the brightest future ahead of you'. 'Oh, thank you', I reply, 'that's very kind of you to say!' 'No, it's the truth – I hope you don't mind, but I've been overhearing your conversation, and the way that you ask such philosophical questions, take such an interest in your friend, and really listen to what she has to say…it's a gift, it really is'.

Oh, Debbie, stop it! I'm not convinced that you're an actual psychic, but I do know that you're certainly a charmer! You're making me blush! Before Debbie can say any more nice things about me, I quickly launch into my Huw Edwards 'I've got 101 questions to interrogate you with' mode. I quiz Debbie on her life as a psychic and her beliefs about what exists beyond the spiritual world. I want to know all about her psychic skills and, as she calls them, 'gifts'. To our delight, Debbie happily chats away about her journey to 'discovering' her psychic powers. However, she, unfortunately, seems reluctant to disclose any of her secrets across the table in Macclesfield's Café Nero!

'Anyway, I must go' says Debbie, finishing her large cappuccino and putting her little dog down by her feet. 'But I must just say before I go – you really do have a gift, and you have the brightest future ahead of you…I can see it, I can sense it. But the most important thing to know and remember is this: wherever you go, and whatever you do…make sure that you enjoy the journey'.

And with that, Debbie was gone. Erin and I stare at each other in disbelief. 'How much sugar is in those caramel waffles?' I ask, genuinely concerned, 'am I having some kind of adverse reaction to caffeine and sugar right now?'

'Debbie!', exclaims Erin, 'what an absolute queen!

I have never forgotten – and I will forever remember – Debbie's wise words of advice. We don't know where Debbie came from or where she went! But I know that I will always treasure her words of wisdom:
Whatever you do and wherever you go…always remember to enjoy the journey.

The title of my story, 'Road to recovery', might potentially sound as I believe there is a destination for us all to arrive at. It might give the impression that there is an ultimate goal or location to reach. I hope that, as you read my story, you'll realise that this is not – by any stretch of the imagination – the case. It is essential to have goals, dreams, and aspirations in life. But it is vital to realise that the journey is so much more important than the destination. Life is about progress, not perfection. Every day is another opportunity to learn. Every experience that you have presents you with another chance to grow. And every moment of your life offers you another opportunity to spread love, be self-confident, and dare to live a fearlessly authentic life.

This book is the story of my journey. It begins with my hospitalisation with anorexia, aged 12, and it concludes as I start my third year at university in London. This is a story told with brutal and unfiltered honesty. I have included unedited diary entries, clinical records, and as much honesty as I possibly can. I have strived to bring you the most honest and frank account of my struggles with mental illness and sexuality. I have strived to fill every page with entertaining anecdotes and empowering lessons for life! And I have made it my mission to share with you all of the wisdom, inspiration, and life lessons that have helped me get to where I am so proud to be today.

I hope that you'll enjoy reading every page of the story. And I also hope that it might encourage you to share your own! I passionately believe that the secret to overcoming stigma is starting conversations. Every story deserves to be shared. And every truth deserves to be told.

Wherever you are up to on your journey through life, be proud of who you are. Acknowledge your accomplishments and know with confidence that you are more than capable of achieving all your dreams for the future.

Whatever you're going through, keep going. Even in the darkest of times, there is always light at the end of the tunnel. More than anything else, you deserve to live a genuinely happy and fearlessly authentic life.

And that begins with knowing your worth and striving to enjoy every single step of your journey! This is our only lifetime, so let's aspire to live every single second of it to the absolute full! Dare to put yourself out there, and dare to live your truth.

Be fearless, be confident and be proud of your journey. You are an absolute icon! You were born to live your best life. This lifetime is your chance to shine – so live your life to the absolute full! You've got this!

1. STARVING TO DEATH

How are you supposed to react when a doctor tells you that you are starving yourself to death? How are you supposed to reply when they follow this up with the question, 'is that what you want? Do you want to die?' I can sum up my response to both of these questions in one word that I think goes to the very core of battling with the eating disorder Anorexia Nervosa: denial.

It's October 2012, and I am sitting in a private room on the children's ward of Macclesfield hospital. To say I am not happy to be here would be an understatement. I am incandescent with rage that these medical 'professionals' think there is something wrong with my eating, weight and mental health. I am desperate to escape this room, which is filled with doctors, nurses, child psychiatrists and my mum. Why are they all ganging up on me like this? What have I done to deserve this kind of treatment? I am determined to get out of this room and out of this hospital. There is absolutely nothing wrong with me, and the sooner these doctors and psychologists realise this, the better. I want to go home.

Unfortunately for 12-year-old Ben, the Consultant paediatrician at the hospital has other ideas. It turns out that I will not be going anywhere anytime soon. They have received blood test results, and alarm bells are ringing. They have calculated my BMI and have discovered that something is seriously wrong. I am so underweight and dangerously ill that they have decided I will be immediately admitted to the ward. I will be placed under strict 24-hour observation and banned from leaving my bed.

My mum is in floods of tears, whilst a children's psychiatrist is reassuring her that this is the 'right... the ONLY – thing to do'. I feel angry and overwhelmed. I don't want this. This isn't fair. They can't do this to me; they can't make me stay here! As I am led away by the child play therapist, fury rushes through my veins. I need to call my dad – who is at work – and tell him what they're doing to me. But the play therapist won't let me. I have to get into my bed, she says, and order something from the hospital canteen food menu. Oh, of course, I bloody do. Here we go! I instinctively order the lowest calorie options on the menu, opting for the soup of the day and a carton of orange juice. I may only be 12 years old, but I have an encyclopaedic knowledge of calories and nutritional information. I am a professional calorie counter, and avoiding calories is my full-time job. If this play therapist thinks she's going to win this one, she's got another thing coming. I'm not giving up without a fight, I think, as I sit on this bed feeling more agitated and angry than ever before. Where is my mum? Why can't I call my dad? Why are these people doing this to me?

It turns out that there is a very good reason that 'these people' are doing this to me. On this day that I am admitted to hospital, just one week before my 13th birthday, I weighed 24kg. To put this into perspective, the average 13-year-old boy weighs 45.3kg. My blood test results are incredibly alarming, and the doctors are genuinely shocked that I've not collapsed or become seriously ill yet. The medics are very clear – if they don't intervene right now, I am going to die. They are saving my life. If they let me carry on like this, my body will not be able to cope. I am severely malnourished and dangerously underweight. My essential organs can't continue functioning. I am a ticking time-bomb and practically knocking at death's door. Perhaps most shockingly of all, I am completely and utterly in denial that there is absolutely anything wrong whatsoever.

For the past six months, I have been charging headfirst towards a catastrophic mental health crisis. Whilst the nation has been enjoying the 2012 Olympics 'summer of sport', I have been starving myself to death. Whilst families across the country enjoyed BBQs and the BBC's Olympic coverage; I have been descending into the depths of anorexia. I have been throwing away food, militantly restricting calories, and obsessively exercising at all hours of the day. Deep down, I have known that what I'm thinking and doing is entirely irrational and dangerously self-destructive. But I have been unable to do anything about it. My mind has become completely and utterly taken over by the most extreme and irrational anorexic thoughts. I cannot go for a single second without obsessing about calories, food and the size of my waistline. I am utterly obsessed with the idea of getting both my hands around my waist – I am desperate to keep losing more and more weight. I believe that all of my problems, worries and anxieties will disappear if I can just become even skinnier and skinnier.

On my walks home from school, people have started shouting things at me. 'Go back to Ethiopia', one boy yells, as his mates snigger around him. 'Does your mum not want to feed you?' shouts another, failing to realise the irony of what he's just said. Yes, my mum does want to feed me – she is so beside herself with worry about my refusal to eat that she has dragged me to the GP at least twice. The GP has not been interested in what she has to say – 'boys don't get anorexia', the GP tells her, adding 'just give him a good meal, and he will be fine'.

My mum knows that her son is not going to be 'fine'. She has been onto me for months, watching her son starving himself to death and unable to do absolutely anything about it. She has attempted to monitor my food consumption – or, more specifically, lack of food consumption– like a hawk, but I am always one step ahead. I have fool-proof strategies for getting around her efforts to feed me. They include hiding food in tissue paper, feeding whole meals to the dog, and excuses for claiming 'Oh I've already eaten…' ready to deploy at all times. The more that she attempts to help me, the more I start to resent her and view her as a controlling, interfering and force-feeding monster. She is trying to save her son, but I am so wrapped up in anorexic thoughts that to me, she is Public Enemy Number One. It's only years later that I will realise just how amazing she is and just how much gratitude I owe her.

Let's return to the story now because, at school, teachers have begun to talk. My Head of Year – the most fantastic business teacher, Mrs Moulsdale – has been summoned by my PE teacher to come and see me in the Sports Hall. I am skin and bones, standing there shivering in my sports kit. The teachers are desperately concerned and ask the school nurse to meet with me. I attempt to palm her off with my now well-rehearsed 'I'm fine' routine, but she is not buying it. She sees straight through it, and sends me straight to CAMHS, the Child Adolescent Mental Health Service. She calls my parents into school and expresses her concerns. I'm that malnourished, and underweight that the school think my parents could be abusing me. My mum is relieved that someone is finally listening to her concerns. Unlike the GP, the school nurse is taking her seriously. Very seriously, in fact. At first, she is confused by my height and weight statistics – they can't be right, she tells my mum, because my BMI is ludicrously low. She is refusing to believe the statistics my mum gives her. So she calls the GP surgery, who in fact confirm the statistics are correct. The school nurse is mortified and immediately launches into action. This action saves my life.

The next day I am dragged into CAMHS. Now, CAMHS is notorious for its six-month waiting lists, but the nurse has called them with my BMI statistics, and I've been fast-tracked to the very top of the list. I am furious about all this fuss, and the anorexic thoughts inside my head convince me that everyone is trying to cause me harm. I am in complete and utter denial – I may be severely underweight and malnourished but, in my head at least, I am fine. And, as my mum has found out, anyone who tries to question me had better is prepared for the fight of their lives. Fortunately, the CAMHS team know exactly what they're dealing with. Lin, Sarah and Dr Andrew Weaver can see straight through my delusional denials and my defensive outbursts of anger. They are ready to fight against my anorexia with every drop of energy that they've got. I may be fighting back against them, but they know this eating disorder well enough not to take it personally. They are launching into battle and doing everything that they can to save me, even if I am insistent that I do not need to be saved.

I am dragged into a CAMHS room and asked questions that I refuse to answer. They are not surprised. I am asked to complete a 'tick the box' questionnaire, which I wholeheartedly take in my stride. I think that I'm winning – I think that I can pull the wool over their eyes. I take pride in lying my way through every single one of the twenty-eight questions. If you ask someone with anorexia **'have you been deliberately trying to limit the amount of food you eat?'**, they are not going to tick the box that says 'yes – every single day'. Anorexia is too clever for that. Denial is in anorexia's DNA. Deception is a fundamental component of living with anorexia. The deeper you sink into the depths of despair, the more insistent you become that 'I'm completely fine, thank you for asking'.

And so, I breeze through al of these twenty-eight 'eating disorder' questions. I answer a total of zero questions truthfully. Do they think that they can trick me this easily, I think to myself? How dare they accuse me of having an 'eating disorder' – whatever that term means! Why are these people so bothered about me? Why do they care what I'm eating – they're the ones with the problem, not me! Do I look like these stupid adults will control me? Do they think that they can outsmart me like this?

I am in-and-out of these appointments for the next few days. The CAMHS team become more and more concerned with every single appointment. They can see exactly what is going on, and they know that time is now absolutely critical. My mum is completely beside herself with worry. I am completely and utterly in denial. I hate these people, I hate their questions, and I hate the fact they've cottoned onto my eating disorder. I visit CAMHS; I visit the school nurse. I spend PE lesson time with the family liaison officer. Dr Andrew Weaver arranges blood tests, and he is alarmed beyond belief at the results. He immediately gets on the phone to my parents, and I am rushed out of school and taken immediately to the hospital. I don't know it now, but I won't be leaving this hospital ward for a very long time. And, when I do, it will be with the knowledge that these people I have been fighting against have quite literally just saved my life.

****

I have been spiralling to new depths of denial, deception and despair for months. Anorexia has been taking root and spreading its poison throughout my thought processes for a long time. I have lost all interest and enjoyment at school. During drama lessons – formerly my favourite thing in the entire world – I hideaway and avoid attending. I don't want people watching me perform; I don't want to play these stupid drama warm-ups or exercises. People had always mocked me and thought that I was 'different' because I was a boy who loved drama so much. I had spent so many years feeling alienated because I was the weird boy who liked acting. Why couldn't I like football like the other boys? Why did I have to be so, well, dramatic? Maybe everyone would be happy now that I hated drama. Maybe I'd stop being judged and labelled now that I was wasting away. Surely people wouldn't notice me now that I was a shell of my former self. I don't want any more glances, jokes or feelings of exclusion – I just want to hideaway. I'm fed up of the exhaustion, and I am fed up of the exclusion. I'm going to disappear and do my own thing. And by my 'own thing', I mean starve myself and control my food intake. It's the reason I wake up in the morning and the only thing I can think about all day.

I continue to disappear, both figuratively and metaphorically. My life becomes completely overwhelmed by a brand new purpose: calorie control. Every day is defined by my obsession with what I eat. At every moment, I am looking for new opportunities to get out of eating – all that I ever want to do is restrict my food intake. I might not be able to control what other people think about me. I might not be able to change the fact that people see as this weird outsider who isn't a normal boy. Still, I can control how many calories I am going to put into my body. Nobody likes me, and nobody pays me any attention. Nobody takes me seriously, and nobody wants to include me—nobody, except the anorexia. Anorexia is my inner ally. Anorexia is the only one who is interested. It's me and anorexia against the world. How dare they try and take anorexia away from me – it's not like anybody cares about this 'gay' and 'dramatic' little 'gossip'.

Except they do care. And 'they' – my parents, the teachers, the CAMHS therapists, the doctors – are trying to do everything that they can to save me. I am not having any of it. I am perfectly fine, thank you very much, and the only thing I need saving from is people's interference with my life. As the appointments and concern continue I – or, instead, my anorexia – continues to put up a good fight. I am like a clam superglued shut, and I am adamant that nobody is going to crack this case anytime soon. My façade continues, and yet deep down, I know that I can't carry on living like this much longer.

I must be consuming no more than 300 or 400 calories a day, and I am obsessively exercising like someone in training to become an Olympic athlete. I go for ridiculous runs at night and spend hours doing star-jumps in my bedroom. My body is struggling to manage with the basics of just breathing and existing, never mind this kind of exercise. I am completely and utterly exhausted. My body is on the brink of collapse. I am severely malnourished, dangerously underweight, and I utterly unable to think clearly. Every waking minute is entirely preoccupied with my obsession for counting calories and my determination to maintain an absurd regime of starvation and self-punishment. It's October, and I am always ice cold. I sit in lessons shivering, I can't concentrate, and I don't want to communicate. What kind of existence is this? How much longer can I continue spiralling towards self-destruction? Why won't I let my parents, my teachers, or the medical professionals help me?

I am now a ticking time-bomb. At any moment, my body is going to give up. My organs are failing, and my body is wasting away. I am now nothing but skin and bones, and yet I am still convinced there is absolutely nothing wrong with me. I refuse to let anyone even mention the word 'anorexic' in my presence. The GP telling my mum that 'boys don't get anorexia' is music to my ears. This is exactly what my deceitful and control-obsessed eating disorder wanted to hear. How dare someone – especially my mum – label me as an 'anorexic'! You heard what the GP said; boys don't get anorexia! I don't have it! There's the evidence! How dare she try and give me another label that I do not want! I am sick of people commenting on my life, and I am fed up of being the object of people's judgements! All I want is for everyone to leave me alone. I want to control, and I want freedom from my pain. I want people to stop judging me and excluding me. I want to be understood and, if I can't be understood, then I want nothing but complete control over my body. Nobody is going to stop me, and nobody is going to stand in my way. I don't want any more judgement, anymore mocking or any more feelings of inferiority. I want to control, control and control. Nobody cares, so what's the f*cking point? It just shows how toxic the anorexic mindset can become once it has infiltrated into your thought processes. This is especially the case at such a young and impressionable age. As your body gets weaker, these anorexic thoughts and 'voices' get stronger. You don't just lose weight – you lose your sense of self, sense of perspective and ability to think rationally. Anorexia is like a drug or addiction. It is compulsive, all-consuming and shockingly self-destructive. It eats you alive (no pun intended!) from the inside out. It's no wonder that Anorexia Nervosa has the highest mortality rate of any psychiatric disorder in adolescence. It's no surprise that eating disorders, in general, have the highest mortality rate among psychiatric disorders.

As my 13th birthday approaches, it becomes highly doubtful that I will reach it. As I walk around the park on another one of my weight-loss regimes, someone shouts something about me looking like a Holocaust survivor. I'm too starved and exhausted to care. I've given up caring about people's opinions. I've realised I can't control the fact everyone has a problem with this 12-year-old boy no matter what he does. They had something to say about the love for drama, and now they have something to say about the weight loss. I thought everyone was supposed to like you once you were skinny? I thought this is what made someone desirable and valuable? As I say, I am beyond caring. I've got bigger things to worry about than some random man's outbursts in the park. What does he want; an award for tasteless and deeply offensive attempts at 'humour'? I'd shout back if I had the energy to do so. But I barely have the energy for this walk, let alone any confrontations with this man. I should be in a hospital bed, not exercising in the park.

As I make my way home, I feel a sharp pain coming from somewhere in my stomach. Is it my lungs? Is it my kidneys? The pain intensifies each time I inhale. Each time I breathe in, I find myself clutching my emaciated stomach even tighter. I know I need to get home – fast. And so I clutch onto my stomach and focus on putting one foot in front of the other. What the hell is this pain? Why do I feel so dizzy and disorientated? What is happening to me right now?

By some miracle, I make it home. I immediately run to the kitchen cupboard and reach for the sweetcorn relish. I squeeze perhaps ¼ of the entire bottle directly into my mouth. I've started doing this a lot recently. After realising that one serving contains just 25 calories and 0.5g fat, I have been reaching for this sweet and supposedly energising relish every time that I start to crash. I've done the same with BBQ Sauce and Tomato Ketchup as well – I squeeze the bottle directly into my mouth, desperate for the salty and flavoursome taste. It is disgusting, but it is the only way I can get a fix of energy and flavour. As I swallow the sweet relish, I feel a temporary relief from my now omnipresent feeling of hunger. I feel so smart to have found a way of getting this energy rush without having to consume any calories. I feel so smug to be cutting my calorie consumption like this, and I search the internet for new ways of supposedly 'cheating the system'. I look for new ways to cut corners – what other low-calorie foods can supply me with the energy boost I am desperately needing? How many calories can I afford to consume for the sake of some temporary reprieve from my exhaustion and despair?

Later that evening, I lie in bed, unable to sleep. I am – yet again – freezing cold and utterly starving. Since I woke up this morning, I've consumed:

- Half a Weetabix at breakfast with a tiny drop of milk
- Lettuce leaves – perhaps with some kind of dressing – and carrots at lunch
- Sweetcorn relish, Tomato Ketchup, BBQ sauce directly from the bottle
- Probably ¼ of the dinner my mum has made me – usually just the vegetables. I have given the rest to the dog or wrapped it up in tissue paper

I lie in bed and will myself to fall asleep. The faster I can fall asleep, the less likely I am to go looking for food. The faster I can fall asleep, the less time I will have to spend lying here feeling so cold, so empty and so weak. The faster I can fall asleep, the less time I will have to spend listening to those anorexic thoughts and voices racing around inside my head. Yet, despite my exhaustion and my best efforts, I am unable to fall asleep. The feeling of hunger consumes my body. And, at this moment, I realise that it is not just a hunger for food and nutrition that is consuming me. It is a hunger for escape, a hunger for acceptance, a hunger to be understood and a hunger for control. I am starving for self-acceptance, self-confidence and self-love and, as a result, I am starving myself to death. Right at this moment, I can see no light at the end of the tunnel. All I can see is calorie counting, defensiveness, and despair. I have dug myself a hole so deep that there is no hope of escape. I have gone so far down this path of self-destructing that it is a miracle my body keeps soldiering on. I am alienated from everyone, and everything – my family, friends, all my previous passions and interests.

All of my desire to make connections and all of my self-confidence has been utterly extinguished. I am a shell of my former self, and I am barely able to survive each day. When people see me, they see skin and bones. When people talk to me, they receive a vacant stare. When people try to help me, they are dismissed as controlling and interfering. I am completely isolated, and I am completely overwhelmed by utterly irrational thoughts. I am starving myself to death, and I am desperately in need of urgent medical intervention. This is the reality of anorexia. This is the reality of living with an eating disorder. This is what it is like to be a 12 – almost 13 – year old boy who has spiralled to such depths of self-hatred and despair that they haven't eaten, socialised or functioned properly for months. I finally fall asleep, my body essentially passing out from utter exhaustion. I have miraculously made it through another day. Time is running out, and yet I am still aggressively refusing all help.

2. HOSPITALISED AT 13

In the 12 months to October 2013, official statistics reveal that the age at which boys were most commonly admitted to hospital for an eating disorder was 13. This is somewhat ironic because it was in October 2013 – just days before my 13th birthday – that I was myself hospitalised with anorexia. It just goes to show that my story is not just some isolated exception. Indeed, the reality of the situation is this. There is an epidemic of eating disorders destroying lives across the UK, and we need to do something about it. Thousands of young lives are being ruined – many are even being lost – because of the explosion in eating disorders. That's why I want to share my story here – with complete and unfiltered honesty – in order to raise some awareness and shine a spotlight on this so-often misunderstood issue. I hope that, by being so honest, I can offer some hope to anyone suffering.

I would describe the day that I was hospitalised by doctors at Macclesfield Hospital as the most significant day of my life so far. I don't want to say 'most important' or 'best day of my life', as that would give the wrong impression about my feelings at this time. Too many people get away with describing mental illnesses, and especially eating disorders such as anorexia, as nothing but 'attention-seeking'. Let me be very clear: on the day that I was hospitalised, it was the very last thing that I wanted to happen. I was kicking and screaming in protest – I was, as you know, completely in denial about having any kind of 'issue' with food. Anorexia had completely taken over my thoughts and mind. Anyone looking at me would have realised I had a major physical health problem. But most people do not see – or understand - the psychological health problem that is the cause of the physical malnourishment. I was so consumed by anorexic thoughts and beliefs that I genuinely did not understand why I was being hospitalised. It was like being possessed. I had sunk so deep into the depths of denial that I was no longer able to distinguish between my anorexic beliefs and reality.

I was furious to have been backed into a corner by these medical professionals. Doctors telling me that 'you are anorexic and we are going to control everything that you do and eat' was not music to my ears! But here's the thing: that angry, furious and defensive 12-year-old was not the real me. It was the anorexia within me, desperately trying to fight off the doctors and maintain complete control over my thoughts and behaviours. Looking back now, I can say that this was the most important – and, yes, I would say the best – day of my life. By hospitalising 12-year-old me, these doctors not only saved my life, but they also transformed my life. I'll talk more about my belief that 'breakdowns lead to breakthroughs' a little later in this book. Still, for now, I'd like to just say this: my hospitalisation came at exactly the right time. Any later, and I would most likely be dead. It was equivalent to divine intervention – it was, and I hope you can understand what I mean by my use of this phrase, too good to be true.

That's because the doctor's decisive actions – which they took despite my protestations and my masterclass in the art of denial – undoubtedly saved my life. They had taken one look at my heart rate and one look at my blood test results, and they had known there was no option other than to immediately admit me to the ward. Dr Hussain would later tell me that the test results had shown my liver and heart rate to be half of what they should be. I was severely underweight and dangerously malnourished. As I would write in a diary entry on the day that I was discharged, *"I am so grateful and lucky that they saved my life…I know now I would have died without them [admitting me to the ward]"*.

As I have mentioned, I felt everything but grateful on that day I was first admitted. Looking back now, I feel extraordinarily lucky, blessed and overwhelmed with gratitude for those doctors and what they did for me. But back in 2012, I was not rushing to thank anyone anytime soon! With the anorexic thoughts and beliefs still commanding complete control over my mind, I was instead extraordinarily angry and furiously incandescent with rage. I do not want this, I kept repeating to myself, and I was desperate to escape from this level of supervision and control. Unfortunately for my anorexia, I wasn't going anywhere anytime soon. Once my mum had finally left the meeting room, she came straight to my bedside and hugged me amongst a tsunami of tears. I cannot even begin to imagine how worried sick she must have been. She had been fighting to get me help for months – and I had been fighting right back against her, accusing her of projecting her problems and issues with food onto me! Here was her 12-year-old son, lying in a hospital bed having been asked by doctors 'do you want to die?'

My next visitor was a nurse with all the details about my time in the ward. I was informed:

- I would be on strict bed-rest at all times (other than to go to the toilet, when I would have to collect urine samples so that they could be measured). I would have to keep my curtains open at all times, and I would have a set of 'observations' – blood pressure and temperature – every four hours, including through the night.
- I would begin with eating ¼ portions of food, before moving to ½ portions, ¾ portions, and then full portions. After not eating for months, my body would need to slowly get used to food consumption again.
- Every day, I would be able to select my food from the hospital menu. I would make my selection with the help of a nurse, and I would get one chance to do this – I would not be able to change my decision once it had been made. My nursing management plan stated this: **"Ben will do a daily meal plan with his named nurse. Once meals have been chosen, they cannot be changed".** In addition to my breakfast, lunch and dinner, I would eat three 'snacks' a day – morning, afternoon and evening. Each mealtime would be fully supervised by a nurse who would sit next to my bed whilst I ate.
- If I refused to eat the food, there were several courses of action: in the first instance, I would be given a liquified version of the meal that I would have to drink. If I refused this, I would be force-fed the meal using a tube. Or to use the jargon on my nursing management plan: **"If Ben does not finish the meal, it should be removed, and Ben should be given the drink supplement…If Ben does not comply with either of these stages an NG tube would need to be passed and Ben would need to receive the supplement via this route".**
- I would be heavily limited in terms of visitors: at first, only my parents would be able to visit, and only at certain times (and not at

mealtimes). According to the nursing management plan: ***"Mum/Dad will not be present at mealtimes. Visiting is for immediate family at present this will be reviewed weekly and will be dependent on weight gain".***

Faced with the threat of a tube being forced down my throat, I felt quite certain that I needed to go along with the instructions of the nurses. And, as the first afternoon in the ward went by, I noticed a slight shift in my attitude. Perhaps it was some sense of relief – deep within me – that it was now doctors in charge and not my anorexic thoughts. My exhausted body – and mind – were perhaps simply delighted to have finally escaped the terrifying and soul-destroying treadmill of anorexic thoughts, feelings, and behaviours. Whilst the anorexic thoughts and beliefs were still able to exist within my mind; they were no longer capable of controlling my behaviours. I simply didn't have the option to avoid eating, hide food or obsessively exercise. The anorexic thoughts could not fuel such destructive and toxic behaviours any longer, because I was

In time, as I lay there in my hospital bed, I became extraordinarily relieved. As my body finally received some food and nutrition, I regained some strength. And as I regained this strength, I regained some sanity in my thinking. Anorexia takes full advantage of your constant exhaustion and inability to function. It is when we feel at our weakest, lowest and most physically frail that the toxic anorexic beliefs can infiltrate your mind and distort your thoughts. In the moments of clarity that I enjoyed from my hospital bed, I felt utterly relieved that this hell on earth was over. Of course, the anorexia hadn't just 'gone'. Indeed, I would be in therapy for those anorexic thoughts for literally years to come. But the gruelling physical regime was no longer able to continue. The cycle of self-destructive anorexic behaviours had been broken. I came to think like this: *'well I have to eat now – I don't have a choice – so I might as well enjoy it!'*

As I regain a little more strength, I think this. If the doctors – the medical experts – are telling me that I am seriously malnourished and dangerously underweight, then maybe they might be right? And if they are telling me that it's not just 'okay' to eat – but that I need to eat to get better -then maybe I can eat and indulge without feeling so much guilt and disgust?

A mantra I keep being told – in particular by a play therapist who I took an instant disliking to - is that 'food is your medicine'. This is a completely alien concept to me. For months, I have become sucked into the 'diet culture' of 21st-century social media. I have fallen for this narrative that weight loss is the secret to all happiness and success in life. I have completely bought into the narrative that calories are the enemy. I am convinced that certain foods are inexplicably bad for you. I devoutly believe that you should always look for the 'healthiest' option on the menu. Fewer calories equal more happiness! I devour news articles about the 'obesity crisis'. I am shocked by the statistic that 1 in 5 ten-year-olds are classified as obese, failing to realise that this means 4 in 5 are not. I read magazine interviews about celebrities who have found love and success now that they've lost weight. I'm convinced that the answer to all my problems in life is weight loss, even though I do not have any more weight to lose! Is it any wonder that so many people in our world today have such a distorted, unhealthy and toxic relationship with food? The media is so obsessed with the minority of people who are overweight. As a result, every single person in society – the vast majority who are not overweight in the slightest - are made to feel guilty for having a normal appetite. The average mentally resilient person can remain unaffected by the constant barrage of diet adverts and obesity awareness messages. Yet kind of media exposure is toxic for somebody already suffering from an eating disorder. Your irrational eating-disorder mind seizes every opportunity to provide so-called 'evidence' that your fixation with calories and weight loss is justified. Every single 'diet' or 'obesity' message you are exposed to is seized on by anorexia. The anorexia uses it as a piece of so-called 'evidence' that your anorexic beliefs are justified.

Here's a quote from my therapy notes, more of which I will share with you later: **"Ben was arguing with his mum about there being an obesity epidemic in the UK and that his biggest fear is becoming overweight".** My anorexic mind had seized on the news stories and media messaging about obesity. Anorexia was trying to use the 'obesity crisis' coverage as a justification for those anorexic behaviours. Whilst I am not criticising the messaging itself, I am simply asking this. Can the media not become more mindful of the fact that their obsession with weight loss may be fuelling an epidemic of eating disorders? We talk about the problems caused by obesity, but where is the awareness campaign about how dangerous it is to be underweight? Why is the media so obsessed with telling us that EVERYONE is going on a quick-fix weight loss diet (which is never going to work)? The majority of people do not need to lose any weight at all! And, regardless of that fact, surely the focus should be on having a healthy and balanced diet? My anorexic mind convinced me what 'healthy' really meant was 'weight loss'. If you want to be healthy, I believed, you needed to be constantly restricting your food consumption and continuously keep losing more and more weight. Food is not medicine; my anorexic mind tells me. Food is the enemy and food is the number 1 thing you have to avoid… at all costs. Weight gain is a weakness. Weight loss is the fast track to being approved by society and, most importantly, actually liking yourself.

As I lie in my hospital bed, the free CBBC channel playing on screen, I have a moment of clarity and realise how ludicrous this entire belief system is. I realise that it has never crossed my anorexic mind that food could ever be a good or positive thing. I have become so wrapped up in the anorexic voices that I can't imagine a universe in which you could have a slice of cake or eat a chocolate muffin without feeling guilty. My anorexic mind has convinced me that the societal weight loss message is being directed to me. Your worth, your attractiveness, your success is all based on your ability to lose weight. If you want to be liked and if you want to be attractive, then you have got to deprive yourself - at all times. But then I have another moment of clarity: is this starvation an attractive look? Is it a case of 'the skinnier, the better'? Will people be more attracted to me if I resemble nothing more than skin and bones? Can you live a happy life when you are enslaved to calorie counting and unable to think about anything but food? Can that be a fulfilling way to live your life?

The anorexic mind is a very dark, distorted, and deceptive place indeed. Any piece of information – such as a statistic about obesity or a calorie count on a chocolate bar – can become lodged in your mind. These statistics, statements and ideas become your brand-new obsessions. You simply cannot shake them off. As an anorexic, you are trapped in an endless cycle of irrational thoughts, feelings, and behaviours. The thoughts fuel the behaviours, and then the behaviours fuel the thoughts. It is a never-ending spiral into depths of self-destruction and self-delusion. It's like you're on a giant hamster wheel that cannot be stopped – you just keep going round and round, constantly becoming more exhausted and constantly feeling worse. And the worst part of it all is this – there is absolutely nothing you can do about it. As those thoughts, feelings and behaviours become further ingrained, they completely take over your life. The hamster wheel speeds up, and you completely lose not only your sanity but also your sense of self. When you are consumed by anorexia, you lose all ability to get some perspective on your life. This level of delusion and deception can have all-too-easily have catastrophic consequences.

I strongly believe that I would never have recovered from anorexia if I had not been hospitalised. Being hospitalised was like somebody pressing the 'emergency stop' button on my giant hamster wheel. The whole cycle came crashing down. I was no longer able to compulsively engage in anorexic behaviours. The chain between anorexic thoughts and anorexic behaviours was broken. I cannot stress this to you enough; I passionately believe I would be dead if it hadn't been for my hospitalisation. With my physical health in such a shocking condition, I was living on borrowed time. That destructive cycle would never have ended. Without the drastic intervention of this kind, it would have continued until I was dead. Left to my own devices, I would have continued losing more and more weight. The problem was, I did not have absolutely any more weight to lose. I was skin and bones. My skeletal appearance was shocking. I could not walk five steps without being out of breath. I could not focus, think or concentrate. I was a walking corpse. And yet I was still determined to lose more weight. No matter what the GP, CAMHS therapists or doctors said to me, the only voice I was listening to was anorexia. Without the dramatic and decisive hospitalisation, nothing was ever going to change. That cycle of destruction was never going to be broken. I would have attempted to pull the wool over everybody's eyes – including my own. The denial, deceit and delusions would have continued. It breaks my heart to think that this is what it came to, but I thank my lucky stars that this intervention happened. I was not in any position to be taking responsibility for my health and wellbeing. I am so thankful that the doctors, therapists and my family believed in me at the time when I had completely lost myself. I was so fortunate to have this real 'golden ring of steel' around me. They provided me with the most incredible support when I was at my absolute lowest point. They fought against 'me' – or, more specifically, they thought against the anorexia that had completely taken over my life. In doing so, they saved and restored the real me. They gave me a chance to live and a chance to conquer my demons. Every single day, I thank God that they did.

Let's return to my hospital bed, and we're now just days away from my 13th birthday. Oh, what a party this is going to be! What better way to celebrate your birthday than on a hospital ward with observations every four hours and the threat of a force-feeding tube hanging over you?! On a serious note, and without getting too cliché or philosophical here, the greatest birthday gift I received for my 13th birthday is my life. And the doctors have certainly delivered on that one! I have received the most incredible gift from these healthcare professionals. They have saved my life. They have saved me from myself. I think that beats anything you can get on Amazon Prime, don't you?! They are still extremely concerned about my physical health, but I am now in the best place in the best possible hands. There had been talk of me being moved to an inpatient unit in Chester, should things not improve, but so far and so good.

I'm still here, and I'm gaining some control back from the anorexia. I'm able to smile again, relax again and chat away again. I'm feeling so much happier in my skin, even after just a matter of days. Perhaps it's because they've got the heating on full blast and I'm feeling a lot of love from the kind nurses, doctors and my family. Everyone is genuinely so lovely, giving me big smiles and making small talk conversation. I'm able to eat – and actually enjoy - more than half a Weetabix without feeling guilty. I am actually eating little bits of real food, rather than surviving on sweetcorn relish squeezed straight out of the bottle. I'm sitting down and eating an actual meal for the first time in, well, forever. It feels so good to feel this food nourishing both my body and my soul. I look forward to eating the food I'm given -my body is desperate to replenish itself with nutrients, calories and fuel. I don't feel guilty when I eat and – to my absolute shock – I enjoy doing so! In my head, it feels okay to be eating, because this is what the doctors ordered. I know that I need to put on weight and, although I don't want to think about that, I know I can take time to enjoy what I'm eating.

I already know that the hardest part of my recovery will follow my discharge from hospital. I'm kind of seeing my time in hospital as like a mini-vacation. It's the time that I can eat what I want without any of the guilt. I've been starving myself for so long, and so I can 'afford' to over-indulge for a couple of days. But there's still an anorexic voice in the back of my head, reminding me that you can't go on eating like this forever. It's when I'm back home and responsible for my food consumption that I will face the hardest challenge of my life. Like a recovering drug addict or alcoholic, I will have to re-learn a healthy relationship with food. I will have to break free from my toxic compulsions, thought processes and behaviours. I will have to find rehabilitation and restoration, as I battle to reform my relationship with calories, carbohydrates and control. I will have to learn that my worth is not defined by my ability to limit food intake, and I will have to realise that food is not the enemy. I know I have such a long way to go. But right now, I am happy. I never wanted to be in this hospital bed, but I am now so extremely grateful that I am.

As I lie here in this bed, I realise something extraordinary – I deserve to be happy. I deserve to feel good about myself, and I deserve to love my life. Life doesn't have to be defined by never-ending inner turmoil and a struggle over calories and control. I realise that there is light at the end of the tunnel – there is a way of breaking free from these anorexic thoughts and rediscovering a love for my life. I can make peace with my body image, and I can let go of my overwhelming fixation on calories. As CBBC plays on the TV screen and a nurse arrives with my evening snack and milk, I feel good about the future. I can see a life beyond this giant hamster wheel of starvation, obsession, and control. I can picture a future filled with happiness and laughter. I have hope for a calorie and control free future. And I feel a warmth inside that I haven't felt for a very long time indeed. I feel comfortable and content in my own skin. I feel loved and cared for. I feel safe. I feel like I could end up being a survivor. There might just be a life waiting for me that is free from the plague of anorexia.

3. TURNING 13 IN HOSPITAL

It's Saturday 27 October 2012 and about one week into my time as an inpatient on the Children's Ward. I've just been woken up for my morning observations, the first of six I'll have today, and a nurse is bringing breakfast over to my bed. CBBC is on the TV, and presents, balloons and unopened cards surround my bed. Oh yes, I suddenly remember, it's my birthday. I'm finally 13! And who could have predicted that I would be celebrating this birthday just feeling lucky to be alive! I was relieved to be feeling so safe and protected – protected from myself and my anorexic behaviours – in a hospital bed. As I am served by breakfast (two slices of toast with jam and a bowl of rice crispies cereal, in case you were wondering), I feel excited for my day ahead.

For the first time as an inpatient, I am being allowed visits from my grandparents. My grandparents are my absolute world. There are no four human beings who I love, admire, and care about more. I am the luckiest grandson in the world, and not just because they never fail to provide the very best Christmas and Birthday presents! I'll get a visit from my Grandma and Grandad – my amazing grandparents on my dad's side – and a visit from my Granny and Grumpy, my wonderful grandparents on my mum's side. They're all from a generation that doesn't quite grasp the 21st-century language of 'eating disorders' and 'anorexia nervosa'.

Nevertheless, they are all filled with the most amazing amount of unconditional love, compassion, kindness and concern. My granny arrives wielding one of her famous chocolate birthday cakes, which just weeks before I would have avoided like the plague. I write this in my diary: ***"Gifts from mum & dad, lots of cards & even gifts from Children's ward (Ben 10 Comic maker)…gran and grumps just been…great to see them and can't wait to have grans cake".***

Today, in a celebration of my birthday (and also in celebration of my fightback against power anorexia) I enjoy not one but two slices of this famous cake (one for my 'afternoon snack', and another as dessert after my dinner). After depriving myself of anything sweet or 'indulgent' for so long, this cake tastes delicious. Whilst I do feel guilty as I eat my slice, I do also think to myself 'just enjoy it!' My mum, dad and brother Sam all spend the day at my bedside, whilst the doctors and nurses make a fuss over their 13-years-old patient. In particular, I'm delighted with the DVDs I've been given. They include a Keeping Up Appearances boxset, a My Family DVD, and set of comics (this is back in 2012, please remember my dear reader!) I emphasise in my diary that I have received *"Money – (Over £100)"*. I was clearly delighted to be spending my 13th birthday on the brink of becoming a multi-millionaire. As I watch My Family on DVD, I feel that happiness within my soul once more. It is such an unfamiliar – and yet very welcome – sensation. For months, I have felt nothing but coldness – both literally and figuratively. Today, I feel such warmth. It's comforting, it's reassuring, and it's a feeling I never want to end. I want this birthday to be a turning point – I want this birthday to be an opportunity to move on after months of self-inflicted starvation and suffering. I want this to be a moment of re-emergence, a chance to be reborn and to take back control of my life. It's a miracle I'm alive to see my 13th birthday, and I intend to never take the blessing that is my life for granted ever again. I want to get better, and I want to appreciate my amazing grandparents, parents and brother more than ever before.

Before I go to bed, I write this in my diary: *"Clocks go back tonight. Great chat with Claire [one of the nurses]. What a fab day. 13! Yay! Now reading Beano Halloween comic before bed ☺"*.

***

The next morning, I wake up to another day in the ward. My dad arrives – as he has done every day that I've been in hospital – with the day's newspapers. I may be only 13 years old, but I am on my way to giving Fiona Bruce a run for her money. I am loving reading the newspapers every day – it gives me a sense of perspective on what's going on in my life. I find that the world of news reports gives me a welcome escape from my thoughts. I also love the familiarity, routine and reassurance that comes from reading the daily newspaper, with its regular features and distinct writing style. That afternoon, I am allowed to go for my first home visit since being admitted to the hospital. It's only for a couple of hours, but it's a chance to feel just a little bit of normality in my day. I write this in my diary: *"Have been told to measure toilet trips and stay sat down at home this afternoon"* and later add: *"At home – great to see the dog. Just want to be able to stay. Don't take me back to the hospital! Love being at home".*

I return to the ward, and I find that the staff are starting to be more candid in their discussions with me. Things are on the up. I know I've been putting on weight (even though I'm refusing to look at the scales myself). I've been recovering at a steady rate. One of the doctors does a 'body examination' and blood tests. They tell me that, when I was first admitted, by BMI (Body Mass Index) was just 5. To be classified as 'healthy', your BMI needs to range between 18.5 and 24.9. It's finally starting to sink in why these medical professionals were so concerned about me. Today, my BMI is 13.5. We're getting there – or so I thought.

The next day, it's arranged. I will go home for bonfire night fireworks in the garden. Might you think I'm delighted with this news? Here's what I write in my diary that morning: *"For some reason, I think it's the anorexia, I don't want to go home…know I will have to eat lots and I don't like that. Sam [my ten-year-old younger brother] will be eating less than me which I am really unhappy about…worried about roast dinner – don't want a big roast. Anorexia taking control and making me not want breakfast etc. at home".*

I then write: *"Dietician was here at 1.30 to meet with mum to talk about what food to give me during 'recovery process' – e.g. what meals, for example, lunch two pieces bread used for beans on toast, and tea ¾ fish fingers. Still milk with every snack one and massive breakfast!! How long left?!"*

I've hit a wall with my ability to keep putting on weight. We've had a good run, but the anorexia is fighting back. As I approach the 'healthy weight' BMI, something inside me is rebelling against it. I don't want to be a 'healthy weight'. I don't want to put on any more weight. When will this weight gain end? How dare they make me put on so much weight? What if I don't want this? Why are they trying to fatten me up? I don't want to be like other people – I don't want to be another 'healthy BMI'. They can't do this to me. I will get around them. I will get around this.

And I do. The fun and games begin on bonfire night, when I'm spending the night at home and write this in my diary: *"Had a big roast dinner then bread and butter pudding. Had a row with mum about not [being] allowed to go to [the] toilet after eating, and what type of milk I should be drinking. Don't want to be back!"* Milk has become my new control issue – I am desperate to have semi-skilled green milk, instead of 'full-fat' blue milk. The anorexia is asserting restriction and control over any area of life that it can. If that means demanding a lower calorie type of milk, then so be it. My stubborn side comes out in full force – I refuse to let anybody tell me what kind of milk I should be consuming. If I can cut the calories in my milk – and I have to have three glasses a day – then I will do it.

The next day I return to the ward and write this: *"Doctors talking saying my weight has dropped. Dr Hussain has spoken to me about home leave and is going to do bloods in a bit…[one of the nurses] is so stupid, ordering full-fat milk for my snack on the phone when, in fact, I can have semi-skimmed instead".* I have turned milk-gate into a fully-fledged saga. My anorexia is clawing around for any control. If I can cut the calories from anything, I will. There is a struggle within my soul, like the angel on one shoulder and devil on the other. Is this the start of a slippery slope? Will I start refusing more things and attempt to take back control of my calorie consumption? Or is this just a passing phase, like a minor 'growing pain' or obstacle on the road to recovery?

I'm weighed the next morning again, and I scribble this in my diary: *"Weighed. My weight has gone down. Oh my god. Worried about what will happen. Not allowed home? Worse?"*

Here's how the diary entries continue:

"8 am – was worried [about weight], anxious about weight loss. Calmed down a bit now, whatever will be will be.

8.10 am – Anne Marie [one of the nurses] sorting my breakfast out. She says she's giving me some of her bread from home because she wouldn't feed the hospitals bread to the ducks. She also asked whether I wanted a cup of tea! So she gave me her seeded batch toast with blackcurrant jam!!

9.30 am – DOCTORS ROUNDS. The doctors are confused about my weight. They don't know what's going on. Waiting for CAMHS [Child Adolescent Mental Health Service] to inform them of the plan – they don't know. They are doing to work out what's happened with my weight and may get the dietician to re-do my meal plan. So basically they are clueless, and CAMHS are meant to be phoning with a plan…will I get home leave tonight? I reckon NO.

10.30 am – I'm not worried about weight anymore. What will be will be. Waiting for snack. The moody wheelchair girl who demanded a cubicle is now demanding she is moved again – as her telly doesn't work.

12.20 – Sarah from CAMHS has phoned the hospital. Turns out, I can go on home leave from today until Friday, when I need to be back for bloods, weight and breakfast. Then a meeting with Sarah in the afternoon".

It's now the evening, and I'm back at home with my family. We're about halfway through November, and it's my favourite time of year. There's something that I just absolutely love about the Autumn and Winter seasons. I love the cosy evenings in, the feel-good Saturday night TV, and the big build-up to Christmas. It's strange to be back in my bed once again. The last time I was lying here, I was a frail and frozen 12-year-old child. Tonight, I lie here feeling so much more self-confidence, self-love and warmth. I feel good about life for the first time in forever, and I find that I am taking enjoyment in things that I had always taken for granted. I laugh away as I watch a 'My Family' and 'Keeping Up Appearances' DVD. I love feeling so warm, safe, and cosy inside my fairy-light illuminated room. I realise that life is about the simple pleasures and the little things that you can enjoy as you go through your day. I resolve to start appreciating the little things more. I resolve to find genuine enjoyment in the everyday activities of my life. It dawns on me that I appreciate my life for the first time in forever. How on earth did I get to this point? What the hell has happened here? I realise how lucky I am to be alive and how blessed I am to be surrounded by so much love and support.

****

My thoughts drift to the topic of school. I've not been in lessons for months now, and I'm worried about falling behind. It's only Year 8, but I still feel so concerned about how much I might be missing. The plan is for me to have a tutor who will come to the house and give me lessons in Maths and Science. My school-teachers will all email work for me to complete at home, meaning I can keep up with everything whilst I recover at home. I wonder what everyone at school thinks? Will they be talking about where I've disappeared to? I wonder how shocked they became to see me wasting away before their very eyes, walking around as little more than skin and bones in a uniform? I need to get back into the classroom; I need to keep up with my lessons. But the doctors say it's far too soon – my body is still vulnerable and frail, I am still required to rest and be kept under constant supervision. For now, a tutor and emailed work will have to do.

I return to the ward the next morning for more observations, blood tests and to be weighed. I am moved to another unit in the ward, a good sign that I'm going to be discharged very soon. Part of me doesn't want to be discharged. I don't want to have to go back to the real world. Everything feels so safe and positive in here. I can eat what I want, the loveliest nurses surround me, and I do not have a care in the world. I love the routines of the hospital day – the regular observations, the mealtimes arriving like clockwork, the shift patterns worked by the doctors. The ward has become a safe, secure, and comforting place to be. This is the place where I came to recover. This is the place where I was saved from myself. I have been here for several weeks, and it feels like a home. But a hospital cannot become your home. You cannot become institutionalised; you cannot live your life from within the walls of a hospital ward. At some point in time, I know I have to face the real world. And that is when the hard work is going to have to start.

But here's the thing: I want to get better. I genuinely, in my heart, want to get better. This is very good news, indeed. Here's something I believe very strongly about anorexia: unless the patient genuinely wants to get better, there is nothing anybody can do to help them. Doctors can force-feed you and section you, but unless you want to recover, things will just keep going back to square one. You will get caught in an inescapable cycle of 'recovery' and relapse, like a reoffending prisoner being released before going straight back to jail. The habits, compulsions and behaviours that drive an eating disorder do not just disappear overnight. To overcome this crippling eating disorder, you need to genuinely want to get better. If there is even the slightest doubt in your mind, then the anorexia will quickly creep back. This, in my opinion, is the reason why eating disorders have the highest mortality rates amongst psychiatric disorders.

I, therefore, feel so lucky to be in a headspace where I genuinely want to get better. As a result of the exceptional care I receive, my eyes are opened to the extraordinary kindness that exists in this world. That alone gives me something incredible to live for. And I have become so aware of the preciousness, fragility, and beauty of human life. I have been well and truly shaken up – I will never take one blue sky, one walk to the paper shop or one evening watching a good DVD for granted again. Being asked by a consultant paediatrician 'do you want to die?' has made it very clear to me that I do not. As William Chapman wrote, 'Words cut deeper than knives. A knife can be pulled out; words are embedded into our souls'. The doctor's words will remain in my mind for many, many years to come – perhaps for the rest of my life. They will motivate me at my toughest points and empower me in my darkest hours. I realise I have so much to live for. And so, I'm confident that, no matter what I go through when I get back home, I will remain resilient. I don't, for one second, expect anorexia to go quietly. I know that I'm in for a rocky ride. I know that this is going to be a turbulent and testing journey. But do you know what? I'm ready for it. I'm a fighter, and I'm a survivor. I want to get better. I want to defeat anorexia and get my life back. I want to recover. And I want to help anyone going through the hell I was going through. In the same way that total strangers saved my life, I want to do the same for others who might be going through the same ordeal. I want to use my story to help inspire, empower and support anyone in the grips of a painful and paralysing eating disorder. I need to get better to show those suffering in silence that there is a light at the end of the tunnel. I want to change lives, and that has to begin with changing mine. I realise that I'm not just doing this for me – I'm doing this for everyone who saved me, and I'm doing this for everyone who might need saving themselves. And I have never felt so ready, resilient or determined in my life. F*ck you, anorexia, I want my life back.

****

It's now 3 pm on Friday 9 November 2012, and I have just been discharged from the Children's Ward. I am sad to be leaving this new home and safe space, but I am excited to get my life back. I will not miss being woken up every four hours for a temperature check and blood pressure reading! I will not miss having to take a measuring jug every time I want to go to the toilet! I will not miss sleeping with the lights on and curtains open! But I will miss the incredible doctors and nurses who have saved my life and shown me so much love, kindness, and care. They have truly gone above and beyond in their efforts to care for me. They have shown me there is a lot of goodness and kindness in this world. They have demonstrated the absolute best of human nature and have showcased the absolute best of the human spirit. They are true heroes and genuine inspirations.

I am discharged by Dr Hussain, who sets me a ten-week weight target of 34kg (5 st 4lb). I write this in my diary: *"3 pm – Following meeting with Dr Weaver & Sarah [therapist] I have been discharged from hospital! My 10-week target weight is 34kg. Dr Hussain says [the] reason I was kept in was because of liver and heart rate being ½ what it should [sic]. They have all been great at the children's ward in helping me to recover…I am so grateful and lucky that they saved my life…I know now I would have died without them [admitting me to the ward]. DISCHARGED!!!"*

4. ROAD TO RECOVERY

What do you do when you are two full-time working parents and have a son recovering from anorexia who needs looking after? You call in granny, of course!

I have always had the best and closest relationship with my gran, or Queen Wendy as I like to call her. My gran is, quite simply, my number one inspiration and my absolute world. She is the most amazing human being I have ever met in my life, and she is a never-ending source of kindness, acceptance, calm and love. I love nothing more than a walk around Alderley Edge woods with my gran and Flash, the dog, followed by a coffee and good catchup back in her gorgeous kitchen. Nothing makes me more excited than the prospect of a trip to M&S Café Handforth Dean with my mum (Queen P) and my gran. Every trip consists of a very familiar routine: we split up and wander around the shops, before heading off to M&S café, where we can be guaranteed to argue over who should pay and what coffee granny should have (she has still not grasped the fact that 'just a normal coffee' is not an acceptable answer in the age of Cappuccinos, Lattes and Frappes).

My gran is, as I say, my biggest source of inspiration and love. She radiates wisdom and truly has a heart of gold. Every single Saturday - for as long as I can remember - Mum, Sam and I have spent the day visiting gran and Grumpy (he gave himself this title, so I hope he will not be suing me for defamation of character!) In my mind, Saturdays are synonymous with afternoons spent in front of their roaring fire, a cup of tea in hand and the day's newspapers sprawled across the kitchen table. And I have the happiest memories of Easter holidays spent at gran and grumpy's caravan in Trearddur Bay, North Wales, with Queen P, Sam, and Tessa, her dog. We would enjoy walks down to the little 'Boat Bay' and drive to see the ferries arriving at Holyhead harbour. My absolute favourite part of the holiday was our visits to the 'big Tesco' about twenty-five times a day (this was an exciting day out back in the days before HD television).

I love my gran to pieces. She is my absolute favourite human being in the world. However, I must be honest; her understanding of eating disorders is comparable to my understanding of model aeroplanes (in other words, non-existent). This is not her fault in the slightest – eating disorders were not even a 'thing' for the vast majority of her life! And her 'table manners' etiquette was a product of its time! Growing up, my cousins and I were informed that we could not leave the table until we had finished everything on our plates. Well, I just could not stand some of these meals (sorry Gran, I love you but not your pies) and so, aged just eight or nine, I got into the habit of hiding food. I would sit there wrapping it up in paper towels or feeding it to the dog under the table. Now let me be very clear: I do not – for one second – correlate my dislike for the granny's cottage pie with the development of my anorexia. Of course, I don't! But I do know that these mealtimes were not something I looked forward to. And I think that they give an early indication of my sometimes difficult relationship with food.

So it is – at first – difficult to be back at this kitchen table, being told to eat certain portions of meals once again. My gran – like most – likes to make sure that everybody is well fed and looked after, and so she takes great pleasure in buying out the M&S bakery aisle. I am presented with a selection of carrot cakes, flapjacks and other M&S classics. My gran has a heart of gold and goes above and beyond to look after me. She is never overbearing but always instinctively caring. We go for walks in Alderley woods and drink coffee (with plenty of sugar) whilst reading the day's newspapers. And we would go off to Wilmslow garden centre and look at the ever-growing selection of Christmas decorations. I have the happiest memories of my Mondays and Tuesdays spent with Queen Wendy! This is precious time with my gran that I know I'll never get to enjoy again. And so I am thankful for this opportunity, even though the circumstances are not necessarily ideal! I cherish this opportunity, and I cherish her unconditional love and unwavering kindness even more.

On Tuesdays, Angela, my home tutor, comes to visit. When I say that Angela is an icon, what I mean is that she would give even Gemma Collins a run for her money. Angela is a bubbly, outgoing and truly fabulous human being. She is a ray of sunshine and a fantastic tutor. She teaches me algebra in Maths and white blood cells in Science – the sessions go quickly, and I genuinely enjoy her tutoring. It's not quite the same as being sat in a classroom at school, but it does mean I can ask as many questions as I want, and go over the concepts I don't quite grasp several times. And when it comes to me learning algebra, you better believe that more than a couple of attempts at explanation are required!! It's good to have some routine and order back in my daily life – I thrive off routine, and I like the fact I have things to do every day of the week. It keeps my mind busy, meaning I can't start overthinking the calories, and it means the anorexic thoughts can't take over once again.

In the weeks and months following my discharge from the hospital, the anorexic thoughts are still very much present. They weren't driving all of my behaviours as they had before, but they were still 'there', hiding away in my mind. You may have made a physical recovery (in terms of weight gain and an improvement in your heart rate, organ functions, etc.). But this does not mean you have made a psychological recovery as well. You can't just click your fingers and wake up with a whole new mindset! The physical recovery certainly helps – once you have regained strength and have begun delivering essential nutrients to both your body and brain, you can think more rationally and clearly once more. But after months of anorexic thoughts, feelings and behaviours, it is ludicrous to imagine you might be back to 'normal' overnight. I saw this time in my life as a 'new normal'. I didn't want to return to how I had been, even long before anorexia had taken hold of my life. Throughout my childhood, I always struggled to feel happy in my skin. I didn't fit in at school, I struggled to make sense of my identity, and I often responded to situations and stressors in very emotionally unintelligent ways. I have always been a sensitive soul, and I had a habit of taking absolutely everything extremely personally.

I very much saw my discharge from hospital as an opportunity to rebuild my life. This was an opportunity to leave behind the anorexic thoughts, feelings and behaviours for good. I was also my chance to have a brand new start. I could finally leave behind the unhappiness and sadness that I had experienced for many years before developing an eating disorder. One thing that my hospitalisation and discharge brought me is the most incredible amount of self-awareness. Before my eating disorder, I had never been a relatively thoughtful, philosophical or reflective individual.

Instead, I was rather impulsive and very driven by strong feelings of emotion. I was extremely sad not to be 'popular' at Primary school, and I would feel an enormous amount of emptiness and loneliness in my life. I felt very judged, very rejected by my peers, and very alienated. I was unable to connect with other people, and I struggled to understand the differences between us. I knew I was different – I was a boy who loved acting and couldn't stand football. I was sensitive but also very self-centred, as well. In my head, everything was all about me – I was a victim who had been excluded by the other boys. And life wasn't fair because nobody paid me any attention on the playground. Looking back now, it's all absolutely pathetic! I want to shake my younger self and shout 'get a grip!' But at the time, I was unable to take a step back or put things into perspective. Every emotion entirely consumed me, and I was consequently unable to exert any direction, control or responsibility for my own life. This all came to a head with my eating disorder. I became utterly consumed by my calorie control project, and I became so overwhelmed by anorexic thoughts that I lost all autonomy over my own life.

My hospitalisation and discharge changed everything. I, therefore, believe that my breakdown led to the best breakthrough of my life so far. Whilst my eating disorder was the most shocking and scary time in my life, it also produced the most positive changes in my life. If I hadn't had this 'breakdown', I would never have had the 'breakthrough' of self-awareness. I passionately believe that I wouldn't be where I am today without having this extraordinary breakthrough. If I hadn't, I would still be living on an emotional rollercoaster and consumed by deep unhappiness, anxiety and alienation. Or, in the worst-case scenario, I would most certainly be dead as a result of my anorexia.

This breakdown and breakthrough, happening aged just thirteen years of age, was the most significant and transformative moment of my life so far. This may sound weird (and I imagine many people will not understand this), but I am so immensely thankful for this lifechanging experience. I could not be prouder of the person I am today, and I know I would not be this person if my breakdown and breakthrough had not happened. For this reason, I believe that everything really does happen for a reason. What doesn't kill you, as they say, makes you stronger. Well anorexia may have nearly killed me, but it did not – instead, this experience transformed my entire life…for the better. Following my hospitalisation and discharge, I was able to - for the very first time - step outside of myself and 'look down' on who I was. I was learning how to press pause on what had been a lifelong emotional rollercoaster. I was finally able to objectively observe the thoughts and feelings that had been driving my self-destructive behaviours. All of this kindness from the nurses and doctors on the ward shook me out of my self-absorption. Having seen so many patients come-and-go on the ward, I had become acutely aware of what a cocooned existence I had been living in Macclesfield. And having read so many stories of suffering, tragedy, but also redemption in the daily newspapers, I had realised how restricted and self-centred my world view was.

One of the best sources of self-awareness was my weekly therapy sessions with Sarah from CAMHS. My physical recovery was well underway, but my mental rehabilitation journey was only just beginning. I had made so much progress and regained so much of my health and strength. However, if this progress was to be sustained, then my physical health needed to be matched with mental wellness as well. I remember first arriving at the CAMHS building, back in September 2012, and feeling so angry and frustrated to be here. Back then, denial and deception had been my order of the day. I had lied my way through eating disorder assessment questionnaires, and I had refused to respond to the therapist's questions about my eating behaviours. Walking back through these doors, several months later, I genuinely feel like a completely different person. Today, I want to be here. I genuinely want to get better. I no longer see these therapists as the enemy – they are my lifesavers. As I say, you can only recover from an eating disorder if you are genuinely willing to. To beat this mental illness –a condition heavily characterised by denial and deception – you have to be wholeheartedly willing to cooperate. If you do not want to recover, you will never recover. It's as simple as that. To escape the chains of anorexic thoughts and behaviours, you have no option but to let down your guard, relax your defences, and open your mind to what your therapist asks you. The doctors have decided that I will now be weighed weekly at CAMHS, and so the first thing I do once Sarah has greeted me in reception is head for the scales.

This is a new weekly ritual that fills me with anxiety and fear. I am fearful for two very conflicting reasons. Firstly, I am terrified I have not made sufficient weight gain and so will get into trouble with the doctors. I'm aware of the programme the hospital has created for me, and I genuinely want to keep on track with the weight gain targets. But secondly, I am so anxious about putting on weight. To put it simply: I don't want to put on weight. In my head – and this may be the anorexia, or it may be the constant media messaging – any kind of weight gain is bad. When Sarah weighs me, I don't look down at the scales. I don't want to see the number – I just can't do it. Sarah notes my weight down and adds it to a BMI chart.

When we go off into a therapy room, Sarah wants to know how I am. She's interested to know how I feel about being weighed, and I volunteer to her the information that I find weight gain extremely difficult. Like any good therapist – and Sarah is fantastic – she wonders out loud why this might be the case. I try to justify my fear of weight gain, both to myself and Sarah, like this. The media, and society as a whole, is utterly obsessed with weight loss and diets. We are constantly being told that there is an obesity epidemic and that everyone needs to eat more healthily. Society says we should all be counting calories and we should all be cutting down on the carbohydrates! It is therefore not a good thing to put on weight – weight gain is something to be seen as unhealthy, toxic, embarrassing and wrong. After I have articulated my thoughts and opened up like this, Sarah gently challenges and asks questions: 'why is weight gain objectively wrong?', she wants to know. 'Could it not be that if someone is underweight, putting on weight is the healthiest thing that they can do?' It's questions like these that lead to what I like to call 'lightbulb moments', or 'mini breakthroughs'. Of course, she's right, I think in my head. Yet I am so conditioned to believe that 'putting on weight' makes you unattractive and a failure in the eyes of society. As a result, I cannot comprehend what she is saying. I cannot get my head around the concept that weight gain could be a good thing. In a world that worships weight loss and skinniness, how could putting on weight ever be anything but horrifying?

Sarah is extremely good at her job, asking the right questions at the right time. 'What comes to mind when you think of weight gain?' she asks. At first, it seems like an easy question to answer; getting fat, being seen as unattractive, being unhealthy, being judged by society. The reasons why I think weight gain is the enemy just keep on coming! Sarah then continues with one of her follow up questions, which are designed to probe and challenge those anorexic thoughts. 'Is that a rational or helpful thought?', Sarah wants to know, 'or could that be an anorexic thought that is not a true reflection on reality?'

This kind of questioning goes to the heart of 'Cognitive Behavioural Therapy', or CBT as it is commonly known. CBT is all about exploring the relationship between your thoughts, feelings and behaviours. You firstly identify your cycle of thoughts, feelings, and behaviours. As a result, you can work on challenging the anorexic thoughts that are fuelling the anorexic behaviours (such as starvation, calorie counting, excessive exercise, need for complete control). The CBT therapist is not here to tell you what to do or what to think – CBT is all about helping you to help yourself. This, again, is why it's so important to actively want to recover from your eating disorder. To be successful in the long term, your recovery has got to be self-directed, and your wish to get better has to be 100% genuine. By asking good questions and paraphrasing your words back to you, a good CBT therapist will allow you to identify your irrational beliefs. They will teach you how to observe - for yourself - how these beliefs have been fuelling your very toxic and unhealthy behaviours. It is an exercise in self-awareness and self-discovery. By identifying what's going on (and what's going wrong) in your thought processes, you can learn how to think and function in healthier ways.

What Sarah is saying makes sense. The questions she is asking are leading to genuine breakthroughs inside my brain. I'm starting to realise that all of these anorexic thoughts and beliefs cannot be rational. Weight gain is not objectively bad! Calories are not objectively evil! The purpose of life is not just to be as skinny as you possibly can! The thick cloud of anorexia is slowly beginning to clear. I'm having more and more moments of clarity. I finally see the light at the end of the tunnel, and I'm finally seeing that the purpose of life is much more than being as skinny as you possibly can!

Towards the end of the session, Sarah sets me homework. Sometimes, she'll give me a worksheet on identifying and challenging irrational thoughts as they pop into my head. Other times, she'll give me a task to do or something to research. After one session in which we'd discussed perfectionism, she had handed me an information sheet on perfectionist traits and how to handle them.

Today, she wants me to go away and research something called 'Mindfulness'. I've got to be honest; I'm not entirely convinced by what she's saying about this. It's all about 'doing what you're doing'. If, for example, you're making a cup of tea, then you've got to be 'mindful' about pouring in the milk and stirring in the sugar (in my case that's a lot of sugar!) Or, if you're going for a walk, then you've got to take time to listen to the sounds of nature and connect with the fresh air. I promise that I'll look into this whole 'mindfulness' thing. I'm not convinced that it is going to be anything helpful, interesting, or important. Why, I think to myself, would you just focus on breathing? Do you not just get bored and want to get on with your day? My mum arrives to collect me after my session comes to an end. Sometimes, she'll come into the therapy room for 10 minutes. However, I'm still not keen on any of my family getting involved with my CBT sessions. From my 13-year-old point of view, this is all very private and very personal. I hate - more than anything else in the world – the thought that people are interfering in my life.

I don't want my mum putting her ten pennies worth in, and I don't believe that she has a right to do so. I don't quite know why, but I know that I do feel very strongly about this. I know that I don't want absolutely anybody else involved in the therapy. I don't want people having opinions on my mental health and wellbeing. It's a control thing, I think, that comes down to my autonomy for my own life. I want to be in the driving seat – at all times. And so I argue that my parents - or anybody else for that matter - have no right to start speaking about my eating habits or my mental health. It's my body and my brain, I tell Sarah, and I want to retain as much control of this situation as I possibly can. And so, my mum isn't coming into the session today. I'm relieved – I don't want her 'ruining' it all. Is this me talking, or is this the anorexia? She is, after all, the one who kept dragging me – kicking and screaming – into the GP's surgery all of those months ago. To my anorexia, she is public enemy number 1. To anybody looking in, she is my saviour and the reason that I am alive today! Today, she isn't coming into the session. Instead, she's sat waiting for me in the reception area, lanyard and teaching uniform still on. She's just here to collect me and take me home. Probably the wisest decision, I would say, if she wants to avoid World War 3 with her defensive son! She doesn't need a therapy-session showdown after getting through a long day at work! So, I arrange a time with Sarah for next week and say goodbye. I promise that I'll do some 'mindfulness' research when I get home, fully intending to spend no more than thirty seconds writing down the definition from Google. It really can't be anything I'd be interested in, I think to myself. I don't have time to be researching this concept - I've got the news programmes to watch and newspapers to read as soon as I get in.

***

Once I'm home, I keep myself busy whilst waiting for dinner. I read through the newspaper – which I now go and buy every morning – and I film a video of me presenting the news for YouTube. I've called my channel 'BW LATEST' and my dad, bless his resourceful soul, has painted me a (bright red) backdrop to present in front of. I love standing here in my bedroom, reading the BBC News website headlines to the world. Once I've finished thinking I'm Huw Edwards, I remember that Sarah has asked me to research mindfulness. I've got a few minutes before the tea is ready, so I think 'well why not?' I type 'mindfulness' into Google and, of course, go straight to the Wikipedia entry. Nothing interesting or captivating here. It all sounds very ancient and abstract to me. Why on earth does Sarah want me to research this?

I return to google and find another link. Again, nothing very-interesting here. But then I click onto a website with the name 'Dalai Lama' in the title. The name sounds familiar; I think I read a BBC News article on him a couple of days ago! Well, I'm intrigued to find out what this Tibetan Monk has got to do with mindfulness.

Quite a lot, it turns out. I discover that the Dalai Lama (or Jetsun Jamphel Ngawang Lobsang Yeshe Tenzin Gyatso; born Lhamo Dhondup, if you were interested in his full name) is the leader of Tibetan Buddhism. He is known worldwide as an inspiring spiritual leader. As I read about him on the internet, I learn that the Dalai Lama has a very simple yet extraordinarily inspiring message. He says this: the purpose of your life is to find genuine happiness, and you can achieve this genuine happiness by living a life of compassion. As I read these words about the Dalai Lama and message to the world, something just feels so right within me. There is something about this message of kindness, compassion and love that resonates with me in an extraordinarily powerful way. Perhaps it's all the pain and suffering I've been inflicting on myself over the past few months. Perhaps it's all the love, warmth, and kindness that I've been shown by the doctors and nurses on the children's ward.

Whatever it is, there is something about the Dalai Lama's message that feels so right. I am not, in any way, a religious person. I have attended a Catholic pre-school, primary school and now secondary school, but my Church attendance has been limited to one annual Christmas Eve Carol Concert (and we only went to that because Queen P 'thought it would be a lovely thing to do as a family'). I am not religious, but this feels like a kind of Saul to Paul conversion experience. I'm on my road to Damascus, and some kind of divine intervention has just struck me. This man is speaking to me. Not literally, I must clarify, but I feel in my heart that compassion, love and happiness are what life should be all about. Why have I never thought like this before? Why have I never felt this way about life before? I Google more about the Dalai Lama, his message of compassion, what he has to say about mindfulness and the teachings he gives on finding happiness. I feel so warm and so good inside. After months of self-punishment and after years of feeling that the world is a cold, judgmental and alienating place, this message is like sitting by the roaring fire on a cold winter's day. My soul feels nourished; my worries and anxieties feel tamed. Why have I spent so many years feeling so victimised, so alienated and so angry that nobody seems to like me or accept me? Why have I never discovered the transformative power of approaching the world with an attitude of compassion, love and kindness? Where was mindfulness and the Dalai Lama when I needed them?

It's now later in the week, and I'm looking around The Works. Searching for bargain books in this shop is one of my favourite things to do when in town with my mum! I have developed an obsession with stationery, and I have started getting into my reading. I have recently been watching the twenty-four-hour news channels and have been scouring the newspaper websites for world news. I'm now obsessed with buying current affairs books. I've just picked up Sky News journalist Alex Crawford's 'Colonel Gaddafi's Hat', an account of her time reporting on the 2012 Libyan uprising. As I glance across the rest of The Works' book selection, I see a face that looks a little bit familiar. I crouch down for a closer inspection. Beneath the AMAZING VALUE! £1.99! bright blue sticker, I see the unmistakable face of the Dalai Lama. 'The Art of Happiness', the cover reads, listing the authors as 'His Holiness the Dalai Lama and Howard C Cutler'. It's divine intervention (yet again), I think to myself, grabbing a copy and loving the fact that I've found yet another bargain book in this store. I head to the till and pay, before heading off to find my mum (usually to be found either trying on everything in FatFace or complaining about the lack of good clothes in M&S).

That evening, I sit down to see what 'The Art of Happiness' is all about. I turned to Part One, The Purpose of Life, and Chapter One, entitled 'The Right to Happiness'. I read the first line: "*I believe that the very purpose of life is to seek happiness. That is clear. Whether one believes in religion or not, whether one believes in this religion or that religion, we are all seeking something better in life. So, I think, the very motion of our life is towards happiness…*" It's another St Paul conversion moment. Another lightbulb flashes to life in my brain. This makes everything in life make sense. This is what life is all about. It's literally like these words were written exclusively for me. Over the next few hours, I race through the first half of the Dalai Lama's book. I read about 'inner worth', 'deepening our connection to others', 'training our mind for happiness', 'shifting perspective' and how to overcome 'self-created suffering'. Every single page enlightens me. Every single sentence illuminates my life.

I feel enriched, educated, and like my eyes have suddenly been opened. This £1.99 book is – I am sure of it – going to change my life. Just by reading a little bit about what the Dalai Lama believes, I already feel a new sense of perspective and newfound connection with the universe. This incredible book is, I am sure of it, going to provide a solid foundation for my brand-new approach to life. I'm going to do as the Dalai Lama says and start approaching people with compassion. I'm going to train my mind for happiness, and I'm going to discover a real sense of purpose in my life! I go to bed that evening feeling both content and invigorated. It's like the scales have finally fallen off my eyes, and a new zest for life is rushing through my veins. I drift off to sleep whilst listening to the BBC World Service Newshour on the radio. I'm feeling good, and I'm feeling ready to create a meaningful, loving and positive life. Little 13-year-old me is ready for a rebirth, revitalisation, and reincarnation. It's time to start thriving through life!

5. BACK TO SCHOOL

It's now well into 2013, and things are going well. My weight is continuing to increase, my anorexic thoughts are much more under control, and I am feeling good about life. I've told Sarah about my interest in mindfulness, and I've started beginning each day with 30 minutes of meditation. At first, I found it impossible to sit still for longer than 5 minutes. But now, I find myself looking forward to half an hour of calm before the day ahead. The more that I become aware of my thoughts, and the more that I practise mindfulness in every area of my life, the happier I find myself feeling. I start to realise that life isn't all about calories, weight loss and control. I start to discover that there is more to our existence than worrying about what other people think. There is more to our lives than obsessing about whether you can fit both your hands around your waist. Perhaps most importantly, I realise that the thoughts you have in your head are not necessarily 100% accurate. I am no longer at the mercy of the anorexic beliefs that have been driving my unhealthy habits and behaviours. Instead, I am slowly learning how to become the master of my destiny.

Don't get me wrong; many of those anorexic thoughts and beliefs are still there. They continue to creep into my thought processes, and they continue to fuel strong feelings of anxiety and anger. But I am learning to detach myself from these previously all-consuming thoughts. I am beginning to discover how to challenge, question and critique my own beliefs. Instead of believing the anorexic thoughts, I look for evidence that will back up my beliefs. Instead of continuing to believe that eating one piece of cake will make me 'fat' overnight, I force myself to consider more rational and realistic perspectives. Instead of simply accepting as 'fact' the idea that 'putting on weight is bad', I learn to question my thoughts and look at their origins. *'Is this thought helpful or rational?'*, I am starting to ask myself, *'or is this an anorexic belief that is supported by no evidence whatsoever?'*

I am making good progress, and CAMHS decide I can start going back into school. My parents go in for a meeting where it's decided I can start by attending two lessons a week. I am excited to be going back and having a completely fresh start. However, I am still apprehensive about what people are going to think. They're still going to have memories of seeing me emaciated and fragile all those months ago. And, of course, people are going to notice when someone they've not seen since September suddenly reappears! My head of year, Mrs Moulsdale, says she will talk to my class ahead of my return. Mrs Moulsdale is the definition of an angel. This woman is the most incredible teacher I could have ever asked for, both as my Head of Year and later as my Business Studies teacher. She has a heart of gold and is the most amazing human being. She is one of the biggest blessings to have ever come into my life. I am so humbled by how she truly went above and beyond to ensure I was okay. Certain people come into your life and make the most monumental and unforgettable difference – and she is undoubtedly one of them.

I was extremely relieved that Mrs Moulsdale was going to talk to everyone and, in particular, ask them not to make a fuss. Any attention was the last thing that I wanted. Of course, I knew that people would have questions. It's only human to be inquisitive about changes happening in the world around you. But I wasn't ready to share my 'eating disorder' story with my family members, never mind 30 people in my class at school! They had, of course, seen my deterioration over the previous academic year. So they would have had a pretty good idea of what was going on. But eating disorders are extraordinarily complicated for an outsider to understand. There is so much misunderstanding, and there are so many people who, quite simply, just do not 'get it'. They can't understand why someone would seemingly starve themselves in this way. Many people think it's just attention-seeking or a silly 'phase' that someone will snap out of when they choose to. I may well have believed this if I hadn't gone through my first-hand experience! There are so many myths and misconceptions perpetuated, especially on social media. And eating disorders do continue to be shockingly misunderstood by society as a whole. The stigma around mental illness contributes to a shocking amount of suffering for those battling an eating disorder. It is so important to remember: an eating disorder is a very serious mental illness. It is not a phase, a lifestyle, a body type or a choice. It is a serious mental illness, and we need to take eating disorders seriously.

Mrs Moulsdale spoke to my class about not making a fuss and, with the Doctor's permission, I started returning to school for certain lessons I had chosen. I cannot even begin to tell you how much I enjoyed getting back into a daily routine. And I was relieved that everybody – to my face at least – was extremely kind and understanding. Nobody caused a fuss, and I did not feel like the centre of any unwanted attention. But equally, I didn't feel ostracised or alienated – a feeling I knew all too well. I just felt, well, normal. People smiled and made conversation, but they knew not to grill me on the shocking weight loss and personality transformation that they had all witnessed. I felt included and supported but not overwhelmed and interrogated. Mrs Moulsdale was constantly looking out for me but also knew how to give me just the right amount of time and space. The support I received over the next few weeks and months was truly extraordinary. It was incredible, and I will forever be overwhelmed with gratitude for kindness and support of my teachers, students and – of course – Mrs Moulsdale. I can tell you, and I say this hand on my heart, that I had the most positive experience of returning to school possible.

Looking back, I am extremely thankful to have been in a class, and on a side of the year, that was so kind, considerate, and accepting. As I say, they didn't overwhelm and interrogate, and they didn't isolate or alienate. The balance was perfect – I was utterly over the moon. I felt like I was a new and improved version of the 'old' Ben, and I felt like I had been handed a whole new opportunity at life. My teachers were fantastic, as was Pam Shatwell, the Family Liaison Officer. Pam is another one of those individuals who come into your life and transforms it in the most positive way possible. The word icon is an understatement – she is the most incredible human being with the kindest heart and the most generous soul. When my parents were at work, Pam would come and pick me up from home and drive me into school. She knew I was a big fan of business and reading the papers, so one day she bought me Richard Branson's biography. It was little gestures like this which demonstrate what a caring, compassionate and amazing woman Pam is. A true blessing and ray of sunshine in this world. She would reassure me and chat to me as we drove the 10 minutes down the road, before waving me off as I went in through reception. It is individuals like Mrs Moulsdale and Pam (as well as the other teachers who I'll introduce to you later on) who have made who I am proud to be today. Their unconditional kindness, support and genuine care touched my heart and changed my life. Without the kindness and support of individuals like Mrs Moulsdale, Pam, Sarah and the nurses on the ward, I wouldn't be where I am today. I will never cease to be grateful, and I will never cease feeling inspired by what they selflessly do, every single day of the week.

The Summer term flies by, and everything goes well. I'm not back in school fulltime, but I'm attending for lessons that I enjoy, and I'm feeling excited to start GCSEs in September. Before we break up for the summer, it's time to choose our options. Alongside the compulsory English, Maths, Science and Religious Education, I select as my GCSE options: Business Studies, Drama and Geography. I make a note to start reading up on my subjects over the summer, and as we break up for the summer holidays, I feel good about what's ahead. This time last year, I was descending deeper and deeper into the depths of an eating disorder. Today, I feel that the only way is up – I feel eternally grateful to be alive, and I feel genuinely excited about what is ahead. It's a real moment of joy and celebration.

6. PROGRESS MAKES PERFECT

It's September 2013, and there are only three words that could be coming to mind right now – Back to School! Year 9 will forever hold an extraordinary place in my heart. It was, without doubt, the best year of my time at school. Whilst I would love the rest of Key Stage 4 and Sixth Form, this was the year that I really found myself and genuinely fell in love with life. It was the beginning of my rebirth and reincarnation! I put my love for Year 9 down to three things. Number 1, I was still on a high after the wake-up call that my hospitalisation has given me – I'd realised life is precious. I was not longer taking absolutely anything for granted. Number 2, I was genuinely in love with my subjects. I'll make no secret of the fact that I'm an absolute Business Studies nerd. And, as you can imagine, I loved nothing more than 90 minutes spent in the Drama studio twice a week! And number 3, this was the year that I began discovering the amazing friends who would become my rocks for many years to come.

As I wake up every morning, I genuinely feel excited to go to school. GCSEs are still feeling brand new, and being in all these new classes means meeting new people I've never crossed paths with before. Before my hospitalisation, there were certain characters I felt terrified of seeing. I was not one of the 'popular' kids, and I made it my mission to avoid them at all costs. There were some very nasty kids in their 'popular' group, some of whom I'd known in Primary School. I had avoided this group of people like the plague, and I had deeply resented the fact they seemed so confident, outgoing and…well…popular! But my battle with anorexia has provided me with a brand new perspective. I've realised life is too precious and too short to be wasted worrying about what people think. I've also been shown so much kindness and compassion, from nurses, therapists and teachers. My time in therapy, as well as my brand new interest in mindfulness, has done me a whole world of good.

As I wake up every morning and head into my new classes, I'm feeling excited about meeting all these new faces. Having spent months watching daytime TV, I now seem to think that I'm the next Holly Willoughby. I'm confidently starting conversations with whoever find myself sitting next to and have a great time chatting away! I secretly hope that the seating plans will put me next to someone popular so that I can make conversation with them (very sad, I know!) I've discovered that I'm quite good at entertaining people and that I'm quite good at both starting and sustaining conversations. My ability to talk – to anybody about any topic – becomes my number one strength in life! In the past, I had been labelled an attention seeker, a gossip, and a drama-seeker. Whilst it was never my intention to be these things, looking back, I do realise that I was so self-absorbed. I was so desperate for validation that I probably did come across as this loud, insecure character who was annoying and irritating. But, these days, it's very different. I've seen how Phil and Holly make guests feel comfortable on the This Morning sofa, and I seek to emulate what I've seen!

I am much more interested in asking people questions about their lives, rather than giving them a monologue or performance based on mine. I've discovered that the way to win someone's interest is to take an interest in them. And so I make it my new mission to ask people questions about their lives and their interests. Small talk becomes my new specialism – I feel so empowered to make conversation and put a smile on somebody's face. I can't quite believe I'm here making conversation with the *dramatic pause here* popular people! They are talking to me…and I'm making them laugh and smile! Sitting in these lessons, I do feel like I'm in my element. Again, I'm fortunate with the people I'm around. There is nobody overly bitchy or nasty, and there is certainly no bullying to be seen. I'm in the top set and talking to these new people. I'm feeling on top of the world!

My favourite lessons of the week are GCSE Business, Drama and RE. In business, I know the textbooks like the back of my hand. I shamelessly go above and beyond for every single piece of work. I am living my best business nerd life! We get asked to type 1 A4 side of paper giving the answers to the questions, and I regularly fill about 6 or 7 pages instead! I am a shameless Business Studies nerd…and I love it! Whenever I am passionate about a subject, I live and breathe it! I read all the textbooks, do all the research and end up caring more about the subject than the teachers!

In this case, my business teacher is Mrs Moulsdale, and I couldn't be happier. I strongly believe that a teacher either makes or breaks a subject – and Mrs Moulsdale has made business the best topic I have ever studied! These lessons, on a Tuesday and a Thursday afternoon, are my favourite time of the week. I'm sat next to Erin, who I have known since Primary School. We have the happiest memories of performing in shows together over the years, the most recent one 'Bugsy Malone' in Year 6. We haven't spoken much over the past couple of years, but we have the best time in these business lessons. We do not stop laughing – she makes my day! Erin's also in my drama lessons, which are genuinely comedy gold from start to finish. Drama is my opportunity to let go a little, lighten up and have a good laugh – and oh my GOD we do! We only have a small class, but I love it so much.

I remember loving acting as a child, performing in all the school productions and attending one million and one acting classes. Sadly, boys who did drama were not in the same league as boys who played football. I felt very judged, alienated and like people were laughing at me for being so – well – dramatic. Being so passionate about performing made me feel very judged, by both my primary school classmates and also my primary school teachers. The majority of the teachers at my primary school shared a dislike for any child who wanted to express themselves on stage. I found my Year 6 teacher to be particularly dismissive of my love for the performing arts. Whilst loving football meant you were practically the risen Jesus Christ, being interested in shows or performing was nothing but a distraction from your SATs. Her attitude had crushed me, as had the opinions of my primary school peers.

Being interested in performing also meant I was labelled as (a) gay – at the age of about 10, before I even knew what the word meant, (b) going to have a 'sex-change' when I was older – a comment made by a boy in Year 4, aged nine and (c) an attention seeker – a comment made by a boy with the personality of a plant pot in Year 6. At the time, little sensitive Ben took these comments to heart. By Year 7, I believed that going on stage meant you were nothing but a weird, gay, and annoying little attention seeker. As I performed in the school production in Year 7, my anorexia took over my life. The Performing Arts department had cast me as 'Lefou' in Beauty & the Beast. I vividly remember forcing myself to do about 100-star jumps in costume before I went on stage. As a result, my mind associates performing onstage with a lot of negativity, embarrassment and – ultimately – with having an eating disorder.

That's why these GCSE Drama lessons were so good for my soul. They allowed me to perform and get into character, which I loved to do, and I got to do it all within a very safe and accepting space. Everyone in my little class is good fun, even if very few people are here to take it remotely seriously. Let me rephrase that – absolutely nobody is here to take it seriously in any way, shape or form! We giggle our way through the warmups (our teacher pretending to be a cow on the floor doing a 'Moo Off' was a particular highlight). And we laugh our way through the devised performance rehearsals. We find ourselves feeling thoroughly entertained by the whole thing. I genuinely love these lessons – they give me life and a much-needed opportunity to express myself.

I start walking home with Erin afterschool, meaning the poor girl is now not only stuck with me for half the school day but also then for another half-an-hour walking home. There is no escape for the girl! We may only be in Year 9, but we are already having some pretty deep and meaningful conversations. We talk about psychology, mental health, and I find myself opening up about my struggle with anorexia. Erin is a rock – understanding, trustworthy and with a heart of absolute gold. We can talk for hours without running out of things to say and having her in my life makes me feel so much contentment and warmth inside.

In lessons, I am doing well academically. My Geography teacher tells me that my mock exam answer is better than the A-Level work he's marked. Oh, I did put heart and soul into my study of tectonic plates! And my Religious Studies teacher consistently gives me full marks on the tests. I did love reading up on the Catholic. For the first time, I fall in love with learning and education. I feel genuinely interested in what we are studying. So I start spending my spare time looking up mark schemes, searching for exam specifications, and reading around the subject. Reading the daily newspaper also helps with my academic performance. I've got into the routine of walking to the shops at about 7.00 am before school, and then reading through the day's stories every evening when I get home! Each morning, I am served by Lindsey, the loveliest lady, who always greets me with a warm smile and a 'good morning, Ben!' I love seeing her in the mornings – we always have a little chat, and then I walk back home, in full school uniform, clutching my newspaper. I love this little routine and seeing Lindsey every morning – I feel mature, confident, and ready to take on the world.

Reading the newspaper and reading up on my subjects quickly become my favourite things to do in the world. I genuinely love studying…although only in a very select number of areas! For example, I adore English, Geography, RE, Business and Drama. I spend hours reading up on these subjects and genuinely look forward to the lessons. But when it comes to maths, science, and French, however, we have a very different story. I do okay in all these subjects, but I do not feel excited by them…in the slightest. I find them a lot more difficult, and I get annoyed by the fact others pick things up so much quicker than I do. Ever the perfectionist, I decided that if I can't be the absolute best at the subject, then I don't want to care about it at all. It's what we like to call throwing your toys out of the pram! My French is limited to *"Bonjour je'm appelle Ben"*, although I can just about manage *"Un chien vert"* (A green dog) on a good day. Well, this is looking promising!

We're flying through Year 9, and I love every second of it. I'm still seeing Sarah, and walk to CAMHS for an appointment once a week after school. It's been a year since my hospitalisation, but the hard work is only just beginning. Now that I'm getting closer to a much healthier weight, we're starting to explore what might have caused my anorexia. We're starting to talk about what I can do in the future to ensure that it doesn't come back. Anorexia is notoriously difficult to overcome. Only 46.9% - less than half - of Anorexia Nervosa patients are ever classified as 'cured' whilst 30% simply 'improve', and 20% remain 'chronically ill'. Many people believe that you can never fully 'recover' from an eating disorder, but that instead, you can only 'learn to live with it' or 'manage' it. I can certainly understand this belief. There is something about anorexia that, in my experience, means that it completely infiltrates how you think about absolutely everything in your life. However, I am a deeply optimistic person, and I do believe that - with therapy - you can get to a place of genuine 'recovery'. But, of course, it all comes down to whether you genuinely want to recover. Here's what I believe. If you do not genuinely want to be freed from your eating disorder, you will never escape this debilitating condition. If you are not consciously willing to recover, then you never will. It is as simple as that.

I feel like I'm making good progress, both physically and mentally. I still cannot allow myself to think about the fact I'm 'putting on weight'. The concept still fills me with so much anxiety and, if I'm totally honest, an overwhelming feeling of disgust. Why I ask Sarah, would anyone ever celebrate putting on weight? She continues to gently question me and offer counterarguments to the points I am making. It's so helpful to have this 'voice of reason' in the room. Every time you challenge an anorexic thought, you move one step closer to reprogramming your mind and achieving recovery. For me, an important part of my recovery is reframing my relationship with food. For so long, I had seen food as the absolute enemy and had consequently constructed a life characterised by constant restriction, deprivation, and denial.

I tell Sarah that I am still unable to shake off my fear of weight gain. I say that it's because of the 'obesity crisis' and 'weight loss' messaging that I have been absorbing for so long. But is this the truth? Am I using this as a scapegoat or an excuse? Is my anorexia clinging onto anything it can to 'justify' my irrational beliefs and behaviours? Is this the eating disorder's way of deflecting the blame and trying to justify its existence? Whatever the reasons and motivations behind these beliefs, it is clear that they are toxic and that they are causing me an enormous amount of harm. These beliefs, therefore, need to be challenged, and they need to be deconstructed. This is a process that will take a lot of time, hard work and effort, and it will require – of course – a genuine desire to get better. It is only once I have been able seen through these toxic thoughts that I will be able to move closer to liberation and recovery. I see this light at the end of the tunnel, and I resolve to work hard at challenging these toxic and debilitating beliefs.

***

There's a phrase that my mum keeps using which motivates me to get better. She keeps saying this - ***'you need to have the energy to do all of the things that you enjoy'.*** I find that it is a very good way of looking at food. It is a perspective that I have never looked at it from before. For so long, I have seen 'food' as being a source of weight gain, obesity and unattractiveness. Anorexia had led to me completely losing sight of the true role of food in human life. Food, I now realise, is all about fuelling your body so that you can function and thrive. This sentiment is especially powerful considering my loves for studying, filming YouTube videos, and all of my dreams for the future. Suppose I want to enjoy all of this success and achievement. In that case, I need to be fuelling my body and providing myself with energy and nutrition. In the hospital, I was encouraged to view 'food as medicine'. And now, as I recover at home, I'm being encouraged to view 'food as fuel'. I find it very helpful to see food as this 'fuel' as opposed to being a focus in itself. This keeps me focused on all of the things that I want to do and enjoy in life, rather than making my entire life all about food, calorie control and eating. At the height of my anorexia, food became my sole focus in life. I would spend my time watching the food channels, reading up on calorie statistics, and thinking about all the food I wish I could eat. Everything became about food and calories. It was all I would think about, and all I would care about. It is pretty ironic to think I was so obsessed with food, and the one thing I wouldn't do was eat any of it.

Fortunately, I now have other things to focus on. I have my GCSEs, of course, and I have all of these new people that I'm meeting. I also have all of my news and current affairs, which I devour in extraordinary quantities! On a typical evening, I'll watch all of the flagship news bulletins – and then go online to watch even more! I think that I'd love to be a journalist and be interviewing, reporting, and presenting on the top stories. I'm becoming interested in politics, and I am fascinated by reading about the coalition government. I start to realise how much is going on in the world and how much people are going through. It puts all of my problems, worries and concerns into perspective. I remember the Dalai Lama's message of spreading compassion, kindness and love in the world. And I know with confidence that I want to make a difference in people's lives, in the same way, that the doctors, nurses, therapists and teachers have made a difference in mine. I want to use my experiences to help others – I want to, in the words of Gandhi, 'be the change I wish to see in the world'.

But I'm not quite ready to make that worldwide impact…not just yet! I still struggle talking to anybody about my eating disorder. I'm a very happy, chatty and sociable boy – until anyone mentions the word 'anorexia'. Just hearing the word paralyses me. I can't discuss it with anyone but Sarah, my therapist. I hate being asked questions about it. I think part of me is still in a state of complete disbelief and denial about everything that has happened. Part of me refuses to believe that I could be 'anorexic'. It doesn't make sense – I am a teenage boy, not a female model. I can't get my head around it. When someone refers to both me and anorexia, I struggle to believe they're talking about me. I feel embarrassed about it, ashamed that my mental health is being presented as conversational material for the world. The perfectionist within me comes back; I don't want anybody to get even the slightest hint of weakness or vulnerability in my life! I desperately want to control the narrative – I don't want anybody to talk about me, or to see me as anorexic. I've still not fully accepted what has happened, and the anorexic beliefs still bubbling away within me are still implementing 'Project Denial'. I, therefore, refuse to answer questions or discuss 'the a-word'. I almost feel like I'm battling with a severe dose of something comparable to 'imposter syndrome'. I simply cannot get my head around the concepts of 'Ben' (me) and 'anorexia' (the eating disorder) being connected or associated in any way.

Despite these struggles to fully understand and accept my experience with anorexia, I continue making good progress thanks to the support of Sarah and the love of my family. School is going well – I love the subjects, I love the routine, and I love feeling productive. I enter a public speaking competition on behalf of the school…and win! I am on cloud nine, delighted to have done so well at such a prestigious and highly-regarded event. I'm confident talking to teachers, to my peers and strangers out and about in public. I'm feeling good about life!

I decide that I want to start volunteering in Macclesfield hospital, where I had spent all those weeks being cared for on the children's ward. I start working Sunday mornings in the WRVS hospital shop, serving on the little till from 9 am until 1 pm. I adore it – I love talking to the staff and visitors, making small talk and bringing a smile to people's faces. I feel like I'm making a positive difference, and I feel like I'm becoming even more confident in my skin. The social skills development and confidence boost this volunteering gives me is incredible! On those Sunday mornings, I am entirely in my element. I feel a real sense of purpose and a real sense of fulfilment – this kind of service is, I think to myself, what makes life worth living! Everything is looking up, and so I'm feeling more confident and content than I have ever felt before.

7. THE G-WORD

Homo. Faggot. Fag. Batty Boy. Gay. For years, I've been relentlessly labelled with labels such as these. Some of my earliest memories are of being stared at in the street, laughed at in the playground and being called names across the road. For as long as I can remember, people have always seen me as different. It is impossible to count have many times I was described as 'acting like a girl', 'so gay', 'flamboyant' or 'gay boy' in the years before secondary school. At no point during my time at Primary School was I taught what it meant to be 'homosexual'. The word 'gay', 'bisexual' or even 'heterosexual' were never mentioned to us. There was, in this school's worldview, just one kind of relationship – and that was between a husband and wife.

I instead received a very different education in the language of 'homosexuality', in particular, the word 'gay'. I was being described as 'gay' long before I knew what the word meant. All I knew is that people thought I was 'gay', and that this wasn't a good thing. It was intended as an insult, and this word was being used against me in a very judgemental way. People were seeing my love for acting, singing, and performing, and they were assuming I was 'gay' – whatever the word meant. People saw my disinterest in football and my inability to fit in with the other boys on the playground, and they assumed I was 'gay'. Children can be extraordinarily cruel, and they certainly do not filter what they think or say. I did not fit the stereotypical expectation for how a 'boy' should act, speak, or behave. And so I was seen as weird, different – I was seen as gay.

Because the word gay was being used as an insult against me, I assumed it was a very negative and bad thing. I therefore instinctively believed that needed to deny that I was 'gay', despite not knowing what the word meant! It had been made very clear to me that to be seen as 'gay' meant I would be disliked and excluded by my peers. As a child, you are desperate to fit in and win your classmate's approval. So it's not the best feeling when your classmates – and strangers in the street – are labelling you as 'gay', or say that you are 'acting like a girl'.

****

I believe that there are three fundamental foundations for the homophobia and homonegativity that are found in all four corners of our planet. They are societal repression, individual ignorance, and a deep-rooted fear of the unfamiliar. Ever since the formation of civilised society, homo sapiens have been subject to an extraordinary amount of repression. And with the development of organised religions such as Christianity, the repression of mankind was significantly intensified.

Religions such as Christianity taught that mankind was inherently sinful, and so human beings required strict discipline and training. Adam and Eve were blamed for bringing the sin of sexual lust and desire upon humanity, corrupting our nature and predisposing us to sinful behaviours. Religious pioneers such as St Augustine associated sex and sexual desire with sinfulness and shame. This resulted in a situation where human beings were being made to feel ashamed of the thing that comes most naturally to them…sex. Humans are sexual animals, and their sexual desires are therefore perfectly natural. However, organised religion insisted on controlling and disciplining homo sapiens, especially when it came to their sexual desires and behaviours. Under the instruction of St Augustine, the Catholic Church began teaching that mankind ought to be ashamed of lust and sexual desire.

And, under the later instruction of St Thomas Aquinas, the Catholic Church declared that sex was only permissible for the sole purpose of reproduction. The only sexual pleasure that was not sinful, according to Aquinas' Natural Law theory, was that enjoyed between a married couple with the explicit intention of creating new life. Even sex that led to a new life was sinful! The Catholic Church teaches that reproduction leads to the transmission of Original Sin, meaning that every single child born into this world is born into a state of inherent sinfulness and selfishness. Not only is 'sex' therefore unquestionably a sin itself, but it is also the cause and reason for all of the sinfulness in the world! Aquinas declared that the pleasures of sexual intercourse 'seriously corrupt the judgement of moral wisdom'. Sex, therefore, could not be enjoyed or be seen as something pleasurable. It is only permissible when the purpose behind it is strictly the creation of new life, within a monogamous and heterosexual marriage. And even within the context of monogamous and heterosexual marriage, sex was still surrounded by shame and stigma. Is it any wonder that society today has such a big problem accepting sexuality and sexual expression?! In my effort to understand why people were so intolerant when it came to making sense of sexuality, everything was now making sense!

Of course, it was not just the Catholic saints who were intent on curtailing their audience's sexual desires and behaviours. Over 2,000 years ago, Ancient Greek philosopher Plato declared that sensual pleasures distracted men from their pursuit of the ultimate truth. Ever since, there has been almost universal condemnation of sexual desire. Lust and desire are seen as distractions from a rational and respectable way of life. They are also seen as critical threats to the stability of society and the sanity of mankind. Sexual behaviour, therefore, has always been very tightly controlled and regulated. It has long been thought strict repression and regulation is the only way to prevent our degeneration back into untameable animals. We are a species, according to organised religion, that is unable to manage our sexual desires and impulses unless we are subjected to strict authoritarian controls. As Immanuel Kant, the 18th century Enlightenment philosopher, famously declared, 'Man must be disciplined, for by nature he is raw and wild'.

Kant was particularly critical of homosexuality. He wrote that, in 'unnatural' sex acts like homosexuality, we become 'beneath the beasts', whose unthinking behaviour is in tune with an animalistic nature. Homosexuality, according to Kant, was the result of 'giving in' to animalistic and sub-human desires, which led to moral degradation and the collapse of civilised society. Kant, unsurprisingly, believed in the importance of strict discipline and rigorous regulation to maintain a respectable, rational and moral social order.

Kant (one of my 'top 3' philosophers, despite his thoughts of homosexuality) was one of many Western thinkers to believe human beings need strict control and discipline. There is almost unanimous agreement that sexual desire is animalistic, shameful, and a distraction from our intellectual and civilised pursuits as human beings. To an extent, I get where these thinkers are coming from. It's obvious that, if we all acted upon our animalistic desires, our civilised society would indeed collapse. And so I agree that we must have certain standards, rules and regulations when it comes to human sexual behaviour. For example, in the same way, that you can't just go around stealing and killing, you cannot go around engaging in sexual behaviours that cause disruption or harm. However, I do not believe that we should, therefore stigmatise human sexuality and sexual desire to the extent that nobody is allowed to talk about or acknowledge sexuality! If we do not create safe spaces in which to discuss sex, we simply drive sexual behaviours underground. And, when we do this, we create a society that is plagued by hypocrisy, and we create a real crisis with regards to people's sexual health! It's all rather ironic that the people publicly banning and condemning certain sexual acts are the ones most frequently engaging in them behind closed doors!

We cannot confuse the sinfulness of *specific* sexual acts (for example, sexual acts that cause harm to other people) with the notion all sexual desire is sinful. Seeing sex as unequivocally 'sinful' is far too much of a black-and-white way of thinking. To put it another way, we need to get more 'sex positive' as a society! There needs to be much less shame and stigma around sex! We need to move away from the shame that surrounds sexual identity, desire and behaviour and move towards a position where we can all engage in frank, open and honest conversations. Businesses know that sex sells, and porn has become the biggest money-maker on the internet. You don't need to be Freud to know that we're all interested in sex and thinking about sex! Furthermore, we all know that we are only here on this planet because two people decided to have sex. So why are we not acknowledging sex and discussing sexuality?

Our fear of being frank about sexuality is a recipe for disaster. When we don't talk about something, we turn it into a taboo. This is precisely what has happened when it comes to sex and sexuality. Today, we live in a society that is ridiculously repressed and irrationally reluctant to talk about sexuality. This is storing up trouble for future generations, especially in the digital age. If we don't give our young people expert advice and safe spaces for discussion, then they will end up learning everything from non-experts online.

From a very early age, the vast majority of people are conditioned into a state of continuous repression. They are brought up to believe there sexual desires and feelings are shameful, sinful and embarrassing. We fear the naked body, for example, or we shy away from frank conversations about masturbation. I think that homophobia is just one small part of the whole rainbow of problems that arise from this stigma around sex and sexuality.

I cannot emphasise to you enough how important it is to get comfortable thinking about your sexuality. Nothing matters more than being comfortable in your skin, and that starts with an ability to acknowledge and reflect upon your own identity as a human being. A huge and valid part of your identity is your sexuality! And reflecting on your 'sexuality' is not just a task for holding a minority sexual orientation, such as being gay or bisexual.

Instead, every single person – even the most heterosexual person on the planet – deserves to feel informed, aware and secure in their sexual identity as a human being! We need to get comfortable thinking about our sexuality and talking about our sexuality! Being open and honest – even if it's just with ourselves - is the only way that we can find confidence and self-acceptance as human beings!

8. PRIMARY SCHOOL PROBLEMS

My years in Primary School were, if I'm honest, years that I would be more than happy to forget completely! To say that I did not enjoy primary school would be an understatement – I hated every single thing about it. The teachers were archaic in their approach to young people, and the school did nothing to encourage individuality or diversity. The school may have been 'Ofsted Outstanding' on paper, but in reality, I felt that it was a hell on earth. I felt completely lonely, excluded and 'other'. The fact that I was a boy who preferred drama to football was seen as a problem, and I would leave school every day feeling utterly inferior and excluded. There were, of course, many moments of genuine happiness and joy, for example performing as Bugsy in our school production of 'Bugsy Malone' alongside Erin and Harriet. Mrs Scott, our school music teacher, was fabulous and encouraged me to pursue my passion for performing. But she was a very rare gem in a sea of rather closed-minded and uninspiring educators. If I had been a football-loving and 'straight acting' boy, then of course none of these problems would have arisen. But nobody, in particular, can be blamed for this – it was just an unfortunate set of circumstances and a lot of bad luck! It was the perfect storm and a recipe for disaster. We had individual teachers who were getting away with teaching styles that have no place in the 21st century. We had judgmental and bitchy classmates. And we had a wider societal context within which a lot of prejudice and ignorance still existed.

Looking back, I do feel a little bit sorry for my younger self – but I am not one for the self-pity and sympathy party! There were plenty of positives to celebrate – for example, at least I had the most loving and accepting family at home. I believe that there was a greater purpose behind these experiences. Here's how I see it: I would not be the person I am today if I had not had this experience at Primary School. So I am grateful for this time in my life. I could not be happier to be where I am or who I am today. So I am genuinely thankful for this early-life character building and self-development! I certainly didn't have things anywhere near as bad as so many others. And, having now come through the experience, I can look back with gratitude for the insights gained and lessons learned.

I admit that I do still feel extremely bitter about what happened in primary school. Still, I believe that it has made me the person I am proud to be today, and I am also aware that my early experiences could have been a lot worse. As I've mentioned, I do think our society still has a long way to go in terms of promoting acceptance, understanding and inclusivity. We need to keep fighting for the respect and acceptance of all the people in our communities. Schools must be at the front of our fight against racism, sexism, homophobia and every other kind of discrimination in this world. I wouldn't wish my primary school experiences on absolutely anybody, but – actually - I also wouldn't wish them away. As I say, I feel extraordinarily confident, resilient and empowered in my life right now, and I think that this is thanks to the tough times I have been through. I always say this: *'You grow through what you go through!'* And there's one thing that I know for sure: I will never let anybody make me feel so ashamed, embarrassed or excluded ever again! And I will never standby if I see any young person being persecuted because of who they authentically are. So I am thankful for my primary school experiences because they taught me invaluable lessons about the importance of resilience and standing up for yourself!

***

A couple of years ago, I wrote about my primary school experiences in a blog post for the Huffington Post website. I'll talk a little bit more about this later, but for now, allow me to share a couple of paragraphs here:
"**After a lifetime of being bullied for acting gay – whatever that word meant to the children doing the name-calling – I developed the most intense rejection and fear of the idea that I could actually be gay. My only understanding of the word 'gay' during childhood was when the term was being used to bully, insult or mock someone…usually me! I had no understanding of what it meant to actually be gay, having never been taught about homosexuality, gay couples, or never having been introduced to somebody who was openly gay**".

I continued: "**For so long, I have been relentlessly bullied and mocked for 'acting gay', whilst never actually knowing what 'gay' really means. It was being used as a label for my mannerisms and an insult towards my character. As a result, I've never been able to independently establish my sexuality. Being mocked for 'acting gay' led to me fearing and rejecting homosexuality as some dark insult. I saw being 'gay' as something everyone was repulsed by – and so I should be repulsed by as well. Being 'gay' meant you were laughed at, excluded and rejected by everyone in your class. As a result, I've lived a life of suppression, embarrassment, insecurity, and denial**".

I do appreciate the lessons that my early years taught me. But I must admit that it does still make my blood boil to look back on a childhood spent defending myself from accusations that I was 'gay'. How the hell can you label an 11-year-old boy as homosexual? How on earth can you tell a Year 6 student that you know their sexual orientation better than they do? Who on earth thinks that they are entitled to appoint themselves as the gender identity police?

I think that my problems all came down to one single word: repression! In a society where everybody is repressed, anybody who 'stands out' is instantly seen as a 'problem'. The fact that I wasn't conforming to society's ridiculously restrictive – not to mention irrational – gender stereotypes and expectations meant that I was sticking out like a sore thumb. People are drawn to difference like bees are drawn to honey – and they very rarely think that difference is a good thing!

During my primary school years, I did have a real problem with identity. It was not about sexual orientation – you cannot determine someone's sexual orientation based on their mannerisms, interests or how they talk. Sexual orientation is about innate sexual attraction and the sexual behaviours this results in. When I think about the people who would label me as 'gay' at primary school, I want to ask them this. Are you telling me that you imagine what sexual behaviours a ten-year-old child – or younger - is interested in? Should you really be spending your time speculating on what a pre-adolescent child might want to do in the bedroom in several years time? How insecure do you have to be in your own sexuality to spend your time obsessing about somebody else's?

The problem that I was encountering was my inability to conform to society's gender stereotypes and 'norms'. I was being labelled as 'gay' because I did not conform to people's preconceptions of how a 'boy' should walk, talk, act and behave. This is something I still get to this day – people will ask me 'are you a boy or a girl?' or wonder out loud 'why don't you act or talk like a boy?' People, it seems, feel threatened by the fact I don't conform to their narrow-minded and ignorant idea of what a 'boy' should be like. Here's how I see it. If I had been a stereotypical boy (complete with football kit, laddish characteristics and a hatred for anything pink), then nobody would have labelled me as gay. Even if I *was* homosexual in my sexual orientation, like many rugby players, builders and footballers are, people would never, ever have said a thing. The idea that I might be sexually attracted to men would never have crossed their minds – it would have been unfathomable! A quick thought experiment for you: If you show people a male dancer and a rugby player and ask them which one is more likely to be gay, who do you think they'll pick? It doesn't take Einstein to predict which of the two candidates people will pick, without even giving the question 0.1 second of thought. We are all guilty of letting stereotypes completely shape our world view! People do not realise that sexual orientation is completely separate from personality. And people do not realise there is nothing wrong with effeminacy in a man or masculinity in a woman. People's problem with me was not necessarily my sexual orientation, which is an intrinsic, invisible thing. Their problem was with the fact I didn't conform to their gender stereotypes and expectations. This clearly made people feel uncomfortable and threatened. This really isn't surprising; insecure, ignorant and repressed people cannot cope with difference and diversity! These ignorant and repressed individuals felt very threatened by my individuality and self-expression…I almost feel sorry for them!

As a child, I was labelled as 'gay', and it was made very clear to me that being given this label was not a good thing. To be honest, I might as well have been given the label 'different' or 'unusual'. The people who are labelling me as 'gay' are not actually labelling my sexual orientation or preferences. You cannot tell what someone likes in the bedroom from one glance at them in the street! Instead, they were noticing stereotypes, and they were drawn to the fact I appeared very different from their idea of a 'male'. Difference is not a bad thing! As I say, the human mind is drawn to anything or anyone who doesn't blend in and conform. This is human nature, and there is nothing we can do about it, other than resolve to start celebrating difference as a strength, rather than fearing it as a threat. As humans, we fear anything that 'rocks the boat'. Familiarity is the greatest source of comfort, and conformity to gender stereotypes and expectations is something everyone takes very much for granted. No boy is born liking blue, and no girl is born loving pink – we condition our children to like certain things, act in certain ways, and wear certain colours. All of this is because of the societal stereotypes that govern all of our lives. It is only when we finally become aware of how limiting all this labelling is that we can stop being slaves to conformity and start living life on our own terms instead.

No matter how hard I tried, I was unable to conform to the stereotypes or blend in with the other boys. Perhaps if my parents had forced me to stop enjoying acting and had instead sent me off to a football boot camp, things could have been very different. They could have very easily moulded me into a 'mini-me' of my dad, your classic football-crazy, DIY-expert heterosexual man.

But, actually, why should they have done? Whilst this might have protected me from bullying or name-calling, it would have caused much worse problems later on down the line. When you raise your child to be somebody they're not, you sabotage their future happiness and completely damage their self-esteem. Suppose you want to raise a happy and healthy child. In that case, you must give them unconditional acceptance. After all, the secret to a happy life is living with nothing but fearless authenticity. I am so lucky in the respect that my parents have always given me nothing but unconditional acceptance. They have always given me the absolute freedom to do whatever makes me genuinely happy.

Within our home, I was free to play with whatever toys I liked and to pursue whatever interests I enjoyed. And so I went to drama lessons, learnt to play the piano, and sang my way around the house (plastic microphone in hand). Whilst my younger brother Sam went off to play football; I staged performances in our living room. Whilst Sam went off to watch Macclesfield Town Football Club with my dad and Grandad, I auditioned for productions and got involved with local shows. My dad would then come along and help backstage at these productions, whilst my mum would also get involved as a backstage chaperone. Both my brother and I were utterly and unconditionally supported in pursuing our interests and doing what made us happy as individuals. It just so turned out that he was naturally inclined towards football and sport, and I was naturally inclined towards performing in shows. In a way, you could say that he was lucky! He didn't choose to love football, any more than I chose to be gay!

I mean, just imagine a society where everything was in reverse. We could so easily have ended up with a world where boys wore dresses and any boy who played football was seen as weird! It's just the luck of the draw, so I really don't think that we can take it personally! And I don't think we can take the stereotypes and 'gender norms' of today too seriously – they could all be completely different in just ten years!

At home, I was free to be myself without any judgement whatsoever. My parents had open-minds and loving-hearts; the fact that his son wasn't obsessed with football did not threaten my dad's masculinity in the slightest! I was not told how to act or informed 'that's not what boys are interested in'. Instead, I was encouraged to do more of what made me as an individual happy. The problems only began when I would arrive at school and find that the other boys didn't share my same interests (and, of course, as a boy you weren't allowed to go anywhere near the *gasps* girls!) I am fully aware that this was nothing personal. I am wide awake to the fact that I had it very easy in Primary School. I knew that millions of young people have it a million times worse than me! They go through so much more than simply feeling that they don't quite fit in! I was very lucky. I do realise this! Suppose you do find that you can to relate to this feeling of being an outsider. In that case, I do hope that you know you are not alone – and that there is absolutely nothing wrong with you!

As I have mentioned, my teachers – excluding Mrs Scott - were not impressed with my love for performing. And many of the other parents – who were wonderful actors themselves at playing the role of a good, committed Catholic – exuded an attitude of judgement at pick-up time as well. I have always been a little bit of a 'drama queen' with a serious serving of 'sass' and 'flamboyance'. To be 'flamboyant', it felt like it was being made clear to me, was a serious problem. To be a 'drama queen' meant you were an embarrassment. 'Get back to your repression immediately', these people might as well have been shouting! And to be a boy with personality, sensitivity, and femininity was like signing my own death warrant. Children, parents and teachers alike were not impressed.

Everybody had decided that I was gay before I had even been taught what the word meant. The word 'gay' means, of course, 'homosexual', which is defined as a 'person sexually attracted to people of one's own sex'). When you consider it like this, that effectively means my classmates and strangers judging me in the street had decided 10-year-old Ben is 'sexually attracted to other boys and men'. Well, thank you very much for letting me know! I'd love to know why you think sexual orientation could be assumed based on the way somebody walks or talks…especially as a ten-year-old! Why were people imposing stereotypes and assumptions on a 10-year-old child? The fact that I was 'different' was very apparent. People would laugh at me, stare at me and mock me. I thought I was just my 'normal' self, but I was sticking out like a sore thumb. I didn't want all of this staring and sniggering – I desperately wanted people to just be nice to me! Is that really too much to ask as a 10-year-old child? I was a very sensitive little soul, and I was seriously affected by this feeling of rejection and ridicule. As a result of all this labelling and judging, I refuse to even think about the word 'gay'. It's like I've been conditioned to associate being 'gay' with being laughed at, mocked, belittled and excluded.

****

Whenever anyone would use the 'gay' word against me, I would feel absolute panic and horror. The word cut deep into my core. It never failed to have this extraordinarily powerful and paralysing effect on me. I felt like a rabbit in the headlights, and I genuinely couldn't understand why so many people were attacking me with this insult. In my head, I just didn't understand what 'gay' meant. I didn't think about sexual attraction, relationships, who I wanted to have sex with or even who I wanted to get married to. In my head, I was just 'Ben'.

I didn't know any different to the way I acted and behaved. I just did what made me happy and what came naturally to me. If that meant performing in shows or being a little bit dramatic from time-to-time, then so be it! My parents instilled in me the message of doing 'whatever makes you genuinely happy'. I wasn't trying to be 'gay' (I was a pre-adolescent child who wasn't having sex with anybody, of any gender). I wasn't trying to 'act like a girl' or 'become a girl'. And I wasn't trying to be dramatic or different. I was just myself! It became very clear to me that people did not approve of or appreciate that. They took one glance at me and labelled with those three all-defining letters – GAY. And, no, they didn't intend this as a genuine diagnosis of my innate sexuality. Or as a compliment!

The label, totally based on my personality and mannerisms, really triggered something within me. I resented it with every bone in my body. I didn't understand why I was being labelled as 'gay', and I didn't understand why 'gay' was such an awful thing in the first place. All I understood is that being labelled as 'gay' – which was happening all the time – was making me a very lonely, mocked and alienated young boy. And you don't exactly rush to start embracing such self-diminishing and insulting labels, do you?!

As a young boy, I was unable to take ownership of my sexuality or just identity in general. I was too sensitive and so desperate to be included by others that I lived every day on a complete rollercoaster of emotions. My self-esteem was, for some reason, entirely dependent on what other people thought of me – and what they thought of me was not very good! I was desperate to be anything but this 'gay sissy' who 'was acting like a girl'. I just wanted people to like me! I just wanted people to be nice to me! Instead, I felt judged and excluded every time that I opened my mouth.

For a long time, I had taken refuge in the theatre and performing arts. But that had become another source of ridicule and rejection. Boys, I was told, are meant to play football and sports…not get dressed up and dance around in a musical. And so, 11-year-old me ended up having quite an identity crisis. I hated being singled out and sniggered out – why couldn't I be like the popular boys, who went round to people's houses and were centre of attention on the playground? That feeling of rejection and exclusion left, I believe, a lasting impact on my psyche, with two particular consequences:

- I was determined to never be put down, excluded, or ridiculed by anyone ever again. I would become extremely defensive and assertive.
- I could not stand seeing anybody being rejected or excluded. I made it my mission in life to ensure everybody felt included and valued. I could not stand seeing anybody being bullied or ridiculed – I became seriously passionate about calling out bullies and empowering young people.

****

I arrived at secondary school ready for a new start, but still not ready to think about the 'gay' word. I genuinely was not thinking about sexual attraction, relationships or sexuality – at all. Everyone else had decided I was gay. Meanwhile, I was stuck in a mode of denying the label whilst still not understanding what it even meant in the first place. All I knew was that 'gay' felt like a derogatory insult designed to isolate me, single me out and put me down. It was a barrier to forming friendships or gaining acceptance and inclusion by the group. I was being labelled as 'gay' because I was not conforming to the masculine stereotypes. I think that the problem lies with societal attitudes to gender roles and stereotypes, not with the morality of same-sex sexual acts and behaviours.

After all, why should a child in the school corridor be concerned with what consenting adults might get up to in the privacy of their own bedroom? I realise that my presence is offensive to so many people because they are so repressed in their own lives. I am just here 'being me', and I am just following my parent's guidance to 'do whatever makes you happy'!

It starts to dawn on me that so many of these kids who are name-calling me cannot be not happy in themselves. They are so enslaved to stereotypes and so desperate for approval that they have lost all their individuality and identity. They look to the others in their group for constant approval and reassurance. They feel threatened by someone who is a little bit different or presents some kind of challenge to the stereotypes enforced upon them as they grew up. You don't choose your parents, and you don't choose how they will shape you during your formative years as a child. I strongly believe that cannot become a judgmental person unless you have been cruelled judged yourself in the past. I feel blessed that my parents are so loving and unconditionally accepting of my interests and mannerisms. Still, I feel frustrated that the rest of the world can't be the same.

Why is it so hard to fit in? Why is it so difficult to make friends? Why don't these people just talk to me normally? Why do they define me by the fact they think I'm 'gay'? Who will give me a chance to just 'be me'? Will anyone ever like me for 'being me', or am I going to spend the rest of my life being rejected, labelled, and alienated?

The next thing I know, the anorexia has taken over. Could the anorexia be a response to my feelings of alienation and my desire to have back some control over how people perceive me? I honestly couldn't tell you. I've thought about it over and over, but I just cannot make sense of it. I think sexuality is often closely linked with self-esteem and body image. And I think that battling with anorexia does perhaps highlight deep-rooted difficulties concerning authenticity, self-acceptance and self-awareness. In my personal experience, I found that anorexia is very much about appearance, control, and denial. It is about a lot more than weight loss – it is a manifestation of your internal struggles with identity, control, relationships, and appearance. It is extraordinarily compulsive, seriously deceitful, and utterly overwhelming. Did speculation and self-doubt about my sexuality all get too much for me? Was I struggling to deal with my feelings of rejection, alienation and the endless labelling? I certainly felt very lost and very misunderstood in the world. I was seriously struggling to understand who I was. I had all of these strangers taking one look at me and ridiculing, mocking and labelling me for the way that I walked and talked. In my attempts to take back control and manage all those feelings of anger and pain, had I been especially vulnerable to a crippling and debilitating eating disorder? Was it the case that anorexia was very easily able to exploit my insecurities and make me obsessive about my eating?

Although I didn't want to talk about my sexuality during therapy sessions with Sarah, I can vividly remember it coming up in conversation once. It must have been about one year into my recovery, and I must have said something about people's comments concerning my personality and mannerisms. Sarah asked me 'have you ever thought about the fact that you could be…might possibly…be gay?' I instantly became extremely defensive and shut the conversation down. Even after a year of CBT – which is all about that self-awareness and insight – I could not bear to hear the word 'gay' brought up in my presence. This was the word that bullies and strangers had used to attack, belittle and hurt me for the first 14 years of my life. I associated this word with so much rejection, unpopularity and inferiority. I had been conditioned – by all this name-calling – see 'gay' as the label people use for somebody who is disliked, excluded and weird. I hated being that alienated and excluded person. I hated people judging me so harshly and cruelly, without even knowing a single thing about me. If they were going to label me and reject me, as 'gay', then I was going to protect myself in whatever way possible. This meant refusing to think about or discuss the 'g-word', and so I focused on my studies instead.

Over time, however, something changed. Perhaps that's just what happens as you get older and become more aware of yourself, of your sexual identity and other people around you. As I say, I had never expressed any sexual interest in either sex. Well, I was too busy performing in shows, setting up sweet stalls at the bottom of the garden and, later, reading the daily newspapers! But as I got older, I did begin to think about the future and, in particular, the prospect of relationships. I did enjoy my own company, and I was indeed extraordinarily self-sufficient. Having spent most of my time at primary school feeling very alone, I had become very independent. I was at my happiest – and I still am to this day – when I was doing my own thing and left to my own devices. I remember feeling so lonely and rejected on the playground or in the year six cloakroom – I had never wanted to feel like that again. So I had become my own best friend. I lived in my own little bubble, where I was quite happy to keep busy and keep myself entertained. But, like all of us, I did start to think about relationships and romance. And after getting through anorexia, I realised that life was too short to let other people's judgements, opinions and assumptions hold you back. Having nearly died from an eating disorder, I was only too aware of the preciousness and value of human life. If I could survive anorexia, I could survive anything! And I needed to make sure I appreciated every single second of my life!

My experience of anorexia really had given me a brand-new perspective on life. I was feeling so thankful to be alive that I stopped caring so much about what other people thought of me. I put all of those worries about being labelled or judged into perspective – after what I'd put my own body through, and after what the doctors had said to me, I had realised that the things unkind kids said and thought in the corridors were the least of my concerns. We are so fortunate to be alive, I would think to myself, that we need to stop taking our existence for granted and start living life to the full instead. I had almost lost my life to self-hatred – I was not going to endanger my existence like that ever again. And so, as I went into year 10, I started allowing myself - for the very first time – to think about sexuality. The memories from Primary School were still incredibly painful. Yet, I wanted to make sense – and make peace with - of all this name-calling and labelling.

I was so fortunate to be surrounded by the most loving, kind, and unconditionally accepting friends imaginable. Even though I hadn't breathed a single word about sexuality in their direction, I felt their unconditional support. So many of the most important messages are the ones that are transmitted unspoken, and I felt extremely accepted and supported by those around me. I was also becoming a lot more confident in my own skin – I knew what subjects I enjoyed, I cultivated an ability to talk to anybody about anything, and I was living my life with a greater sense of meaning and purpose. I would start every morning with 30 minutes of meditation before reading from the pages of Dalai Lams's 'Art of Happiness'. As a result, I felt very mindful, and I felt that the meaning of my life was to spread kindness, love, and compassion. Subsequently, I felt invincible; I knew my worth, I knew my purpose, and I knew that I had a strong group of friends around me.

I was also so fortunate to have the most amazing teachers and educators. They would prove to be incredibly inspiring and empowering. I now had

Mrs Connor, the Deputy Principal, for Business Studies, and I found myself deeply inspired by her incredible teaching and leadership. Mrs Connor – along with her work ethic, commitment and, let's not forget, effortless glamour – was a key source of inspiration during my high school experience. She inspired me to pursue a career in teaching, in particular in school leadership (well you know me, I don't like to do things by halves!). I know that I would not be who I am or where I am today without her. She would say that she was just 'doing her job', but anyone who has met her will be able to testify that it is in her DNA to go 'above and beyond'. When I look back at my journey over the past few years, I am most thankful for the ***people*** who have inspired and empowered me along the way. And for Mrs Connor, I am extraordinarily thankful. I was also lucky to have been taught English firstly by Miss Gerrard, and then by Mrs Williams. They were two exceptional teachers whose energy and dedication (not to mention their 'power outfits', as I liked to call them) inspired me to teach myself. And in Religious Studies, the angelic Mrs Sutton was another source of inspiration and support. Mrs Sutton was another outstanding teacher whose commitment to her subject and genuine concern for her students made the most extraordinary difference in my life. Thanks to these teachers – and many more – I felt safe, supported and valued at school. I felt excited about the future, and I realised that life is all about making a positive difference in people's lives. I saw how these teachers had changed my own life, and I wanted to go on to make that powerful difference myself.

But I wasn't standing in front of the classroom myself yet! Instead, I was the one still learning, both academically and personally. Our school, like every school, had its fair share of bullies and bitches. I can remember one particularly vile little boy impersonating how I talked and shouting about me being gay (what a surprise!) But I'm aware that I got off very lightly – I've heard some real horror stories about the bullying and abuse some young people face on the school corridors. I was, I can see now, living in a lovely little Cheshire bubble. And, with my friends and classmates, I was blessed to be surrounded by the best of the best. In my lessons, I had a friendly top set class which I felt confident and comfortable to be around. I was enjoying chatting to all these new people who I would have been afraid of back in year 7! I had now formed some amazing friendships, in particular, Erin and Becky. They would become my absolute rocks and remain my best friends to this day. I was blessed to have so many genuinely lovely friends – and I was genuinely shocked that these people wanted to spend time with me! I couldn't believe that, after the way I had been treated in Primary School, people genuinely liked me and wanted to be friends with me! Looking back, I feel genuinely blessed that the universe brought me amazing friends like Douglas, Harriet, Poppy, Emma, and (Café Nero) Erin. I genuinely could not be more thankful for the amazing support system, love and kindness that I had around me. And it was only within this loving and supportive framework that I could dare to consider the subject that filled me with so much fear and horror – my sexuality.

9. IGNORANCE, REPRESSION & SELF-EXPRESSION

The biggest problem I had was this idea that being 'gay' meant you were going to be alienated, excluded, and rejected for the rest of your life. This was, I cannot emphasise this to you enough; the only understanding I had of the word. I did not understand 'gay' as sexuality; I understood 'gay' as an isolating insult and a taunt that was being used by bullies. In the same way that I'd had to challenge my irrational anorexic thoughts and beliefs, I had to challenge these irrational – and self-limiting - beliefs about my sexuality. I had to separate the bullying I had received for acting in a way that people deemed to be 'gay' from the reality of being homosexual in sexual orientation. Let us not forget that it was illegal to be gay in the UK just 50 years ago! 'Coming out' is never going to be the easiest thing to do in the world, especially considering that much of the world is still extraordinarily homophobic and intolerant of homosexuality. Gay relationships are still criminalised in over 70 countries worldwide, with the death penalty still enforced as a punishment for same-sex sexual acts in some. Humans have been participating in same-sex sexual acts for literally thousands of years. Despite this, the world today has a big problem with any behaviour that challenges the patriarchal hierarchy of modern society.

As I say, I believe that three key things fuel the homophobia we see endemic in the world today. They are individual ignorance, societal repression, and a perfectly natural 'fear of the unfamiliar'. Homosexuality, for many people, represents a shameful and sinful kind of lust, and promiscuity that threatens to challenge the order of society and undermine their pre-existing ways of life. Sex and sexuality are surrounded by so much stigma and shame. This means that so many people are never able to explore or make sense of their own sexual identity fully. Our world never gives people the framework within which to explore their sexuality and fully understand who they are.

As the 20th-century philosopher Ludwig Wittgenstein famously said, 'the limits of my language are the limits of my world' – we're still living in very repressed times. So we are all still incapable of articulating and understanding what it means to be a sexual being. I do believe that sexuality is a lot more fluid and flexible than society would like us to believe. Human beings are very fond of putting people into categories and boxes when, in reality, nothing (not least human sexuality) is ever that black or white. Reductionism of this kind is futile!

Perhaps the most interesting – yet unsurprising - revelation is the fact that the people who are the most critical of homosexuality are the ones secretly having the most frequent homosexual trysts! There's a famous life-coaching saying that 'whatever triggers you the most reveals what you need to heal'. If you were truly secure in your heterosexuality, why would you be so personally offended by homosexuality? Suppose you were truly confident in your own identity as an individual. Why would you be so unhappy about others being confident and comfortable in theirs? Of course, secret homosexuality is not the sole explanation for all the homophobia that we see in the world! A lot of homophobia is ingrained into whole societies and belief systems. This means that, for many people, believing homosexuality is 'intrinsically disordered' is as factual as believing that there are seven days in the week. Many people are raised to believe that homosexuality, sex before marriage and masturbation will all result in eternal punishment in Hell. We, therefore, cannot be surprised when these people express homophobic or homonegative views! But I also don't think we can lose sight of the fact that homophobia can be overcome. In the words of Nelson Mandela, **"No one is born hating another person because of the colour of his skin, or his background, or his religion. People must learn to hate, and if they can learn to hate, they can be taught to love, for love comes more naturally to the human heart than its opposite."**

This 'teaching' is very important. When it came to making sense my sexuality, I cannot overstate just how important and empowering education has been. Indeed, I would say that reason I am so confident in my sexuality today is because of the education I gave myself about sexuality aged just fifteen. All I can say is thank God for Google – my ability to accept my sexuality is all thanks to the research and studying that I did back in year 10 and 11! They say that knowledge is power. Well, I found gaining the knowledge that homosexuality is natural and normal to be the most empowering process in the world. I am a strong believer in John Stuart Mill's 'non-harm principle', which he devised back in the 19th century. Mill says this: **"The only purpose for which power can be exercised over any member of a civilised community, against his will, is to prevent harm to others"**. In other words, we should all be free to do whatever makes us genuinely happy, as long as this does not involve causing harm to anybody else. When I read this quote for the first time, it genuinely transformed my entire world outlook. I have never felt so empowered, emboldened or liberated from the judgements and criticisms of society! Almost overnight, I realised that despite the name-calling and the mocking, being 'gay' would not cause harm to absolutely anybody in the world. How were my sexual preferences in the bedroom anybody's business but my own? In what way was my love life an issue of national security?

Thanks to Mill's 'non-harm principle', I 'woke up' to the realisation that the problem was with the homophobia, and not with my *potential* homosexuality. My mind was opened to the fact that being 'gay' did not mean social suicide, as I had subconsciously believed for so long. I realised that it was not right for me to continue living my life in fear of people's opinions and judgements. As the Dalai Lama had written in 'the Art of Happiness', the purpose of your life is to be happy. And I – just like anybody else – deserved to be happy! How dare people bully me, belittle me and make me feel so inferior! How dare they get on with their lives whilst not allowing me to do the same! I felt both angry and empowered. I felt ready to make sense of who I was. I felt ready to stop feeling so threatened by people's snap judgements and assumptions, and I felt ready to take full ownership for my life instead.

This is a crucial point. I believe very strongly that it is only when we finally take responsibility for our own lives that we can find true happiness in this world. Up until this point, I had lived my life in this self-pitying victim mindset. I went through life with a real chip on my shoulder, almost looking for somebody to criticise, judge or be 'mean' to me. I became my own worst enemy and the single biggest barrier to my happiness in life – I was refusing to take any responsibility for myself. I was blaming everybody and everything else that I could for my unhappiness and misery. Well, I now think enough is enough! I need to pull myself together, take responsibility for my existence, and become the master of my destiny! I cannot keep feeling like a victim to other people's opinions! I cannot keep complaining and crying my way through each day I have on this planet! This is my one lifetime and, unless I take action now, I am going to waste all of it as a prisoner. A prisoner to my emotions, fears and other people's opinions!

I needed to make peace with my memories of being labelled 'gay' in a way that made me feel being gay was an inherently bad thing. My vision and understanding had been totally clouded – my early experiences had completely corrupted my understanding of the word 'gay'. My Catholic Primary School never taught me about the existence of loving and monogamous homosexual relationships – they never mentioned the words 'gay' or 'LGBT' to me once! Instead, my education came entirely from the playground and my experiences in public (where I had been labelled and ridiculed as 'gay').

I realised that I needed some serious re-education and rehabilitation. More specifically, I needed to rethink my relationship with the word 'gay totally'. I could not continue fearing this three-letter word. I could not continue burying my head in the sand. I needed to forget everything that I had absorbed from both societies and the people around me. I needed to face my fears, move beyond my insecurities, and ask myself the question – could I actually be gay?

Once I was prepared to consider this question, in a completely non-judgemental and entirely open-minded way, the scales instantly started to fall from my eyes. It sounds so cliché, but it was literally like these dark storm clouds had cleared. I could see clearly for the very first time! In the same way that I'd had to become aware of my anorexic thoughts in order to confront and overcome them, I now had to become aware of my internalised homonegativity. (Internalised homonegativity refers to the process whereby lesbian, gay and bisexual persons internalize societal messages towards gender and sex – often unconsciously – as part of their self-image).

I started to realise the extent of my internalised homonegativity. I quickly realised how deeply ingrained repression and suppression is within modern society. Everybody is having sex – but absolutely nobody is talking about it! Everybody is going through the same journey of making sense of their own sexuality – but nobody is discussing that journey with anybody else! No wonder so many people were struggling with their sexuality, battling with repression, and unable to live an authentic existence! Discovering this was like taking the blinkers off and seeing clearly for the very first time. I was finally waking up to the fact that the majority of people sleepwalk through life in a very sexually-repressed state! I finally realised that the people doing the name-calling and staring were not the 'perpetrators' but victims themselves – they were victims to repression and ignorance. And I felt very sorry for them indeed! If you go through life with such a closed-mind and with so much intolerance towards other people, then you surely cannot be living a genuinely happy life! I wanted to help these people realise that there was another way to live their lives. I wanted to help them wake up to a world of acceptance, openness and personal freedom!

***

As I have said, I am blessed to have the most accepting and non-judgmental family in the world. I did not 'dislike' gay people; for a start, I had never actually met or known a single openly 'gay' person. There were no openly gay teachers, TV characters or role models who I could see. My only experience with the word 'gay' had been in a name-calling context. All I knew was that – according to people in my class and people in the street – the way I was walking and talking meant that I was 'gay'. And they felt the explicit need to bring this up, single me out, and mock me because of it. I hated being labelled and singled out in this way. And (I can see now) I was struggling with a heavy case of 'internalised homonegativity'.

LGBT+ people are one of the most stigmatized groups in society. There is still an extraordinarily high level of intolerance towards LGBT+ individuals, undoubtedly because of society's continual repression of sexuality in absolutely any form. Thanks to St Augustine and his aforementioned belief that human lust and desire are sinful, our society is deeply embarrassed by sex and sexual desire. This is even though it is a completely natural and normal part of human behaviour. It shocks me to think that homosexuality was still illegal for much of my grandparents lifetime. This means that this generation is only the first to grow up in a society that does not universally, by law, condemns homosexuality.

This inevitably means that an enormous amount of stigma, intolerance and unkind judgement will remain – this is just the beginning of the journey towards a society of complete acceptance, inclusivity, and diversity. For many people, homosexuality or non-conformity to simplistic gender stereotypes remains a reason for condemnation, rather than celebration. Social change takes time, and we cannot expect to wake up in a perfect world where everyone is kind, loving and unconditionally accepting. Most people live very repressed lives, blindly conforming to societally-imposed stereotypes and gender expectations. I just thank my lucky stars that I am so fortunate to wake up in a household where this unconditional acceptance is not the case. I realise now how incredibly fortunate I have been to live in a home where I have always been unconditionally loved and accepted. The number of children thrown out of home and disowned because of their sexual orientation is shocking and sickening.

Why are people so homophobic, and why is there so much homonegativity? I think it all comes down to those two key factors: societal repression and individual ignorance. We have been conditioned to believe that sexuality is sinful and that we should be ashamed of our sexual desires. We have an innate fear of anyone we deem to be 'different'. It, therefore, should not come as a surprise that people fear anything – or anyone – that they don't understand. Homophobia, of course, literally means 'fear of homosexuality'. People are afraid of anything that appears different or might present a challenge to their normative world view. We are tribal creatures who feel safest when surrounded by people just like ourselves. So when someone rocks the boat and presents a challenge to your pre-existing world view, we don't like it one bit!

Homosexuality, of course, is a minority sexual orientation, and so there will always be this fear and misunderstanding. But there is, I believe, a solution to homophobia – and it is through education and exposure! I strongly believe that 'you can't hate anybody whose story you know'. When people realise that gay people are normal people with feelings, emotions and families just like themselves, they will stop feeling so threatened by minority sexualities. If you feel secure in your skin, I truly believe that you will not have a problem with other people's sexuality. It is only because many people are so repressed themselves that they are unable to be comfortable with people expressing who they authentically are. The solution to the problem of intolerance is through encouraging all people to become the very best and most authentic version of themselves. We need to make sure people are exposed to inspiring and hard-working individuals who just so happen to be homosexual. When we meet gay doctors, lawyers, teachers, priests, business owners and politicians, we realise that sexuality is nothing to fear. We realise that diversity is a strength, not a weakness.

Homophobia is fuelled by stereotypes, prejudice, misunderstanding and stigma. The only way to combat this plague of misinformation and intolerance is by rolling up our sleeves and starting conversations that will build bridges in our everyday lives. We need to give inspiring LGBT+ figures a platform. Just by being a visible LGBT+ presence or ally, I believe that you can become a catalyst for change. Just by giving people a safe space in which to explore their sexuality – something which 99.9% of people have never been given a chance to do – we can bring enlightenment and empowerment to all four corners of the world! A sexual liberation will benefit every single one of us – men, women and non-binary individuals alike will feel instantly much more accepted and understood! We are all human beings, and we all have the same needs for sexual expression!

***

I began to gain conscious of and work on understanding. My 'internalised homonegativity'. I became genuinely confused about why homosexuality was seen as such an intrinsically bad and awful thing. I couldn't quite grasp why people felt so strongly – and so negatively – about other people's sexual orientation. I genuinely could not understand why society felt so angry, threatened, and furious about people's sexual orientations. At this time, the internet became my greatest source of education, information and empowerment.

The internet is, in my opinion, humanity's greatest invention. It is the greatest way to connect, educate and empower human beings. It gives us all equal access to practically limitless amounts of information and opportunity, all at the click of a button. Whilst my primary school did not teach me a single thing about sexuality in general – never mind about homosexuality! – the internet was an endless source of knowledge, insight, scientific studies and opinion. Thanks to the articles I was reading, I was able to understand my own 'internalised homonegativity'. And I was finally able to make sense of the way that people had been treating me.

For example, I read Office for National Statistics reports which revealed that 93.2% of the UK population identify as heterosexual/straight (2017), meaning that almost 7% of people did not. Yet the statistics said that only 2% said they identified as lesbian, gay or bisexual (2017). I start to realise I am not the only person in the world who is on the receiving end of this homophobic name-calling bullying. This realisation is incredibly empowering and genuinely liberating. Instantly, I no longer felt so alone, isolated and misunderstood. Reading these statistics gave me a newfound feeling of self-assertion and self-assurance – I realised, perhaps for the very first time, that I was not alone! If I was, in fact, gay, then I wouldn't be the only person on the planet who was! It sounds stupid writing this down now, but at the time, it felt like a major epiphany moment in my life. Up until this point, I had genuinely felt so alienated, misunderstood, and lost. The idea that being 'gay' might be – dramatic pause for effect here – a normal and perfectly acceptable thing was a bombshell and a half. My little brain couldn't quite comprehend it! And with this realisation, everything changed. With this breakthrough, the blinkers covering my eyes fell off. It was as if my ignorance was evaporating. I realised that 'gay' was not some scary insult that meant a life of nothing but exclusion, inferiority, and rejection. Instead, I was realising; homosexuality is something perfectly natural, normal, and acceptable.

As I continued my reading and research, I realised that being 'gay' does not define you or demean you as a human being. For so many years, I had felt the burden and weight of this label on my shoulders. I had consequently carried around the very self-limiting belief that 'nobody likes me because they think I'm gay'. In my head, people didn't like me because I wasn't acting like the other boys. They didn't like me because of the way I walked or talked, and the assumptions that they made as a result of this. As I continued to do my research into homosexuality, a thought suddenly came into my mind. Why I asked myself, am I letting these people put me in a box and put me down in this way? Since when was it acceptable to give people the permission to label and belittle you in this way? In what universe is it healthy or acceptable to give other people so much power over your self-image and self-esteem?

I started to realise my insecurities were fuelling an inescapable state of self-hatred and self-sabotage. I was desperate for everybody to like me, and I could not handle it when it transpired that they did not. And, let's be real, many people did not. That's not necessarily a problem – not everybody in the world has to like you! The real problem was the fact that I was taking this rejection and ridicule personally. I was effectively outsourcing my self-esteem and validation to kids in my class and strangers in the street. Why did I care so much about what they thought of me? Why was I so worried about their opinion of me? Why was I assuming that they were right and that I was the one who needed to change? Could it not be that they were the ones with the issue, and not me?

Of course, we all want to be accepted and included. The 'herd mentality' is a basic human instinct because we all know that we will be safer when we are part of a larger group. Human beings are social animals who have evolved from tribes of hunter-gatherers dependent on the protection of the group to survive. However, there is a very clear difference between the healthy desire to 'belong' and irrational fear of being 'disliked'. I needed to learn that somebody not liking me was not the end of the world – my whole universe would not collapse just because I was not one person's cup of tea! To develop this kind of self-confidence and resilience, you must learn to accept who you authentically are. If you do not genuinely like and accept yourself, then you will go through life as a very sensitive a. If you take every rejection and remark personally, you will not be able to cope with life in the modern world we live in today!

I knew exactly what I needed to do. I needed to unconditionally accept myself, grow a thicker skin, and stop caring so much about what irrelevant strangers thought about me! I needed to become a master of my destiny and take back control of my life. Other people could not continue dictating my self-image and self-esteem!

As I continued scouring the internet for information and knowledge about homosexuality, I could feel my entire world view changing. I am waking up, opening my eyes, and providing myself with the most amazing education imaginable. As I scroll through the search results, I read articles about footballers, rugby players, business CEOs and television stars who are homosexual. Never in a million years had I imagined that a footballer or rugby player could be 'gay'. I had been completely consumed by the 'homonegativity' that is endemic throughout our society. Sexuality is completely independent of your personality, I realise! Of course, there must be millions – hundreds of millions – of people who are lesbian, gay and bisexual. Being 'gay' is not an insult, problem or an attack – it is a naturally occurring and harmless human sexual orientation. It does not – or should not – limit you in any way, shape or form. It does not mean you cannot live a positive, happy, successful and fulfilling life. It does not diminish or demean you as a human being. It does not mean you deserve to be ostracised, dehumanised and vilified by the rest of the world. Instead, it just means that the gender of the person you are sexually attracted to is the same as your own. That is it. And what on earth is so awful, disgusting, or offensive about that?

As I start to realise that there is nothing whatsoever wrong with being gay, I begin feeling incredibly angry. Rage and fury are bubbling away within me. I feel as if I've been conned – all of these people have made me feel so small because I was acting 'gay' when there is absolutely nothing wrong with acting gay! How can society be so cruel and unjust? How dare all these people think that can decide my sexuality and then completely belittle me because of that sexuality they have assumed? What right did they have to cause so much harm, self-hatred, and unhappiness? What precisely was their problem?

This is an extraordinary turning point in my life. It is a moment of a total transformation. I have gone from a fear of being labelled as 'gay' to feeling a genuine fury about the fact people have made me feel that being 'gay' is wrong. As I keep scrolling, I come across a psychology article explaining something called the 'Kinsey Scale'. I clicked onto the article and became instantly enthralled in reading about this research. The Kinsey Scale, I discovered, is used in research to describe a person's sexual orientation. The scale ranges from 0, meaning exclusively heterosexual, through to 6, meaning exclusively homosexual. I was fascinated to read that (according to 'Sexual Behaviour in the Human Male', published back in 1948) at least 37% of males – 1 in 3 – 'had experienced at least some overt homosexual experience to orgasm'.

What's more, this 1948 study had found that 10% of males were 'more or less exclusively homosexual' (See the Kinsey Institute website for more details on this study!) That was 1 in 10 men! How could there be so much hostility towards homosexuality when so many people were – or at least knew someone who was – gay!

Sexuality, I started to realise, was a complex spectrum that went well beyond the labels, stereotypes and name-calling that I had encountered during my childhood. Again, this was an earth-shaking discovery. I had suddenly realised that sexuality was so much more than stereotypes and assumptions based on how somebody acts – sexuality is not a 'way of walking' or a 'way of talking'. Sexuality was not as simple as 'he's acting like a girl; he's gay'. Sexuality was instead a complex spectrum that every single person in the world has a place on. All these people labelling me as gay could, I started to think, be themselves enjoying plenty of male-on-male bedroom action! The people who appear to be the 'straightest' in the room (e.g. the best at conforming to society's gender stereotypes and expectations) could be having more gay sex than anyone else! How dare all of these people go around labelling me and belittling me as some weird and abnormal reject when every single one of us sits somewhere on the sexuality spectrum! They might have looked more 'heterosexual' than me (according to those societally imposed stereotypes). But that didn't mean they had fewer feelings of same-sex attraction than I did. You cannot, under any circumstances, assume somebody's 'sexual orientation'. And actually, do we even have a set sexual orientation? Surely human sexuality is too complex to be reduced down into three mutually exclusive categories of 'straight', 'bisexual' and 'gay'?

Labelling sexuality, I read, was a very new phenomenon. Back in the days of Jesus Christ and the Ancient Greeks, sexuality was never labelled in the way it is today. Over 2,000 years ago, for example, Greek men would regularly have sex with boys, and these same-sex sexual practices were seen as completely normal and fine. Ancient Greece was the birthplace of Western Philosophy, and Ancient Greek philosophers such as Plato and Aristotle have completely shaped the entirety of Western Civilisation! I am not suggesting we should ever endorse this Ancient Greek practice of pederasty (sexual acts between men and boys). But I am very interested in the fact that Greeks saw sexuality in a very different way to us. It proves the issue of homosexuality is a lot more complex than many people seem to realise! At what stage did society suddenly decide that the 'normal' way to express 'love' is through a monogamous, heterosexual relationship? I think it's a little bit like open relationships – why has society decided that there is something so morally wrong with people sleeping with multiple different people? We have so many societal norms – mainly related to regulating and controlling our sexual practices and relationships – that we are just expected to accept and adhere to without question. I wanted to know why everybody had a problem with my supposedly 'effeminate' mannerisms, and behaviours. Why did they assume my sexuality based on my appearance and personality, and why was someone homosexual a problem in the first place?

The biggest shift in my thinking came when I realised that it was the homophobic people judging me who had the problem, not me! For so many years, I genuinely believed that there was something wrong with me. I thought that it was somehow my fault all these people were treating me as weird, different and inferior. But now (as I realised that homosexuality was something natural and normal within a diverse human population) I realised being 'gay' was not something I needed to apologise for. And I realised that there was nothing wrong with the fact that I was a little bit more 'effeminate' or 'flamboyant' than the other boys! After spending years apologising for my 'over-the-top' and 'too much' personality, this was a very liberating discovery indeed.

10. KNOWLEDGE IS POWER

It was around this time that I began to get interested in philosophy and psychology, two subjects that would become my absolute passions in life. My interest had been initially ignited as I read the daily newspapers when I become interested in human behaviour and political debate. I was already conscious of mental health as a result of my own experience with anorexia. Still, I was noticing the issue in the papers more and more. I also became very interested in human behaviour – and specifically, motivation – as a whole. In Year 9 Business lessons with Mrs Moulsdale, I had loved studying the 'Business and People' module. I was fascinated by Maslow's hierarchy of needs theory and spent hours researching other theories of human motivation. I became utterly obsessed with human behaviour and understanding 'what makes people tick'. I began reading so much about social psychology, explanations for certain behaviours, and what makes people do the things they do. I think half of me was interested in making sense of my own life experiences and struggles with mental illness. And half of me was fascinated by getting to know people and understand what is going on 'beneath the surface'. Every single one of us is projecting an image and performing for the outside world. Even the loudest and most confident person in the room has there share of fears, insecurities, and anxieties. We only ever see the 'tip of the iceberg', and it was my new passion to understand what is going on people's minds and lives.

A bit part of what shapes an individual is, I soon started to discover, their core beliefs and values in life. Our core values and fundamental life principles massively influence our outlook on the world and how we conduct ourselves. This demonstrates how the values we inherit from our parents fundamentally shape how we live our lives. Discovering how much values and beliefs so heavily shape people led to me exploring, in quite some detail, the basics of philosophy and religion. I became genuinely interested in what people believed – about everything from politics to sexuality – and how these beliefs had formed. I wanted to understand why people were so hostile towards homosexuality, and I wanted to know how people's different attitudes to life had been formed. At our Catholic school, we were regularly reminded of the school's 'five core values' and mission statement, which was to 'aspire not to have more but to be more'. I love this ethos. It has shaped so much of what I think and do in my life to this day. But I had never been brought up religiously, despite my Catholic education. So I felt as if I was taking a 'birds-eye' perspective looking in on this entire belief system. I was fascinated by how we had to pray, attend masses, and go into the chapel. I found the rituals and routines very comforting and empowering. I really did feel a sense of connection with both the Christian values and with these Christian rituals. They seemed to give me a sense of purpose and a feeling of empowerment – everything was very ordered, which I liked, and I felt a sense of belonging to a larger cause. But did I believe in these miraculous stories of angels, prophecies and resurrections? Did I honestly believe that when we had to sit there and pray the 'Hail Mary', a woman up there on the clouds was listening to every single word I was saying? I struggled to take many of these teachings seriously, and I just did not think any of it was credible. But the values spoke to my heart, and the rituals gave me a real sense of comfort. So I became fascinated by religion and, in particular, the teachings of the Catholic faith.

I became very interested in making sense of both religious teachings and also wider philosophical ideas. I found attaining knowledge and understanding to be extremely empowering – the more I discovered, the more powerful I felt. People had always thought I was this sensitive, annoying and silly little boy who acted like a girl and thought he was amazing at performing in shows. But actually, here I was, taking a genuine interest in current affairs, Christian theology, and the development of Western philosophy! I loved nothing more than learning more about the world – in particular, psychology, philosophy and religion – and I loved sharing my newfound knowledge with others. I was not content with just surviving through life. I wanted to understand what it meant to be a human being. I wanted to know what it meant to 'thrive' as an individual.

I think my life experiences –battling an eating disorder and accepting my sexuality– were a major catalyst for studying philosophy. I had lots of questions – about both who I was and also about my place in the world – and I wanted to understand why things were the way they were. Why was a boy with flamboyance seen as such a bad thing? Why had I ended up in a situation where I was starving myself to death and being completely overwhelmed by the most irrational thoughts? I suppose you could call my hospitalisation with anorexia a sort of 'near-death experience'. It had woken me up to the preciousness and fragility of human life. My survival – and realising just how poorly I had been – had left me seeing the world around me in a whole new light. I felt so much gratitude for my existence and so much love for the people around me. And I experienced so much genuine happiness when enjoying the simple pleasures in life. Feeling so blessed to still be alive, I wanted to live my life to the full. And this meant asking lots of philosophical, psychological, and ethical questions. I was not content with just surviving through each day – I wanted to ask all these questions and have all of these deep, philosophical questions.

Usually, it was my poor Granny who drew the short straw and ended up on the receiving end of my deep and philosophical questions. We would walk around Alderley woods, and I would quiz her on the meaning of life and the lessons she had learned over the years. I saw her as a source of infinite wisdom and insight, and I wanted to interrogate her on every single topic imaginable! We would be sat in her kitchen, and I would quiz her on her life experiences. Or I would subject her to a sermon about a book on anthropology I had just purchased! Some weeks, I'd launch into a sermon about what I'd been reading in the news. I'd sit there telling by poor gran about the development of western society or the implications of globalisation! With a cup of coffee and the morning newspapers in hand, I would interrogate Granny over a chocolate digestive about the day's news, or about something I'd been reading in one of my books.

One book that totally and utterly changed my world outlook was the simply phenomenal 'Sapiens – A Brief History of Humankind'. This book, without doubt, changed my entire world outlook. I would even go so far as to say that it changed my life! This book ignited this insatiable interest in the human race and sparked my passion for philosophy, psychology and making sense of our human existence. I mean it when I say that I learned more in 15 minutes of reading this book than I had learned in 15 years of education combined. I cannot put into words how incredible this book is! Every single page left me feeling enlightened and with a newfound enthusiasm for studying the big questions about what it means to be a human being. It shook me out of myself and the little bubble that I had been living it, humbling me as I realised I was just one of the billions of homo sapiens to have ever lived! Our lives are so insignificant and short – we are like tiny ants in this enormous, ever-expanding universe! I don't know if some people might find this depressing, but I found it liberating! It was a reason to really 'get over myself' and stop taking myself so seriously. It was a reminder that what we know as human beings is a drop in comparison to what we don't know, which is an ocean! I felt even more inspired to study, question, discuss and learn about what it means to live as a human being.

'Sapiens' really is the most extraordinary read. It talks you through the development of humanity from the hunter-gatherer days, via the agricultural and cognitive revolutions, right through to the technological revolution and the present day. I could – and indeed would – talk about this book and what it had taught me for hours. What's more, I had discovered that the author – the incredible Yuval Noah Harari – was in fact, gay. I couldn't believe it – here was the most intelligent man, authoritative academic and internationally bestselling author…and he was openly gay! It just showed that being 'gay' didn't mean being a reject, an embarrassment, a caricature or an outcast! If he could be a man of such credibility, intelligence and achievement (and just so happen to be 'gay')…then so could I! This planted a very positive seed in my teenage mind.

***

The more that I would learn, for example, from reading the papers and reading non-fiction books, the more confident that I would become. I loved discussing anything deep. I have never felt more alive than when studying or talking about philosophical ideas, a cup of green tea in hand! Philosophy and psychology energised me. They allowed me to ask probing questions, and they gave me opportunities to look for answers! My vocabulary and my ability to articulate myself were rapidly improving, which provided me with an amazing boost to my self-esteem. I had a newfound passion for life, and I felt so energised by an interest in these big philosophical questions. I do believe that knowledge is power, and that philosophy is empowering.

The more I would read and learn; the more empowered and self-confident I would become!

And, as I became somewhat of a novice 'armchair expert' in world politics, Christian theology, basic human psychology, I started to feel as if I was on top of the world! I started to realise that people's prejudices, judgements and unkind behaviour all came down to one thing – ignorance. And I realised that the answer to ignorance was therefore found in one thing and one thing alone - education!

****

I became increasingly passionate about the importance and value of education. I genuinely loved learning, and I was evangelical about the importance of expanding your mind. I discovered 'growth mindset theory', a concept first devised by Dr Carol Dweck. Mindset theory is based on the idea that intelligence is a skill that can be learnt, cultivated and developed over time. We shouldn't fear failure, and we should never impose limitations on our capabilities – life is all about growth, learning and discovery. As Dweck says herself, 'A growth mindset is when students understand that their abilities can be developed'. I saw this firsthand – the more I was reading, the more my grades were improving. The more that I watched BBC Parliament and the BBC News Channel, the more informed and articulate I became.

Most importantly, the more that I read, researched and watched these politicians and powerful people speaking, the more confident I became in myself. Indeed, I was now confident enough to contribute in class and, to my delight, people were starting to notice that I had something insightful and intelligent to say. It felt like I was no longer the annoying, attention-seeking 'gay' boy (although I'm sure plenty of people still thought that about me!) Instead, I felt as if I was being recognised for having intelligent insights and an ability to talk about serious topics. I found this instantly rewarding, and it gave me the real motivation to become even more informed and articulate.

In time, I started to think that I would like to be a teacher. It genuinely felt like my dream job – I would be able to make a difference and help empower young people through education. I had seen the positive transformation that education and knowledge had achieved in my own life. And I wanted to help others to achieve that in their own life as well! Furthermore, I saw teaching as not just a career, but a calling. I thought that I might be able to use all my experiences of the past to make a positive difference in the future. I could show young people that they too could overcome mental illness, bullying and rejection! If they worked hard and believed in themselves, then they could also live their best life! I started to feel this burning desire to do something that could make a positive difference in the world. I felt like teaching would be a genuinely fulfilling and rewarding career. I thought how much I would love to be a Business Teacher and Head of Year like Mrs Moulsdale, who always appeared so organised, well-put-together and in control. She radiated positivity, professionalism and had a real sense of presence whenever she entered a room. And so I dreamt of living her life of power outfits, delivering assemblies, teaching classes and coffee breaks! Of course, I knew there was so much more to her job, but I loved what I saw of the role and dreamt of doing that job myself.

Dreaming of a teaching career wasn't an entirely new feature in my life. I could remember going to my Grandma and Grandad's house on a Saturday morning and 'teaching' them 'lessons' sat at their dinner table. I would make worksheets – such as spelling tests for my Grandma and maths quizzes for my Grandad – and stand in there lounge writing on a little whiteboard I had brought along. I bought them exercise books from Rymans and 'well done' stickers from Sainsbury's. I loved these mornings – I would look forward to 'teaching' my lessons all week. When Saturday morning came, I would feel absolutely in my element. Grandma and Grandad were exceptionally good sports and went along with the whole thing without comment or complaint. They even did the homework tasks I had set them, and put up with me 'teaching' them the basics of primary school literacy and maths!

I loved these mornings, including our little tea break at 10.30 am when my Grandad would put the kettle on, and my Grandma would put together a plate of biscuits. There would always be Happy Hippos, Teacakes, Chocolate Chip digestives and custard creams. I'd always have two sugars in my tea, just like my Grandma, and no matter what time of year it was, she would always insist on putting the fire on. We'd then watch the Saturday morning television when Grandma would always complain about it always being a cooking programme. After a cup of tea and a biscuit (or two!), we returned to the dinner table, and I continued my lesson! My poor, poor grandparents! If they had thought they'd be able to enjoy their retirements, they had another thing coming for them! Afterwards, we'd go for a walk to buy Sausage Rolls and Pork and Apple pies at their local butchers, before we would sit down to have lunch and then they would drop me off back home. Looking back now, I can tell you that Grandma and Grandad had the patience of saints – how they put up with me instructing them to write sentences and do spelling tests I will never know! But I do know that I loved these Saturday mornings more than anything else. I think they reveal that there's always been a little teacher within me, itching to write on that whiteboard and mark those homework tasks!

***

Thanks to my education and my new ambitions, I was feeling liberated from my insecurities of the past. I felt genuinely invigorated by this wish to make a positive difference in society. I had found empowerment through education and liberation through learning. And my study of growth mindset was helping me to start seeing the world in a much more positive and optimistic way. I loved my GCSE lessons in school, and I was starting to feel much more secure in my skin. I was finding my voice, believing in my Whilst I wasn't ready to fully accept the idea that I was gay, I was no longer *terrified* of the idea. That alone was a monumental amount of progress that took the enormous weight off my shoulders.

I was finally challenging the internalised homonegativity that had been weighing me down for so long. And I was feeling so incredibly liberated as a result. Meanwhile, the anorexic thoughts have been disputed into submission. I am feeling genuinely happy and content in myself for the first time in forever. I finish Year 9 with a spring in my step and a smile on my face. It starts to look like my future might be filled with happiness and good health – and what more could you possibly wish for?

11. GOOD TIMES IN YEAR 10

September comes around, yet again, and – as always – I'm already feeling excited for Christmas. It's the start of Year 10, and a lot is going on. I'm (finally) starting to make sense of my sexuality, I'm working hard on my GCSEs, and I'm finally getting there in my fight against anorexia. I've discovered my amazing 'guardian angels' – Becky and Erin - and I'm feeling more socially confident than I have ever felt before. I still feel relatively anxious when meeting new people or mixing with people I perceive to be more 'popular' than my little self. Still, I feel confident in my ability to hold a conversation and walk into a room with my head held high – an achievement in itself!

I've been attending CAMHS for a while now – it's been at least two years – and I'm starting to wonder if I'll ever leave the service. I feel so thankful for all of their help and support. But I am also itching to get on with my life, and leave my battle with anorexia 'behind me'. I'm aware that I need to remain vigilant against an eating disorder resurgence. Still, I also want to make an effort to 'move on' with my life. So many people fail to realise that overcoming an eating disorder does not happen overnight. As we have found out, only around half of the people with an eating disorder are ever thought to properly 'recover'. It takes hundreds – if not thousands – of hours to challenge irrational thoughts, overcome toxic beliefs, and rehabilitate your relationship with body image, weight and food. I discuss my journey towards discharge from CAMHS with Sarah, and also with my mum, and we start to talk about the plan going forwards.

Here's how I see it: I am determined to fight off this illness and live my adult life to the absolute full. I don't want these anorexic thoughts, beliefs and behaviours to overshadow – and potentially ruin – my adult life. I'm convinced that, with early intervention, there is absolutely no reason someone can't challenge their anorexic thoughts and turn their life around. I genuinely want to get better, and I genuinely want to live a happy and fulfilling life. I do not want to be defined by my eating disorder. And I am determined to do what I can to help anyone else battling against this crippling mental illness. And I know that to help others, I have to get myself to a very strong and empowered place myself. This becomes my new motivation for recovery and rehabilitation – I want to get better so that I can help others get better as well. I want to turn my experience into something very positive – and I want to make a genuine difference after everything that I've been through. And so, I am prepared to put all of my energy into fighting off these anorexic thoughts. I am ready to get busy getting rid of those anorexic behaviours for good.

I discuss all of this with Sarah, hoping that she believes I can carry on my journey without needing the support of CAMHS. I am, I realise, also trying to convince myself – I know deep down that this journey will not be a walk in the park. I know that I will probably cling on to many anorexic thoughts and behaviours for years to come. But I want to prove – to both myself and everyone around me - that I am capable of reclaiming my sanity and living a healthy life.

But that is not the only thing making me crave a discharge. To be brutally honest, I was also unwilling to put on any more weight. I knew that staying with CAMHS meant having to keep on meeting higher weight targets – and I did not want that number on the scales to keep on climbing. I was struggling with the constant weight gain, and I wanted to keep my weight at the amount it was at. I was still underweight, but not to a dangerous extent. In my head – and this was an anorexic thought that I had still not shaken off – I wanted to remain underweight. I loved the idea of weighing less than everyone else. It gave me – I thought - a feeling of victory, empowerment and control. And so, as you can see, it became clear that whilst I was moving forwards in a very positive way, I still had a lot of obstacles to climb. I could tell that my mum was not convinced by my requests to be discharged from CAMHS, and I knew that I needed to sell my 'recovery credentials to Sarah'. After one of the appointments, in which we discuss my discharge from the CAMHS service, Sarah sends this review to my GP:

"During his time at CAMHS, Ben's weight has slowly increased, but he has remained underweight. In the appointment, I discussed with Ben and his mum the concerns of this and the potential consequences in relation to his physical health on a longer-term basis.

Ben felt he is happier than he has ever been. He expressed no concerns at home, school or his academic achievements. He informed me that he is able to accept chocolate from his friends whilst previously would have declined. He expressed no concerns regarding his mental health. Mum mentioned that Ben gets highly stressed about his exams, but he did not want to discuss that at the appointment.

Mum reported that Ben continues to count calories and restrict types of food he eats. Ben continues to have anorexic thoughts and this was evident during the session when Ben was arguing with his mum about there being an obese [sic] epidemic in the UK and his biggest fear is becoming overweight.

Mum's main concern is Ben losing weight, becoming physically compromised and having to require hospital treatment. Mum has discussed that her role is to keep Ben well and not let him get ill again. Mum reflected that when he was ill at the beginning, she was told that he was ok when she knew he was not. Mum felt that the needs to take responsibility as no one else would.

During the appointment, Ben strongly disagreed with mum about her perspective. Ben discussed how he no longer wants to come to CAMHS and that he has been coming over the past couple of years. He is frustrated about being told what he can and cannot do and does not want it to be focused on his weight.

Ben described that he wants a fresh start next year and not come to CAMHS. Mum is concerned about his physical health and requested that he be reviewed by a doctor, and if the outcome of that is that his physical health is not compromised by being underweight, she will accept Ben's decision.

Formulation and plan: Ben is reluctant to engage with CAMHS, and he feels he is in a much better place than at the beginning. Mum is concerned about him being underweight and the implications of this on his physical health. Mum felt that he should continue to come to CAMHS but understands that Ben would want to have goals to work towards which he does not have".

How do I feel about what Sarah is telling my GP? I am furious about the phrase 'Ben is reluctant to engage with CAMHS'. Or, to be more specific, the anorexic thoughts still clinging on in my brain are furious about this phrase. She is, of course, completely correct – and this makes me anorexia even angrier! As my physical health is improving, I am no longer seen as a serious health risk. Let me be very honest with you here. This 'physical recovery' gives someone who appears to be recovering but who is inwardly still suffering a dangerous opportunity to 'play the game' and 'cheat the system'. Remember, anorexia is all about control and deceit.

Deception is in this mental illness' 'modus operandi'. It is very easy to fake being 'fine', especially when your weight is within medically 'safe' boundaries, (even though you are suffering more than ever before inside). I think it's very easy to forget that anorexia, and any other eating disorder for that matter is not primarily a physical illness. It has serious physical effects, of course, but the illness itself is not visible. And so your recovery cannot be assessed by your physical appearance. Remember, this is a psychological illness that has physical side effects. Many people suffering from an eating disorder actually weigh within the 'healthy' range for their height and age. Yet, their thoughts and behaviours are anything but 'healthy'. This is just part of a major problem with eating disorder treatment as a whole. If a patient's weight is not seen as threatening to their physical health, then they are not seen as a serious case in need of urgent care or treatment. They can very easily slip through the net and never receive the psychiatric treatment they so desperately need. Due to the high demand for eating disorder treatment, young people can be left on waiting lists for six months….and often longer.

I am still 'underweight', according to the BMI chart, and yet I do feel both physically and psychologically stronger than I have ever felt before. And so, I continue to talk about being discharged from the service. Part of me feels well enough to keep moving forwards without needing regular meetings. And part of me is just absolutely fed up of being weighed every week! I feel controlled, and as if I'm being watched like a hawk – I want freedom! The critical thing is this: when I do 'take back control', whatever that means, I need to make sure it is me (Ben) that is taking back that control as a healthy, rational and responsible human. In order words, I cannot risk anorexia being the one that takes back the control and consequently takes over my thoughts, feeling and behaviours once again.

I am genuinely worried about the prospect of anorexia once again taking over my life and sending me straight back down to that dark path towards self-destruction. The one thing that reassures me is this: I know that I want to be genuinely happy in life, and I realise that the anorexic thoughts and behaviours are the opposite of happiness. The fact I am aware of the anorexia is an enormous breakthrough in itself. As long as I am not in denial about my vulnerability to an eating disorder, I feel that I will be able to maintain vigilance against relapse. I know in my mind that my anorexic ways of the past have caused nothing but destruction and pain. I have learned from this experience that life is so precious, fragile, and short. And so I want to seize every single day and live every single moment to the absolute full. And – most importantly – I now know how to identify those anorexic thoughts, feelings and behaviours. Thanks to my Cognitive Behavioural Therapy, as well as my enjoyment of meditation, reading, and journaling, I am more self-aware than I have ever been before. I believe that I'll be able to 'be my own therapist', challenging any anorexic thoughts and managing my mental health in a very positive way.

And so, it's decided that I can be discharged from the CAMHS service. My mum still has reservations, as does Sarah. Still, I am adamant that, after so many years, I am ready to take full responsibility for my mental health. I am starting to feel like a burden on NHS resources – I have been reading about the waiting times for mental health treatment. I feel bad for taking up so much time when some people are stuck on a six-month-long waiting list. I need to take responsibility, and I need to get myself together. I am eternally grateful for everything Sarah has done, but now I feel it is time to move forwards.

As we start working towards my discharge from the service, Sarah sends over an email in which she summarises some of the key points from our discussions:

"**- We have explored the events leading up to your experience of anorexia. You felt that it started when you starred in a school production and were playing an overweight character and had to wear** a large costume. When you started to perform, you did not want the audience to think that you were overweight, so you became conscious of your body shape. This was when you started to cut down your food intake and increasing your exercise. You noticed the more weight you lost, your personality changed, you became less social. You described that at the time you were oblivious of what was happening

-We discussed that you choose less calorific food and you deny yourself food which you consider calorific. We have discussed how you can challenge this by choosing the food you want to eat rather than making the decision on calorific content

-We have discussed during the sessions that you continue to be underweight and that your weight gain during your sessions at CAMHS has been gradual. I have discussed with you that you are growing taller and that your body has to compensate for you being underweight.

-We have explored whether you have perfectionist traits, and you felt that you could identify with most of the traits on the worksheets. We discussed how you could acknowledge and be more aware of these traits.

-We discussed that you feel you have two parts to you and how this relates to how you see yourself and what type of career you would like in the future. We have discussed that you have a caring side and talk about becoming a nurse and the other part of you that is ambitious and have money [sic]. During these discussions, you found it difficult to think of a balance for you in this decision.

- Part of you places pressure on yourself to achieve a high standard, and you have been concerned in the past of pressure to maintain your grades and school work. We have discussed that you will put pressure on yourself to work and we completed an exercise using a pie chart to represent your current work balance and how you like to balance this out with enjoying yourself and not worrying about eating.

- We discussed how you can achieve more balance in your life by completing activities you enjoy, such as reading, listening to the news, and how you should not feel guilt for not working. We have discussed mindfulness techniques you have tried, you commented on feeling calmer and sleeping better from practising this

- You have discussed how you feel you are 90% recovered from anorexia and want to get to 95%. This would include you wanting to feel comfortable with choosing and eating food you want to.

- We have discussed that there are health implications to being underweight as there are being overweight. You continue to be concerned about news articles stating that there is an obesity epidemic and you are worried that if you eat too much you will become obese. We have had discussions around people being obese exceed the recommendation of calories/lifestyle choices. Still, you continue to worry about this".

I have told Sarah that I feel 90% recovered. However, there was still plenty of work to be done in terms of releasing me from the chains of those anorexic thoughts, beliefs and compulsive behaviours. Those fears about an 'obesity crisis' and an irrational belief that I could suddenly become 'fat' overnight still play on my mind. I still worry about eating the 'bad' foods that we are regularly told pile on the pounds. For example, I still can't touch a muffin, cake, or a burger without thinking about how I will be able to make up for this the next day. But these anorexic thoughts are no longer taking over my life. I am now much better at managing these thoughts, and I am much better at 'seeing the bigger picture'. I now know that my life is about so much more than calorie control. For example, I have my studies to do, my sexuality to make sense of, and my friends to keep entertained! I want to live each day to the full, help as many people as I possibly can, and live a genuinely happy life. And I can't do any of this with anorexia calling the shots on my life!

There are big hugs, tears, cards and presents as I say goodbye to Sarah. This woman has changed my life – and, for her, that is all in a day's work! I am once again amazed at the kindness and goodness of human beings. I have spent so many years fearing people's opinions and assuming the worst about people's intentions. I feel shocked – in the best way possible – by the kindness and care that human beings have shown me. It is the strangest thing to think that this person now knows so much about me (more than any other human being alive!). Yet, I will never see her or communicate with her again. People are often divided over whether this is a good thing or a bad thing – is it easier to open up to someone you know well or someone you don't know at all? I found therapy with a total stranger to be the best thing I have ever done, even if I was determined not to engage with it back at the start of my illness. Therapy transformed my life in the best ways imaginable. And I found the fact that I was speaking to a trained professional – who was a stranger – to be extraordinarily beneficial. I felt free from judgement, and I never once felt like a burden. This lovely and judgement-free stranger was paid to listen to my problems. I didn't need to worry about what they might be thinking, or whether they might be bored by what I was saying. And I didn't feel like a burden or an embarrassment. Instead, I felt free to pour out my heart, talk through all of my thoughts, and really open up about everything I was feeling. There is no way I could have been so open with somebody I knew or had a close relationship with. I would have too vulnerable, too embarrassed and too much of a burden.

Having therapy saved my life. Not only did the CAMHS service save my life, but they also totally transformed my life as well. I will never be able to thank them enough. I will never tire of evangelising about the benefits of Cognitive Behavioural Therapy! Indeed, here's what I now passionately believe. Every single person should get some therapy, even if you believe you are 100% psychologically well. It is the greatest exercise in self-awareness, healing and empowerment. The insight it gives you into your thoughts, feelings and behaviours is incredible.

If I were Prime Minister (now there's a thought!), everyone would regularly see a therapist on the NHS, in the same way, that everyone regularly sees a dentist. This would – I have no doubt – lead to an incredibly positive transformation across the whole of society. Crime rates would plummet, life satisfaction ratings would soar, and mental illness would finally get the investment it requires. We need to normalise the conversation around mental health, and we need to make life-changing talking therapies accessible to everybody across the country. I hope that, by sharing my story here, I might be able to play my part in normalising these important conversations. I hope that my honesty might remind anyone going through a little bit of a tough time that there is light at the end of the tunnel. You deserve to be happy, and you deserve to thrive through life. And guess what? You can, and you will. You've got this. Whatever you're going through, keep going. There is a bright, colourful, and genuinely fulfilling future awaiting you – all that's required is some self-belief and recognition of your inner strength. I believe in you!

***

Year 10 will always be incredibly special because of the people who came into my life during this time. I was becoming closer to Erin, and I was starting to speak more to Becky, who had begun walking home from school with us. I loved my walks home with these two girls – I would genuinely spend all day looking forward to walking home with them! I do think some people are just meant to be in your life forever, and I realised very quickly that Erin and Becky were these people. We instantly clicked and connected – they gave me the biggest boost to my self-confidence and self-esteem. I always wonder how different my life would be today if I hadn't ended up in business and drama lessons with Erin in Year 9. And I always wonder how my life would be today if Becky hadn't decided to start walking home with us in Year 10. These two unquestionably changed my life in the most positive ways imaginable. These Year 10 walks home planted the seeds for what I know will be a lifetime of friendship, and I thank my lucky stars for this every single day!

With these two amazing girls by my side, I felt ready to take on the world. And that is exactly what I decided to do…

12. PARIS, NEW PEOPLE & PASSING EXAMS

Where on earth does the time go? Another year has flown by, and here we are again, it's September! As you know, September marks the start of my favourite time of year, the glorious arrival of autumn and the long build-up to Christmas. There's something about the leaves falling, the temperatures dropping, and the seasons changing that I just absolutely adore. I love the cold mornings, and I love the Saturday night entertainment shows (always best enjoyed with a hot drink in hand and the central heating fully turned up!) As the Christmas chocolates and festive cards start filling up the supermarket shelves, I start to get excited about the countdown to Christmas. I love an excuse to dig out the fairy lights and start watching my favourite Christmas movies! There's something so warm and comforting about it all, and it leaves me feeling so wonderfully content inside. The Danish have a word that describes this feeling – 'hygge', which means "A quality of cosiness and comfortable conviviality that engenders a feeling of contentment or well-being". There's nothing I love more in life than this festive cosiness and warmth!

There is something very different about this September because it's finally my last year in High School. I cannot believe that I've made it – I'm finally in Year 11! I can still remember my first day arriving at All Hallows back in year seven, terrified by all of these tall and confident teenagers. It dawns on me that I am not one of those terrifying year 11's who I so desperately wanted to be all those years ago! I feel a sense of pride and accomplishment – I've made it, I think, and I'm ready for the next chapter in my life! I have already decided that I want to stay on at All Hallows for Sixth Form. I genuinely love every second of school, and I know that All Hallows is a place I feel safe, happy and secure. I love the teachers, love the people, and I love the place itself – school genuinely feels like a home away from home. I am happy to be staying somewhere that I feel so safe and secure. Still, I am also excited about it being something different. I was happy about the fact Sixth Form would be a very different experience, whilst at the same time still feeling very familiar and reassuring.

For a start, I'd be in business dress and not the All Hallows uniform. I was already excited about being able to - *shock and excitement* - wear my suit and pick different colour ties to wear each day! And I would finally be able to sit in the big and scary Sixth Form Common Room, which had seemed like the most exciting and exclusive place back in my year seven days! I can remember glancing through the Common Room windows as a young year 7, wondering what it would be like to be allowed in such a big, cool and grown-up place! They had their café, comfy chairs and they all looked so important! Well, I was about to find out – that would be me striding into the common room in just 12 months! I felt excited, if a little apprehensive, and was, it dawned on me, finally growing up – and I was very much excited about this prospect!

Don't get me wrong; I had thoroughly enjoyed the past two years of education. I had the time of my life during those English, Business, RE and Drama lessons! I loved getting home from school at 4 pm and doing extra research on the laptop, whilst sipping a green tea and enjoying a piece of toast (with butter and jam, my all-time favourite snack!) Life was very straightforward, and I very much enjoyed living in my little school bubble! I was laughing my way through lessons whilst getting good grades in my mock exams, and I was surrounded by the most amazing friends who were giving me so much love. But, at the same time, I was also itching to get out into the world and start achieving my dreams and goals.

I was a very ambitious young boy, and I had my sights set on big things from a very early age. My diary entries from my high school years are filled with debates about what career I wanted to pursue. I was particularly torn between journalism, being a TV presenter, teaching, or being a therapist. I remember sharing my indecisiveness and anxiety about this with our school careers advisor. She had tried to reassure me by repeating the mantra "no big decisions!" about one hundred times in the space of five minutes! It's funny to look back on my frustration at being unable to decide on what job to pursue. It feels like I have ended up doing a little bit of everything (if you replace 'TV' for 'YouTube'!) in the years since finishing

High School! I had seen the difference that doctors, therapists and teachers had made in my own life. And so I was determined to find a career which would enable me to make a similar difference. I wanted to do a job where I could help people and make a real difference. And all of those hours watching the TV News had left me desperate to be sat behind a newsdesk! I would film my own news bulletins on a webcam in my bedroom, and practice reading through the headlines before pretending to interview important guests!

I loved the excitement of a 'breaking news' story flashing across the screen, and I had dreams about presenting my own evening news programme! I became utterly obsessed with current affairs. Each morning, I would walk to the Co-operative just around the corner and buy the 'I' newspaper. I'd chat to Lindsey, the lovely lady who worked on the till every weekday morning, before walking home to read the headlines. In the evenings, I would watch the BBC, ITV, Channel 4, Channel 5 and Sky News bulletins. I would then spend hours scouring the news websites for any information or stories I might have missed. Looking back, I wonder where on earth I found the time to do any of my actual GCSE revision! Practising these news bulletins – and binge-watching all these news programmes – gave me a lot of self-confidence, not to mention access to a very wide-ranging vocabulary. I soon found that aged just sixteen, I was talking in the same language as the BBC Economics Editor or the Channel 4 News Political Correspondent. I was absorbing a whole new vocabulary and way of speaking like a sponge plunged into the kitchen sink. This love for news and current affairs provided me with the most amazing – and unintended – benefits, both for my confidence and also for my academic performance.

I was now writing eight mark exam answers as if I was a journalist at the Daily Telegraph. And I was making conversation –with anyone who would give me five minutes of their time - about the Prime Minister, the economy and the latest problems to hit the coalition government. I became very keenly interested in politics and world affairs, which led to an interest in psychology and philosophy. In my head, I was Huw Edwards and at the helm of the BBC's flagship evening news programmes. I had to be kept informed on the latest current affairs! And I loved nothing more than asking people their views on the day's latest news stories! Thomas Jefferson once wrote that 'knowledge is power', and I could not agree more. The more that I read The Times watched Sky News and listened to the BBC World Service, the more confident and articulate I became.

I soon discovered that reading the newspapers and watching the news channels was my 'secret weapon' for success. And it had come at just the right time – I had GCSE exams to sit, and a place in Sixth Form to apply for. I felt so informed, so aware of world affairs and, as a result, so confident. I knew that I could hold a conversation, and I knew that I had a good grasp of how the world worked. I felt very secure and very certain that I could achieve, and it was all thanks to my news channel addiction!

***

From the very start of September, the thought of GCSEs was very much present in my mind. I wasn't necessarily worried or anxious, but I was certainly aware that the clock was ticking! I felt organised and in control, which meant I felt confident and prepared for the May exams. A school trip to Paris was a very welcome distraction, and it was also a fantastic boost to my confidence and self-esteem. I genuinely had the best few days, spent with the best and loveliest people. We had set off from school at midnight, taking the coach down to Dover and arriving around 5 am. I was sat with my gorgeous friend Lauren, who I had known since the very first day of Form in Year 7, and we had both attempted (and largely failed) to get some sleep on the journey. We then boarded the ferry – travel sickness tablets in hand, I can assure you – and headed over to France. We had the best few days exploring Paris. We saw Notre Dame and the Eiffel Tower, we spent a day in Disneyland, and we even took in the incredible views from the Sacre Coeur. My only previous experience of a residential school trip was the Year 6 trip to the Isle of Man, which had been absolute hell on earth. I had hated the teachers, despised the activities (I mean, do you see me thriving at archery or abseiling?), and didn't get on with any of the people. It was genuinely my worst nightmare, and it had scarred me for life. This trip to Paris was the perfect rehabilitation. Everyone was lovely, the activities were much more sophisticated and cultural, and I felt that I was able to completely be myself.

I became particularly close with Poppy and Emma, who I had known for a couple of years. I had laughed through business lessons with Poppy, whilst I had bumped into Emma at a couple of house parties. These girls completely took me under their wing – they showed me nothing but kindness, love and complete acceptance. As a 16-year-old boy struggling to work out their sexual identity and find a secure place in the world, I cannot overstate how much this support meant to me. We would stay up late chatting about our lives, and I still have a picture of us all posing in the Palace of Versailles gardens on my wall to this day! Paris was simply incredible, and I loved every second exploring this beautiful city. But it really was the people who made this trip for me – spending time with such kind, friendly and caring people made me feel so excited to get back home and start forming more genuinely meaningful and fulfilling friendships.

The Paris trip had left me feeling more confident and connected than ever before. It was the biggest boost to my social confidence – I had spent this time with all these people in my year, and they hadn't hated me! I think they had found me quite friendly and entertaining! This was in stark contrast to the Year 6 trip, which had left me feeling like an unwanted reject who nobody liked and everybody thought was an annoying waste of space. It had been the worst end to the worst Primary School experience imaginable! 5 years later, everything has been completely transformed. I feel able to finally shake off the memories and feelings associated with that fateful Year 6 trip – it was rehabilitation and rebirth, and it felt incredible.

So, I returned to little Macclesfield with a spring in my step. Erin started hosting house parties, which meant an opportunity to meet new people and, as I like to say, 'put myself out there'. I would turn up in a little blazer, and spend the night drinking tea or diet coke! 16-year-old Ben was incredibly innocent and was living life in a little bubble! Everybody, as you'd expect on Erin's guest lists, was lovely and nothing but kind, friendly, inclusive and accepting. Nobody said a word about my blazers or my choice of a cup of tea (they knew they'd have to answer to Becky if they did!). These house parties were yet another boost to my social-confidence and another opportunity to form meaningful connections. I do have to thank Erin, Becky and another lovely girl from my Primary School, Emma, for actually launching my social life! At their house parties, I was able to 'put myself out there' and socialise without fearing rejection, judgement, or humiliation. I have the happiest memories of these parties – Halloween in particular – and it is impossible to overstate how much they achieved for my happiness and self-esteem!

As the year progressed, the pressures surrounding GCSEs grew. We had received our final mock results and, a few months later, our exam timetables landed on our desks. Although I was very much aware of their impending arrival, I never felt anxious about these exams. I think that my experience with anorexia had taught me to keep everything in perspective and remember that your health and happiness must always come first. And I believed that, after going through so much, I was not going to let an exam paper upset me. I knew that I was keeping my brain active by reading the daily newspapers. And I knew that it was beneficial to be maintaining my strict revision schedule. Self-discipline and routine have always been my strong points, and I found that I was very good at motivating myself to revise, study and work hard. I genuinely loved my subjects, and studying was something I genuinely enjoyed. Suppose I wasn't in school, reading the newspaper or volunteering in the hospital shop on a Sunday. In that case, I could be found creating my own GCSE worksheets on the laptop! I may have been sixteen, but in my head, I was already a teacher with worksheets, mock exam papers and even PowerPoint lessons to prepare!

This love for 'teaching' came in very handy for my revision. It turns out, according to the so-called 'Learning Pyramid' that, whilst you only remember 10% of what you read, you remember an extraordinary 90% of what you teach. And so by making 'teaching' my revision method, I was not only helping others, but I was helping myself as well! Indeed, I was able to revise in a very efficient and enjoyable way! It meant I could help other people and, at the same time, actually help myself as well! I wanted to share my resources and my revision with others. To be honest, this was because I wanted to help people, and partly because I wanted someone to headhunt me for a teaching career! I was producing all of this revision, and I had become quite an expert in my favourite subjects. Mrs Sutton let me teach a lesson in RE, and my class were genuinely very kind to me. I was not – I don't think – arrogant or 'nerdy' in my classes. Instead, I had enthusiasm and a genuine desire to help, support and include everybody that I could. It worked very much in my favour – people, I think, liked the fact that I wanted to help people, and they also liked the fact that I wasn't taking myself too seriously.

I was getting A*s in my mock exams, and I was feeling excited about the real thing! I had, by this stage, decided that I wanted a career in teaching. Or, more specifically, I had decided I wanted to be both a TV star and a headteacher (as I say, ambition seems to be hardwired into my DNA!). I can vividly remember approaching Mrs Connor and our headteacher, Mr Billings, whilst they were standing in the school hall. 'How do I get your job?' I asked Mr Billings, informing them of my intention to become a secondary school headteacher by the age of 28. They didn't bad an eyelid and were more than happy to offer words of advice and encouragement. I had decided that I would be on TV as the 'Brian Cox of philosophy' (these were my exact words to the Head of RE, Mr Keane). At the same time, I would also be running a secondary school as the 'Executive Principal' (I've always loved an important-sounding job title). Ambitious little me had decided that my 'TV meets teaching' career would begin on YouTube, where I could share my revision sessions with the world. It wouldn't be the first time that I posted on YouTube – back in Year 8, I had uploaded those 'BW Latest' videos of me presenting the BBC News headlines. My brother Sam even made the odd appearance to present the sports news! Fortunately, I can confirm these videos have been wiped off the internet and safely stored away under lock and key! But this would be the first time I used YouTube properly – and I was extremely excited, but also nervous, about the whole thing.

In English, we were studying the play Journey's End, a 1928 war play by RC Sherriff. By the final term of Year 11, I knew this play like the back of my hand. I had annotated every single word, bought every single revision guide, and Googled every single bit of context. I felt confident enough to go through the entire play line-by-line discussing the language use, character development, writer's intentions and wider historical context. And this is exactly what I did! I'd set my little laptop up on my windowsill, meaning I had the benefit of natural light flooding in behind the camera. I sat down at my desk – which was up against the window – and looked straight into the webcam. When I say that I loved this feeling, I did channel my inner Huw Edwards! I'd put on one of my favourite shirts (it was a favourite at the time - when I look back today I call it a fashion disaster) and had made myself a big cup of tea. For the next hour, I spoke directly into my webcam, with an annotated copy of the play in one hand and a fluorescent coloured highlighter in the other. I felt like a newsreader and teacher – and I loved it!

The video ended up being around an hour-long, and by the end of it, I was exhausted. Watching it back, I could see that the lighting was not exactly HD BBC quality, but it would do. I was just so happy to have produced this video all by myself! Teaching my webcam all of this information had not only helped me but, I also thought, it might help others as well. I even thought – well, I dreamed – that it might catch the eye on a guy somewhere in the country who might want to then take me on a date! Yes, wishful thinking at it's finest! Even aged 16, I already had men and dating on my mind! So there we have it, I've been exposed: my supposedly noble intention of 'helping the nation revise' was secretly a conquest to find me a man!

This is what I wrote in my diary on the day I posted this 'Journey's End' video:

"…So I seem to have taken to upload a 1 hr revision video to YouTube on Journey's End. I say 'seem' because I may end up not going through with it! Before I do anything, I'm always questioning myself and always worried about how I will be perceived. I am unsure whether this is good or bad – it shows I care and, I suppose, stops me from doing anything stupid on social media. I worry that, when I put something like this out, people think I am asking for attention. It's going to happen. And I think I do want attention, or perhaps I want praise and friends, which I do think we must distinguish from 'attention' or 'popularity'. I have, afterall, achieved, if I may say so, so much more than [name of a 'popular' girl at the school]…yet she would be named as more 'popular' than me!

But returning to the YouTube video, and I always seem to assume the worst about what people are saying about me. Because it is completely inevitable, we all know it, that there will be comments, in the same way

as I comment to my friends about other people's blog posts, photos or status updates. And I'm realising that there are many people a lot meaner, nastier, judgemental, and rude than myself.

I think I must ask myself whether I am going to let [names of 'popular' kids at the school] stop me from achieving or doing anything with my life. Remember the lottery programme 'In it to win it?' – how can I ever achieve if I never put myself out there, create opportunities and take risks? And if it does all go wrong, people will have learnt and grown, and I have the resources, journaling, friends, an online counsellor, walks, meditation, philosophy, relaxing music, 'Keeping Up Appearances' [classic British sitcom I was obsessed with], and so much more to help me 'cope'.

Anyway, life is all about taking risks and gaining these new experiences, and only when you're bold can you become the best. So I think I will go ahead with this video launch. Although these nerves do give me real insight into the insecurity I feel within – about people, being liked, being accepted, being mocked – that have, and I suppose in many ways still do, played a big part in my life.

So as I end today's entry, I am thankful for the experiences I am able to have – thinking forward to Monday next week when I will attend an LGBT group for the first time and then the Monday after that when I sit my first GCSE – and remind myself it's good to take risks, put yourself out there and become stronger because of it. You only live once."

Oh, I really did think I was a life coach! I wish I still wrote so eloquently today! I could do with some writing tips from 16-year-old Ben.

I'm anxious about what people are going to say about me. Still, I was given confidence by the fact my video might help people. Surely they can't criticise you if you're doing something good and helping people to succeed? The next day, I write this:

"Well, firstly a little update; I uploaded the YouTube video this evening – goodness knows how many people will react, but I did enjoy filming it, and it is lovely to be able to share these little things with the world…he says…"

I then move onto a discussion of GCSEs as a whole. Here's what I had to say:

"Well, let's move on to today's topic. Four letters 'GCSE'. I am actually pretty, well not sure of the word really, want to say 'scared' but then its sort of frustrated that we have 13 days to go – I do feel like I should / could have done so much more revision, but I bet everybody, every year, feels like this. I must remember they are just tests for me to enjoy and try my upmost best at, but at the end of the day they do not – by any stretch of the imagination – matter. I will make a success of my life!

I suppose some of it is the thought of Result's Day too, but I really don't have to show or tell anyone [my results]. I do feel under pressure and like I have no time, and then I worry about sleep and being ready on the day – it will be over quickly, and I do think that nightly, targeted revision will help. I was happy with my mock results – I just need to perform to that level again.

I am taking GCSEs seriously, yet I want to keep calm and remember I will achieve great things – books, TV, leadership – irrespective of whether I get a bloody B in maths. I think, as much as anything, it's about proving to MYSELF that I can do it. I am trying to stay detached from the exams (just focused on the course content revision) and not thinking of them as GCSEs. I'm just terrified I'll get in the exam, have a nightmare, and cry on Result's Day if I don't do 'well'. I will certainly NOT be opening my results at school, no way, I will be in my own room with tissues on standby!

But Results Day is a long way away (in comparison to the exams, I feel it's ridiculous how soon they are, although I concede they are nicely spread out and so don't seem too daunting) and I think I should be thankful for my mindfulness and meditation, and religion and my favourite comedy TV shows, that will keep me grounded and focused throughout this time. You do not understand how much of a gift meditation is going to be for me during exam season (and always, I suppose, although now more than ever before!)

So I must stay calm, keep mindful, and remember I have worked hard and, if I do continue to work hard, I will reap the rewards I deserve. And anyway, personal GCSE results are not a reward (isn't that selfish?) life is about so much more – what will I do with myself after this? Oh yes, A-levels!"

Let's stick with the diary entries because the next day, I receive my first ever online 'hate comment'. *Round and applause and cheering here please!* I always think this – if you're not getting hate mail, you're doing something wrong! If you aren't provoking the trolls, then you aren't doing enough! I didn't know it at the time, but this would just be the first of literally hundreds – if not thousands – that would come my way. Today, these comments do not affect or phase me in the slightest. But, as you can see, this first comment did hit a nerve for 16-year-old me:

"Well, tonight I want to share how I reacted to the comment 'fag' being uploaded to my YouTube video (yes, I put it up!). I reported the user, felt shocked and numb, and yes, it did hurt me. But I've tried to forget about it, move on up, and laugh off their sad life…I'm 10,000% more successful than this troll will EVER be".

I am very proud of how 16-year-old Ben bounced back against this troll – I was a very sensitive soul back in Year 11, and I know how much this would have shaken my fragile little soul. It makes me smile to see the '10,000% more successful' line – I just love seeing that, even in Year 11, I was overflowing with sass! I clearly did manage to forget about it, because the next evening I upload another YouTube video:

"Put another YouTube video up – this one a GCSE RE mock, I learnt so much from doing it, and I hope people learn from watching it. I did feel a little apprehensive after doing it. Still, hey, life is for living and its great experience…and a selfless, image boosting thing to do!"

I was so excited to be sharing my revision videos with the world. Still, I genuinely did not expect anything to come from them. It was just me, sat in my bedroom in Cheshire, talking about my revision notes! As I say, I did dream of being a newsreader or a TV journalist. But I didn't envisage these dreams becoming an actual reality! Little did I know what my little YouTube videos might be leading to in the future…

13. THE LGBT+ CLUB DISASTER

The next week – just days before my GCSEs – I go along to an LGBT+ youth support group being held in Macclesfield town centre. It is years before I will step foot inside G-A-Y, work in Europe's biggest gay nightclub, or become co-Chair of National Student Pride. It will be my first experience meeting others openly LGBT+ young people. I am excited, nervous and praying that some of the boys I fancy at school will be there (wishful thinking at it's finest). It's a very bold move for me to be making – it is the first time properly acknowledging my sexuality and doing something about it. I get my mum – my number one flag-flyer and champion – to drop me off outside, and I feel sick with nerves as I ring the bell. The next day's diary entry reveals that the hour that followed did not exactly live up to expectations:

"Oh my God, what a bloody travesty. None of the attendees were in ANY way attractive (one who was clearly coming onto me told me that he had a record of viewing inappropriate images – I tried to make small talk but I just had to get away). I mean where on earth did they find these people – it was more of a drugs, alcohol and weirdos society than anything remotely LGBT. Did they even know what those letters stand for? Not a single attractive boy and I would have so much preferred for it to be a party – can you imagine a gay house part, it would be my dating dream…So no one who will now take me on dates, no one even looked remotely like [names attractive boy I fancied in year 11], **for God's sake. It was ridiculous. Like what on EARTH…**

I was so desperate to find SOMEONE [the story of my life, is it not?!] **But clearly not meant to be – I draw upon my mindfulness, my meditation, and focus on the fact that all will end up being well. Of course, it will. This has been – how shall we put it – a great life experience and has actually distracted me from worrying about exams, which is good. I'll just have to try harder (I am honestly craving an**

LGBT+ house party, although I know I'm only 16) to get there. I just expected something so different, not such an odd set up with such odd people. I exchanged/wanted absolutely NO numbers, I mean oh my God what WAS that! There was not a single fit guy there, I mean REALLY. We'll not get too disappointed, and there is a career in TV, writing, education, and leadership still awaiting. I'm not desperate. I just want a romantic hot date. Surely not too much to ask? Oh come on Ben, ground yourself and pull yourself together!"

The next day I wake up feeling frustrated and upset about my LGBT+ group disaster. I had genuinely expected to walk into the gathering and be swept off my feet by all of these gorgeous, good-looking and charming boys. I'd expected to be exchanging numbers, scheduling dates and planning my wedding. Well, how wrong I had been! I wanted someone to be interested in me, and I wanted to feel wanted. I wanted nothing more than a fit boy's attention, and I was frustrated that this appeared to be impossible.

That day, I was on the internet looking up ways of meeting gay teenagers. I wanted to know where to go and how to find attractive boys I could speak to, get to know and – I hoped – maybe even go on dates with. I'd heard in the news about these online dating apps that everybody was now using. What if I could find love online, I wondered, scrolling the search results and finding hundreds of different 'gay chat' sites. As far as I could see, these were all free 'chatrooms' where hundreds of gay men from around the world could chat, and exchange social media details. I came across one 'gay teen' chatroom that I particularly liked the look of, the sole reason being that there were so many people active in the conversation. I typed in my name as 'Ben – 16 UK' and went into the chatroom. At first, I was shocked at the overtly sexual nature of the main conversation stream – users were talking about all sorts of sexual acts, desires and fantasies. '54 year old looking for teen boy – phone fun' read one comment, 'anyone who wants cam fun now??' asked another. Oh my God, I think, is this what it's always like trying to find someone to speak to? Why is everything about sex, and why are these old men so interested in finding teenage boys? I had my questions, but I also had my absolute desperation to find someone to talk to.

And so, I typed a basic message and sent it to the mainstream of chat, where everybody was introducing themselves (or sharing their sexual desires and fantasies). 'Hey, Ben – 16 year old in the UK ☺' I wrote, hoping that someone might see my message amidst the never-ending stream of incoming comments.

Within seconds, the private message section of my profile was blowing up. I was receiving a new message every five seconds, with users demanding that I 'show face' (sic) or asking if 'got Kik??' (sic). I loved receiving this interest and attention – every though it was from random strangers who did not even know what I looked like! My absolute delight at receiving this kind of interest left me absolutely blind to its origins. It didn't matter – or I didn't even consider the fact – that this interest was coming from 50-year-old men sat behind a computer screen. It didn't even cross my mind that this might not be the kind of interest or attention that I wanted in my life. All I knew is that I was getting attention and interest, which was more than I had got at the LGBT+ youth group the night before! This was, I thought, my only chance of finding someone who might be interested in me. And so, I soaked up and seized absolutely all of this anonymous online attention.

Everyone kept asking if I had Kik, the social media messaging app, and so I, of course, quickly downloaded it from the app store. For someone who prided themselves on reading the daily newspapers and being an armchair 'expert' in psychology, I was ridiculously naïve in the way I was behaving! I think that it came from desperation for validation and a craving for romantic attention. I started giving out my Kik username to everyone on the chatroom who asked for it, and I soon had dozens of messages over on Kik. I uploaded a profile picture and started replying to these new Kik messages. Some were teenagers like myself. Others were older men looking to fulfil their sexual fantasy of messaging a teenage boy whilst their wife way on holiday. I just wanted to find someone of a similar age to me who might be interested in a Disney-style whirlwind relationship, culminating in a Westminster Abbey marriage and kids. Was I really asking for too much? The answer, it appeared, was a resounding yes – the best I was getting was a man asking for 'pics' (sic), and he didn't mean of what I was having for dinner.

In my – let's be brutally honest here – naïve and desperate state, I agreed. I sent one man the pictures he was asking for, and instantly completely regretted it. I was absolutely beside myself. I was crying, filled with self-hatred and felt anger rushing through my veins. What the hell had I done? Why the hell had I sent this? What the hell was going to happen now?

16-year-old me is seriously distraught at what I've done. How can your feelings about something switch so dramatically and so quickly? One minute – in the heat of the moment – I am the one taking and sending the picture. The next minute, I am genuinely devastated at what's happened. I feel I have let myself down and done something really awful. I feel ashamed and embarrassed. I don't know what to do with myself. I'm panicking, and I'm so angry with myself – what the hell have I done? Writing this down, with the full benefits of hindsight, I can see that this is a complete overreaction and gives an insight into my real lack of emotional intelligence. But at the time, in the heat of the moment, I really did feel overwhelmed and out-of-my-depth.

The next day, I have a follow-up/review appointment at CAMHS with the fantastic Dr Andrew Weaver, the child psychiatrist overseeing my care. I write this in my journal: **"I've just had a counselling session with the lovely Andrew Weaver, such a lovely man bless him. Really helpful but the thing I couldn't get off my chest and really needed to was that I had sent images to a man".**

I was desperate to tell someone about what I had done - and hear them reassure me that everything was going to be okay - but I just couldn't find the confidence or the words to do it. I was seriously overthinking the situation and felt genuinely embarrassed and ashamed. What would people think about me? How would this make me look? Would that raise questions about my sexuality, which I did not want to be brought up by absolutely anybody! I felt unable to tell my CAMHS psychiatrist and unable to tell my parents. Even the thought of telling them filled me with absolute horror and anxiety. But I needed to talk to somebody about this; I needed to get this off my chest.

And this is where Kooth comes in. Kooth, in case you haven't heard of it, is an online counselling service available on the NHS for 11-24 year-olds. It is the most amazing service, and I strongly suggest that you check it out! I had first heard about Kooth through Sarah. She had been talking about my discharge from CAMHS and the services that I'd be able to access once I'd finished seeing her for weekly therapy. I had liked the sound of Kooth, because it meant you could speak to a familiar therapist regularly, all from the comfort of your own home. I'd made a note of the details and put the idea to the back of my mind. Well, thank God I did! Right now, Kooth was exactly what I needed. I'd be able to talk to someone about what I'd done with complete anonymity and confidentiality. They wouldn't even be able to see me, meaning that I wouldn't feel so embarrassed and ashamed. I quickly googled Kooth and created myself an account. Once on the page, I found the 'chat' section, where I was giving the option of speaking to an online counsellor. *Yes, please!* I thought, joining the chat queue and feeling good to have been proactive about how I was feeling.

After a short wait, a chat window popped up, and a counsellor called Dana introduced themselves. 'Hello!' I nervously typed back, finding the idea of communicating with a counsellor via an online chatroom novel and new. Dana gave me some basic information about how the Kooth service worked before asking me what I might want to talk to her about today. And, just like that, I told her everything about sending these pictures and how it had made me feel. I was surprised at how easy it was to type every detail about the situation down, and I was also (pleasantly) surprised by how good doing so made me feel. Writing what had happened down was instantly making me feel better. An enormous weight was lifted off my shoulders. Writing down and sharing my experience was incredibly cathartic and calming. Even if I didn't have Dana reading what I had written, I would have still found the process of writing down what I was feeling very helpful.

But Dana did read everything that I wrote, and she then replied with questions that gently challenged me to think 'outside the box' about my situation. 'Why do you think you feel so upset about this?', she enquired, challenging me to challenge my thoughts, 'okay so you have done this – what is the worst thing that can happen now?' Dana then introduced me to a concept and mantra that would transform and revolutionise my outlook on life. 'Whatever happens in life', she wrote, 'know that you can handle it'. It was, yet again, another one of those breakthrough moments that I desperately needed in my life. I had been here acting like the world was going to collapse just because I had sent an explicit picture on Kik. But was this a rational belief? Had the world ended? No, of course, it hadn't! And, whilst I might have felt so upset in the moment, this whole experience would soon be just a memory! But not only that, this experience would teach me about my sexuality and my need for better emotional intelligence! My breakdown had now turned into a breakthrough. And I wanted to use this experience as a positive catalyst for transformation and change in my life. I needed to realise that the world was not going to end just because of one decision – I desperately needed some serious perspective! And I needed to use this experience to work through some of the underlying issues that I had!

Talking through how I was feeling about sending this picture did help me to get this perspective. The hour I was allocated to chat to Dana flew by, and she informed me that our session was coming to an end. 'How are you feeling?' she inquired, and I replied that I was genuinely feeling ten million times better. Even though we might have just been typing to each other for an hour, I felt this enormous debt of gratitude to Dana. She had listened without judgement, helped me to put everything into perspective, and supported me in working through my feelings about the situation. She was amazing! Dana asked me if I'd like to book in for another session next week, to check in on how I was doing. '– yes, please!' I replied, knowing that speaking to Dana had done me a world of good.

This would be the start of three years of weekly online sessions with Dana, who I would speak to every Friday at 5 pm. These weekly sessions genuinely made the most positive contribution to the quality of my life. Each Friday, I would sit down at my laptop and spend up to an hour messaging Dana. Even though I never saw what she looked like or met her in person, I felt as if she knew me and helped to bring out the very best in me. I appreciated her non-judgemental listening and the fact that I could talk about all my worries and fears without any filter whatsoever. In my real-life conversations, I was always so worried about coming across as an 'attention seeker' or a 'burden'. I wanted people to think that I always had it all together. So I didn't want to give the slightest hint of weakness or vulnerability. I would always plaster on the biggest smile and talk to people about how THEY were – I didn't want to be opening up to anybody about my issues and insecurities.

But speaking to Dana on Kooth was different. Like Sarah, I knew that she was being paid to listen to me. As a result, I didn't feel pressure to impress her or put on a façade. I didn't feel like a burden, and it felt as if everything I said was being accepted non-judgementally. I, therefore, wasn't filtering what I said out of fear of making a bad impression. This unconditional acceptance was what I needed. I had been stuck in a constant cycle of beating myself up for all of my apparent shortcomings. This meant that I never felt satisfied or secure in my skin. I was always angry with myself – I wasn't popular enough, I was embarrassing myself, I didn't get any sexual attention etc. It always felt as if every little mistake that I made was the end of the world, and I never felt as if what I was doing or achieving was good enough.

Words cannot express how much it helped me to have somebody just tell me 'you're doing okay – you are enough just as you are'. My mum would regularly repeat this kind of mantra to me, but I never believed her when she said it. She's just saying it because I'm her son, I'd think, dismissing her little 'I am so very proud of you' sermons as shallow sentiments. But hearing this from Dana was different – her words were leaving a very positive imprint on me and my life. Dana was changing my life. She was helping me to become more accepting and understanding of myself, which gave me the space to start daring to be vulnerable in every area of my life. This meant being able to think more about my sexuality. And it also meant being able to think about my hopes and dreams for the future. I started to give myself some more acceptance and love, and I stopped worrying so much about what everybody else thought about me. What made ME happy? What was it that I wanted from life? Who would I be if I wasn't so worried about who I thought everybody else expected or wanted me to be? If I forgot about chasing validation and approval, how would I live my life and express myself? Did I know that I genuinely deserved to live a happy and fulfilling life?

***

Here's how I now feel about this whole 'sending images on Kik' situation: fine! Nobody got hurt, and I learned a lot of lessons! If this 'incident' had never happened, I would not have turned to Kooth. And I would never have discovered Dana. It is the strangest thought because Dana is one of the best things to have ever happened to me! Her online support and words of wisdom have shaped me into the person I am today! I wouldn't be where I am today without her! So, when I look back, I sort-of see the whole Kik incident as a blessing in disguise!

This goes to the core of my entire philosophy for life. I strongly believe that we can learn from absolutely every single thing that happens in our lives. Our mistakes from the past are often our best teachers for the future! You grow through everything that you go through, and you can learn from every situation that you encounter as you go through life.

I wanted to include this situation in this book for a couple of reasons. Firstly, I wanted to emphasise that you should never feel bad or ashamed about the things that you have done. As long as you keep learning and growing, you have got nothing to worry about! I also wanted to share this experience to express my gratitude to Dana and Kooth. If I had never had my experience on Kik, I would never have crossed paths with Dana. Our weekly online counselling appointments did change my life! Here's what I have learned: everything will work out in the end! Everything that you go through will help you to grow! So don't worry about making mistakes and don't regret absolutely anything that you do. Instead, focus on growing and learning from every situation you encounter in life!

I also write about Kik because I want to raise the issue of sexting. We need to start a genuine, frank and honest conversation on the culture of sending 'nudes' online. I do not believe that there is anything wrong with sexting. The only wrong thing is the fact that we don't talk about it! Sexting is not an issue we can brush under the carpet. We cannot pretend that it is not happening. Adolescence is the time we start to explore our sexuality, and young people are increasingly doing this via their smartphones. At the touch of a button, anyone can access hardcore pornography, send their explicit images, and receive explicit images from social media users across the world. Sex education in schools needs to catch up – and keep up – with how sexuality is expressed and explored in the 21st century. Obviously, we cannot police everything that young people are viewing and doing on the internet. However, we do need to ensure that they are as informed and educated about what they're going to stumble across online. Not talking about sexting does not mean it will not happen. Not discussing online pornography does not mean it is no longer there. We need to start a frank and real conversation about sexting! All that silence achieves is the spread of stigma, which leaves our young people battling with feelings of shame and confusion.

As a student of religious ethics, I would love to see more real, honest and unfiltered conversations about online sexual behaviour. Whether this means discussions about porn or conversations about sexting, we need to realise that it's time to talk about sex on the internet! So here's what I urge you: talk to people you trust about your online sexual experiences. Share your worries, talk about your fears, and start a conversation about what you're getting up to online. You are never alone, and somebody who cares about you is never going to judge you. The online world can be very scary and overwhelming. It can also, I have to be honest, be very dangerous. The best way to protect yourself is to talk about what you're seeing and doing online with people you trust.

14. THE ONE WHERE I SIT MY GCSEs...

Fast forward two weeks and it's the night before my first GCSE exam. I've had Becky and Erin around all day doing some last-minute revision for our first exam – RE. This is the big one. I've revised every topic about ten thousand times, and I know more Biblical quotes than any sane human being should ever know of. I'm feeling quietly confident that I'll be able to get full marks. I feel anxious and nervous, but also secure and – believe it or not – excited. Whenever I'm faced with exam seasons, I suddenly become very calm and confident about everything. I am, fortunately, not someone who gets anxious and starts panicking. I thank the meditation for that! I focus on being organised, well-rested and 'in the zone'. I am also very good at keeping things in perspective, and can finally step back and see the 'bigger picture'. GCSEs, I remind myself, are not the be-all and end-all of life! I write this in my diary:

"SO – I feel calm, collect, content and ready to go. This one piece of paper [the exam/results sheet] **will not undermine my future world success (let alone all of the teaching I have done to help so many people). I am just excited for the freedom I'll have after GCSEs – once all this is over, I can't wait to read and write without feeling guilty or needing to revise! An exciting chapter in my life is not beginning...I need to be a Buddha and OWN this experience".**

The next day, the GCSEs begin. Years of mock exams, practice questions, and even now, YouTube revision videos are culminating with these forthcoming weeks. I go straight into the invigilator's good books after turning up with a branded SmartWater bottle that they couldn't get the label off. I don't understand how they can walk around in silence for two hours without getting ridiculously bored. Still, I don't have much time to think about this, because the exam has now started!

When I get into an exam that I feel confident for – such as RE or English – I enjoy the whole 'exam conditions' experience. Whilst the same can't entirely be said for science or maths; I do always find that the exam hall makes me feel extremely calm and at peace with the world. I feel very much in the zone – as soon as I sit down, I feel so focused and calm. I know that there's nothing more I can do, and I know I have been working hard for literally months. I also know that I can write very quickly, and so I do not need to worry about whether I'll be able to finish the exam paper in time! And so I go into the exam with a very Zen headspace and quite happily work my way through the questions. I even actually enjoy it, and I wonder how everybody else might be getting on.

Before the exam, several people have come up to me and thanked me for my Journey's End revision video. I am delighted if admittedly surprised! The Head of Year – Mr Aspinall – has come over to me and had also thanked me for making these videos. It makes me feel as if everything I've been doing has been worthwhile – I've helped people, I think to myself, I've made a difference! This thought helps to take the pressure off my impending exam. It's not all about how well I do, I think to myself, but it's also about how much confidence or help I might have given to other people as well. No matter how well I do on this test, I am secure in the knowledge that I have helped other people during a very stressful time in their lives! The feeling that you have made a difference is ten million times better than any feeling that getting good exam results could ever provide. By focusing on helping other people rather than worrying about my grades so much, I found that I was relatively free from anxiety and able to keep everything in perspective.

***

It was a long, hot summer as we sat through those exams in the school sports hall. Half an hour before each exam, our 200-strong year group would all congregate outside the PE block, textbooks and last minute revision notes in hand! As I say, I found that I enjoyed the routines and rhythms of the exam season. It is so focused and very structured, meaning that I could put my love for scheduling and organisation to very good use! It's like you go into auto-pilot! You get up every single day to do more revision, sit another exam, and then start thinking about whatever exam you've got next. There was very much a feeling of 'we're all in this together' – I was genuinely more interested in helping other people than competing against them. This is what I love about my friends; we all genuinely care about each other, and we all genuinely want each other to do well. I've encountered so many toxic friendships, where someone is only happy with their friends as long as they are doing better than them. These friendships turn everything - exams, their love life, their weight loss – into a competition! This is so toxic! True friends do not see you as a rival! Instead of wanting to compete against you and do better than you, they genuinely want the best for you! They love to see you thrive! This is something that I particularly noticed in Becky and Erin, who were the greatest sources of unconditional love and support. If someone said anything about me, they were there fighting my corner. And if I had achieved something, they were flying the flag and championing me. I hope they'd say that this is reciprocated – I am so proud of them and everything they achieve. Most importantly, they teach me what genuine friendship looks like and feels like, which is the greatest and most valuable lesson in the world. Thanks to these two, I set my standards for friendships high – I know what it means to feel loved, supported and accepted, and I know now that they are going to be stuck with me for life, whether they like it or not!

With Becky and Erin by my side, I'm finding GCSEs to be a smooth and largely stress-free experience. I feel very much 'in the zone' – I'm so busy sitting exams and going over revision notes that I don't have time to think about what I'm doing! This is very beneficial because it stops me from worrying about what could go wrong or what topics I don't know as well as I would like to. On the whole, I feel secure in my knowledge, and I am so thankful that I started revising all those years ago! I do believe that organisation is the secret to success. When you schedule, plan and get yourself organised, you feel very calm and in control of what's going on. I am clued up on the specifications, and I am well practised at answering exam questions. I am, to be honest, quite enjoying going through the papers and ticking each subject off once it's done!

I was also very lucky to have a good sense of perspective, cultivated during my years of CBT! Thanks to my daily meditation, I can 'step outside' of myself and look down on what I'm doing from a birds-eye perspective. And by doing this, I can see that, in the grand scheme of things, these

GCSEs don't really matter. They are not life or death! They are not make or break! I have been reading some more 'Feel the Fear…and do it anyway!', the book that Dana, my online Kooth therapist, has recommended to me. In this book, which contains a mantra Dana has spoken to me about before. It is a mantra that has become my central life coaching message. It shapes my entire outlook on the world. It is, of course:

'Whatever happens in life, you can handle it.'

This mantra allows me to keep all of these exams in perspective – I know with confidence that the world is not going to end if things don't go amazingly well! And I also know that we can learn something from every single thing that we go through in life – remember, we grow through what we go through! – and so even if everything were to go shockingly wrong, I would still gain essential life lessons and become a stronger individual as a result of the whole experience! Don't get me wrong, I would love to come out with As and A*s, and I know that the perfectionist within me will not be happy with anything less. But I also know that these GCSEs are not as crucial as some teachers are making out. I am sitting an exam paper, I think, not completing life-saving brain surgery!

As my mum has repeatedly told me, as long as you try your best, that is all that ever matters. She tells me that I will be a success in life 'no matter what exam results you get', which also helps to reassure and calm me. I'm just happy to be working hard, keeping focused and giving these GCSEs my best shot – I would like to get amazing grades, but I also know that there is more to life than exam results! And I keep in mind my battle with anorexia, which has taught me that nothing is more important than your mental health. As long as I am alive, that is more than enough. As long as I am happy in myself and helping other people to find their happiness as well, then I am doing well in life.

Producing the revision videos on YouTube is also really helping me to keep everything in perspective. I find that by focusing on how I can help other people, I can take the pressure off myself and my performance. I am also now convinced that I'm a mini-celebrity, and I write this in my journal:

"It's a lovely sunny day, and my Unit 8 video has practically gone global – 800+ views…although most like from the year 8s who want to mock me! I mean, I'm practically a mini-celebrity now, so many people have said thankful, and it makes the whole thing worthwhile. Even Mr Aspinall [the head of year] came to say how impressed he was, touching me with a 'well done/appreciated' sort of thing! Apparently, Mrs Garvey [Head of Sixth Form / Deputy Principal] even put one on for her class…she was impressed that I knew what the catechism was!!!!"

I then move onto other exam-related topics:

"Don't ask me how chemistry went…GOD KNOWS! I'm just focusing on doing my best and moving on up…what else can you do? Need to say I am rather worried for maths and the other sciences, but I will work hard, rest well, and hopefully, my effort will pay off. I just can't wait for the whole performance to be over, although I am much more eased into it now. Not that the Tuesday we have drama AND geography or the Wednesday that we have business AND physics is going to be enjoyable! Two exams in one day!

Becky was so lovely saying she needs to get me a gift and thank you card for my help – bless her, I'm the one who should be thanking her for being so kind to me!! I suppose it's a good example of the rewards you do get for helping others, and many people have been so kind about my revision videos. It's genuinely so kind and heartwarming; you don't realise how worthwhile it makes it all! I know SOME people have mocked me and been rude, but the positives MUST outweigh the negatives…and it has made me feel like a mini-celebrity so I couldn't be happier!!! And besides, you are never going to please everybody, and this is a great life lesson for me to learn.

I DO want good grades – I know I'm capable of say 5* - so I want to work hard and do MYSELF justice. Do not care about external pressure! SO excited for Sixth Form too, like you don't understand, although get the impression that English will be a lot of work. Really can't wait for philosophy though, my life long PASSION! Let's do this!

Exams seem to have made me more popular, well known and confident (revision) – I don't want this to go, and I MUST sustain this throughout the summer into Sixth Form. I must be bold, confident and believe in myself. There is no room for negatives!

Will just keep calm, positive, mindful and compassionate…the end of school is in sight, and it's rather emotional!!! And don't mention the PROM word….!!!"

The next day, I have arranged a 'brunch' date for a couple of the people in my business class, so that we can all revise together. Here's what I write that evening in my journal:

"Well I went to the business brunch we had arranged, it was lovely although I feel such anxiety with some of these people…as I feel so much like I don't want to embarrass myself and that I've always got to be impressing them…I have such deep-rooted insecurity that I'm not wanted, not liked, deeply judged and still that tearful, sensitive little boy who [name of boy at primary school] and [name of boy at primary school] could reduce to tears and worthlessness at the click of a finger. I really need to recognise the fact that we've moved on from there, although I know there are always, always people who are going to judge me.

Perhaps this is one reason I am such a bag-of-nerves people pleaser who craves fame – people are always judging, mocking or asking questions, such as 'are you really a boy' and 'are you gay?' It does affect me, it does, I will use the word HURT me, but I do need to see that there will always be people like this in the world, but that it's their problem, not mine, and that I am loved – as events have shown – and that I am liked, I do have friends (even if I do get insecure and defensive when I see them at parties with other people) and that I do actually have a right to be successful and happy".

The GCSEs have finally finished, and I am beyond relieved. It is the best feeling in the world! I don't have to spend all of my time revising chemistry, maths and French anymore! Although I feel quietly confident about how I've done, I don't want to spend any more time dwelling on the exams. I need to forget all about GCSEs – there's nothing more I can do – and I need to focus on enjoying my summer! I want this summer to be a summer of renewal, reinvigoration, and reinvention. I want to make September – when I'll be starting sixth form – a brand new and fresh start. It's time to leave the past behind us – the only way, I tell myself, is up! I want to be able to walk into that common room with genuine self-confidence and nothing but total self-belief. I want to finally overcome all of these self-limiting beliefs and insecurities that have been holding me back! It's time to make friends, make a difference in the world, and make a success of my life! I am not going to let myself be intimidated by anyone, and I am not going to let anybody put me down! Let's go!

15. SUMMER OF 2016

The sun is shining, the crickets are chirping, and my mum is asking me whether I need any-more suncream (the answer is yes…pass me that factor 50!) It's August 2016 and we – my mum, dad, brother and I – are enjoying our annual two weeks holiday on the Greek Island of Kefalonia. Every year, we come back to this same gorgeous Island and stay in the same gorgeous Apartments, where we relax by the pool, eat out at the local Greek restaurants, and go off for long days on the beach.

I love being here in Kefalonia. There's just something about being by a pool in the sunshine that leaves you feeling as though you've not got a care in the world. When we are staying in these gorgeous apartments, located in a lovely and quiet region of the Island called Lassi, it feels as if we're relaxing in a home away from home. The gorgeous staff here, Maria and Effie, feel like family. They never fail to greet us with the biggest hugs and smiles, cook us the most delicious Greek food, and constantly exude so much kindness and warmth. Effie refers to Sam as 'the little one', whilst Maria has to carry dad to bed after serving him one-too-many of her notorious Greek cocktails. As my mum tells them every year that we leave, they make the holiday for us. Their kindness and hospitality is the reason that we keep on coming back, year after year!

The people we meet around the pool are as equally lovely as Maria and Effie serving in the pool bar. After the initial first couple of days – when I'd feel very nervous about what the people around the pool thought of me – I'd strike up a conversation with someone. We'd end up becoming amazing poolside friends. After I'd made the first move by talking to the teenager, my parents would then start chatting away to their parents. Before long, we had new 'friends' to say 'good morning' to as we arrived for breakfast each morning (everyone but Sam, who would wake up several hours later just as I was ordering lunch…)

Over the years, we have met the loveliest people around this pool. It is so strange to arrive for a holiday, not knowing who else is going to be swimming in the pool or relaxing on a lilo! These two weeks away give me a chance to think about my past few years of High School and allow me to look forwards to the future. What will things be like in Sixth Form? Will I make new friends and do new things? Will I step outside of my comfort zone and put myself out there? Will I build on my YouTube revision videos and create more online content? I am genuinely excited about the next chapter in my life, and I feel ready for a fresh start.

One thing that I'm thinking about, as I lie by the pool and read my philosophy books, is my sexuality. It has been on my mind for a long time now, but I've still not spoken about it with anyone but Dana and Queen P. I have mentioned the idea that I might be 'bisexual' to both Becky and Erin, as well as other friends at school, as a kind of 'testing the water' type of exercise. The response I have received has been nothing but positive. This has completely contradicted my expectations that announcing myself as 'gay' would give the bullies and haters 'victory' after all these years defending myself against this label.

***

As I have mentioned, I had spent my whole life up until this point being labelled as 'gay'. As a result, I have kept my head stubbornly buried in the sand. I have had to defend myself against this label again and again, desperately trying to make people like me and want to include me. Ever since my experiences in Primary School, I have associated the word 'gay' with being rejected, laughed at, mocked and inferior. Being labelled as 'gay' has become my biggest fear and cause of anxiety – just overhearing the word in conversation would fill me with absolute dread and horror. Whenever I heard that word – that toxic and terrifying three-letter-phrase – I knew that it would only be a matter of seconds until all eyes turned to me.

Over recent years, however, I feel like I have begun a journey to understanding and accepting my sexuality. As I have said, I had begun to realise how homonegativity had been completely clouding my knowledge of what it meant to live as a homosexual person. I had finally woken up to the fact that people's comments about my presumed sexuality revealed more about them than they revealed about me.

Thanks to my weekly sessions with Dana, I felt able to explore my sexual identity fully. I decided that I want to take some ownership over my life. I was so fed up of other people judging me, labelling me and making me feel so insecure. Why was I handing these haters so much power over my life? My YouTube videos had demonstrated that people actually liked my personality (shock of the year!). And my growing number of genuine friends provided me with actual evidence that I might be a likeable person.

I concluded that I no longer wanted to be a victim of other people's judgement and opinions. Instead, I wanted to take ownership of my life and become a role model for the next generation. I didn't want to be defined by the labels and comments other people were making. I wanted to decide - for myself - how I would live my life and express myself as a human being. I was now stronger, wiser and more empowered than I had ever been before. My years of therapy and reading had put me in a very powerful position. I didn't want to keep defending myself against all this labelling. I wanted to make a genuine difference in the world. Again, I was now very conscious of the 'bigger picture' behind my struggle to understand my sexuality. If I was going through this, I thought, then so must thousands of other young people! I wanted, to paraphrase Gandhi, to 'be the change that I wanted to see in the world'. I wanted to use my newfound voice and newly gained wisdom to help anyone who might be suffering in silence.

It helped me to stop thinking about sexuality as an issue solely about me. It was a cause and an issue that went well beyond my upset at being labelled as 'gay' ever since arriving in Primary School. I had memorised all of these RE quotes about 'blessed are the peacemakers' and being a good steward – well why wasn't I putting any of them into practice myself? It was easy to film a YouTube video on the Islamic concept of being a 'Khalifah' (a good steward in the world). And it was very easy to film a video on the Christian notion of 'whatever you did to the least of these, you did to me' (the parable of the sheep and the goats). But why was I not putting any of this religious wisdom into action in my own life? I had all of this timeless religious and philosophical wisdom written in my textbooks, but why was I not practising what was being preached? I knew that I wanted to make a change in the world. I wanted to be a positive presence who could help those people struggling with accepting their sexuality. After all the love and support I had received – from people like Dana, Sarah, my family, friends and teachers – I desperately wanted to give something back. As our headteacher used to repeatedly say, it's good to *'pay it forwards'* in life!

And so, I felt as if I almost had a moral duty to get a grip! I had, in my head, a clear choice: to continue going through life terrified of the word 'gay', or to tackle the issue of my sexuality head-on. I had, I realised, an extraordinary opportunity to do an extraordinary amount of good. It was my chance to make a difference in the world. I had the chance to help make the world a more accepting, inclusive, and loving place. As someone deeply inspired by the Christian values of compassion and love, I wanted to play my part in making the world a more kind, caring and inclusive place. I knew that daring to put myself out there and be an advocate for acceptance would give me a real sense of purpose in the world. It would allow me to transform all of the obstacles that I had encountered over the years into opportunities to make a difference. Helping others could help to make everything that I had gone through to feel almost worthwhile. It would give a sense of purpose to all the pain, allowing me to move forwards and make a difference in life.

Let me be very clear: I do not think that anybody should ever have to 'come out'. You should not have to announce your sexuality to the world – who you sleep with or who you fall in love with is nobody's business but your own! But I do believe that it can be very helpful to share your story of 'coming out' and 'coming to terms with' your sexuality. There is, in my opinion, so much strength to be gained from sharing our stories. There is so much empowerment to be found by speaking about our journeys. As I say, nobody owes anybody else an explanation about their love life. As long as you are not causing anybody harm, you are free to do whatever you want with whoever you want! But I think that sharing your story can help both yourself and also many people in the wider world. Talking about your experiences is extremely empowering, and sharing your journey can give others some much-needed inspiration. That's why I wanted to be 'loud and proud' about my journey to making sense of my sexuality and coming to terms with my identity as a gay man.

I have always enjoyed keeping a diary. I have always found so much comfort and clarity in this practice. And so, as I soaked up the Kefalonian sunshine, I picked up a notepad that I had packed in my suitcase and grabbed a pen from my bag. I found myself a little table underneath the café-bar canopy and opened up my notebook. As the crickets chirped away and children played in the pool, took a deep breath and began to write. I'd decided that I was going to write down exactly how I felt about sexuality and 'share my story' in print. I wanted to write about all of those experiences of name-calling at primary school and make sense of my journey towards embracing my sexuality. As I thought of my opening line, I decided that I was going to become the next JK Rowling and become the nation's next bestselling author. I had visions of my story being published in the newspapers. Then the movie adaptions would, of course, inevitably follow. Get your popcorn ready my loves; I'll see you in Leicester Square for the red carpet premiere!

Back in the real world, writing down my 'sexuality story' was proving to be a lot harder than I had thought it would be. Where on earth do I start? What is it that I want to say? How do I explain my journey without looking like an attention-seeking and overly sensitive little boy? I took a deep breath, took in the beautiful view of the Greek mountains, and put my pen to paper.

I have, as you've seen, included the first half of the essay I would then write earlier in this book. I want to pick up the essay where we left off:

"I felt it was now time to tackle the issue of my sexuality - and my ability to accept who I am - once and for all.

I asked myself; Do you really want to lie on your death bed and bitterly regret living a lie, hiding your identity, wishing that you had found the confidence to be happy and content in life?

Do you really want to look back on your life and wish that you hadn't let negative comments and hateful homophobia limit you and stop you from living a positive and fulfilling life?

I questioned whether I was really going to let the words of homophobic and hateful individuals result in me wasting my precious lifetime

drowning in self-hatred and fear. Surely, I thought to myself during one particularly philosophical session; life is too short, precious and valuable to spent hating who you are? Life is too futile to waste time not being happy with, and being proud of, who you authentically are?

It was not long before I realised just how much I would prefer to spend my last few hours alive, reflecting on how I'd found the courage to stop fearing the 'haters'. I want to reflect on having lived as my authentic, free self. And I want to die knowing that I have hopefully inspired hundreds, if not thousands, of people along the way.

Empowering others is something I feel deeply passionate about due to the fact that I know I am not alone in my struggle to understand, accept and embrace my sexuality.

It's thought that between one in 10 and one in 15 young people are Lesbian, Gay or Bisexual. This means that three young people in every classroom are potentially gay. These young people are individual human beings who, just like every single other person on this planet, simply want to live a happy, positive and fulfilling life. Yet because of bullying, homophobia - the vast majority of which is ingrained into the very fabric of society - and a culture in which the idea of being 'gay' is still seen as a negative, derogatory insult, these young people feel unable to do something that so many people take for granted without a second thought; accept themselves, believe in themselves and feel comfortable in their own skin.

I have come to realise that being ashamed of my sexuality or personality, is saying that the haters and homophobes are right or that they have 'won'. As a believer that goodness, kindness and love should always triumph, I simply cannot allow this to be the case.

Those who bully, mock or reject others on the grounds of thinking that the way they act is 'gay' need to see that, actually, being 'gay' is not a sign of weakness or something to be mocked for, but that sexuality is just one, small, positive part of who you are.

***

We also need to work to overcome the stereotypes and slurs surrounding the idea of being 'gay'. There is no stereotypical gay person. From high-profile, and very masculine, rugby players such as Keegan Hirst and Gareth Thomas, to top Business Executives such as the CEO's of WH Smith, Burberry, HSBC, Qantas, Monarch and the Managing Directors of Goldman Sachs, Standard Chartered, Visa Europe, Virgin Holidays and Costa International, absolutely anybody can be gay [ALL CORRECT AS OF 2016]. Gay people are normal people, from every walk of life and every single area of society.

By recognising that people from every walk of life and profession are homosexual, we can see just how normal and acceptable being gay is. As a result, see the need to accept and celebrate each person for who they are.

Now, it's one thing to celebrate others who have found the courage to embrace their sexuality. But how can one individual move from a place of pain and self-rejection to a place of empowerment and self-acceptance? What does it take for a young person struggling to understand and accept their sexuality to find the courage, confidence and strength to be themselves? How can they be liberated from the burden of shame, fear and the feeling of being out-of-place in this world?

I think that we must keep in mind that we only have one life. This is not a rehearsal - this is everything we'll ever have, and we have to celebrate and embrace that. For me, I think a great source of motivation for working to find the confidence to embrace my sexuality is the fact that we do only live once; you are never going to get the second you have experienced back.

Therefore, shouldn't you live each and every moment to the full in a happy and positive way? And I passionately believe that the only way we can do this is if we live as our authentic, original selves. As Shakespeare's Hamlet says so well: 'This above all, to thine own self, be true'.

We aren't living this life for the haters. We aren't on this planet to let criticism, rudeness and bitterness drag us down. We are here to be a positive presence and to live as our authentic, original selves. We are privileged to be living in a golden age of acceptance and ever-increasing love and tolerance, and so we have the perfect opportunity to make our dream of living freely as our true selves a reality".

I continued:

"My personal journey of acceptance and empowerment has, I can assure you, not been an overnight quick-fix. It has taken long hours of deep introspection and reflection on how having attractions to members of the same-sex is an integral and positive part of my identity, and that sexual orientation doesn't stop me from doing absolutely anything. I can still enjoy the marriage and children, as well the successful career and happy life, that I dream of.

I have invested a great deal of time and effort in accepting myself and seeing that to be gay (whatever that term means in today's world) ould not make me inferior, a failure or an easy target for bullying. Instead, I have been able to realise, your sexuality and how you walk, talk and behave are simply parts of your identity. You should accept and embrace every aspect of your identity as a positive part of who you are.

I have also been able to realise that being gay causes no-one else any harm whatsoever, and so any homophobia or hatred is simply down to ignorance and an incredibly negative reflection on the perpetrator, not me. Seeing that being gay is not about having a negative label and having no place in mainstream society, but that homosexuality is actually just about which gender you are programmed to fall in love with has given me so much strength, self-belief and empowerment. I have been blessed to see that your sexuality does not define you and should not condemn you to a life of unhappiness, bullying or discrimination.

I feel privileged to have this opportunity to show people that true happiness comes from being positive, kind and accepting. True fulfilment is the result of living as your authentic, original self. This is my chance to live out my philosophy of acceptance and authenticity. We should celebrate who we are, and that the kindest thing we can do for others is to love and accept them for who they authentically are too.

From a personal perspective, being able to accept my sexuality means I can now open myself up to relationships. This means that I can finally experience the love and romance I have been dreaming of ever since I can remember.

Knowing who I am means that there is now a possibility of having a relationship and feeling the love and connection I dream of. What could be more natural, more human or more wonderful?

To accept yourself - in my case, my sexuality - requires that you're bold, that you're frank with yourself, and that you make time to do some serious soul-searching. It first requires that you have the confidence to be fully honest, open and truthful with yourself. You must then use this self-acceptance as the basis for feeling happy, empowered and confident in your skin when out in the real world.

Of course, my head is still swimming with questions. There's still so much I don't understand about my sexuality. And I'm scared by the fact that the world is still filled with homophobia and hatred. Countless people are attacked and even killed, for being gay every day. Yet I now feel as if I am finally ready to close a chapter of suffering and open a new chapter of self-acceptance, empowerment and liberation. I want to get serious about celebrating my identity and letting my personality shine through, without fear of rejection or negative responses.

I feel truly blessed to be able to say that, after so many years of self-hatred and denial, I can accept, and embrace the fact that I am gay. I am also truly blessed to be alive at a time when I will be able to get married and have the children I dream of having.

Whilst I fully expect to face setbacks in the years to come, I feel I now have the confidence, courage, and self-belief to overcome negativity and hatred. I am reading to start responding with love, resilience and compassion for all. The word 'gay' no longer has a paralysing power over me; I no longer see it as a dark insult that makes you inferior, isolated and rejected. Instead, I simply see it as an aspect of one's identity that should be accepted and embraced.

I would urge anyone struggling with their sexuality to spend time cultivating self-understanding, self-belief, and self-acceptance. Realise that we are all incredible, loved and valued human beings! You have a right to live happily and authentically, just as much as absolutely anyone else.

Be proud of who you are, and know that the world is becoming a kinder, more accepting and more understanding place. Your sexuality does not define you, give you a negative label or make you any less of an incredible human being. It does not mean that anyone has any justification for rejecting, bullying or mocking you. Remain strong, keep growing in self-acceptance and confidence, and I promise that, in time, you will find yourself becoming so much stronger and comfortable in your own skin.

May I also urge each and every one of us to work tirelessly to create a kinder, more accepting society, and indeed the planet, leading by example in showing acceptance and love to all and refusing to allow negative stereotypes, mocking and bullying to hold us back from living our lives to the full.

Living as your authentic, original self is the most beautiful and most incredible thing in the world. I feel deeply blessed and privileged to say that this authenticity and freedom is finally now my reality".

As I put down my pen, I felt the most incredible sensation of relief, empowerment and joy. I had done it! I had put pen to paper, and I had declared, for the very first time, that I was gay! This felt like an enormous moment and a genuine turning point in my life! As my mum always says, nobody should ever have to 'come out. Being gay should never be seen as something that you have to 'admit' to people. However, I found that writing this 'coming out' essay was incredibly empowering for me. I felt like I was finally in control of my narrative. I was finally the master of my destiny! And I had finally conquered my insecurities and fears!

After so long, I was finally ready to peace with who I was. I was no longer letting other people label me or judge me. Instead, I was, quite literally, becoming the author of my next chapter. And, let me tell you this – it felt bloody fantastic!

It's no surprise to me that there is a field in therapy known as 'bibliotherapy', which uses storytelling and reading to help individuals to heal. I find storytelling and writing to be the most extraordinarily empowering and therapeutic process. By writing about your feelings and sharing your story, you can take ownership of your life and become the master of your destiny. Never underestimate the power of putting pen to paper and writing about how you feel! My daily journal writing had proven to be my greatest source of support on my journey towards working out who I was and what I wanted from my life.

Once we had got home from Kefalonia, I sat down at my laptop and typed everything I had written up. I submitted my essay to the Huffington Post blog section, and a lovely journalist called Jess got in touch. She suggested that I split my piece down into sections of around 800 words each so that I would be able to publish my writing as a series on their website. I did as she recommended, and my 'four-part series' was born! Oh, I did take it all very seriously! I printed it all off and handed a copy to both Queen P and dad. This would be the first time I ever 'admitted' to either of them that I was gay.

However, there is no doubt that they knew long before I decided to write a four-part series for the Huffington Post! Mum hugged me and dad wiped away tears. They didn't turn it into an episode of EastEnders. They just reiterated how much they loved me and how they were so proud of me for writing it all down. I also gave a copy to Granny and Grumpy, who were just as accepting and loving. Even though they had spent almost half of their lives living in a society where homosexuality was illegal, they showed me nothing but acceptance and love. The fact I was 'gay' was just not a big deal. When I told her about my sexuality, my granny was more interested in telling me about her latest garden centre purchases! That does say everything you need to know about Queen Wendy! Here was the relieving and incredible thing: nobody batted an eyelid, and nobody had absolutely anything to say. Whilst a dramatic 'coming out' story would have certainly added a little bit of flavour to this book; I was beyond relieved by their low-key responses. I know how fortunate I am, and I could not love them more.

***

Making sense of my sexuality did not happen overnight. It was a long process that required a lot of time, patience, and self-love. It required an open mind and a strong support system around me. Most importantly, it required a firm conviction that I deserved to live a genuinely happy life. I needed to realise that I deserved to live my life to the absolute full. Only then was I able to stop worrying so much about what other people thought of me. Only then was I able to finally start cultivating authenticity in my life.

My journey towards accepting my sexuality was made so much more comfortable thanks to the people around me. I have always been the biggest believer in the idea that it is the people around us who make our lives complete. Without strong relationships with other human beings, we would not be able to survive – never mind thrive! To give you a little bit of evolutionary backstory: Humans are, on a very basic evolutionary level, tribal beings. We can only survive as part of a group. This was the case when humans were primitive 'hunter-gatherers', foraging for food on the plains of Africa thousands of years ago. And this is still the case today! As Dr Martin Luther King famously remarked, 'before you have finished breakfast in the morning, you have already depended on more than half of the world'. No man is an island, and no human being is self-sufficient. Without strong relationships and close connections, we would be deeply unhappy and disadvantaged, both physically and psychologically.

I have been extremely blessed to have the most genuinely amazing people around me. First and foremost, my parents have always been the most incredible sources of unconditional love and acceptance. They are extraordinarily open-minded and unconditionally loving, providing my brother and me with a very loving, accepting and liberal home. The same can be said for my grandparents – my Gran in particular. They have provided my brother and I with the most incredible amount of love, kindness, and care throughout our lives. In doing so, they have inspired me and supported me more than they will ever realise or know.

I must also express an enormous amount of gratitude and love for my brother, Sam, who is three years younger and my absolute opposite. Some may say (in other words I say) that we look a tiny bit like twins….but only when I'm having a week off the fake-tan addition. Sam is a typical football-playing 'lad' with an absolute heart-of-gold. I undoubtedly regularly irritate and annoy him with my (let's be honest) divalike and dramatic ways. However, he is the least judgemental and most accepting human being you could ever meet. He is very like my dad, who just so happens to be the manager of Sam's football team, whilst I am very much like my mum, Queen P – and I think that title really does say it all! I could not ask for a better, kinder, or more accepting brother. I am fully aware that the lottery of life has truly blessed me, and I genuinely do thank my lucky stars every day.

Thanks to the unconditional love and support from my family, I did feel I had space, time and freedom to explore my identity. I was given a safe space within which to work who I authentically was. Whether I have been performing in theatre productions, entering Catholic public speaking competitions, filming YouTube videos, or selling cups of instant hot chocolate at the bottom of our drive; my parents have always been there, cheering me on. I can tell you with complete certainty that I would not be here today without them. And I would not be capable of doing any of the things that I am so fortunate to be doing today without their unconditional love and support. I am very aware that everybody is not fortunate in terms of their family's responses. It particularly pains me to read about LGBT+ individuals who have been thrown out of home, or worse, after revealing their sexual orientation. Not only does this anger me beyond words, but it also genuinely blows my mind. The idea that you could treat your child in this way is utterly incomprehensible to me. If you are not prepared to unconditionally accept and love your child, then you should not become a parent. Every single individual deserves nothing but unconditional love, acceptance, and inclusion within a loving, safe, and caring family. I realise how privileged I have been, and I thank my lucky stars every single day.

***

Of course, family extends further than just blood or biological relations. I count my best friends as an integral part of my family, and it is thanks to my closest friends that I am here today. I will introduce you to Freya and Kristina a little bit later on (in keeping with the chronological order of this book!) but for now, let me tell you about Becky. She was my absolute rock and the most incredible source of support during this time of 'working out' my sexuality.

The one person who supported and championed me the most at this time was my best friend, Becky. I had known Becky since primary school, but I had only become close with her towards the end of year ten and the beginning of year 11. To say Becky was – and remains - the biggest blessing in my life is an understatement. This girl was – and is– truly amazing. This stunning and confident girl, with an absolute heart-of-gold, completely took me 'under her wing' after we had started walking home together, with Erin, after school. Even after one 20-minute walk home, I knew that I would be best friends with this girl, whether she liked it or not! There was, from my perspective, an instant connection and 'click'. And our friendship quickly blossomed as we walked home and discussed our life drama's every evening after school. We would put the world – and our Year Group! - to rights, discussing every single topic under the sun. We did not hold back, let me tell you that now! Becky taught me what it means to genuinely care about someone and to have their back, no matter what. We remain the best of friends to this day, and I think one of our greatest moments has to be getting awarded the joint honour of 'Biggest Divas' in sixth form (I mean it says it all really, doesn't it?!).

It's funny to think how different our lives could have turned out if we had not crossed paths with certain people. I cannot imagine what my life would be like if I had not – on one random evening after school – ended up walking home from school with Becky and Erin. This one encounter changed everything, and it blows my mind how easily this encounter could not have happened.

Before crossing paths with Becky and Erin, I had felt very lost and alone in this world. Life before Year 9 had not been filled with meaningful, genuine or fulfilling friendships. As you know, I spent the first 14 years of my life feeling very insecure in my skin. Meeting Becky and Erin completely and utterly changed my life – and I will be forever thankful. It's funny to think that we went to the same primary school, and yet our paths never crossed until the final years of high school. But thank God they did – we were all in just the right place, at just the right time! It was like the universe was sending me a sign, and I have never been so thankful for anything in my life! It sounds dramatic, and she would be mortified to ever read this, but Becky changed my life. As I say, it is the people in our lives who make our existence so fulfilling and our time on this planet feel so complete. And so I may have achieved a lot in my penultimate years at high school. For example, overcoming anorexia, accepting my sexuality and even - as I'll talk about later – having an amazing time in Sixth Form. But I would say without any doubt whatsoever that my greatest achievement was discovering the most amazing friends I could ask for. My final years at High School had led to the discovery of the most incredible friends for life. I finally felt accepted and included, which left me this most incredible feeling of confidence and connection. I had the best friends I could ever wish for and the most amazing family I could dream of having – what on earth could stop me now? As far as I was concerned, nothing was going to stop me…

***

The Summer of 2016 was a time of so much personal growth and positive transformation in my life. It was like I was finally emerging from my chrysalis, ready to become the master of my destiny and live a fearlessly authentic life. There were two key practices that I discovered this summer that I believe gave me the capability to find genuine self-confidence and self-acceptance from within myself. They were yoga and meditation, two practices which continue to play an enormously significant role in my life to this day.

I had, as you know, been meditating every single morning and evening ever since my therapist Sarah had encouraged me to research 'mindfulness. I had found that meditation had the most life-enhancing effect on me – meditation left me feeling so confident, calm, and genuinely content in myself. It gave me perspective, space to breathe, and a newfound love for the gift that is life. Sitting in meditation was literally like hitting a 'reset' or 'refresh' button – I would finish my session feeling so cleansed, invigorated, and inspired! Meditation taught me – and continues to teach me – the value of human life and the beauty of just being present in the present moment. Meditation has different purposes and goals for different people. Some meditate in the hope of training their minds, some come to the practice to attain liberation from the cycle of rebirth, whilst others meditate simply to de-stress. Meditation is what *you* make it! For me, meditation is an indispensable practice that illuminates and enriches my human existence. It is, for me, all about 'waking up' and connecting to the world around us. It is all about focusing on your breath and simply becoming aware of this present moment, and learning to make peace with all your thoughts, feelings and emotions.

The second practice that has transformed my life was yoga. Yoga has been the most positive practice in my life over the past few years. In particular, it has helped me in my efforts to rehabilitate a healthy relationship with my body. I can't quite remember what first got me into yoga, but I do know that I instantly fell in love it. Everything I know about yoga I have learned from Adriene Mishler, the gorgeous YouTube sensation based in Austin, Texas. I had discovered Adriene's series of yoga videos – titled 'Yoga with Adriene' – and I began practising most evenings before bed. I loved absolutely everything about yoga with Adriene – it was so good for the body, mind, and soul! I loved that it improved both your body – I started becoming toned and, eventually, started getting abs! – and your mind as well! The practice felt so healing and empowering, and it also led to incredible improvements in your fitness.

Crucially, I wasn't doing this practice with the sole intention of improving my physical appearance or losing weight (not that I needed to). However, physical fitness was certainly part of the package! Oh, you should have seen the little six-pack I soon had going on! Yoga was proving to be a deeply holistic practice, which felt me feeling grounded, present, and nourished. Every session was like continuing an enriching journey towards self-love and self-awareness. I started to love my body genuinely, and I started to see my life through a brand-new lens. I do believe that discovering yoga – via Adriene's YouTube videos! –transformed my life! As someone with a history of an eating disorder, I found that yoga was a fantastic way of rehabilitating my relationship with my body. I found that I now had a much healthier perspective on my physical appearance, and I felt more connected with every inch of my body than ever before. Furthermore, I now had a toned stomach and the first signs of a mini six-pack! I loved that this positive transformation in my appearance was not the result of an obsession with exercise or eating. Instead, it was the by-product of a spiritually nourishing and life-affirming daily practice! Adriene's videos were teaching me to 'find what feels good' and 'be present in your body. And, at the same time, they were improving my core strength and benefiting my body! It was amazing! I could not love yoga more; it is the most positive and life-affirming practice, and you can do it anywhere in the world!

16. SIXTH FORM: NEW SUITS AND NEW STARTS

It's 6.30 am on a crisp September morning, and I've just jumped out of bed. It's the first day of Sixth Form, and I am both excited and terrified in equal measure. In particular, I am terrified of the Year 13s, who I am scared of facing in the Common Room! How will we know where it's okay to sit? How do we fit into the Common Room hierarchy?

It's a brand-new school year, and it's a brand-new start. And so, I think it's only right that I'm getting into a brand-new M&S suit and putting on a brand-new M&S skinny fit tie! I'm looking, if I may so myself, very smart in my navy blue suit, skinny maroon tie and shoes! I don't know if anyone else finds this, but there's something about wearing business dress that makes me feel like a million dollars! I feel like Kris Jenner, Alan Sugar, and Huw Edwards all rolled into one…and I love it! Others have been complaining about having to wear business dress in Sixth Form. It was not like going off to College, where we would have been able to wear whatever we had liked. But never one to follow the crowd, I genuinely love filling my wardrobe with suits, ties and an array of long sleeve shirts. I take great pleasure walking around Primark in Manchester, picking out different shirts and skinny-fit ties! If you're ever looking for a funky skinny-fit tie, then I urge you to get yourself down to Primark! I had the time of my life picking out my Sixth Form 'power outfit' wardrobe, filled with an eclectic array of patterned and bold-coloured shirts!

As Becky and I walk into school, I wonder what the next two years might have in store for us. I've picked to study English Language, English Literature, Psychology and Religious Studies, and I am excited to find out who will be in my new classes. A-Levels, we keep being told, are hard. 'The jump between GCSE and A-Level is ten times bigger than the jump between A-Levels and University', I keep being told. Great, I think, that's just the positive information I needed! Well, I do love a challenge! And I do, as you know, love a good bit of hard work!

We arrive at school. It feels so weird not to be in the school uniform. We're all grown up, I tell Becky, as we walk through a sea of Year 7s feeling very mature and important! We head to the Common Room, which is already packed with people and feels hotter than a sauna…which is not exactly ideal when you're standing there in a shirt and blazer! Mrs Garvey, the Head of Sixth Form, appears in one of her many power outfits. I love this woman. She is someone who instantly commands respect, admiration, and attention. She welcomes us to the Sixth Form and goes through the basic bits of admin and housekeeping. After that, we go off to our assigned forms, where I have chosen to be with Becky and Harriet. Thank the lord! To my absolute delight, our form tutor is the one and only Mrs Sutton, who greets us with a beaming smile on her face. 'It's like a divine intervention!', I joke to her, feeling genuinely delighted that I'll be seeing her for Form every morning. She has been an absolute angel to me over the past two years, and I am so glad we'll be crossing paths every morning throughout Sixth Form. Her positivity and kindness are just what I need before a busy day of A-Levels!

The first week in Sixth Form flies by in a storm of suits, ties, and A-Level specifications. I genuinely love all of my classes, and I am very happy with my teachers. I am enjoying the smaller class sizes, which allow you to get to know everyone a lot better. The teachers seem to have a more relaxed relationship with us, which I love, and I especially like this idea of being responsible for my own learning. Whilst the teachers will still use 'Show My Homework' to set us tasks, we will no longer be treated like Year 7s – the responsibility to work hard is in our own hands! This is music to my self-motivated ears! I am excited to roll up my sleeves and get down to work! I soon settle into Sixth Form, working hard to keep up with all the reading and essay writing. I am thoroughly enjoying it – I love my subjects, and I love my teachers, which I really do believe makes all the difference.

In Religious Studies, we have three teachers who will each cover one section of the course – Philosophy of Religion, Religious Ethics, and Developments in Christian Thought. Ms O Hagan teaches us Plato and Aristotle whilst Dr Keogh tells us all about St Augustine and Original Sin (he's obsessed!) Meanwhile, the fabulous Mrs Stewart brings Natural Law to life, with her sparkling personality and infectious enthusiasm for a debate! These three teachers quickly become the Holy Trinity of my A-Levels – they are all experts in their field, and they are all infectiously passionate about education. I am instantly obsessed with the Religious Studies course, and I am instantly sure that this is the subject I want to study at university.

Whilst I also love my psychology lessons with Miss Clarke and Mr Howells, I am seriously put off by the maths and science involved... I find psychology content so interesting. To be honest, I find it more interesting than some of the Religious Studies content. And the exceptional teaching I receive helps me to 'get over' my fear of the maths and research methods elements involved! This is where the 'growth mindset' became particularly important. For so many years I had literally dismissed maths by saying 'I can't do maths…it's not for me'. Imagine if I had replaced the word 'maths' with the word 'reading' – nobody would get away with just saying 'I can't read, so it's not for me!' But with maths, things are different. I feel that people are a lot less confident and a lot less convinced that they can acquire and improve their numeracy abilities. If I was going to crack psychology A-Level and get the A/A* grade I wanted, then I had got to make friends with maths! The psychology exam was 10% maths, and 'research methods' was a massive part of the specification – I needed to face my numeracy fears and make friends with the science!

At first, I was not convinced that a growth mindset would be sufficient for improving my maths and science. As I say, I had spent my whole time in education, believing that I simply 'couldn't do' maths. So I now needed to get myself into a headspace of believing that I COULD indeed cultivate these skills! I knew that psychology was going to take me outside of my 'I'm good at writing essays' comfort zone, and I was excited about the challenge.

Over in English Language, I had Mrs Williams for one lesson and teacher I'd never had before, Mrs Davies-McCumaskey, for the other two. At first, English Language A-levels was not my thing. At all. It was, I have to tell you, utterly soul-destroying. I did not want to sit there learning about syntax, grammar, prepositional clauses and pragmatics. Like with the maths in psychology, I felt out of my depth with all this new terminology – and when I didn't get something, I didn't like it! However, I kept going, and we got onto better topics, such as the language used in different occupations and regions around the UK.

My fourth and final AS Level subject was English Literature. I had always loved my English Lit, as my YouTube video on 'Journey's End' must have demonstrated very well! I loved going through set texts and analysing what everything meant – what was the author's intention? How did certain language features shape the narrative? What was the wider context around the publication of the novel? English Literature made me feel very cultural, academic and knowledgeable. I was genuinely interested in studying different texts, plays and novels, and I saw each new book as a new 'mini-project' to enjoy. You would learn so much – about English and the world – just from studying a text in detail! At AS Level, we were studying Othello, Atonement and a selection of poems. One of my two English Language teachers were excellent – I loved studying Othello and poetry with this teacher. The other teacher, however, was not my cup of tea. At all. I found their style to be condescending, abrasive, and unengaging.

Both of these English Literature teachers were very set in their ways and uninterested in evolving their prehistoric teaching styles. But at least I felt engaged and supported in the Othello lessons. I strongly believe that it is the teacher who makes or breaks a subject at school. If your teacher is not passionate or inspiring, then how on earth are you supposed to be passionate or inspired as a student? Teaching, in my opinion, should be all about changing lives by igniting passions, inspiring young people, and unlocking their full potential. You should want your students to thrive, and you should strive to keep your teaching as current, dynamic, and inspiring as possible. Well, these English Literature lessons were not igniting any kind of passion within me whatsoever. Indeed, I would argue that they were doing the opposite. I left these lessons feeling deflated and unenthusiastic – the life, and love for English, had been sucked out of me!

And so, I decided to take matters into my own hands. I was seriously loving studying Othello – it was genuinely my favourite thing in the world. When I enjoy something, I go completely extra with it. I had soon ordered every single Othello revision guide available online, and I had soon covered my bedroom with critical quotes about the play. I began learning dozens of quotes by heart, analysing every language feature used and linking each quote to its historical context. My copy of Othello became a chaotic rainbow of highlighters, post-it notes and arrows! Every single line of the play had been highlighted and annotated! Practically every other word had been linked to either a critical quote or piece of context. I was living and breathing this play – I just loved immersing myself in this world of studying Shakespeare! My essay results were reflecting the level of my passion; I would regularly score at least 19/25 (an A) on the homework pieces I was handing in each week. By contrast, anything I wrote on Atonement would be lucky to scrape 14/25, and that was if I was lucky!

I decided that I wanted to get back onto YouTube, where I had posted my 'Journey's End' and GCSE RE videos a year earlier. I knew that teaching someone else – even if I was effectively just teaching my webcam – would help me massively in terms of my own exam revision. I'd read a statistic saying that whilst you remember 10% of what you read, you remember 90% of what you teach. It was a no-brainer – if I wanted to remember all my critical quotes and contextual links, then I needed to teach them to somebody else! And so, I decided that I'd do an 'Othello revision session' on my YouTube channel. I didn't expect anything to come of it, and I was literally doing it for my own personal benefit. So I didn't worry about the lighting or how the video would end up going! I just set up my webcam, picked up my copy of the play, and started speaking into my webcam. Over the next 75 minutes, I went through the play line-by-line, talking my viewer (the webcam) through every single page. I spoke about the types of language used, the context of certain words and concepts. I kept linking everything back to the theme of my English Literature exam paper, which was 'Love through the ages'. Seventy-five minutes later and I had got through my copy of the play. The final 15 minutes of filming has been a complete blur, fuelled entirely by adrenaline and green tea. I thought nothing of it as I uploaded the video to YouTube, before getting on with my day of reading and revision.

A couple of days later and I'd forgotten all about uploading the video. Well, I was too busy trying to get through all my AS Level revision and coursework to be worrying about whether I might become the next Zoella!

I hoped that it might get one or two views, and I had hoped that it might help one or two people doing their revision. But I certainly wasn't expecting to wake up to a call from Simon Cowell and find my video being broadcast on BBC Breakfast! In a moment of boredom, I mindlessly logged into Facebook for a quick scroll through the news feed. To my surprise, I saw that I'd received several message requests. That's odd, I thought to myself, as I clicked through my inbox. What could this be all about? Well, within seconds, I was reading message after message about my revision videos! I could not believe it! These random people across the country had seen my video…and it had helped them! I could not believe it! I was genuinely over the moon. My Kris Jenner fantasy was finally coming true!

***

When I look back on my time at school and Sixth Form, I do believe that education saved me. Education rescued me and gave me an escape from my troubles. Studying saved me - firstly from my eating disorder, and then from my struggle to accept my sexuality. Knowledge is power, and studying is empowering! Studying, reading and then teaching – in my YouTube revision videos – provided me with a much-needed distraction and escape from my thoughts. The more I learned, the more confident I became. The more I read, the more articulate I became.

There was one subject that empowered and inspired me more than any other. I credit this subject with totally transforming my life. Studying this subject has become my ultimate passion and favourite past-time. When most people hear what subject this is, they genuinely can't believe it. They're genuinely shocked that I would be passionate about this subject. What subject am I talking about? Let's find out…

17. THE UNEXAMINED LIFE IS NOT WORTH LIVING

There is nothing that I love more – other than Kris Jenner, green tea, and Prosecco – than discussing and studying religion, philosophy and ethics. It is my absolute passion and all-time favourite past-time.

When I think back to the beginning of my relationship with philosophy, it was love at first sight. As you know, I started becoming interested in news, politics, and current affairs as I read the newspapers whilst in hospital with anorexia. My dad would bring me the papers every morning on his way to work, and I would spend the day reading the newspapers from cover-to-cover (excluding the sports pages, of course)! I became completely fascinated by news and current affairs. I loved reading about people's lives and the latest political developments, and I loved the feeling of being informed on the latest news stories from around the world. Over the next few years, my fascination with news and current affairs grew and grew. I would buy the 'i newspaper' every morning before school, and I would look forward to reading The Times at the weekends. I could not go a single day without reading the day's newspapers, listening to BBC Radio 4, and catching up on all of the day's TV news bulletins.

At school, I loved being able to bring the latest news stories I had been reading about into conversation, both on the playground and in the classroom. I found that my current affairs knowledge particularly came in handy during Business Studies and Religious Studies lessons. These two subjects, along with English, Drama and Geography, soon became my firm favourites. I particularly enjoyed Religious Studies, despite not being religious in the slightest! We would discuss contentious issues such as global warming, abortion, community cohesion and ethics. I loved exploring and debating these topics, and I became particularly interested in understanding the Christian way of viewing the world. It amazed me how influential Christianity had been in shaping the way things are thought about and done in the UK, and also around the world. It fascinated me to consider how ancient Christian teachings were continuing to shape societal attitudes, values, and beliefs over 2,000 years after the death of Jesus Christ. Although I was attending a Roman Catholic school, our Religious Studies lessons were not about indoctrination.

On the contrary, they encouraged critical thinking and debate. I enjoyed considering moral and ethical problems from both a Christian, Islamic and atheistic perspective. I would spend my evenings reading up on Church teachings about contemporary moral dilemmas. For example, I was fascinated to read what the Catechism of the Catholic Church had to say about homosexuality. And I would spend hours reading the different teachings and doctrines that the Church had created on this issue!

The more I read, the more I realised how much Christianity had to offer society. And the more I read, the more I realised how my Catholic Primary School had completely oversimplified and misinterpreted very complex theological and philosophical ideas. I had left Primary School with a completely distorted and incorrect idea of the Christian faith. We had been taught to conceive of God as this powerful man sat somewhere on a cloud. Key Biblical characters such as Jesus and Mary had been reduced to two-dimensional cardboard cutouts. Today, I read articles about Jesus being a revolutionary social reformer. And I read discussion forums about the true nature of the being theists refer to a 'God'. I soon realised that everything I had been taught to believe in Primary School was wrong!

As I researched more about the origins of Christianity and the moral teachings of Jesus Christ, I stumbled across discussions of something called 'philosophy'. I read about Ancient Greek philosophers such as Plato and Aristotle. They had laid down the (metaphorical) foundations for the entirety of Western civilisation. I read about 'empiricists' such as John Locke. He had argued that to believe something, you must have 'evidence' deriving from your experiences. I came across the ethical theories devised by Immanuel Kant and Jeremy Bentham. I became utterly fascinated by how these ancient philosophers had shaped how we conceive the world today.

I began asking my teenage self some seriously deep and profound questions. Why is the universe here in the first place? How do we know the difference between right and wrong? What does it mean to live a happy and fulfilling life? Out of all the different world religions and belief systems, how do we know which one to be true? As I thought about these questions, I quite liked the fact I didn't have any of the answers to hand. I liked the idea that these questions were so big and so bold that they got the cogs inside my brain turning, and they challenged me to think outside of the box. Just thinking and reading about these key philosophical questions, ideas, and dilemmas gave me a sense of stimulation and a real feeling that I was 'waking up' to the reality of human life.

I began reading endless books on human anthropology, psychology and society. I had this insatiable thirst for knowledge and understanding about who we are and why we are here. Looking back now, I wonder whether this desire for such knowledge about humanity was motivated by a desire to understand myself. As you know, I spent many years feeling judged, misunderstood and out-of-place in the world. By striving to understand humanity as a whole, was I hoping to learn more about myself as an individual?

If this was indeed my intention, then it certainly paid off and worked wonders! The more that I learned about the evolution of Homo Sapiens and the development of human society, the more confident and empowered I felt in my own skin. You know what I say, knowledge really is power! I was learning all these new words and concepts, and I felt as if I now had a real sense of place and purpose in the world. Philosophy is all about overcoming ignorance, which I believe is the cause of all of the hatred and division that exists in our world.

I loved the fact that philosophy encourages us to question, think, and evaluate everything that we would otherwise take for granted. Indeed, it is only when we question, critique and reflect that we can evolve and progress as a species. For example, we need to ask why certain things – such as homosexuality or sex before marriage – are seen as so wrong and taboo within society. What is the justification for this societal attitude? What values and principles underpin these moral positions? I found that studying philosophy provided me with an ability (in terms of vocabulary, language and pre-existing philosophical ideas) to articulate myself with confidence and conviction. For example, I could argue against homophobia by referencing John Stuart Mill's 'non-harm principle'. His principle states that every individual should have freedom and autonomy over their own body. I could use this assertion to defend people's right to love or marry whoever they wanted. And I could challenge those who used Christianity as a justification or their homophobia by discussing the wider contextual and hermeneutical significance of the Old Testament passages that talk about homosexuality.

My knowledge of religion, philosophy and ethics became my battle armour with which to face the world. The more I read and the more I studied, the more articulate, curious, and confident I became.

I was particularly interested in rethinking the teachings of Jesus Christ, which I had been completely turned off by during my time at Primary School. I remember one Year 9 Religious Studies lesson in which our teacher, Mr Nickson, introduced us to the 'Sermon on the Mount'. It is a speech – perhaps the most famous speech in human history - delivered by Jesus to his followers over 2,000 years ago. This speech laid the foundations for the entirety of Christian social and moral teaching, and yet I had never been taught about it before. It is taken from the Gospel, according to Matthew, in the New Testament:

"Blessed are the poor in spirit, for theirs is the kingdom of God.

Blessed are those who mourn, for they shall be comforted.

Blessed are the meek, for they shall inherit the earth.

Blessed are those who hunger and thirst for righteousness, for they will be filled.

Blessed are the merciful, for they will be shown mercy.

Blessed are the pure in heart, for they will see God.

Blessed are the peacemakers, for they will be called the children of God.

Blessed are those who are persecuted because of righteousness, for theirs is the kingdom of heaven". (Matthew 5:3-10)

As I read this extract on one of the GCSE RE handout sheets, Christianity suddenly all made sense. I'm not saying that I suddenly became a devout Roman Catholic, but I suddenly understood what Christianity is all about! I no longer saw Christianity as a silly little fairytale about an angel telling a woman that she was going to have a baby. I realised that Christianity was so much more than the Nativity play that we had performed in school. Christianity, I realised, was so much more than going into a Church and singing a few hymns.

Christianity, I started to realise, was a real, raw, and radical movement that had utterly transformed the entire landscape of western society. Jesus Christ had not come so that the Catholic mums could have a coffee morning in the Church hall every Wednesday. Christianity was not all about getting dressed up for Holy Communion on a Sunday. Jesus Christ was a radical social reformer, not an excuse for a coffee morning! He was a passionate moral activist who came with a serious agenda for social change. He wanted to liberate the oppressed, empower the marginalised, promote equality and preach a message of unconditional love. The Sermon on the Mount set Christianity up like a movement that championed the rights, dignity and worth of every single human being on this planet. Jesus had spent his entire life promoting an obvious message of stewardship, kindness and compassion to every single person who would listen to him! This is what Christianity was supposed to be all about today!

There was another quote that Mr Nickson was particularly passionate about, which he had taken from St Teresa of Avila. It came from a prayer she had written, and it read; "Christ has no body but yours". Again, this was a teaching that transformed my understanding of what it meant to be 'Christian'. Christianity, I realised, was all about rolling up your sleeves and working hard to make this world a better place. That means that every single individual has a fundamental duty to be a peacemaker and promote goodness, kindness, and compassion in the world around them. Every single individual must actively 'become the change they wish to see in the world'. Christianity is not a comfort blanket or set of customs to blindly follow. Instead, Christianity is a radical call-to-action, which is supposed to inspire a very positive and reformist change in your life. I felt invigorated, inspired, and empowered by this practical and positive understanding of Christianity, which made the teachings of Jesus Christ feel so relevant and real. As I say, this is not to say that I was now on the verge of a St Paul style of conversion and transformation. But I was certainly now more invigorated and energised by the Christian teachings than I had ever been before.

***

One of the news stories that particularly spiked my interest in religion – and led to my passion for philosophy and ethics – was the election of Pope Francis as leader of the Catholic Church. I was captivated by the spectacle of the Papal Conclave – the outfits, the secrecy, the drama, and even the white smoke fascinated me. I became intrigued by how organised religion had gained so much power and influence over so many millions of lives. These cardinals were sat here electing the new leader of the world's 1.2 billion Catholics – this was a pretty big deal! I was particularly fascinated by how the Church has been able to establish itself as a leading source of absolute moral authority on everything from euthanasia to homosexuality.

The Catholic Church, I discovered, held the prestigious status of being the world's oldest and largest continuously functioning institution. Over the years, political leaders and ideologies have come and gone. Yet the Church has remained an enduring and authoritative source of moral leadership and ethical guidance for hundreds of years. The teachings of this single organisation had shaped and moulded millions of people's entire lives. And, as the News Channels reported on the election of Jorge Mario Bergoglio (the new Pope Francis), I felt excited by the prospect of history unfolding before my eyes. I loved the pomp and the pageantry that surrounded the election of a new pontiff, and I was utterly in awe of the power, influence and authority held by the Catholic Church. I instantly knew that I needed to learn more about this extraordinarily powerful organisation. I wanted to know how it had become such a powerful institution and how it continued to shape the world that we live in today. As always, I headed onto the internet for some further research and reading. I discovered articles about how the Catholic Church has played an extraordinarily important role in the development of Western civilisation. And I was fascinated to think about what role this institution might play in years to come. I wanted to be at the centre of the action and at the heart of the debate around the role of this organisation. I wanted to start the conversation on its relevance in the 21st century. I was seriously fascinated by how it continues to shape so many millions of lives.

I was captivated by this new 'Pope Francis' figure, who the TV commentators revealed was the first-ever pope to come from the Americas. Despite being the 266th man to lead the Roman Catholic Church, Bergoglio was the first to pick the name 'Francis'. This symbolised a real shift in direction and a new beginning for the Catholic Church, which the commentators seemed very excited to see play out. As he appeared on the balcony of St Peter's Basilica in front of thousands of devoted followers, the newly appointed Pope Francis asked those gathered to 'pray for me'. Here was a man who had just been elected to lead one of the world's most powerful institutions, and he was asking the public to pray for him. This moment set the tone for a papacy defined by humility, compassion, service to others, and mercy.

I think that the prayer of St Francis of Assisi, the 13th-century friar and philosopher, perfectly encapsulates what inspired me about the message of Pope Francis' papacy. This prayer has become my personal manifesto for life and the inspiration for everything that I do in this world. Allow me to share it with you in full:

"Lord, make me an instrument of your peace
Where there is hatred, let me sow love
Where there is injury, pardon
Where there is doubt, faith
Where there is despair, hope
Where there is darkness, light
And where there is sadness, joy

O Divine Master, grant that I may
Not so much seek to be consoled as to console
To be understood, as to understand

To be loved, as to love
For it is in giving that we receive
And it's in pardoning that we are pardoned
And it's in dying that we are born to Eternal Life".

This prayer has become my absolute mantra for life. I do think that these words of 13th-century wisdom have the power to inspire, invigorate and empower every single one of us. They are words of wisdom that can inspire us for life!

I also read Pope Francis' encyclical 'Laudato Si' – 'On care for our Common Home'. I was inspired by his belief that every single individual has a duty to contribute to the common good of humanity. Discovering the teachings of Pope Francis – defined a commitment to the common good and a commitment to the practice of compassion – made Christianity seem both important and inspiring.

As human beings, we have an innate craving for a sense of meaning, belonging and fulfilment. Organised religion has enjoyed so much success as a result of its ability to fulfil our burning desire to make sense of the universe. Religion is so popular because of its ability to make us feel a sense of connection with the world around us. The established world religions provide a successful set of pre-packaged doctrines, practices, and teachings that offer a comprehensive guide and fulfilling framework for living. Christianity, for example, offers it's followers an explanation for how the universe came into existence. It provides an authoritative code of morality and ethics. And it is successful at offering comforting teachings about the purpose behind suffering and about what will happen after death. The Church offers a complete 'cradle to grave' experience, marking births (baptisms), relationships (weddings) and deaths (funerals) with a comforting series of familiar rituals. Added to this, the liturgical calendar allows Christians to track the progress of the year through the observation of annual festivals such as Advent, Christmas and Easter. The Church provides a sense of community and belonging. The church also provides a sense of collective purpose and identity to all of its members. All of this contributes to the success of organised religion as a success formula for providing meaning and fulfilment.

Of course, many people do not have a choice whether to believe in God. Instead, they are brainwashed from birth to believe in creationism and eternal damnation, with religious teachings instilled in their young psyches with no room for questioning, critiquing or evaluation. Religious scripture is taught to children as if it carried the same credibility and authority as scientific evidence, which it does not. It is not explained to young people that religious scripture has to be understood within a wider contextual framework. It is not explained to those reading the Bible that these stories can only be understood as part of a larger landscape of human culture, practice, and behaviour. As a result, young children do not realise that the religion they are being brought up in is just one of many different belief systems. They are not given adequate opportunity to question dogma or think about key philosophical and ethical questions for themselves.

As you know, I believe that ignorance and narrow-mindedness are the enemies of progress and societal evolution! When we brainwash our young people to believe the same things that we believe, simply because 'that is the way things are', we do them a shocking disservice. When be indoctrinate our young people, we severely limit their life chances. Of course, we must provide our young people with strong moral values and principles. It is in their best interests that society offers them rituals and traditions such as the celebration of Christmas or the attendance of Church weddings. Belief brings about a sense of purpose, belonging and identity. Indeed, an enormous part of British national identity is shaped by the Christian faith. The Queen, for example, is Supreme Governor of the Church of England. I would conclude that Christianity has served as a unifying and identity-providing force for good. It has brought people together, and it has brought people a sense of meaning in life.

Here's what I think about the current conversation on religion and faith. We cannot allow adherence to dogma to drown out open and honest conversations about the origins, teachings, and future of religion. Young people should be taught how to think, critique, discuss and evaluate for themselves, rather than simply being told what to think and what to believe. That is why I believe it is essential that we put philosophy and ethics on the school curriculum. This will mean that our young people will be empowered and inspired to take responsibility for their own beliefs and behaviours. Our schools should be teaching young people not what to think, but how to think for themselves. Every young person must be encouraged to question more, think more and, as a result, become more. Young people need a chance to work out who they are and what they want for life – individuality is the essential ingredient for a successful society! As John Stuart Mill wrote back in the 19th century, 'it is only the cultivation of individuality which produces, or can produce, well developed human beings.' It is in everybody's best interests that our young people are handed the freedom to think autonomously and determine the direction of their own lives. Schooling should not be about enslaving young people to a system. It should be about empowering every single individual to develop their skills, cultivate their individuality and, ultimately, live their very best life. This means that every young person must be taught how to think for themselves. This is why the skills of questioning, evaluation, and analysis need to be taught from an early age! We develop this ability to consider different perspectives, evaluate the evidence, and reach an informed conclusion through the study of philosophy and ethics.

It is not fair that children are being brainwashed into believing in religious concepts that carry no empirical evidence or scientific support whatsoever. Education is a fundamental human right, and education should mean the empowerment of the individual, not their enslavement to a belief system. This is why critical thinking and debating skills are so essential; we need to hand our young people the power to think for themselves and become the masters of their destiny! How can you be comfortable enslaving your child to a religious belief system? Surely you would want your child to have autonomy, authenticity and, as a result, genuine happiness in their life?

I think it is because I was given this freedom to decide my life's direction that I have enjoyed such a comfortable relationship with Christianity. I can tell you for a fact that if I had been forced to attend Church every Sunday, I would have rebelled against all religion! However, my parents never once tried to impose their own opinions or world views on my brother or me. Instead, their mantras have always been 'do what makes you happy', 'treat people with kindness and respect', and 'have good manners!' As a result, I was given a lot of freedom to explore and decide for myself what I believed and how I chose to live my life. For example, I once took myself off to the local Methodist Church down the road from our house, thinking that I might like to become a regular Church attendee. Within the first thirty minutes, I had decided that it was not going to be for me. Still, at least I'd had the opportunity to question my beliefs and explore my religious inclinations! Similarly, my parents always instilled in us a strong message of unconditional love and acceptance, with my mum regularly reminding me that I could bring 'a girlfriend, or boyfriend…WHOEVER!' home. She would welcome them with open arms.

My dad is just as accepting and welcoming. My parents are the kindest, most loving, respectful, and accepting people that I have ever known. As I say, this gave the freedom and autonomy to explore my sexuality, my religious beliefs and my outlook on life. I was not told what subjects I had to study at school, and I was not put under pressure to pursue a certain lifestyle or career. I was respected, encouraged, and unconditionally loved as an individual. I could not be more thankful to have been blessed with such incredible parents. The heartbreaking thing is this; I think that my experience may still be an exception, even in liberal 21st century Britain. There are still far too many parents failing to recognise and respect their children as individuals. They continue to impose their worldviews and try to vicariously relive their youths through their children. It is a recipe for disconnection and disaster!

This is why I believe so passionately in promoting the study of philosophy and ethics. It is all about questioning more, thinking more, and discussing more! When we learn how about alternative viewpoints and engage in constructive arguments, we expand our world view and – as a result – become enlightened as individuals. Studying philosophy is a 'wake up' call – it allows you to leave the dark cave of ignorance in which the vast majority of human beings spend their lives! When you study theology and philosophy, I think that you are finally able to 'see the light'. Just five minutes of reading about philosophy will allow you to realise that things are never as 'black and white' as they first seem! We all need to think, evaluate, and reflect more in our everyday lives. We must all commit to constantly learning more, about both ourselves and the world around us. Philosophy, in my opinion, is the perfect vehicle for this journey of self-discovery and self-development. Philosophy equips us with the tools, language and framework for comprehending ourselves, our society and our universe. It gives us the freedom to think independently and, consequently, facilitates our flourishing as human beings. It is a life-changing and life-enriching discipline!

***

As a result of my study of philosophy, I have become confident in my own identity and secure in my world view. For example, I have become very committed to Aristotle's concept of 'eudaimonia', which is the idea that the purpose of human life is to fulfil your potential and flourish as an individual. I have also taken inspiration from John Stuart Mill, Immanuel Kant, Jesus and the Buddha. They immensely inspired me in terms of the personal system of ethics, meaning and morality that I strive to live by. And I also have, thanks to my opportunity to study Christianity through an academic lens, become very committed to the core values of Christianity. I do not believe in the traditional notion of 'God'. And I am not going to start interpreting the Bible literally anytime soon. However, I do believe in the importance of living your life with a strong set of core values and moral principles. And I find that the Christian values and principles – of love, kindness, and compassion – provide me with a real sense of purpose in life.

These Christian values anchor me in a commitment to contributing to the common good. They guide me towards living a fulfilling and enriching existence. I really am so inspired by the moral teachings and core values espoused by Jesus Christ. These Christian teachings and values teach us the key ingredients for living sustained, empowered, and inspired me to live a fearlessly authentic life.

So here's what I think: take some time to figure out your core beliefs and principles! Take some time to decide on your core values for life! Think about what values you strive to live your life by, and get serious about infusing your life with a real sense of purpose!

Real happiness in life is the result of finding meaning and purpose in our lives. Make fulfilment your priority! Live your life by a strong set of core values and moral principles…and find greater happiness than you ever thought imaginable!

18. NEW FRIENDS, NEW AMBITIONS…AND MORE EXAMS

It's New Years Day 2017, and I'm off to a 17th birthday party. The host is Holly Wells, a gorgeous girl who I had first met just a couple of months earlier. We were at a Halloween house party, although I must confess that I had inconveniently "forgot" my costume. Oops! How on earth did that happen? I had very kindly been invited to this party by a girl called Ellie. I'd been invited despite not being in her group's 'circle' at school. I had excitedly – and nervously – arrived, feeling very much outside of my comfort zone but determined to seize this opportunity to 'put myself out there'. One of the first people I bumped into was Holl, who had been to a different secondary school but knew several of the girls from my year. I had known 'of' Holly from social media – I had seen her in Instagram pictures, and I followed her on Twitter. She was a stunning girl, and she had a fabulously sparkling personality. So, of course, my opening line to her had to be: 'Oh my God I love your Twitter!'

Fortunately, Holl took my Twitter-stalking well, and this marked the beginning of an amazing friendship. I spent the rest of the night chatting, dancing, and laughing away, and it genuinely felt so good to be meeting these new people. I was enjoying the social confidence that I have always dreamed of having, and I had to pinch myself to check that I wasn't actually dreaming! Who would have thought it – here I was, living my best life as a little socialite, even if it was just for one night!

Fast forward to the Saturday before New Years Eve 2017, and I am out for lunch in Alderley Edge with my gorgeous friend, Megan. We are sat in Gusto, a beautiful Italian restaurant, enjoying the delicious pizza, pasta and salad. Megan mentions to me that 'we' have been invited to Holly's birthday party on New Years Day. To which I respond 'no, YOU have been invited to her birthday party!!' Megan attempts to convince me that Holly has asked her to bring me along as well and is insistent that we are going together! I feel extremely nervous – I literally won't know anybody there, other than Megan and a couple of the girls from my school. But, at the same time, I know that this is the answer to my prayers – this party, I think, will the best opportunity for me to put myself out there and get to know new people! This is exactly what I have always wanted, and it is exactly what I need as a start the New Year with renewed self-confidence and optimism! Megan and I finish our food at Gusto and agree to go along to Holl's party together on New Years Day.

***

It's cold and dark as we step out of the car and walk down Holly's drive. I've got butterfly's in my stomach, but I am determined to walk into this party with as much confidence as I can muster. It's a new year, it's a new me, and this is an amazing opportunity to meet new people. You can do this Ben, I tell myself, taking a deep breath and walking in through the front door. Holl instantly greets us with a big hug and starts introducing us to people standing in the hallway, before heading off to find us some drinks cups. I decide to head into the lounge, where most people have gathered. Out of the corner of my eye, I see a group of girls sat around the dining room corner. They look stunning, and I feel more than a little bit nervous. What will they think of me? What will they say about my mannerisms, my appearance, my 'campness'? I spot a couple of girls from my school and head over to say hello, relieved to see some familiar faces!

A few minutes later, I have discovered new confidence from somewhere within me, and I have decided to walk over to this group of girls sat around the table. I don't know a single one of them, but I do know that they look stunning and like friendly girls. 'HELLO, I begin, 'I just want to know why you are sitting down and not up dancing?' Fortunately, the girls take this comment in the light-hearted way it was intended. They laugh, and two of them instantly jump up and join me in the middle of the lounge. Once they're on their feet, we all introduce ourselves. These two stunning girls introduce themselves as Freya and Kristina, who happen to be twins in the same year as me, but at a different Sixth Form college. They know Holly from High School and, like me, they don't know all of the people in the room. With Freya and Kristina, it really was like 'love at first sight' – I knew, just from this very first conversation, that we would get on like a house on fire. We chatted about our lives and bonded over our desire to track down the hot men who were, it has to be said, very few and far between. I loved their energy, sense of humour and friendliness and, for the rest of the night, remained glued to these two gorgeous girls. Unfortunately for them, I would remain glued to Freya and Kristina for many years to come…

***

After the party, I had kept in touch with Freya and Kristina. A few weeks later we all go out for food with Holly. This would be the first of many lunch and dinner dates to come! It felt amazing to have made friends from outside of my Sixth Form – it was a new start with new people, who genuinely had the most positive impact on my life. We went for food at Revs – where the Club Sandwich was to die for – or at Pizza Express, where we would spend hours chatting and laughing about our lives in Cheshire. We'd swap sixth form stories, laugh about high school dramas, and update each other about the latest boys we were speaking to. I very quickly realised that these girls thought about life in a very similar way to me – more so than anybody I had ever met before. Freya and I, for example, would start spending hours discussing 'law of attraction' and mental health. We would joke about becoming a life coaching duo who would take our 'banish your self-limiting beliefs' message around the world! We shared a real interest in mental health, and a genuine desire to help people become happier and more confident individuals. They were – like me – extremely philosophical and thoughtful when it came to reflecting on life. Again, this was something I had never properly encountered before, and it filled my heart with so much genuine joy. We could quite easily laugh and joke around about boys or Gemma Collins. Still, we could equally spend hours discussing deep philosophical questions or sharing stories about mental health and wellbeing. We became very close very quickly – and have never looked back since!

Today, I see Freya and Kristina as family. Like Becky, they are the sisters I never had – I just know that they will be stuck with me, for life. This is why it is so crazy to think that our paths could quite easily never have passed. If I had never been invited to that Halloween party, then I would never have met Holly. That means I would never have been invited to her party, and so I would never have crossed paths with Freya and Kristina. I just find this whole fate thing so insane! Of course, we might have bumped into each other one day, perhaps on a night out in Cheshire, but that would most likely never have been anything more other than a 'Hi, nice to meet you!'

I could not imagine my life without these girls – I would not be half the person I am today if it wasn't for their love, friendship, words of wisdom and support. Which is why I always ask – do things happen for a reason? Is meeting best friends like this just a very lucky coincidence, or were our lives always destined to align? I feel drawn to the most rational conclusion that it is just genuinely a very lucky coincidence, but at the same time, I think it just seems too good to be true! You could say the same about romantic relationships or any other kind of relationship that we strike up with the people we meet in our lives. It's always just a case of being in the right (or sometimes wrong!) place at the right time! So much of life is about luck, chance and fate! I find it so scary that I almost didn't go to Holly's party. I could quite easily have said 'no' to Megan, or Megan could quite easily have forgotten to mention the whole thing to me! Yet this one decision, to attend a party, genuinely changed my life. As I say, I would not be half the person I am today if it were not for these amazing guardian angels I crossed paths with on New Year's Day! I cannot imagine my life without them, and it's so weird now to think that I actually did have a life – a whole seventeen years – before meeting them!

Kristina has been my number one skincare guru, introducing me to Mario Badescu and telling me off every time that I touch my face. If I ever need advice on whether a new skincare product is good or not, the first person I call is KM! She knows every ingredient in every skincare product, and she knows exactly what works…and what doesn't! Whether we are in Boots or Urban Outfitters, I always feel reassured to have my beauty expert by my side! Sometimes it really does pay to have best friends with flawless skin!

What lesson have I learned from reflecting on how crazy – and lucky – it is that our paths ended up crossing at this party? I've resolved to never turn down a single invitation ever again! Imagine if I had not gone to that party! Imagine if I had not started that conversation with those girls! No matter how anxious or nervous you are feeling, you have got to always put yourself out there! You have got to be 'in it to win it', and you just never know who you are going to meet next! Life is too short to regret missed opportunities for meeting new people who have the power to transform your life! How do you know that the next person you meet isn't going to end up being your future business partner, best friend, or soulmate? If you don't put yourself out there and dare to strike up a conversation, then you will never know!

I realise how blessed I am to have been at that party and to have started that conversation. Starting that one conversation started the most amazing friendship! That is why I urge you – put yourself out there! Seize every opportunity! Constantly be looking out for connections! Remember that you've got to be 'in it to win it'! Don't let your fears (e.g. about starting a conversation or going to a party) stop you from discovering amazing new best friends! If the friendship doesn't work out, then you will survive! But if the friendship does blossom and grow, then you will absolutely thrive! You cannot lose at this lottery – genuinely, what is the worst that can happen? So; put yourself out there, dare to strike up that conversation, and let the universe introduce you to your new business partner, soulmate, or best friends!

***

The year flies by, and the AS exams are fast approaching. Freya, Kristina, and I meet at Café Nero to revise once a week after we have finished for the day at Sixth Form. We discuss Plato, Aristotle, John Calvin and Jesus Christ. Oh, yes, it's all very intellectual! Each session leaves me feeling very positive about the forthcoming exams! I love creating little worksheets and 'handouts' for us to go through, especially considering how passionate I am about the subject. I have genuinely fallen in love with Religious Studies, and I am always researching university courses where I could go and study more. I start to dream about being a religious studies teacher, and I start mentally planning how I'm going to set up my classroom! I cannot wait to be teaching my lessons on Plato and Aristotle! I cannot wait to be hearing all of my student's discussing big ideas, and to see them thriving as they pursue their passions in life!

This is, of course, a big ambition. Still, I genuinely believe I have the passion, work ethic and determination to get there. I would love to be a leader in education, and I genuinely believe that a career in teaching would bring me so much happiness in life. I strongly agree with Aristotle's philosophy that happiness is the result of 'fulfilling your potential' and becoming the very best version of yourself as an individual. I think that the best way I can fulfil my potential is by helping others to fulfil their potential! Aristotle believed that, when you fulfil your capabilities and live your 'best life' as an individual, you attain a state of supreme happiness known as 'eudaimonia'. And as I sat at my computer, making my revision handouts on Natural Law and Utilitarianism, I knew that my source of 'supreme happiness' would be working in education. Every day at school, I would see Mrs Garvey and Mrs Connor working tirelessly hard and making a genuine difference in countless peoples' lives. They were making their mark as outstanding educators and leaders in education, and I knew with all my heart that I wanted to follow in their footsteps.

I was also massively inspired by Mrs Stewart. She was bringing Religious Ethics alive (even at 9 am on a Friday in a Food Technology classroom). I dreamed of teaching classes with that level of engagement, enthusiasm, and expertise. Mrs Williams did the same during English lessons, bouncing around the classroom with limitless energy and enthusiasm for her subject – of which she had a seriously expert level of knowledge. All of these strong and outstanding teachers became the very best role models I could ever ask for. I saw them excelling in their teaching careers, and I became determined to follow in their footsteps. They looked the partt in their power outfits, and they acted the part in the way that they carried themselves. I wanted to do their job! Every single day, they effortlessly exuded expertise, professionalism, and authority. They looked like leaders and just oozed this glamorous, sophisticated and inspiring 'star quality'. What's more, they appeared to genuinely love every single second of their job – and they were phenomenal at doing it!

And so, I became determined to work harder than ever before to ensure that I got the grades I needed to get into university. And so, I invested hours in making sure I remembered all of the case studies and evaluation points for psychology. My bedroom is soon becoming a shrine to the topics of 'Research Methods', 'Social Influence', 'Attachment', and 'Memory'. I cover my walls in 'scholarly quotes' for AS Religious Studies (Kant's declaration that 'man must be disciplined, for by nature he is raw and wild' remains a firm favourite). And I filled countless notebooks with practice question answers for AS English Language. I feel more driven and determined than ever before, and – most importantly – I am genuinely loving every single second of studying these subjects.

****

It's around this time – as I revise for my AS Levels – that I get to know a couple of the girls in Year 13. Throughout the first six months of year 12, I have found the year 13s to be pretty intimidating and – for what of a better word – scary. They sit in big groups and control the speakers – it's very clear that this is **THEIR** common room, and woe betides anyone who ends up sitting in one of their seats! In the common room, I have always tried not to attract too much attention or tread on anyone's toes. I would usually sit with Becky, Harriet and Erin, along with anyone else from our group who was around at that particular break or lunchtime. Sometimes, I would go and chat with Megan or Alice, who I sat with for English Language and English Literature lessons. I would also go and say hi to Emily, Alice's sister, who I had sat next to in the first lesson of A-levels English Language and have never since looked back. Emily quickly became the most amazing friend. She is one of those people who just brings nothing but positivity, joy and a wicked sense of humour to every single situation. I genuinely adored these three, and I would love going for little coffee and revision dates with them both at the weekends and after school. Having these three amazing friends did me a world of good – I cannot thank them enough for the kindness that they showed me and the confidence that they gave me. We would laugh our way through lessons, and they absolutely made year 12 for me. As I always say, it is always individual *people* who make the most positive and transformative difference in our lives. Life is not about wealth, status, fame or acclaim – it is about these life-enhancing connections and the powerful difference made by individual people! And Megan, Alice, and Emily most certainly did make the most positive difference in my life throughout year 12, which is something for which I will be forever grateful!

As I sat with Becky in our usual spot in the Common Room, I would look around the room and see that we are surrounded by year 13s. They had – of course – taken all the best and most spacious seats, leaving the year 12s squeezed in the middle of the room. Directly to our left, there was a space where a group of stunning year 13 girls would sit at breaks and lunch. I recognised a couple of these girls – one of them, for example, had been in the year above me at Primary School – and I genuinely in awe of their confidence. I would, I thought, have loved to have been friends with them but, as always, I was also seriously worried about what they thought of me. As a result, I'd never make eye contact, and I'd make every effort not to collide with one of them when walking in or out of the common room. I was particularly anxious about what the boys who would sometimes sit with them thought about me. I was still being governed by this fear that straight boys (who seemed to make up 99.9% of the boys in this common room) couldn't stand me. I knew that people thought that I was 'too much' or 'too gay'. They weren't rude or homophobic, but similarly, they weren't used to a boy having as much sass or flamboyance as me. That being said, nobody was ever openly rude, judgemental or nasty towards me. I think that is a very positive reflection of the inclusive environment created by Mrs Garvey through her strong leadership. It is also a positive reflection on the integrity of all the people attending that Sixth Form.

The overwhelming majority of people were nothing but kind, friendly and accepting. Most of my fears – as always – were irrational and had been completely blown out of proportion in my head. Well, I had been coming into this common room for months now, and I was fed up of feeling anxious or worried about seeing certain people. I wanted to be a social butterfly, and yet here I was hiding in my seat because I was so scared of what people might say to me. If I wanted to go and talk to somebody, then why couldn't I go and do that? Why was I letting my fears paralyse and limit me? I thought about my fears about going to Holly's party, and how well things had – despite my fears – actually turned out! Because I had ignored my fears and overcome my anxieties in this situation, I had enjoyed the best night and met the most amazing friends. Surely, I asked myself. Was I really going to let my fears of rejection or being judged hold me back again? I'd managed to overcome those fears once, and it was time to overcome them again! It's a new year, I told myself, which means it's a new opportunity to put yourself out there and meet new people! I wanted to get to know these girls and chat to these girls – so why on earth was I not heading over there and doing it?

And so, during one free period, I was feeling pretty bored doing my psychology revision. I found myself looking around for something to do or someone to talk to. Now, I honestly don't know what then came over me. Still, I found myself suddenly feeling very confident, and I heading over to strike up a conversation with these girls in the corner. Again, this was one of the best decisions that I have ever made. It was another perfect example of how facing your fears and overcoming your anxieties will lead to the biggest breakthroughs and most amazing opportunities in your life! I sat down and began my interrogation, asking Alyce what her 'go-to' order was from the Sixth Form café. I then proceeded to share with Alyce, Liddy and Amy how much I loved the coronation chicken wraps. I then remember moving onto a discussion about how much I loved prosecco (and how wrong Alyce was before she did not). Looking back, it is a miracle that these girls did not instantly get a restraining order in place against me! But thank God they did not – thanks to my questions about the café, we struck up an amazing friendship. It felt so good to be chatting away – with confidence – to these gorgeous girls from (dramatic pause here) the year ABOVE! I felt so bold, so daring, and so confident! And, more importantly, I genuinely loved these girls. I loved their energy, their confidence, and felt this 'sixth sense' that we would connect. Well, just call my Mystic Meg, because it wasn't long before we were all heading off for cocktails and nights out!

Now Sixth Form, I had to remember, was not just a social occasion. I was there, of course, to work hard and get the grades that would secure me a place at university. What's more, I genuinely loved the studying side of things at Sixth Form – I was loving my subjects and genuinely loved putting in all the work. As I have said, Mrs Garvey and Mrs Connor continued to inspire me, and my teachers continued to energise me. Sixth Form was not just an education in A-levels. It was the best education in socialising I could have ever hoped to have received! Year 12 was the first year that I was fully 'out' as a self-defining homosexual. It was also the first year that I was finally putting myself 'out' there as a confident, friendly, and chatty individual. It was the best boost to my confidence and self-esteem imaginable! It felt good to feel so authentic, so accepted and so able to talk to anybody that I liked. Don't get me wrong; I was still feeling a lot of anxiety about people's opinions. I was still far too sensitive about whether people liked me or not, but I could see that I was making some positive progress. I was becoming so much more articulate, conversational, and finally embracing my authentic identity. Whilst that common room may have filled me with a lot of fear, it also facilitated a lot of my flourishing as a human being. It gave me opportunities to meet new people, step outside of my comfort zone, and forge new friendships. I feel like my first year of sixth form was, without being to cliché, the beginning of the rest of my life. And it is entirely thanks to the people around me – in terms of both friendships and teachers – that I was able to feel self-confident and genuinely thrive.

As the AS Exams approached, I started working even harder than ever before. If there's one key thing that I learned during sixth form, it's that hard work is the secret to success! Studying for AS / A-levels was not an area of life where you could cut corners! If you wanted to succeed and make it to the very top, then you had to be prepared to put the hard work in. Fortunately, I loved putting the hard work in, and I would spend hours reading and revising for my subjects. When you are pursuing your passions, I honestly believe that hard work is the most enjoyable and rewarding thing in the world. That is why I always advise people to study subjects that they are genuinely interested in and passionate about. Try and find subjects that you *want* to study, rather than ending up with subjects that you *have* to revise for. A massive part of being authentic is pursuing your passions and putting blood, sweat and tears into making a success of your favourite subjects! So discover subjects that make you excited to wake up in the morning, and thoroughly throw yourself into studying them!

As it got closer to exam season, the views of my Othello video skyrocketed. I'd posted on YouTube before, of course, with my revision videos for 'Journey's End' and GCSE RE. But the response to my Othello video was on another level – people across the country were messaging me on Facebook and Twitter. Dozens of people were commenting on my video about how much it had 'saved' and 'helped' them. I was baffled that my little revision project could have made such a difference. Still, I was also delighted that people were finding what I had created useful. The positive response made me even more determined to have a career in education – I wanted to make a positive difference in young people's lives through teaching. I imagined that there was nothing quite as fulfilling as knowing you have helped somebody to learn, study and, as a result, achieve their dreams.

The exams themselves came very quickly and, like with GCSEs, I quite enjoyed the exam season. It helped, of course, that AS Levels did not carry any weight or importance, other than determining whether you could continue studying at Sixth Form the following year. They were, essentially, nothing more than mock exams, which we had already sat several times that year. I didn't like the fact that a whole year's worth of work came down to just one 90 minute exam. Still, I felt confident in the knowledge that everybody in the country was in the same boat. We were all in this together! And I felt confident knowing that I had done everything I possibly could have done to prepare.

****

Once AS exams were over, it was back to Sixth Form to get started on the Year 13 work. The actual Year 13s had now left, which meant our year group now had the common room to ourselves. It all felt very weird – this time next year, I would be leaving Sixth Form and stepping out into the real world. On the one hand, I could not have felt more ready – I had finally found my authentic self, and I was ready to get out there and show the world what I was all about! But on the other hand, I was genuinely terrified by the prospect of actually leaving education…for good! After all these years in a bubble, it would be time to stand on my own two feet and make a success of my life!

So what did I want to do after Sixth Form? Where did I see myself heading off to this time next year? As much as I loved living in our family home here in Cheshire, I knew that I needed to step outside of the little bubble I was living in. I felt like I was becoming a big fish in a small pond – my big ambitions and big personality needed to be somewhere bigger. I wanted to expand my horizons and, as I say, make a genuine success of my life. In a way, I also think that I wanted to prove myself – to both myself and the world. Even though I had felt so much love and inclusion in Sixth Form, I was still pretty fed up of feeling like an outsider. As my disastrous evening at the local LGBT+ group showed, I was keen to meet more LGBT+ people and, of course, find a future boyfriend. I didn't believe, despite my best efforts, that Cheshire was going to be the place I discovered the absolute love of my life! I would love to have said it was, but sadly the local gay scene was best described as non-existent!

Whilst I was very happy living at home in Cheshire, I did feel rather repressed. I felt as if there was a whole world out there waiting for me, and I wanted the opportunity to get out there and live my very best life! My first thought was that I wanted to move to Manchester. The city was just 20 minutes away on the train, and I had spent countless days shopping in the Arndale Centre over the past couple of years. I had also walked down Canal Street – Manchester's famous gay district – several times, imagining what it would be like once I turned 18 and could go out in these clubs. Manchester felt big, bustling, and vibrant, and it also wasn't too far from home. I could certainly see myself in Manchester, and I was excited by the prospect of being in a big city.

But I started to think about going one step further. I knew I wanted to be in a city with a thriving gay scene. I wanted to be somewhere that I could pursue my ambitions, be my authentic self, and feel as if I was living my very best life. In my mind, there was one place in the world that said ambition and opportunity more than any other – and that place was, of course, London. London was *the* big city – it was the place to be, the place to thrive, and the place to live your very best life. Compared to little Macclesfield, London felt like the most daunting and enormous place in the world. Even compared to Manchester, it felt incomparable. London was *the* place – it took big and bustling to the next level! I had been down to

London several times with mum, dad, and Sam, for day-trips and weekends away. We would go down on the Virgin Train, check into a Travelodge near Covent Garden, go for walks along the Southbank, and head off to watch West End shows. I had the happiest memories of these family trips down to the capital, the first of which was in 2008 when we had seen 'Joseph and the Amazing Technicolour Dreamcoat'.

Back then, I had been completely mesmerised by this enormous city, and walking around felt like entering into a parallel universe. Everything had seemed so big, and everyone had seemed so busy. I was genuinely shocked by how anybody could ever consider finding their way around this incredible place! As I thought about where I wanted to be one year from now, it felt like an absolute no brainer – I wanted to be in London. There was, in my mind, absolutely no other option. I had to be in London, it was calling my name, and there was nothing anybody could do to change my mind. I dreamt of my fast-paced London lifestyle; I'd be jumping on the tube, walking by the Thames and dating all these gorgeous boys! I'd finally feel able to fully express myself, and I'd finally have all of the opportunities and experiences that I had ever dreamed of having. London, I thought, is where dreams come true and where people live their best lives. I loved the thought of being able to say that I lived in London – what an achievement that would be! Who would have thought it; little Ben Wardle, the annoyingly camp boy who nobody at Primary School liked, has gone and made a success of his life in LONDON! I was sold, and I wasn't going to be told otherwise – London was calling my name, and all I needed to do now was find a course that I could study down there!

***

I had been busy googling different courses that I might be able to study in London. I had my sights set on the capital, and now I needed to find the course that would give me a reason to be amongst the bright lights of the city! I looked up courses in philosophy, religion, psychology and even media, journalism and English. My heart was very much set on becoming a teacher – of either philosophy or psychology - but I also fancied the idea of making it onto BBC News! I also considered the idea of becoming a mental health counsellor or therapist, and I would have dreams of owning my empire of therapy clinics across the country! I quickly discounted doing a degree in psychology due to the amount of maths and science it would require. Instead, I became more interested in the prospect of studying philosophy and religion. The philosophy courses were looking too 'logic' and 'methodology' heavy, which gave me nightmares of having to do some kind of maths equation as part of my degree. That, let me tell you, was the very last thing that I wanted!

One evening, when I was scrolling through different London universities and course descriptions, I came across the King's College London website. I had heard of this university before, and I thought that it sounded like a very prestigious institution. I had vivid memories of sitting on the top deck of a London bus many years ago, driving past the King's campus on the Strand and seeing the massive red-background photographs on former alumni on the outer windows. I was having a lovely time scrolling through the courses that King's had on offer. There was one in particular that sounded perfect for me (probably because it had the same title as my A-Level course!). 'Religion, Philosophy & Ethics' read the course homepage. Well, I instantly liked what I was seeing!

I scrolled down and read a little bit about the course; sample modules included 'Elements of Ethics', 'Thinking About Evil' and 'Introduction to Buddhism'. I was instantly in love! These modules sounded like the titles of books I would read! These were topics that I was genuinely fascinated by and interested in! I became extremely excited about the course. It was at a prestigious university, located right in the very heart of London, and it was offering modules that I would genuinely love to study. I was sold, and I was very excited! There was only one thing left to find out – the entry requirements! I prayed that they wouldn't be too high and that getting the grades the university wanted would be manageable for me. 'A-LEVELS ENTRY REQUIREMENTS – AAB', I read, a smile forming across my face. That's not too bad, I think to myself! I can do that…there's nothing impossible about these grades!

From that moment, I had a very clear goal in my mind. It was if the stars were aligning and everything was falling into place. I had found my dream city, my dream course…and I knew what I needed to do to get the required grades! It was an epiphany moment, one of those moments when everything seems to fall into place and make sense. That is where I'm meant to be, I say to myself, as a print off the course information page and put it into a plastic wallet. I am going to get myself to that big city, and I am going to make a name for myself amongst the bright lights of London. I will work harder than ever before – I will do whatever it takes – to get those grades and get myself to London. Big Ben watch out, I think to myself, because a certain Ben Wardle is about to arrive! I don't think London could ever be ready for this incoming whirlwind! Macclesfield, it's been an absolute pleasure…but I do have places to be…

19. FIVE STAR SERVICE

It's the end of July and, although we have broken up for summer, I am back at All Hallows, helping out with a performing arts summer school. I've been coming in to help with this summer school – designed for students from local Primary Schools - for several years now, and I love every second of the two weeks. It is just one of several programmes that take place at the school every summer. It's all overseen and co-ordinated by Mrs Connor, who I am delighted to see. It's been a busy week, as always, and we have made it to the Friday of the first week. Friday is always the busiest day because there are two performances of the production for all the student's proud parents. Today is an especially busy day, however, because in between the two performances, I am sneaking off, in full suit and tie, for a job interview.

A couple of weeks ago, I had applied for the job role of 'receptionist' at Mottram Hall, a four* Hotel located with 270 acres of the most beautiful Cheshire countryside. Mottram is the most stunning venue and is very much seen as the jewel in Cheshire's crown. The hotel, champagne bar, garden room and grand staircase all regularly provide the backdrop to Real Housewives of Cheshire functions and events. On top of this, the hotel's 11 luxurious suites regularly play host to VIP guests from across the globe. I had been looking for a part-time job for a while and, when I saw this position being advertised on the Indeed jobs website, I just had this feeling that it would be perfect for me. A couple of days later, the Reception Manager had emailed me to thank me for my application. Whilst I had applied for the role of receptionist, she asked if I would be interested in applying for a 'concierge' position instead.

I must be very honest with you – I did not have an absolute clue what on earth 'concierge' meant. Still, I was not about to miss out on this opportunity to secure a job interview. And so I instantly replied:

"Thank you for your email! Thank you very much – that would be brilliant, please let me know which date would be most convenient for you!"

Well, it transpired that the most convenient date would be next Friday afternoon, and so my mum picked me up from school and drove me the 10-minute journey over to Mottram Hall. As we drove down Mottram's famously long driveway, I had butterfly's in my stomach. As the main property came into view, I could see that it was beautiful. The Hotel, a Grade II listed building, had once been a grand manor house. The grounds were now home to an 18-hole Championship golf course, swimming pool and spa, plus a newly constructed golf course bar and brasserie. My mum gave me a quick pep talk – 'you'll be fine, don't worry about it' – and I gave my tie one final check, before jumping out of the car and heading straight towards the entrance door. Once inside, I headed over to the reception desk. I gave my name and took a seat in the lobby. I then saw a familiar face – it was Serena, here on an apprenticeship, and spending the day working on the reception desk! Serena wasn't the only familiar face working at Mottram; Alyce and Liddy, from the year above, were working over in the golf club bar and brasserie. And Abby, who I had performed with in shows since the age of 8, was working down in the Carrington Grill, the hotel's main restaurant.

The reception and HR managers soon came along and took me off to one of the conference rooms for my interview. Walking through this gorgeous hotel in my suit was all very exciting – I loved the grandeur, the glamour and the sophistication of the place. Being here felt so important and so fabulous – I loved it, and I knew with certainty that I **had** to work here. It was glamorous, beautiful, and luxurious - it was exactly where I belonged!

I'd had about ten green teas so far this Friday, and so I was ready to answer any question that Odell and Bryony asked me. I'd never had a job interview before, so I didn't know what to expect. Forever a bit of a perfectionist, I'd fully researched 'interview questions' on Google. I had been concerned to discover questions such as 'if you were a biscuit, what biscuit would you be and why?' I prayed that I wouldn't be asked to explain why I thought I resembled a bourbon or a custard cream. However, I did try and mentally prepare answers to such a question, just in case, my similarities to a chocolate digestive did come up during the interview!

Odell and Bryony were lovely, and I felt as if everything was going well (e.g. they had not mentioned a biscuit barrel once). They asked me about good customer service and my previous job experience. I entertained them with a tale about my three years volunteering at the RVS shop in Macclesfield hospital. And – in a very promising sign that the interview had gone well – when I would be able to start. They told me about what the concierge role would entail, including 'meeting and greeting' guests on arrival, booking taxis, and assisting with guest's luggage. I joked that whilst I might not be a bodybuilder, I was looking forward to a good workout helping guests carry their bags up the grand staircase! As a Grade II listed building, it was impossible to offer lift access to half of the bedrooms. It would, they explained, therefore be my job to keep guests happy by helping them with their luggage. I would be there, ten Louis Vuitton bags and cases in hand, guiding the guests up to their rooms. I had visions of myself balancing the bags on my head, visions that would prove not to be too wide off the mark.

I said goodbye to Odell and Bryony, and also waved bye to Serena on reception. I also had a quick conversation with one of the Reception Supervisors, who said that her name was Ella. I instantly loved this girl. She was energised, ambitious and had an absolute heart of gold. I left with a real spring in my step, confident that my interview had gone well and that I'd done everything I could to secure this job. A few days later, I found out the good news – I'd got the job! I'd told Odell and Bryony that I was off on our family holiday to Greece the next week, but that I'd be available to start anytime after I got home. They sent across all the paperwork, and I spent about ten days trying to find out my National Insurance number. This is all very exciting - I've actually got a job…and it's meeting and greeting guests at a 4* Hotel! I am living the dream!

***

It's two weeks later, and my mum is dropping me off for my first day of Mottram, suited and booted whilst sporting a glowing Greek tan. I walk into reception, where Odell and Ella greet me and welcome me to the team. Serena insists on taking me for a tour of the hotel, and takes me around the main function rooms and points out the quickest ways to the different bedrooms. It turns out that there are over 120 of them, all of which I need to remember the locations of. Don't worry, Serena tells me, you'll soon pick it up. Let's pray that's true, I laugh! Serena can't quite believe I have been given the job role of concierge, expressing genuine concern about my ability to carry guest's luggage and bags. As long as it's Louis Vuitton I'll be fine, I joke. I'm already wondering how on earth I am going to carry guest's gigantic suitcases up the hundreds of stairs around the hotel. I'll just have to be very good at the meeting and greeting, I think to myself, and charm these guests into carrying their *own* bags to their rooms!

We arrive back down at reception where another girl who has just started on concierge is busy tidying up the lobby area. 'Hello, I'm Jemma!' she beams, and I am instantly in love with this girl's energy. Let me tell you about Jemma – she is the kindest, most genuine, and lovely human being you could ever wish to meet. Her smile and laughter are infectious, and she can light up any social situation or room within 0.5 seconds. I just know that we are going to get on like a house on fire…and I just hope that she's going to enjoy carrying bags around the hotel more than me!

I don't have to wait long until it's time to launch into action with the meeting, greeting…and bag carrying! As guests arrive through the main entrance doors, I welcome them with a confident 'Hello, how are you!? Welcome to Mottram Hall!' I make small talk about the reasons for their stay and their plans for the rest of the day, before guiding them over to the reception desk so that they can check-in. I log into the computer at the Guest Services desk, where Jemma talks me through the concierge emails. She shows me where to find details on restaurant opening times, breakfast times, local taxi phone numbers and other essential 'concierge' information! After that, she takes me off to help with some guest's bags, which quickly turns into some kind of 'Carry on Concierge' sitcom routine. You should have seen me climbing up what felt like ten-thousand flights of stairs with what feels like ten-thousand different suitcases. In reality, I was climbing ten steps with one bag in each hand, but in my head, I was here climbing mount Everest with a giant elephant attached to my back. It's fair to say that there was never a dull moment when Jemma and I were carrying bags around the hotel, or rather when Jemma was carrying bags. I was usually to be found leading the way, very bravely carrying something like a scarf or a coat hanger.

Poor Jemma must have been seriously traumatised by my arrival, because within days of our first shift together, she has got herself a new job! That's right; my Jemma is leaving…after less than one week working with me! This is the effect that being stuck with 'I-don't-carry-bags Ben' had on the poor girl! She insists that her departure (no hotel pun intended!) is absolutely nothing to do with me. To this day, Jemma and I still go for food and drinks with Ella. Together, we make up a dream trio, and I could not love or appreciate these gorgeous girls more. We can usually be found in our favourite Alchemist (I order the 'peaches and cream' prosecco and a Chicken burger every single time without fail) in Manchester. Our time working together was the literal epitome of 'short but sweet' – we may have been working together for only days, but these days it really does feel like I had known Ella and Jemma for a lifetime. Other than the fact that I'd miss Jemm immeasurably, I was also seriously concerned about the prospect of being left on Concierge duty on my own. What on earth am I going to do about all these bags! At least I won't be needing gym membership anytime soon, I think!

Jemma says goodbye, and it's over to me to run the Concierge show on my own. I love these summer days working at Mottram, and I soon get to grips with the layout and workings of the hotel. Ella – or EP, as I like to call her – is a phenomenal Reception Supervisor, and we get on like a house on fire. She stoically puts up with my sass and diva moments, which are coming thick and fast every time that she asks me to carry someone's luggage to a bedroom. The fact that assisting guests with luggage is on my job description does not appear to cross my mind. The prospect of hauling this baggage up the stairs is just not appealing to me…in the slightest! So I focus on doing my 'meeting and greeting', and rename myself as 'Guest Services'. As I was saying, it was quickly becoming an episode of 'Carry on Concierge'! Fortunately for me, I was pretty good, if I may say so myself, at the whole 'meet and greet' package. I was starting to get TripAdvisor name mentions, with guests thanking 'the enthusiastic boy who welcomed us at the door'. One TripAdvisor review stated:

"Reception staff all very helpful and friendly, in particular a young man (I think called Ben) who had such a gift of greeting people with enthusiasm and really made me smile! He is in the perfect job to deal with people, a very warm and friendly personality".

I'm not sure if this lovely lady would have held the same opinion of me if had she seen the look that I just gave Ella when she asked a couple if they would like me to carry their bags! But it was so lovely – and morale-boosting – to receive this kind of feedback from the guests! It really did leave me feeling as if I was living on Cloud Nine! I was very lucky that, whilst I might not have been the nation's number one bag carrier, I was living the dream 'meeting and greeting' people on the door. I genuinely loved every single second of it. Standing at the end of that red carpet, welcoming all of the guests into the hotel, was exactly where I belonged. It was like a dream come true, and I would wake up in the morning seriously excited to be welcoming people into the hotel. I thought that I was Kris Jenner hosting one of her extravagant Christmas Eve parties, and I saw myself as this 'host with the most' adding all of this sparkle to each person's stay. In my head, I was taking five stars to the next level; wherever I went, I was all about offering glitz, glam and first-class service! I really did pride myself on my appearance – in my little grey suit – and in my professionalism as a 'host'. I wanted every single person to feel warmly welcomed to the hotel, and I made it my mission to live and breathe the mantra 'service with a smile'. This attitude instilled in me the most positive work ethic and commitment to providing outstanding hospitality, which continues to serve me well to this day.

September was fast-approaching, which meant I would back at Sixth Form during the week. I arranged to work Friday evenings and Saturdays at Mottram, meaning I will be able to work but still have time for studying and revision as well. I loved working weekends when there would always be beautiful weddings, as well as countless other parties and events. I would start at 9 am on a Saturday which, as an early bird, suited me perfectly, and work through until 6.30 pm, just as the night's wedding celebrations were getting into full swing.

One of my favourite things about working was working with Jane-Marie. Jane-Marie is the kindest and most gorgeous lady, who was working at Mottram after many years working as Cabin Crew in First Class for British Airways. Jane-Marie, who was working parttime whilst she looked after her little girl Scarlett, oozed ridiculous amounts of glamour, elegance, and sparkle. It's fair to say that I was absolutely in love with this absolute icon. She would arrive at 7 am looking more flawless than a Breakfast TV presenter. For the next eight hours, she would effortlessly glide around the hotel in her sky-high heels, charming every single VIP guest who walked through those reception doors. Not only did I love Jane-Marie and her effortless class and glamour, but I also learnt so much from working with her. She was phenomenal at customer service, unsurprising considering her past role as a First Class Cabin Crew Manager at Britain's flag-carrying airline.

I have the happiest memories of Saturdays spent working with Jane-Marie. She instantly realises that my strength as an employee was not carrying bags around the hotel (maybe this is part of the reason why I love her so much?!) She nicknames me 'Mr Meet & Greet' and encourages me to be a 'lobby lizard'. This meant focusing on chatting to the guests and assisting with any of their inquiries whilst they wait to either check-in or check out. Jane-Marie was not only phenomenal at her job but she also never failed to have me in hysterics as well. I vividly remember the two of us having to go to a suite at the very top of the hotel (up three separate flights of stairs) because there had been a flood in the guest's bathroom. I want you to imagine Jane-Marie (in full glam, maxi-dress and sky-high heels) climbing these flights of stairs with bright yellow gloves, a mop and bucket, and 'CLEANING IN PROGRESS' signs in hand! I followed behind, juggling about 100 towels and rolls of toilet paper. This moment was made for TV! 'We are now the Guest Services Glam Squad', Jane-Marie informed me as we climbed to the very top of the hotel, as tears of laughter streamed down my face. The sight of my gorgeous and glamorous Jane-Marie on her hands and knees in the bathroom of room 445 will forever be filed under the 'ICONIC' moments section of my memories.

Another favourite Jane-Marie moment was when the Qatari national football team had checked into the hotel. Jane-Marie was on the reception desk, whilst I was busy sorting out local attraction leaflets and making small talk with any guests in the lobby. The football team arrived and, let me tell you, Jane-Marie was absolutely in her element. They were mesmerised by this tall, gorgeous blonde who was handing out their key cards. And Jane-Marie knew how to handle this kind of VIP guest. Oh, she was an absolute expert at delivering that 5* service! The professionalism and charm with which she told these footballers where they could find breakfast, and how they could use the gym facilities, was a masterclass in 5* service. She then proceeded to offer her personal help with their luggage, which just so happened to be the biggest suitcases you have ever seen in the world. These Qatari football hunks had no choice but to stand back and watch as Jane-Marie came around the reception desk, sky high-heels still on, to grab their massive suitcases. I quickly ran over to help, feeling quite flustered by the sight of all these tall and handsome men in their national team tracksuits. Jane-Marie led the way as we took the captain and another player to their bedrooms. As we walked down the corridors, I attempted to make small talk about the Cheshire weather and the size of the…hotel (don't be cheeky now!) Jane-Marie and I became quite the Guest Services double act, bouncing off each other as we provide nothing less than a 5* service. I loved the fact that she was so effortlessly glamorous and just radiated such 5* energy, and I loved the fact that she just 'got' me. She taught me so much about customer service, handling difficult customers, looking after VIPs…and about how to conduct yourself with sophisticated, glamour and class at all times, whether it was 7 am in the morning or 7 pm at night!

*

One night, after Jane-Marie had headed home (looking forward to watching Strictly), the Operations Manager came running into the lobby area. He came bearing news that a very VIP guest was about to arrive. Well, you know me; my ears instantly pricked up, and I was suddenly very interested in what he had to say! He showed me the day's Arrivals sheet, which named this VIP as 'Belcalis Marlenis Almanzar'. The name did not, I have to tell you, ring any bells. Well, they can't be that famous if I haven't heard of them, I thought, although I was very excited to hear that they were bringing an entire entourage of people with them. Someone googled her name, and up flashed a singer called 'Cardi B'. Again, this name rang no bells. But I was still very excited by the imminent arrival of this pop star and her entourage. So I text my dad and tell him that I'll be finishing work late. Well, I didn't want him waiting in the car park whilst I waited for this pop star to arrive! And I certainly was not going to be leaving until I'd experienced at least five minutes inside a VIP celebrity circus!

Thank God I'd text my Dad about not coming to pick me up yet because it was now 90 minutes since I was supposed to have gone home, and there was still no sight of the tour bus down the driveway. I went off to the kitchen to make myself a cup of tea, hoping the caffeine would psyche me up for mingling with a pop star. When I returned to the door, the operations manager told me that the entourage was only about twenty minutes away, having just left Manchester Airport. They were coming straight to Mottram from the airport, after a long day of travelling.

Twenty minutes later, and Cardi B plus 20+ person entourage have arrived. Minibuses and blacked-out cars all pull up outside the main entrance, as dozens of giant suitcases start being wheeled into the lobby. This is so exciting, I think, as I rush outside with the Operations Manager to welcome them all to the hotel. The security team introduce Cardi B, who the Operations Manager and I then walk inside. We have got the key to her room – a gorgeous groundfloor suite – ready to go, and so I promise to take care of all her luggage and then walk her down to her room. She has specifically requested one of the four-poster beds. As we walk to the suite, I make conversation (or, in other words, I babble on) about the history of the hotel and the cold, wet weather in Cheshire. Cardi, who has just got off a plane after a long day of travelling, does not look as interested in my history of the hotel as I had hoped. Her security man smiles at me. I think this could be code for either 'I love hearing about the fact this is a Grade II listed building' or a signal 'can you please shut up… she could not care less about who used to live in this house two hundred years ago'. I like to think that this lovely security man was genuinely intrigued to learn that the Hotel had preserved some of Hall's original 12th-century wood panelling. However, I will let you reach your own conclusion on whether Cardi was impressed!

We arrive at Cardi's room, and I open the door, relieved that I have got the right key card and it works! Well, leaving a pop star standing in the corridor whilst you run back to reception for a new key card would not quite be ideal! I switch on the lights and show Cardi around the room, pointing out the four-poster bed (as if this wasn't obvious), complimentary mini-bar, walk-in shower and terrace outside. I ask if there's anything she needs (other than for me to leave her in peace and stop telling her how to switch on a light). She says no, and so I run off, promising to be back with all of her luggage. I run back to reception, buzzing on excitement and adrenaline, where the team are getting ready to do the bag drop. I quickly grab Cardi's luggage and dash back to her suite with it, wishing her a good night's sleep and a pleasant stay. I then dashed back to reception to help with taking all of the entourage's bags to their bedrooms. Well, I didn't mind carrying bags every once in awhile…especially when it was for a global pop superstar!

An hour or so later, I finally leave the hotel and head out to find my dad waiting in the car park. I've been here for 12 hours, I think, and I've loved every single second of it. The adrenaline is still pumping as I ask dad if he has ever heard of this 'Cardi B', and he says he hasn't either. As we drive home through the Cheshire countryside, 'Bodak Yellow' plays on Capital. It doesn't register – at all – that *this* is the popstar I have just taken to their room. It's not until I tell Becky about my weekend that I am informed that Cardi B isn't just some random 'singer'. It's only after Becky's horrified **'YOU DON'T KNOW WHO CARDI B IS!!!'** reaction that I realise she is an international pop sensation. I have just given her a completely unrequested monologue on 12th-century wood panelling and the rain in Cheshire. It's another one of those moments when I just think, 'Only at Mottram!'

Working at Mottram is genuinely the best thing that could have ever happened to me. Meeting and greeting all these guests, working with phenomenal customer service experts such as Ella and Jane-Marie, and just being here in this incredible four* hotel gives me the biggest boost in confidence and social skills. I am learning to talk to absolutely anybody, and I am learning how to be an articulate, charismatic and confident professional communicator. I am being paid to talk to guests, and I am being paid to deliver a 5* hosting service. Not only in this my dream job, but it is also the best education in social skills and self-confidence. Working at Mottram does me a world of good and, without being dramatic, totally transforms my life. I am loving – and learning something – every single day. Jane-Marie and Ella give me opportunities to cultivate communication skills, become a confident host, and play my part in delivering an exceptional level of customer service. These skills will benefit me for the rest of my life. And the memories I have of strutting down these corridors with Jane-Marie will last a lifetime!

Nothing excited me more than waking up on a Saturday morning and getting suited and booted ready for a day at Mottram Hall. As you can see, I did take it all very seriously! I was utterly obsessed with the glitz and glamour of it all. I felt as if I was joining Jane Marie in First Class on a British Airways flight somewhere hot and sunny. In reality, my feet were staying very firmly planted on Cheshire soil, with an omnipresent risk of wind and rain! I loved being part of the 'backdrop' to people's big days, and I loved finding ways to make people feel as if they were worth a million dollars. 'Guest services' became my new favourite mantra, and I started going through all of my life with what I called the 'Meet and Greet Mindset'.

I wrote about this 'Meet and Greet Mindset' in a chapter for my first self-help book, Live Your Best Life. I wanted to share it with you here in full:

"Back when I was 17, I had the time of my life working at a 120-room 5* hotel. My job was to 'meet and greet' the guests as they arrived at the main reception desk, welcoming them in and guiding them around the hotel. It was my role to make them feel welcomed and to ensure that their stay was smooth from start to finish. It was also my role to help guests by carrying their luggage up the flights of stairs - however, as I'm sure you can imagine, this part of the job was not exactly my area of expertise (or enthusiasm)... On early morning shifts, I would say 'good morning!' and direct my guests to the restaurant for breakfast. Whilst on a Friday night, I would point guests to the Champagne Bar or book them a taxi into Manchester.

My favourite shift of the week was a Saturday when 200 wedding guests would arrive at the hotel. They would all receive a glass of Prosecco as they walked down the red carpet and through the main reception doors. They would all spend hours posing for pictures in the 270 acres of land around the hotel, perfecting the best Instagram poses and showing their glamorous wedding outfits off to the world. As I'm sure you can imagine, I absolutely loved the buzz of welcoming all these people into the hotel, doing what I could to add a little bit of sparkle to their stay. Getting this incredible job was the best thing that could have ever happened to 17-year-old me. It was literally like a divine intervention - it came at just the right time and completely transformed my entire life! It gave me the most amazing people skills and the most extraordinary boost of confidence that I will forever be thankful for. During my time in this fabulous job, I devised what I now like to call the 'meet & greet mindset' (as you should know by now, I'm very extra like that!) This mindset is the secret weapon that I deploy in every single social situation that I face in my life today! And I hope that it might be able to help you out in terms of your social confidence as well… So what is my 'meet & greet mindset'? Allow me to explain! In every social situation, I imagine that I am back at work standing in the main entrance door to the hotel. With the click of my fingers, I instantly snap back into the role of being the 'host with the most'! I remind myself that it is my job to warmly welcome every single person that I see. I remind myself that it is my job to make sure that every single person I interact with feels happy and at ease. It is my job – which I am being paid to do– to make eye contact, plaster on my biggest smile, and give every person I meet the warmest greeting that I can muster. It doesn't matter if I'm scared of what someone might think about me or whether I fear that someone might potentially end up being dismissive of my friendliness. It is my JOB to say hello and to ask them how they are!

In my first few weeks in the job, I remember feeling so much anxiety about having to speak to certain groups of people. I'd see people – usually groups of men – who I assumed would mock me or ridicule me. As a result of my insecurities and fears, I would instantly assume that they wouldn't want to engage with my attempts at making conversation. I'd expected that they would make comments to each other about how 'gay' I was, or even start making nasty impressions of how I spoke. When these groups of people walked towards the entrance to the hotel (where I was waiting to greet everyone that arrived), it felt like all of my worst nightmares coming true. And quite literally walking straight towards me! My heart would start racing, and my palms would start sweating. In those moments of overwhelming panic and anxiety, I could quite easily have run away from the door and have pretended that I'd never seen those 'fearsome' guests arriving. I could have quite easily slipped off for a quick toilet break, or made myself look busy organising local attraction leaflets in the champagne bar. But that wasn't what I stood for as an employee. 17-year old me took my commitment to delivering 5* service very seriously indeed! I, therefore, knew that I had to pull myself together and realise that this situation wasn't about me. I was here to do a job, and do that job was exactly what I was going to do! It did not matter what these people thought of me - my job was to meet and greet them, and I was going to give them the meet and greet of their lives! I had to realise that I wasn't standing here in the hotel foyer to be subjected to an assessment of my character or to face an appraisal of my personality!

No, I was here to do my job - which I loved more than anything else -,, and I was committed to doing it in STYLE! And so I made it my mission to not let my fears and anxieties hold me back from delivering that full 5* service! I, therefore, allowed myself to acknowledge those feelings of anxiety. But I then also myself to stoically remain rooted to the spot! I was not going to be defeated by my fears - I was going to 'fake it until I made it' instead! So, instead of running away from these scary groups of people at the door, I forced myself to make eye contact and plaster on my biggest smile! I didn't let myself think about it for one second - I simply got into character and got down to business! I greeted all of those intimidating guests with a massive smile and a cheerful 'Hi, how are you today?' or a 'Hello, good evening...welcome to Mottram Hall!' I completely faked my confidence, and I completely concealed all of my fears and insecurities. Looking at me, any of these guests would have assumed that I was the most confident person on the face of the earth. They had absolutely no idea whatsoever that I was secretly terrified on the inside!

And guess what? The 'fake it till you make it' approach 100% paid off! Every single time that I made myself snap into character and fake this social confidence, I found that it got easier and easier. I soon realised that these guests didn't all start attacking and mocking me right before my own very eyes. I found that instead, they responded to my friendliness with…guess what…FRIENDLINESS!!! I couldn't believe it!! And I no longer needed to fake my social confidence. Instead, I now had a genuine level of self-confidence and absolute love for every aspect of my job! Of course, there were always that tiny minority of guests who would exchange a judgemental glance with one another. Still, I was determined not to let it phase me. It was my job to greet them…and greet them I would! I was no longer faking my social confidence - I was radiating a genuine love for meeting & greeting new people! I was being paid to do it, after all, and 17 years old me wanted all that dollar! I was determined to be a true professional and become the dazzling King – or should that be Queen – of the meet and greet!

And so, I got into the habit of swallowing my anxieties, face down my social fears, and plastering on my brightest smile. My 'meet & greet mindset' technique worked absolute wonders. Each time that I went through the 'meet & greet' motions', I found that talking to people became easier and easier! It became second nature to make eye contact, plaster on a dazzling smile, and exchange those small talk pleasantries. Meeting & greeting became something that I didn't even need to think about before doing. Every single guest would automatically receive what I soon self-titled the 'FIVE STAR BEN WARDLE EXPERIENCE'.

I saw myself as a character in a Disneyland parade, who was being paid to make dreams come true by spreading a little sparkle and joy in people's days. And whilst my lovely suit was not quite a Mickey Mouse costume, it felt like my battle armour! And so every time that I got ready for work, I'd get myself straight back into character as Mr Meet & Greet. In my head, I was this beaming and beautifully bronzed (I was in the middle of a fake tan addiction) host with the most. I always had a bottle of champagne in hand and a confetti canon exploding above my head. When I was in this mindset, I truly believed that every single thing that I touched instantly turned into gold. I believed that every person I met was instantly made to feel like a multi-millionaire VIP.

Well, let me tell you, this meet & greet mindset soon started revolutionising every single area of my entire life! At sixth form college, for example, I started confidently gliding down the corridors and making small talk about the weather with anyone who I encountered! When I went into Tesco, I'd not only buy my newspapers and meal deal, but I would also now have a good chat with the staff and tell them to 'have a great day!' At parties (which had previously filled me with so much anxiety and fear) I now entered the room safe in the knowledge I was 'Mr Meet & Greet'! I was confident that making people feel at ease and spreading a bit of sparkle was something I was an expert at. And so, I had nothing to fear and had no reason to feel intimidated! As with everything in life, practice did make perfect when it came to deploying my 'Meet & Greet' mindset! The more that I'd chat to people, make small talk, and get into the mindset of being this fabulous host with the most, the easier it would become to talk to anyone! I do believe that charisma, confidence, and charm can easily be cultivated and perfected with even just a little bit of regular practice!

As I got more and more confident in my 'meet & greet' mindset, I was starting to give Kris Jenner a run for her money! And these days, I'll quite happily make conversation with a brick wall - and it's all because of my meet & greets mindset! I still deploy this trusted mindset in every social situation today. And so can you! When I walk into a room, I strive to provide that 'BW 5* EXPERIENCE' to every single person I encounter! There are no excuses for not acknowledging someone or starting a conversation – see it as your my job to talk to everyone! Think of yourself as a professional socialite or an expert host with the most! With this attitude, it is so much easier to get over those inevitable feelings of awkwardness and anxiety that we all feel when entering a social situation! It is so simple! Just tell yourself 'IT IS MY JOB TO BE A PROFESSIONAL AND GIVE EVERY SINGLE PERSON THE 'MEET & GREET' EXPERIENCE!'

Even if I had endured the worst week or was feeling a little worse-for-wear from the night before, I would always make sure I got straight into the role at work. I consistently delivered that full meet & greet experience! It was my JOB, and I had to be a professional providing that full meet and greet package to every single person that I saw! Even if it was 6 am, or I was 16 hours into a shift, I always made sure that I'd had my green tea and that I consistently provided that sparkling 5* level of service! Looking back, I must admit that it did help to keep a lot of sugar and a lot of concealer nearby at all times!

Start applying the 'Meet & Greet mindset' to your social life and reap the rewards! Become the host with the most and the 5* greeter that you were born to be! Give everyone eye contact, an award-winning smile, and some seriously smooth small talk. Make everyone feel a million dollars – and stop worrying about what they think of you! You've got a job to do – so spread some sparkle and give people the five-star treatment that they deserve! Get into the meet & greet mindset and get out into the world…you are the host with the most, and this is your time to shine!"

I fell in love with everything about Mottram Hall, and the hotel will forever hold an exceptionally special in my heart. The same goes for the incredible people I met whilst working here. Especially Ella, Jemma (even if for just one week), Vicky (another cabin crew angel), and Jane-Marie. Then there was Joel, Carmen (the most iconic housekeeper you could ever wish to meet) and all of the staff at the hotel. Everybody was so genuinely kind, and Mottram felt like a home-from-home. The icing on the cake was the beautiful building and grounds, which are simply incomparable to any other resort or hotel I have ever visited. Everything about Mottram – the beautiful Cheshire countryside, the glamorous event and, of course, the champagne - was just so bloody fabulous and luxurious. It was all very BW!

This job undoubtedly made me who I am today. It was the most incredible education in people skills and social confidence. It gave me an insight into a glamorous and luxurious world that I never want to forget about or leave! As you know, nothing makes me happier than a gorgeous glass of prosecco in beautiful surroundings! It also showed me how happy being busy makes me. This job taught me that I thrive when I am hosting people and ensuring that they are having the best time possible. I hate being the guest at any function; instead, I love to be the host or the person making sure that everybody else is having a good time. I strive to always be the 'host with the most', and I am extraordinarily grateful to Mottram for allowing me to live out my 5* Kris Jenner hosting fantasy! And carrying all of that baggage wasn't always so bad…not when it was Louis Vuitton!

20. THE ONE WHERE I BECAME HEAD BOY

As much as I have loved my summer at Mottram Hall, I do have something called Sixth Form to be getting on with as well! It's now September, and that means it's the start of year 13. It's finally my final year at All Hallows! I'm starting this year with a very clear goal in my mind – I am determined to get the grades for studying Religion, Philosophy and Ethics at King's College London. I am prepared to work harder than ever before to turn this dream into my brand new reality. I was determined that I would be moving down to London in a year. So I bought out the Tesco Handforth Dean stationery aisle and covered my walls in psychology evaluation points, philosophy quotes, and English language theorists. I had a clear goal in mind, and I was ready to work harder than ever before to turn my dream into my brand-new reality!

Towards the end of August, we had received our AS Level results in school. I was delighted with 'As' in English Language, Psychology and Religious Studies, but I had been devastated by a 'C' in English Literature. This was not what I had been expecting, at all. It turned out that I'd got an 'A' – almost full marks – on my 'Othello' exam paper, whereas my 'Atonement' paper had barely scraped something like an 'E'. Something was obviously wrong, and the whole situation gave me a bit of a fright. I'd been quite complacent about my English Literature, and thought I'd be able to rely on this subject to get me the exam grades I'd need for university. As I looked at my results list, it was very clear that this was not going to be the case! The attitude of the English Literature teachers was that they couldn't care less. 'Oops' was probably the best way of summing up their attitude, along with a cheery 'never mind; these things sometimes happen!' Well, I was not happy about 'these things' happening, and I immediately decided to drop English Literature. Looking back, this was a great shame, because I had loved the subject through GCSE and into AS Level. But, having been spooked by my grades and having been taught by teachers who I just didn't connect with in any way whatsoever, I whipped out those scissors and said ciao to the Othello and Atonement study guides! This meant I was now down to English Language, Psychology and Religious Studies. This felt like a very manageable mix, and I was excited to throw myself into these subjects.

***

Talking of throwing myself into things, there was another opportunity that had caught my attention at school. This was the opportunity to become the 'Head Boy' of the school and sixth form, a role which carried a lot of prestige at All Hallows. Ever since Year 7, I had seen – and admired - the Head Boy and Head Girl, two Year 13 students elected to organise events and represent the school. The Head Boy and Head Girl always seemed like very important and powerful people within the school ecosystem. What's more, they always got to present the 'All Hallows Has Talent' show every Christmas. I had dreamed of being able to present this show ever since the first performance I had seen back in Year 7. I naturally believed that I could easily give Dermot O Leary or Ant and Dec a run for their money!

Mrs Garvey has started asking people whether they are planning on running for the roles of Head Boy and Girl. I know in my heart that I would love to be Head Boy. It's not just, believe it or not, for selfish or egotistical reasons. However, I do like the sound of putting the title on my UCAS application! I do want to make a positive difference in the school and sixth form. I have got a lot to say about mental health, sexuality, and how to create a more accepting and inclusive world for everybody to live in.

As you know, I have been reading the daily newspapers for years, and I am genuinely interested in British politics and decision making. In addition to this, I am passionate about getting teaching. Being Head Boy is the closest I am going to get to being a school leader before qualifying as a teacher in however many years! I feel like a natural leader and believe that I am somebody who enjoys motivating, energising and getting the best out of the people around me. I feel like I could do a lot of good, and I also feel like the role would do me a lot of good as well.

But, when Mrs Garvey asks me if I'll be going for the role, I tell her that I'm not sure. Inside, of course, I am very sure that I would love to do the role. I am one million per cent sure. But, as I think about it, I seriously doubt whether I would end up getting the role. And the one thing I hate more than anything else is failing at something – failure (and the embarrassment that I think comes with it) is my biggest fear in the world. I do not feel confident that I would get enough votes to win the vote, and I'm terrified of being left embarrassed. Of course, I know now that there is nothing to fear about failure. I now know that 'whatever happens in life, you can handle it'! But, at the time, I was a prisoner to my fears. As a result, I almost didn't put myself forwards for the role.

Here's how the selection process works: each candidate gives a speech to years 11, 12 and 13, plus the sixth form tutors and the school leadership team. Each person in the room then casts their vote for who they would like to be the next Head Boy and Head Girl. The voting is split into three categories; school (the year 11s), sixth form (years 12 and 13) and the school leaders (Headteacher, deputy headteachers). Whichever boy and girl receive the most votes become the Head Boy and Head Girl, whilst the second-highest become Deputy Head Boy and Deputy Head Girl. Looking back now, the whole thing seems so trivial and over-dramatic. Still, at the time it genuinely felt like a U.S. Presidential Election.

There were lots of people considering putting themselves forward for the role, including Megan and Emily, my best friends from English last year. Before deciding that I would put myself forward for the role of Head Boy, I wanted to be certain that I had a good chance of actually getting the role. I thought that I'd be able to make a very positive difference. Still, I was not convinced I had the popularity to get elected in the first place. And nothing would have embarrassed me more than giving a speech and then not getting the role – I was such a sensitive and fragile little diva back in the sixth form days! Don't get me wrong, I was not the public enemy number one in the common room, but being elected as the head boy was not a done deal. This was because a boy from the 'popular' group in our year had decided he was going to run for the role, which was fair enough. My friend, also part of this 'popular' group, had decided to run for 'Head Girl'. So their group prematurely christened them as the King and Queen of the Common Room. From their perspective, there was absolutely nothing whatsoever wrong with what they were doing. Anyone, I'm sure, would have done the same for someone in their friendship group. And I don't think they were taking it that seriously, either.

But sensitive and fragile 17-year-old Ben was unable to see the bigger picture. I had always felt very insecure about popularity, and seeing all of this going on made me genuinely angry and upset. I took it far too much to heart, and it totally put me off, throwing my hat into the ring. I had found a couple of the people in this 'popular' group – just like any group you find in a high school – to be quite rude and bitchy. So I interpreted everything that was going on as if it was a personal attack. It wasn't, but that was the insecure lens through which I saw the situation at the time. And so, I told Mrs Sutton that there was no way I would be running for Head Boy – what was the point, I asked her, when these people would do everything in their power to make sure that their friend got the role instead of me? One girl had even openly been saying to people 'I really hope that Ben doesn't get it…he thinks he's good at everything', which I had totally taken to heart. I was desperate for everybody to like me, failing to realise that this is just absolutely impossible. I was still to learn that, if you want to succeed in this world, you have got to toughen up and grow a very thick skin indeed. You cannot take what people say to heart, and you cannot go through life desperate for people to like you. This experience was a much-needed lesson in the need to take people's opinions on the chin and focus on doing what you think is the right thing. Focus on doing what you want to do, instead of worrying about whether other people might like you for doing it!

****

It's the night before the 'Head Boy' and 'Head Girl' speeches are taking place in school. I'm talking it all through with Queen P, and I am genuinely conflicted about whether to go for it or not. I have put my name down to give a speech in the morning, but I am seriously questioning whether to even go into school. Becky, Erin, Freya and Kristina have been trying to rally me, but I am being a diva and have completely thrown my toys out of the pram. I don't want to do it, and I am all for throwing in the towel. I want to make a point, and I want to show all of these people that it will be there loss I am not running for Head Boy! Oh, I'm such a little diva! I am determined not to embarrass myself by running for this role and not getting it. My ego is too fragile to risk what I imagine would be the most humiliating experience of my life! I am feeling so down, so annoyed, and so over the whole thing. Mum tries to offer me some words of wisdom, although she does stress that 'whatever you decide to do, you have my full support – do what you think is best for you!'

All these people I had been trying to impress were saying they weren't voting for me and wanted, as anyone would, their friend to win. It sounds so petty to say it now, but it felt like the biggest kick in the teeth. I had been trying to impress these people, and it was like everything was being thrown back in my face. I was taking it far too seriously, and I was reacting far too sensitively!

Fortunately, I managed to get myself out of my ridiculous mood and pull myself together. One minute, I was moping around declaring that 'nobody likes me it's not fair'. The next minute, I am suddenly marching out of the house declaring that I am 'ready for battle'! 'They better be ready for the speech to end all speeches!', I tell Queen P. And so, the next morning, I marched into school feeling riled up to give the speech of my life. I'll show them all, I think to myself, they're all going to be sorry! This perhaps wasn't the best attitude, but it certainly worked in terms of getting me into school and giving the best speech of my life. After the speeches had finished, I marched out of the hall and went into hiding in the library (of course I did!) I was determined to avoid the Common Room like the plague, but I did make sure I saw Becky and went to speak to Mrs Sutton. I've done it, I told them both, trying to get them to predict, on a scale of 1-10, my chances of victory. 'I honestly think you've got it', says Becky, to which I reply 'you're just saying that…but thanks!'

After break time I have a free period, which I spend hidden in the library pretending to do work. At lunchtime, all the candidates have got to go to the Principal's office to find out the results, before we all go home for our weekly Wednesday afternoon 'enrichment' activities. I've planned to go to Café Nero with Erin Lamb, which we always do on a Wednesday. 'We're going whatever the result', I tell her, 'whether it's celebrating or complaining, we're going to need caffeine and caramel waffles!' As the lunchtime bell rings, I meet Erin and drag the poor girl up to the Principal's office with me. 'I'm not doing this alone', I tell her, 'you might have to intervene if I start telling them all what I really think of them!' We arrive at the office, and all the candidates are called inside. We sit around a large meeting table, and the Principal and Mrs Garvey start talking about how well we've all done and how proud we should be. 'Oh my god please get on with it', I think to myself, not taking in a single word they are saying (sorry Mrs Garvey, I'm sure they were lovely sentiments!) They finally cut to the chase and start dishing out the badges, my heart beating and palms sweating. 'And Ben, you're going to be Head Boy' says Mrs Garvey, as eyes dart in my direction and I feel as if I'm about to pass out. Oh my God, I think, absolute relief rushing through my entire body. I pulled it off, I think to myself, despite thinking everybody is out to get you, they have just elected you Head Boy!

Everyone congratulates each other on their new roles. I am genuinely delighted for Emily (who has got Deputy Head Girl) and Megan (who is now Head Girl). They have been the best friends I could have asked for over the past year, and they could not deserve this more. Mrs Garvey and the Principal congratulate everyone and ask Megan and me if we can stay for a couple more minutes. After a quick chat about our new roles, we say thank you and head out into the corridor, where a crowd has now gathered. I run straight in Erin's direction and tell her to 'RUN!' before we bump into anyone I don't want to bump into (e.g. everybody crowded in that corridor!) I tell her the good news, and she is delighted, 'Oh my God I knew you would' she tells me as we walk – well, I practically skip – into town for our Café Nero date.

Café Nero is my spiritual home. There's something about the cosy chairs and the relaxing ambience that makes it feel so welcoming and homely. Erin and I love our weekly Café Nero dates every Wednesday afternoon when we watch the world go by whilst catching up on each other's lives. We order our drinks – always a breakfast tea for me! – and sit down to celebrate my election.

'I actually can't believe it…I just feel so much relief!' I exclaim, adrenaline still pumping through me. It doesn't feel like a victory or an achievement – it just feels like a massive relief. I was genuinely doubting whether I'd end up getting the role, but I also didn't know what I would do if I hadn't got it! Always the dramatic diva, I had genuinely been considering moving schools – yes, even in year 13 – if things hadn't gone my way! I do think that it's the perfectionist within me, unable to cope with feeling embarrassed or beaten at something. Whilst I love this fighting spirit and military approach to achieving success, I do think that I would be a lot happier if I didn't take things like this so seriously! I might even have done me a world of good not to get the role because it would have given me an important wake-up call that you don't need to win every race to have worth or be a 'winner' at life! But that was now beside the point – I had achieved my dream, and I now needed to get serious about making a positive difference. I genuinely had so many things that I wanted to do for the school. I wanted to put the student's mental health on the agenda, I wanted to promote diversity, and I wanted to be a positive role model for younger students. There was no time for being a diva and getting worked up about who had voted for who! I had been handed an amazing opportunity to make a difference. And I intended to seize it with both hands.

As Erin and I chatted, Amy – who had been Deputy Head Girl last year – came into Café Nero. She instantly came running over and asked me how the voting had gone. 'Did you get it?', she asked, convinced that I had. 'Oh my God Amy…I got Head Boy!' I told her, as she climbed over a chair to hug me. 'I'm so proud!' she told me, 'I knew that you would, I said that you would do it!' It felt amazing to have this love and support from the most amazing friends. This was yet another wake-up call that I needed to stop being so dramatic and start appreciating the amazing people I had in my life! I also needed to appreciate the caramel waffles and large mug of tea I had in front of me, which had cost me about three weeks-worth of Mottram Hall pay!

I went home that evening, feeling so relieved and delighted. Mum was thrilled, as were Sam and Dad. Again, it was a reminder of what's truly important in life – your friends and family! I spoke to Becky, who was also delighted, and I told her that I couldn't have done it without it. It was true – if I hadn't had Becky cheering me on, I wouldn't have got through the whole situation. Whether it was accepting my sexuality or supporting me in becoming Head Boy, Becky was always the most loyal and supportive friend. She is one of the biggest blessings in my life and was my absolute rock throughout Sixth Form. I FaceTime Freya and tell her the news – she is equally as delighted for me – and, after what genuinely feels like the longest of days, I sleep so well. Tomorrow, I think, the hard work begins! It's one thing giving a speech and getting elected, but it's quite another thing practising what you have preached and delivering on your promises! I had achieved my dream, and now I needed to let go of any anxieties or bitterness I was still irrationally clinging onto! I needed to put my heart and soul into getting the job done…oh, and I needed to be getting on with my A-Level courses as well, of course!

***

The first half-term of Year 13 flies by as Autumn arrives and the nights get darker and darker. It's soon a couple of weeks before my 18th birthday, and I don't have a clue how to celebrate it. I can't believe that I'm going to be 18 – I'm finally going to be an adult! I am very much ready to finally reach this milestone. And I am very much keen to do it in style! I decide that I want to have a meal at my favourite restaurant, the Alchemist in Alderley Edge, and set about inviting my 15 best friends to join me. I ask Granny if we can all meet at her house (just a 30-second walk from the restaurant) for drinks beforehand. It just so happens that she and Grumpy are away that week anyway. So we have got her lounge to ourselves, which works out perfectly. It is so lovely to have a glass of bubbly in hand and all of my best friends together in one room. We have a couple of drinks, have the obligatory photoshoot on the staircase, and then head down to the restaurant. We have a gorgeous long table at the back of the restaurant, and I genuinely have the best evening. The good food, good company, and good cocktails – that I can finally drink! – make for the perfect celebration. This, I think, is what life is all about. This is what it means to be happy – nothing matters more than being surrounded by the best friends in the world. At the end of the night, I give everybody a big hug and thank them for everything that they have done for me over the years. I have never felt so much gratitude, love and genuine joy. I know that I have found friends for life, and I know that nothing matters more than being surrounded by this type of kind, genuine and truly iconic individuals.

After that rather civilised and classy affair in Alderley, there was something else that I was keen to do now that I was finally eighteen. And I didn't expect this one to be quite as civilised of an affair as dinner and cocktails with my girls…I was desperate for my first night out in Manchester's gay village!

As I've mentioned, I had wandered down Canal Street a couple of times over the last year. I would walk along the street, refreshing my dating app profiles as I passed each club in the hope that it would mean I'd get more messages and attention! I had always glanced through the doors and wished that I could be going out in one of these venues. Well, I now finally could! I was desperate to dress up (or, I must admit in my case, dress down to practically my underwear) and get 'out there' on the gay scene. It wasn't just that I wanted to meet guys to get with (although that was most certainly at the top of my 18-year-old agenda!). I just wanted to meet other gay people who I could become friends with! Whilst I loved Macclesfield, it wasn't exactly known for its thriving gay scene! And so, when I was in Manchester, I wanted to make friends, meet new people, and – yes okay I'll admit it – catch the eye of a sexy man!

I obviously did not have any idea of what to expect on a night out on Canal Street. My most adventurous antics to date had been going to our local Pizza Express and staying there until past 10 pm! I did not have a clue what it was actually like inside these venues, although – to be honest – I don't think there's anything that can actually prepare you for your first night out in Manchester! I was seriously excited and itching to get on that dance floor, blissfully naïve and unaware of what I was about to walk into.

I absolutely loved it. The first club I went to was G-A-Y Manchester, which was nothing but iconic. I loved the music, the atmosphere, the raised platforms, and the screens that lined every wall. I also loved the attention that guys were giving me on the dance floor! I felt as if I was totally in my element, and I felt as if I had finally arrived where I was meant to be! I danced, I flirted, and I bought far too many drinks. By the time we were heading off to the twenty-four McDonalds, I was on cloud nine. And no, that wasn't just because of the prosecco! I had enjoyed the best night of my life, and I was already planning when I could come back. It was so liberating, so empowering, and so enjoyable. I'd had so much fun, without a single worry about what people might think of me. And I'd loved actually getting male attention – for the very first time in my life! I could get used to this, I think to myself, as we jump in the Uber and head back to Cheshire. Little did I know what the future would hold for me…

***

The rest of Sixth Form flies by in a blur of revision, mock exams, and Head Boy duties. My dream of presenting 'All Hallows Has Talent' finally comes true, and we pull off an impressive three shows in one day! Each of the shows opens with our performance of Mariah Carey's 'All I want for Christmas is You', which I'm sure poor Sam was delighted to witness!

It feels so strange that Sixth Form is already coming to an end. I am studying more than I have ever studied before, and my Saturdays at Mottram provide a very welcome break from the textbooks. I am determined to smash these exams, get the entry grades that I need, and then be able to head off to London!

All Hallows has been the best school I could have ever attended. I've had the best teachers, and I've made the best friends I could ever ask for. As our last day finally arrives, I hug all of my teachers and say goodbye. 'Thank you so much for everything', I tell them, 'what on earth would I have done without you?!'

21. THE RESULTS ARE IN….

Light is creeping through my curtains as I wake up, as usual, at 6.30 am. It's a Thursday morning in August, towards the end of a seasonably warm Summer. For a few seconds, I remain blissfully unaware of the significance of this day. And then it hits me. I am immediately wide awake. Oh, my God. Today is the day. It's finally A-levels Results day.

For the past few months, I've put the thought of this day to the back of my mind. I've been busy working at Mottram Hall, going out to the local nightclub with my girls, and even topping up my (natural) tan on the Greek Island Kefalonia. We've been coming to the same resort for years, and this year I was reunited with a gorgeous girl called Hannah. She had been at the same apartments with her family in years before, and we had instantly struck-up a fabulous poolside friendship! Hannah and her parents – Kay and Richard – were absolute angels with hearts of absolute gold. Seeing them around the pool had made my holiday. It just goes to show that you never know where you are going to meet amazing friends and inspiring human beings!

I've been trying to forget all about receiving my A-Level results, whilst at the same time wishing Results Day would just hurry up. The night before Results Day, I write this in my diary:

"Results day tomorrow oh my f***king God – more scared than I have ever been in my life oh my god feel sick thinking about opening that envelope…something always goes wrong for me! My focus is on God, goodness and meditation – I am an aspiring life coach, and headteacher and philosopher like everything will work out no matter what results you get…have some perspective, Ben!!!

Need to be more CONFIDENT in me – with boys, socially, speaking in groups, with straight boys etc. I need to stop doubting that people like me because I am camp – they love it!!! Self-esteem needs a boost!!"

As you can see, even on the night before Results Day, I appear to have been more interested in my love life than my A-Level results! Boys really are a great distraction technique! It's also interesting to see how I turned to God in my hour of need! It appears that there's no need to believe in God until you need to believe in a divine plan or reason behind everything that is outside of your control!

***

It's the morning of 16 August 2018. My tan is fading, and the reality of Result's Day is dawning. I have, surprisingly, slept very well. I think it's because, deep down, I am feeling quietly confident about my results. I'm not panicking; I'm just desperate to know what I had got! I'm safe in the knowledge that, to take up my place reading Religion, Philosophy and Ethics at King's College, London, I needed the grades ABB. These are more than manageable – there is nothing unrealistic about this set of results. I know that, after months of hard works and revision, it is well within my capabilities of getting grades. In fact, something would have to have gone seriously wrong for me to end up getting anything less than three As in my results envelope. In mock exams and practise questions, I had been achieving As in all three of my subjects (philosophy, psychology and English language). And so I was quietly confident that I'd be moving down to London in just under a month. But I wasn't just hoping to get the grades I needed for university – I was secretly hoping I'd achieve even more. Ever the perfectionist, I was secretly praying for at least three As, and even an A* in philosophy. My fingers were crossed that all of my blood, sweat, ink, and tears would pay off. Well, I was about to find out!

The plan was to go into school, with Becky, when the doors opened at 8 am. It was like de ja vu; we had gone in together for our GCSE Results two years earlier. I had found that taking our usual walk to school had been very calming and comforting before opening that envelope. This time, however, I was not prepared to wait until I got into school before finding out my results. GCSEs didn't carry any serious consequences or expectations – we had all just wanted to get the grades we deserved! A-Levels, however, undoubtedly had a lot more gravitas behind them! There pressure about getting into your university of choice, and there was a lot of expectation around your grades. I did not want to open my results whilst surrounded by a whole group of nosey people. I did not want to have to react to my grades as if I was playing the lead role in a performance. I had never understood why students would agree to open their results live on BBC Breakfast or ITV's Good Morning Britain. Surely, I'd think to myself, they must have been told their results beforehand…or they must just be absolutely mad!

I hated getting any kind of results back in front of an audience. I had always hated that inevitable **'what did you get?!'** question once everyone in the classroom had got mock or practice papers back. Whilst I don't mind a bit of healthy competition, I hated the classroom comparison culture that would emerge when it came to exam results. Human Beings, I believe, seem to be obsessed with comparing themselves – we compare anything and everything, including height, weight, social media following, income and academic performance. We always like to know how well we are doing in comparison to the people around us. Many of us find that we are slaves to public opinion and are desperate to maintain a positive public image at all times. We are so keen to conceal any potential weaknesses that we fear will embarrass us in front of others.

As I say, I do think that some degree of competition is both healthy and necessary. For example, it is good to be inspired by – and indeed be kept on our toes by - other people's successes. I do think it's important to be mindful of how other people perceive you. And it is in our best interests to be acting in a friendly, likeable and approachable way! But it is ridiculously easy to end up taking this comparison and competitiveness too far, especially if you have those perfectionist tendencies in your DNA. In my therapy sessions with Sarah, I had identified these perfectionist tendencies and traits. I came to believe that my personal insecurities had left me desperate to achieve an unrealistically positive self-image at all times – I was desperate to be liked by ***everybody.*** I was completely afraid of failure, rejection or mistakes. If I wasn't good at something, then I couldn't be interested in it. I was so scared of people seeing me trying – and then 'failing' – that I went into my default method of defensiveness, where I avoid failure or rejection at all costs. Take, for example, my relationships with people that I mee. If I am scared that somebody is going to judge, ridicule or be rude to me, then my default response has always been to attack them first. It's such a toxic way to be! If I think that they have the potential to make me feel small or inferior, then I instantly put up these big walls. Without consciously choosing to, I will instantly start being extremely cold, rude, hostile and even confrontational towards this person…before they have even opened their mouth! I am so scared of being rejected and ridiculed that I am prepared to write somebody off before spending even just five seconds with them. It all comes down to this fear of failure and this obsession with perfectionism. If somebody looks like they might not like me, then I automatically default into defensive mode before even giving them a chance.

But here's what I've had to learn: you cannot be so afraid of failure. Indeed, you need to fail to thrive. There is nothing wrong with getting things wrong – we must make mistakes! I am a strong believer that our 'biggest mistakes of the past are our best teachers for the future'. If things don't go wrong, we will never learn, and we will never grow. You cannot become the best version of yourself without going through the worst times in your life. You cannot fulfil your potential from within the confinements of your comfort zone. And I have had to learn to make friends with failure and get comfortable with making mistakes. The most important part of this journey has been learning to stop worrying about what other people think of me. I have always felt this perfectionist pressure to 'perform' – I always want to live up to expectations and not 'let anybody down'. And so, when we got mock results back, I would be desperate for an A* - not just because that's what I expected of myself, but also because that's what other people expected of me.

In my mind, nothing would be more embarrassing than everybody talking about the fact I hadn't been 'top of the class'. Nothing would be worse than everybody discussing the fact that I hadn't got the grades I was always expecting. Of course, I have since realised that nobody actually cares – in the slightest – about what grades you get. People might be interested in a bit of gossip – for a solid five seconds – but, other than that, they really could not care less. As I say, everybody is the main character in their own life. They are not sat up at night worrying about your life or your exam results – so why are you worrying about the fact that they might be worried about you? I had to learn that my academic success and performance was for me, and me alone. As my mum has always said to me, *'as long as you are happy and have tried your best, that is all that matters'*.

Indeed, I am a strong believer in the mantra that *'the only person you should compete with is who you were yesterday'*. As long as you feel happy about your results, then that is all that matters! There is always going to be somebody who has done better than you! And there is always going to be someone who has done worse than you. We all want different things in life, and we are all on different journeys. Some people excel at maths; some people excel at a sport. We cannot all be amazing at everything – it's about being happy within your own self. If you put every ten people in a room and asked them to define the word 'success', you would get ten very different answers!

As I got ready to go into school on Results Morning, I was not feeling happy about having to open my results in front of other people. I like to be in control of a situation, and the idea that I would have people crowding around me as I opened this envelope filled me with absolute horror. What if the results were really bad? What if I hadn't got into university? I needed to be prepared, and I needed to know exactly what was coming. So I logged onto the Parental Gateway – thank God for the parental gateway! – and looked at my Results online. As I clicked onto the 'view results' button, my heart stopped. This is it, I thought, the wait feeling well and truly over. Ignorance had certainly been bliss, but I felt sick to my stomach, but oh my God was I desperate to know:

PSYCHOLOGY – A*

RELIGIOUS STUDIES – A*

ENGLISH LANGUAGE – A

EXTENDED PROJECT QUALIFICATION (EPQ) – A

Oh my GOD. THANK THE BLOODY LORD! Was my first thought, as relief rushed through my veins. THANK GOD! AMEN! I was ridiculously relieved and genuinely delighted with my A*s in psychology and religious studies. My perfectionist's brain was instantly drawn to the A in English Language (of course it was). This is the thing with perfectionism – it has this incredible talent for ensuring that you never feel satisfied or happy! But I quickly snapped myself out of my sulk, and I got back to celebrating my success. My hard work had finally paid off! My hours of revision had resulted in success! And, most importantly, I was now going to London! I was over the moon!

Here's what I wrote in my diary:

"So happy A*A*A results – absolutely over the moon, f***king buzzing, beyond my dreams and expectations. So proud of myself, Ben, you actually DID IT!!

Now need to get London ready, feel confident and be 100% happy in my own skin! I am so bad – never had a relationship, get so moody and defensive…I hate being so defensive…but I need to remember: I am alive, I am here, I have amazing friends and now amazing A-levels – I'm all about good vibes now, and all about CONFIDENCE! I get so nervous, and it needs to stop before London…it's time to be confident!

I am scared to move away – I love my little bubble and life, but I suppose I can go and succeed in London. If I am kind, funny and friendly – surely people will like me? Can't go wrong if you enjoy it – enjoying this experience is what it's all about!

I log into Kooth and send this message to Dana: "Hey Dana, so sorry to have missed you this evening!!! [I had missed a booked online counselling session] I just wanted to let you know I got A*A*A in my A-levels – so happy, thank you for all your amazing support I couldn't have done it without you!! So I'm going to go to King's College London!! Speak to you soon. Thank you SO much for everything you have been truly amazing" (sic).

Dana replies: "That is such amazing news – I knew you could do it and I am so pleased for you!!"

***

That evening, Becky, Freya and Kristina go out in Macclesfield to celebrate. I am so proud of them all, and I am so excited about our next chapters. 'Where do you think we will all be in 12 months?' I ask on the dance floor, realising that everything in our lives is going to change in just a matter of weeks. I hadn't let myself think this far ahead yet, and it was now dawning on me that I was actually off to London! I was going to be getting in the car and driving 175 miles down to the capital city…and I would be living there for three years! It was the most surreal, terrifying and exciting thought in the world. 'Let's get more drinks', I say to Kristina, and we head off in search of the bar!

The next week, I am checking into a Premier Inn with Liddy, several bottles of wine in hand. We are in Manchester for the Manchester Pride weekend, and I could not be more excited for my first ever pride. I do not have any clue what on earth to expect, but I cannot wait to find out. All I know is that I plan on having plenty of drinks and showcasing a range of outrageously provocative outfits. These include a tiny mesh crop top and bright red running shorts. In other words, it will be a miracle if Greater Manchester Police do not arrest me. My fake tan is, for the first time in my life, actually looking good. And Liddy and I are in good spirits as we head off towards Canal Street.

It is the best end to my summer, and it is the best boost in confidence before I head down to London. I have never felt happier, and I have never felt prouder of who I am. I cannot wait to see what life in London will be like. I cannot wait for a brand-new start in the big city. I'm going to face my fears, make new friends, and be fearlessly authentic! Is this happening? Am I actually about to move down to London…for three years?! Yes, I think to myself, I actually am! This is my time to finally find my feet and start living out my dreams. I could not be more excited about what the future has in store!

22. LONDON'S CALLING

I have never felt so nervous in my life. It is Saturday 15th September 2018, and I am sat in back on my dad's car. We are on the way down to London, and I could not be more terrified. I am surrounded by bedding, cushions, kitchen utensils, jars, toiletries, clothes, and books. I cannot believe that this day has finally arrived – I am driving down to London, where I will be living for the next three years. Before this 175-mile move, I have only ever visited London for a day or two of sightseeing with my family. We'd first come down when I was aged eight and Sam was aged 5 to watch 'Joseph and the Amazing Technicolour Dreamcoat'.

The memories that I have of London are of a busy, bustling, and enormous city that was both terrifying and exciting at the same time. As a young boy, I was mesmerised by the bright lights and the never-ending bustle of this electrifying city. Walking around London with my parents, everyone seemed important and everywhere seemed exciting. I loved our hometown back in the suburbs of Cheshire, but there was something magnetic about this massive city. I remember returning to London several times over the years and becoming obsessed with the city. We did all of the cliché tourist attractions – the London Eye, Buckingham Palace, Covent Garden and the West End shows. As I sat in the back of my dad's car, surrounded by half of Ikea and with enough pasta to last thirty years, I thought back to these little trips down to London. I knew, of course, that living in the city would be extremely different from visiting for 48 hours! And I knew that I'd be spending my time in Lidl, not riding the London Eye. But I was excited about experiencing this new side of London! And I was so looking forward to being one of *those* busy people jumping on and off the tube! I couldn't wait to be one of those people racing around London with somewhere to go and someone to see! I was excited to meet all of these new and exciting people, and I was excited to call this extraordinary city home!

As we arrived in Stratford, where my student accommodation was located in the gorgeous Olympic Park, I felt sick to my stomach. I need a drink, I thought, as the Olympic Stadium came into view and it finally dawned on me that there was no turning back. I could no longer just swan around Macclesfield thinking 'I'm going to study at King's College, London' – I now had to well and truly walk the walk!

As I stepped out of the care, my hands shaking, I thought back to the last time I was in Stratford. It was almost exactly six years earlier when my parents had brought us down to London to watch the 2012 Paralympic Games. I had deep into my battle with anorexia at this time, and all I can remember is being so cold, frail and unwell. A picture of me standing on the Olympic Park main bridge – looking like nothing but skin and bones – still haunts me to this day. The last time I was in this Olympic Park, I was so desperately ill and sick. I can vividly remember sitting in the Olympic Park McDonalds – the world's biggest at the time – and eating nothing more than two chicken nuggets and carrot sticks from the Happy Meal. That Summer, known as the UK's Golden Summer of Sport, was the lowest point and darkest time of my life. It is heartbreaking to think back to that desperately ill and unhappy young boy who was walking along this very path into the Olympic Park just six years ago. As I walked towards the student accommodation, I thought for a moment about how far I had come. In those past six years, I had managed to turn my life around. I didn't recognise the ill 12-year-old boy who had posed in this Olympic Park all those years ago. I had been on, I realised, quite a journey! And I needed to be so proud of how far I had come!

Things had come full circle – if only 12-year-old anorexic Ben could have seen me now! Where was that crystal ball when I needed it?! I genuinely couldn't believe it; here I was in Stratford, somewhere that was once the backdrop to my battle with the eating disorder that nearly claimed my life. How much had changed! I was back, but this time I was here as the very best version of myself. This time, I was a confident, positive and successful 18-year-old who took mental health seriously and genuinely appreciated the gift of their life. And I wanted to walk into this new chapter of my life with nothing but confidence, positivity, and genuine self-belief.

So my mum, dad and I – just take a guess who was carrying all of the luggage! - walked into the Stratford One reception. This was, of course, in the pre-Covid world (yes, I'm that old!) The place was heaving with students arriving from all four corners of the globe. There were suitcases, parents and – of course – students everywhere. I felt a little overwhelmed, but I was resolutely determined to make a good start and positive first impression of what was now my new home. I checked into the residence before heading off with my parents to find my brand new room. There were over 24 floors in the property, and I was looking forward to a panoramic view overlooking the London skyline. It transpired that my first-floor room had a delightful view overlooking the Stratford International Eurostar train lines. I even had a glimpse of the DLR train track and, on a good day, could see the builders and their cranes constructing some swanky new flats on the other side of the train line. I may not have been able to see Big Ben, but I did get to hear the inspirational *'the next train to arrive on platform two does not stop here…'* announcement every 5-10 minutes. I was living the dream!

I got over my lack of panoramic skyline view and headed into our kitchen. We had two fridges, two ovens, plenty of cupboards, a lovely sofa and breakfast bar. And, from our first-floor window, we had a lovely view of the London Stadium and Orbit statue. In the distance, we could see the skyscrapers of Canary Wharf. Looking beneath us, we could see the Red London Buses as they came in towards Westfield. It felt – to state the obvious – like London! This was a more Instagram-friendly photo opportunity! My mum helped me unpack all of these strange and never-seen-before kitchen utensils that she had taken great pleasure in buying for me.

Meanwhile, my Dad completed another couple of trips to get my stuff out of the car (the poor man!) We got to work making my room as cosy and homely as possible before I sent my poor parents on their way. I was desperate to say goodbye to them before I could get too upset about being away from home. And I wanted them off the premises before they could embarrass me in front of any new flatmates! My poor dad had just driven 175 miles down to London, and I was sending them both back to the car again in little more than 17.5 minutes. I believe that they went off to grab a McDonalds in Westfield – they were living the dream – and then headed home, wondering how I would get on living my brand-new life in London.

With everything unpacked and my room feeling a little more like home, I was ready to start mingling and meet these brand-new flatmates. I also wanted to get a feel for the local area – I had, of course, been in Stratford once before, but I did not have a clue where anything was. I knew that the enormous Westfield shopping centre was right next door, and I knew that the Olympic Park was right across the road. Still, other than that, I was in very unfamiliar territory. I wanted to get a feel for my new surroundings, and I wanted things to feel a little bit more like home. That evening, the accommodation ambassadors were hosting a 'pizza party', where everyone could gather, get to know other residents and enjoy some free pizza. The offer of free pizza is, as any student will tell you, one that is too good to refuse! So I headed down to the 'pizza party' and got my best small-talk conversation starters ready!

At the pizza party, I meet a lovely couple of girls who radiated nothing but positivity and kindness. I instantly felt more at ease – there are nice, kind and friendly people here, I thought! One of them reminded me of Freya, my best friend back home, which meant I wanted to cling onto her for dear life! We had some pizza, chatted to some other students, and went off to explore the building. I still hadn't met anyone from my flat at this stage, so I was making as many friends as I possibly could! It's so strange when you enter a new social situation, don't you think, because you do not know a single thing about a single person! You just want to make as many friends as you possibly can – only time will tell if they become friends for life or if you forget about each other within a month! You chat to so many people, and you try to make as many friends as you possibly can, networking away as if your life depends on it! Well, I suppose you could say that your social life depends on it, and so it makes sense to take your 'Hi, what are you studying?' small talk questions seriously!

I must have made a good impression because the next night the girls asked me if I wanted to go to a King's Residences BBQ with them. The BBQ was taking place at Guy's Campus, which was just next to the Shard. I was so excited! We had to order purple t-shirts that said 'STRATFORD ONE' – fashion at it's finest, don't you agree. We were told to meet in a communal area at Stratford One so that we could all travel over together. We all met, as planned, in our purple t-shirts and, in my case, the skinniest pair of black jeans I could find. I needed to try and save this outfit somehow, I thought! We then all headed off to Stratford tube station, where we jumped on the Jubilee line and headed off to London Bridge. I had used the tube with my parents before – we had once stayed out in Harrow. We spent about two hours on the Bakerloo line travelling into Oxford Circus! But I was most certainly no Tube map expert – not by this stage, anyway – and so everything went by in a complete and utter blur!

We arrived at London Bridge and headed into Guy's campus, where a whole rainbow of different colours met our sea of purple t-shirts. Every residence had been assigned a different coloured t-shirt. So everyone was now wandering around, looking for food and drink, in a mass of different colours. As we joined the – very long – queue for the BBQ, we realised that the group in front of us were also wearing purple Stratford One t-shirts. Well, you know what I'm like, I had to strike up a conversation with these girls. It turned out that they were all staying in a first floor flat – just like me – but over in Block B. Their kitchen was the next window along from my own! And so we all became one big group of purple t-shirts. I remember complaining about the length of the BBQ queue and our inability to track down any hot boys from any of the different Residences. Well, these girls revealed that their strategy was to track down a boy in a light blue t-shirt because 'light blue' meant they were staying in an accommodation called 'Atlas'. Atlas, they informed us, was the place to be – they had a gym, swimming pool and a very high weekly rent to pay! From that moment on, we were united by our shared mission of tracking down the Atlas boys and securing access to that exclusive swimming pool!

Later on, we finally get our hands on the BBQ food. We're still busy trying to work out where on earth these Atlas boys were all hiding. A couple of the girls needed to go off and collect a ticket for a Freshers event they were going off to. And so I was left sitting under a tree with Morgan, who I thought was a stunning girl who radiated the most positive energy and class. Immediately, I launched into my go-to Freshers question of the year – how is your love life? I started asking about boys and whether she had a boyfriend. 'No, I have a girlfriend' she replied, leaving me, as she will tell you, speechless for a solid 0.5 seconds. I hadn't thought of that one! I regained my composure, made a mental note to stop asking such assumptive questions, and knew from that very second we would become the best of friends. And we did! Without giving any spoilers away, we would spend the next year ditching LGBT+ society bar crawls to go on our own Prosecco-fuelled outings, leaving chaos in our wake and returning to Stratford One unable to open our flat front doors! We'd later live together in Stratford One during the second year, spending our evenings drinking prosecco and eating Lidl chicken nuggets! Unfortunately, the coronavirus lockdown struck before we had a chance to become Stratford's answer to Jamie Oliver! That's an absolute hate crime if you ask me!

Anyway, back to the first year, and I am feeling so incredibly blessed to have found Morgan. Morgan very quickly became my rock, best friend and Prosecco partner-in-crime. I am also delighted to finally meet Maisie and Carl, who have also just moved into our Flat 105. We quickly bonded over the angry notes left for us by our long-suffering cleaner Ava-Maria, as well as our shared love for the iconic memes produced about Kim Woodburn, Katie Price and Kerry Katona. These are two of the most intelligent and politically-aware individuals you could ever to ever meet. Carl is studying medicine, and Maisie is reading Liberal Arts. As well as being so intelligent and bright, these two are also the friendliest, most down-to-earth and sociable people in the world. It is a lottery who you end up living with at your student accommodation, and in our lovely (not to mention iconic) Flat 105 I had absolutely hit the jackpot. We laughed our way through the first year, and I mean it when I say that I could not have asked for better flatmates!

Along with Maisie and Carl, we also had several other lovely flatmates, including Phoebe and Janssen. I loved how friendly, genuine and easygoing everyone was. How on earth they managed to live with me (and my daily fake tan fiascos) for an entire year is completely beyond me!

I spend my first week living in Stratford trying to make sense of where I am and get settled into London life. I head out and about in the Olympic Park, Westfield Shopping Centre, Stratford High Street, and even into Central London. At first, I find the tube map utterly daunting and confusing. I jump onto a Westbound Central Line train, and hope for the best! To my relief, it turns out that I'm heading in the right direction, and I soon arrive at

Tottenham Court Road. I head out of the tube station – which will end up feeling like a home-from-home for the next three years –, and I'm on Oxford Street, the bustling heart of the capital's retail industry. I'm here today on a mission – to find a job! In my hands, I'm clutching about 12 copies of my CV, which I'm planning to hand out. As I make my way down Oxford Street, I see all of Britain's biggest high street brands. There's an enormous M&S, a brightly illuminated Sports Direct, and, of course, a massive Primark. I walk along amongst the tourists and workers, wondering where on earth I should start. Could I see myself working in any of these stores? Would they appreciate me walking in and handing them my CV?

As I continue my internal debate, I suddenly have an idea. I remember that Soho – the beating heart of London's gay scene – is just five minutes away. I'd walked through Soho before when I had come down to London for a university induction day. I had been so excited and, of course, had constantly been refreshing my dating apps to see who was nearby! It was now about 12 pm, which meant I could walk through Soho and post my CV under the doors. I start to get excited about the idea of working in a gay bar. Not only would it mean that I could find the gay friends that I craved, but it also meant that I'd be in the perfect place to be meeting guys. I would, I thought, be getting paid to have a night out and flirt! As you can imagine, I was sold! And so I pulled out my phone and checked how far away Soho was. It turned out Oxford Street was quite literally thirty seconds from the heart of Soho. It's meant to be, I thought to myself! It's a divine intervention! I followed the on-screen instructions, and, before I knew it, I found myself in Soho Square. This Square would become a regular destination over the years ahead, as you can imagine!

I excitedly walked through Soho, nervously posting my CV through the letterboxes of the bars I encountered. After my summer nights of nights out on Canal Street in Manchester, I wanted nothing more than a job working in one of these LGBT+ venues! I was too scared to start any conversations or directly ask anybody for a job. So I made sure my CV contained my phone number and email address, and I hoped that at least one of these venues would get in touch! I finished my CV distributing, and I headed back to Tottenham Court Road. I manage to find the Eastbound Central

Line platform, and I am soon back in Stratford (19 minutes later, to be precise!) I love that Stratford has so much greenery and feels very spacious, and yet it is still only 20 minutes on the tube from the very centre of London! I felt like I had found somewhere I could feel safe, secure, and yet also so well connected to Central London! It was the best of both worlds, and I felt as though I was living the dream!

***

The next morning, I receive an email from the Bars Manager at Heaven Nightclub. That's quick, I think, I didn't expect a response so soon! Then I realise that I hadn't posted my CV through a bar called Heaven, and I remember that I'd actually applied for this job weeks ago online! I had been getting excited about moving to London, and I'd been looking on Gumtree – or another one of those job websites – for parttime jobs I could apply for. I'd seen an advert for 'bar support staff' at a venue called Heaven which, according to Wikipedia, is 'a superclub in Charing Cross' with a 'long association with London's LGBT+ scene'. That was all the information I had needed! I had quickly submitted my CV and applied, before forgetting all about it…until today! The email was inviting me to attend the venue – located just off Trafalgar Square – for an interview. My heart was beating faster – of course; I would love an interview! I quickly replied and agreed to attend for an interview at 8.45 pm on Monday.

***

Monday night comes around far too quickly. To say that I am terrified as I jump onto the tube at Stratford station is perhaps the understatement of the century! I arrive in Central London at around 7.30 pm, making sure that, considering the (extremely likely) possibility of getting lost, I have plenty of time to spare. I walk down the Strand and past King's College London, where I am set to attend my first lecture the following Monday. It doesn't get more central than this, I think, walking past Waterloo bridge and taking a quick glimpse at the iconic London skyline. I reach Charing Cross Station and look around. According to Google Maps, the club is just off the road here. That's all well and good, I think, but all I can see is a Sushi restaurant, train station…and Trafalgar Square! I decide to walk down a road towards Embankment Tube station, looking around for any kind of clues that might reveal the whereabouts of this nightclub. My heart is pounding, and my palms are sweating. I'm feeling extremely anxious. I'm anxious because of my inability to find the venue, and also because I'm about to have a JOB INTERVIEW IN CENTRAL LONDON! I have absolutely no clue what on earth to expect. I know absolutely nothing about working in a nightclub, and I know absolutely nothing about this venue. What am I doing right now? I am an 18-year-old boy who has been in London for no more than four days, and here I am, standing in the centre of the city on my way to a job interview at Europe's biggest LGBT+ nightclub. I take a moment to just ask myself, what on earth is going on?!

I give myself a little pep talk, commanding myself to 'think positive' and 'exude confidence'. 'You've got this', I tell myself, 'just go in there and shine'. I eventually find the club, hidden away under the arches of Villiers Street, and I command myself to stay calm. I walk towards the entrance, where security is setting up barriers for the busy night ahead. I remind myself that this is a gay club, and so I should be in my absolute element! I surely don't need to worry about being seen as 'too much' or 'too gay' here! I put on my biggest smile, make eye contact with one of the bouncers, and deliver the most confidence 'hello, how are you?' I can manage. Here we go, I think, let's do this!

Before I know it, I am being escorted down the stairs and into the nightclub, which is about one hundred times bigger than any club I have been in before. We walk through the main room, which is easily bigger than the sports hall and assembly hall back at my high school. I get a glimpse at the labyrinth of different rooms, corridors, bars, and stages around this enormous club. The venue is genuinely massive, and I am taken up another flight of stairs and into the backstage area and offices. As I walk, I imagine what this club must be like on a typical Saturday night. I have never been out in London before, and I can only imagine what the crowds and atmosphere in this venue must be like. How amazing it would be, I think, to be working here at the very heart of the London nightlife and the epicentre of the London gay scene. I enter the office where the two bar managers are waiting to interview me.

The interview goes well, and I'm offered a trial shift that Friday night. Hallelujah! I've got to arrive for 10 pm, I am told, and I'll be working through until around 5 am. Oh my God, I think, realising that I had not considered the hours involved in working at a nightclub! These hours could potentially present a problem for my sleep schedule. On a typical weeknight, I would be tucked up in bed and drifting off to sleep by 10 pm…not starting a seven-hour shift at work! Despite my sleep-cycle concerns, I nod and smile at this information, deciding that I'll sort out my sleep situation at a later date! I'll be working on the 'coffee shop' bar which – and yes, I am genuinely serious now – sells sandwiches, crisps, tea, coffee and Ice Creams. That's right, the club is so big that there are not only dozens of drinks bars, but there is also a coffee shop squeezed in there as well! You may laugh, but I actually love the idea that I'll be selling sandwiches and ice creams. And I could not be more relieved not to be going anywhere near an actual bar! I leave the interview with a spring in my step; I am on cloud nine and beyond excited to have secured this trial shift. I've made it, I think; my love life starts right here! I walk through Trafalgar Square and head into McDonald's for a celebratory Mayo Chicken. By now, I'm already dreaming about all the guys I'll be getting with! Of course, I am! I'm also excited about all the new gay friends I'll be able to finally make! So I call my friend Emma and tell her the good news, before calling Queen P to give her an update as well. She is slightly concerned that I am wandering around Central London on my own at almost 10 pm but says she is 'so pleased' for me. Never mind the degree, I tell her, my love life starts right here!

I get back to Stratford on an absolute high. I've done it, I think to myself, I've gone out there and got a job! And it's not just any random job – I'm going to be working in a gay nightclub! On a Friday night…in the coffee shop! I simply cannot wait.

23. WORK HARD, PLAY HARDER

I spend the next few days feeling giddy and excited, and I try and decide on what I'm going to wear. I've been told to wear all black, so I head to River Island to buy the skinniest fit black shirt that I can find. Friday soon comes along, and I pull on my new skinny fit shirt and my super spray-on skinny fit black jeans. My fake tan is looking fabulous, and a quick spritz of my favourite CK One aftershave gives me the confidence boost I need. It may be 8 pm, but my night hasn't even got started! On nights out back at home, I would always be the one sneaking out of the club at about 1 am or 2 am. Well sneaking off wasn't an option tonight, I told myself! I was going to need a lot of caffeine to keep me going through until sunrise, I thought, genuinely wondering how people manage to work night shifts four or five days a week!

I arrive in Central London with plenty of time to spare, and I find that the Saturday night atmosphere in Soho is absolutely electric. I am nervous, excited and giddy with adrenaline – I just want to get in there and get started!

I genuinely don't think anything can prepare you for your first night out in Heaven, whether you are working or partying. There is nothing quite like it. From the balloons drops and confetti cannons to the live performances and screaming crowds, Heaven takes 'going out' to a whole other level. I was working with the loveliest boy, Pauric, who had drawn the short straw and been tasked with training me up in the Coffee Shop. The job was very straightforward, and I soon managed to work out how to use the bottle opener (I wish I was joking, but it's true!), work the till (unlocking it with the key was harder than it looked, let me tell you!) and do all the stock checks and tasks. By about 1 am, I was getting into my stride. Pauric dared to leave me alone for five minutes, and he looked seriously relieved to return and find that the coffee shop was still standing! By around 3 am, the tiredness was beginning to kick in. 'How do you do it every night?!' I asked Pauric, making myself a cup of tea with the coffee shop kettle and adding around twenty sugars. I was absolutely loving being here – I loved the buzz and the atmosphere of the venue – but I was also starting to feel very tired!

Nevertheless, the adrenaline powered me through, and we made it – by some caffeine-fuelled miracle – to 5 am. Pauric talked me through the stock count, cash up and how to lock up the coffee shop. As I took the rubbish bag out, I was overwhelmed by the atmosphere. Thousands of people, covered in confetti and clutching onto empty plastic cups, were here dancing the night away. I love this, I thought to myself, hoping that I'd done enough to secure myself the job.

After security had come to escort Pauric to the office with the night's cash takings, I headed backstage to see the bar managers. They said that they'd like to offer me a job and asked me if I could start the next night, Saturday. I thankfully and delightedly accepted, before heading off to navigate the night tube and get back to Stratford. As I arrived back at Stratford tube station, it was already daylight. It was now about 6 am, the time I would usually be waking up after a blissful night of sleep. I got back to my room, shut the curtains and passed out on my bed. I was utterly exhausted, but I was desperately excited to do it all over again in little over 12-hours-time. I'm going to need a lot of caffeine, I thought to myself, as I drifted off to sleep, just as the rest of the world woke up.

***

After about six or seven hours of a deep sleep, I woke up – feeling confused and disorientated – at about 1 pm. It took me a few seconds to realise where I was, what I was doing, and why I was waking up halfway through the day. As you know, I have always been an early bird who loves nothing more than 6.30 am starts! And yet, here I was, waking up at 1 pm…I didn't like it one bit! I was not used to this lifestyle at all…now, I thought, I know how my brother feels! I dragged myself out of bed, which felt like mission impossible, and jumped straight into the shower. I then pulled on some clothes, made myself a green tea, and tried to decide what to eat. Was I supposed to have a bowl of cereal and see this as breakfast time, even though it was now almost 2 pm? Or did I move straight onto lunch, despite the fact I had only just woken up? In the end, I am that hungry and tired that I end up having both, leaving my body clock and stomach somewhat confused! I then drag myself out for a walk around the Olympic Park, knowing that some fresh air would help to wake up and revive me.

The rest of the day is somewhat of a sleep-deprived blur, and before I know it, it's 8 pm and time to head off to work. I jump back on the Central Line and Westbound towards Tottenham Court Road. There, I change for the Northern Line, which takes me straight to Charing Cross. As I walk down from the station, I still can't believe that this is my new job! As if I am just one week into my time in London and I am now working in this massive gay club in the centre of London! I cannot believe it…and I love it! I'm soon back inside the venue and stocking up the coffee shop as almost 2,000 people come pouring in through the main doors. I love the fact that I'm able to work inside the nightclub, but that I have not been plunged in the deep end working on one of the busy bars. The teas and coffees aren't quite as in demand as the Vodka shots and jager bombs, but I am very happy with working in this role! It means I get to be here, soak up the atmosphere and meet new people, without people screaming at me to hurry up with their drinks! There is no way on this earth that I could work on one of the proper bars, where you'd constantly have hundreds of people shouting at you for a drink. I was only just managing to open a bottle of Desperados with a bottle opener. So imagine me trying to make ten vodka red bulls and ten rum and cokes within sixty seconds!

As the night went on, I kept myself busy and tried not to think about how tired I was feeling. I loved the job, but I did not love feeling so tired! I knew right then that I'd be unable to sustain this night after night – one 5 am had nearly finished me off, never mind two in a row! I made a mental note to ask the bar managers about whether I'd be able to just do one night a week. I'm then kept busy making myself another cup of tea (yes, a cup of tea in a nightclub!) and tidying up and sorting out the stock. All of a sudden, two faces appeared at the coffee shop. It was two boys, who introduced themselves as Darragh and Alfee. They worked on the promotions team for the venue and were doing the balloons and confetti cannons all night. I instantly liked these two – they were friendly, outgoing and seemed a lot of fun. We chatted away until they had to go and do their next balloon drop, leaving me to keep busy running the coffee shop.

I make it to the end of the night and, with a security escort, take the night's cash takings to the management office. The managers ask me how the night went, and I ask them about only working one night a week. At first, the answer is no but, by some miracle, they agree to let me do just Saturdays. I am delighted, knowing that I'll only have to face a 5 am finish one night a week. I thank them profusely, so thankful to have this opportunity and get ready to head home. By this stage, I am well beyond tired and, I think, starting to go a bit delirious from the sleep deprivation. I then bump into Darragh and Alfee, who have also just finished and are planning to go out for breakfast. I am genuinely shocked by how anybody could have the energy for anything other than sleep by this stage. Oh, I envy their total lack of tiredness! I like the look of these two and think about how much I would love to get to know them more. They are exactly the kind of friends I've been hoping to make ever since arriving in London! And so, I pluck up the courage to ask them if they fancy going out for food and a drink later in the week. To my surprise – and relief – they agree, so we exchange socials before I practically sleepwalk my way out of the club and get myself onto the night tube home. With the sun rising and the birds tweeting, I arrive back in Stratford feeling like I could hibernate for months. I fall straight into a deep sleep, despite the caffeine, adrenaline and sugar still buzzing around in my brain, and I don't wake up until around 4 pm the next day. When I do finally pull myself out of bed and get something to eat – a mix of breakfast, lunch and dinner all in one - I think back to the past week and everything that's happened. I may have only been in London for seven days, but it feels like I've been here for seven weeks or even seven months. I've managed to take on the tube, make some new friends, track down the nearest Lidl, and get myself a new job at the heart of London's gay scene. So far, I think, so good! There's only one thing left to get into, and that's my university degree…the whole reason that I am here in London in the first place! I wonder what the teaching will be like, what the people will be like, and whether I'll be able to find my lecture theatres (I'll be honest, I'm not holding my breath!)…

Right now, I'm delighted to have had some sleep, and I'm proud to have found my feet over the past week. Everything is going well, and things are about to get exciting! All of my dreams are coming true, and I could not be more excited. Let's do this London!

24. LECTURES, READING & RUSH HOUR IN LONDON

It's 9 am on an Autumnal Monday Morning, and I have just made it to my first ever university lecture on time. When I say that it this feels like a modern miracle, I do mean it. I had left Stratford in what – I had thought at least – was plenty of time. I made sure I was at Stratford tube station by 8 am, which would give me a whole hour to get into Central. It only took 16 minutes to get to Holborn, leaving me with plenty of time to walk down to Campus, and find my lecture theatre. On paper, it sounded like a perfect, totally stress-free plan. In reality, it was absolutely anything but.

The fun and games began when I had arrived at Stratford tube station amid the utter carnage of the early morning rush hour. Why had I not considered that I might not be the only person in London with someone to be at 8 am on a Monday?! I made it through the ticket gates and down to the Westbound Central Line platform, which was a complete sea of commuters, builders, and everyday people. The platform was packed with people – there were at least seven rows of people between me and the edge of the platform! How on earth was I supposed to ever make it onto a train, I wondered, especially considering that all of the trains pulling into the platform were full to the brim already? Trains would come and go, but the number of people impatiently waiting on the platform seemed to constantly remain the same. After three trains had been through, I was finally making progress towards the front of the platform. It felt like a World War and military battle – it was every man, woman and commuter for themselves in the battle to get onto the Central Line! I finally made it to the front, just as the next train – they were, fortunately, coming every 30 seconds by this stage – pulled into the platform. The doors opened, and absolutely nobody moved. The carriage was packed to bursting point. People were practically standing on top of each other and clinging on for dear life. This was not the kind of intimacy that I needed with the commuters of London at any time of the day, never mind first thing on a Monday morning! Taking advantage of my 5"6 and slim build, I was able to squeeze my way amongst the sea of people, just delighted to be on board a train that was heading in the right direction.

Well, this is very cosy, I think to myself, as I feel a man's breath on the back of my neck and I desperately try not to fall into the poor woman standing in front of me. There was literally no room to move, and I just prayed that I would remain upright as the train hurtled around corners and arrived in the next station, Mile End. Here was the next opportunity for some early-morning excitement. That's because it now turned out that half of the carriage wanted to get off here, whilst a whole mass of people wanted to pile off the Mile End platform and onto the train. I clung onto my bag as I was jolted and hustled about by people fighting to get on and off the train. Oh my God, I think to myself, this is some next-level endurance challenge! What a way to start your Monday! I fight just to stay on the train – no mean feat when you're being pushed in every direction – and I genuinely breathe (or try to breathe!) a sigh of relief as the doors close, and we depart. This commute was making my leisurely walks to school with Becky look more relaxing than a Himalayan Buddhist meditation retreat. The London commute is cut-throat, sink or swim! Suppose you're not prepared to practically fight your way into Central London. In that case, you do not have a chance of going anywhere near Zone 1 anytime before 10 am!

Fourteen minutes later and Holborn is finally the next station. I realise that I haven't considered how I am going to get off this train, and I somehow don't think that just whispering 'excuse me…oh I'm so sorry!' is quite going to cut it! Well, I think, I'm going to have to just get in the zone and go for it – I've got a lecture to get to, and there is no way I am being stuck on this Central Line all the way to West Ruislip! Fortunately, God appears to have decided that he has tested me enough this morning, and it just so happens that the doors I am clinging onto for dear life just so happen to be on the right side for this platform. Halleluiah! I pull myself together, take a deep breath and jump off the train at the earliest opportunity. I follow the one million and one other commuters also heading up the escalators and tapping out in the ticket hall.

I step outside, inhale as much fresh air as possible, and head straight in the direction of campus. Now that I'm in Central, it really feels like I am in London. I walk past the Lyceum theatre, where Queen P and Dad brought us to see The Lion King many years ago. I catch a glimpse of Waterloo bridge, which provides some of the best tourist photo-opportunities in London. It doesn't get much better than this, I think, although I really should focus on being on time for my lecture! I check the university app to find out where I'm going and head in what – I think – is the right direction. A wild goose chase around the Bush House building later, and I've miraculously ended up outside the right lecture theatre. I feel like I have run about ten triathlons and been subjected to ten major life traumas, and it's not even 9 am! Relieved, and ready to pass out, I head into the lecture theatre

This morning's lecture is for the module 'Elements of Ethics', which is one of eight modules I've picked to date during my first year studying at King's. We study four modules a semester, with each module a total of ten weeks long. My eight modules for this academic year are:

Eight module selections for my first year studying theology:

- **Study Skills (compulsory)**
- **Introduction to Islam**
- **New Testament: Origins, Meanings & Contexts**
- **Elements of Ethics**
- **Theology and Culture – Christian Perspectives**
- **Introduction to the Philosophy of Religion**
- **Introduction to Religion and Politics**
- **Introduction to Buddhism**

The lecture begins, and I am instantly not a fan of the lecturer. He is rude, abrupt and overflowing with attitude. He describes me as 'extraordinarily camp', and he has picked on me to answer a question which he thinks I look too stupid to answer. The look of shock – and newfound respect – on his face when I deliver an impeccable answer explaining the concept of 'metaethics' makes having got up so early this morning worth it! I love proving people wrong like this. I love being able to defy all of their stereotype-based assumptions about me. I am fascinated by how human beings so easily take one glance at someone and instantly place them in a box. We are all, I think, guilty of having made split-second judgements about people that have turned out to be wrong. For example, some people take one look at me and assume that I am an unintelligent, bitchy, and lacking in any substance as a person. They caricature me and see me as nothing more than a stereotype, expecting me to talk about nothing other than reality TV, fashion and makeup. Now, don't get me wrong; I am more than happy to discuss Kris Jenner, skincare and the latest celebrity gossip now and then. But what people don't realise is that I am also more than capable of discussing the big questions in politics, philosophy, ethics, psychology, sociology and current affairs. I see this underestimation as a real strength – it's a 'secret weapon'! I take advantage of the fake that people are so quick to underestimate me and put me in a stereotype-shaped box. If they aren't capable of seeing beyond the stereotypes and assumptions, then more fool them! Indeed, mum has always taught me the value of being the 'underdog'. Whilst people are busy labelling you and underestimating your talents, you can be working hard to get ahead and achieve success!

I survive my first lecture and, despite being put on the spot by the lecturer, I am excited for the semester ahead. I head off the campus and out onto the Strand, looking forward to a busy day in London. The first thing I've got planned is a coffee date with a lovely-looking girl I have met online. Her name is Shadi, and she first got in touch with me after watching one of my English language revision videos on YouTube. She had messaged me saying that she was always starting at King's that September, and asked whether I fancied going for a coffee. I would love to, I had replied, and I was excited to meet a new friend in this big city! I can vividly remember standing on the Strand and waiting for Shadi when I suddenly spot her little red beret coming into view! 'Hello you angel!', I exclaimed, embracing her with the world's biggest hug. 'I hope you don't think I'm a total weirdo for messaging you', she says, 'but I just loved your English language videos!'

We sit down with a cup of tea and croissant in Pret and immediately start putting the world to rights. Within seconds, I am absolutely in love with

Shadi. She is gorgeous, intelligent, and is 100% on my wavelength. I love her attitude and her aura. We instantly get off like a house on fire. Little to we know it, but this ends up being just the first of hundreds of coffee dates here on the Strand. We chat about our lives and our first impressions of our new courses. It quickly becomes apparent that Shadi is an absolute angel. She genuinely has the best energy and, as I say, she is completely on the same page as me. It's so refreshing – and reassuring – to find someone who is exuding so much wisdom, kindness, and common sense. 'I'm going to be clinging onto you for dear life over the next three years', I tell Shadi. And - quite literally three years later - I think she might have now finally realised that I wasn't joking!

***

Thank God I had found Shadi, who introduced me to her equally angelic – not to mention gorgeous – friend from Brighton, Farah. The three of us became a formidable trio, enjoying regular coffee dates and even a night out or two along the way! In my first few weeks in London, I was fortunate to quickly make friends with some of the loveliest people in the world. I would enjoy countless Pret dates, lunch dates and cocktail dates over the weeks and months ahead. But there was something, how can I say this, just not quite right about the atmosphere on my course. Nobody seemed to want to talk to anybody new – or maybe they just didn't want to talk to me! People seemed overwhelmed by my desire to make conversation and socialise. A lot of people seemed very quiet, reserved and unconcerned with meeting new people. There is, of course, nothing wrong with wanting to keep your head down or sit with the people you already know. But I had expected the first few weeks at university to be a frenzy of people starting conversations, exchanging social media handles, and forging as many new friendships as possible. This did not seem to be the case on my course! At the end of the day, I think it's complete luck who you end up being put in lecture theatres and seminar groups with. Unfortunately, it just was not my lucky day! If I'm brutally honest, it felt as if these people had started social distancing a whole two years before the Coronavirus had struck! They did not appear to appreciate my attempts at friendliness! And they did not seem interested in my offer of going for an after-lecture drink! Now, don't get me wrong; they were lovely people. They just did not seem to quite be on my personal level or wave-length.

So thank God that I was busy making friends at Heaven, in my accommodation, and over coffee in Pret! If you're starting university, then let me just give you some advice. Don't worry if the first people you meet don't become your new best friends for life! Don't worry if everybody you cross paths with doesn't happen to be your cup of tea! You are going to have plenty more opportunities to make friends, meet new people, and find your crowd! So just keep positive, remain confident, and keep putting yourself out there! You will – I promise – find your people soon!

Most importantly, don't think that the problem is with you! It's just one of those (unfortunate) things! Everything will work out if you just keep putting yourself out there! And if anybody doesn't want to be friends with you, just remember that it's their loss and not yours! You will found your crowd soon enough! So keep being yourself, and keep putting yourself out there!

25. JUST CALL ME NIGELLA?

Moving into a self-catered university residence was a big step (even if I didn't realise it at the time) in terms of my eating disorder recovery journey. For the first time in my life, I am being left entirely left to my own devices. I will be fully responsible for the food that I will be eating every single day of the week. I would be entirely responsible for my weekly shop and my daily meals – it was all completely under my control. This would be interesting in terms of my relationship with food. If any anorexic impulses or tendencies were hiding away deep in my mind, then surely this would be there opportunity to resurface and take root once again? With my family 175 miles away and all the stresses of moving into a brand new living environment and routine, this could have been the perfect opportunity for anorexia to return with a vengeance.

I genuinely love nothing more than doing my grocery shopping in Stratford. Somebody get me on Real Housewives of Cheshire immediately! I get an extraordinary amount of pleasure from wandering around Lidl, mooching around Sainsbury's, and meandering around Waitrose. It's such a therapeutic, relaxing and enjoyable experience! I love seeing what's on offer and planning what I'm going to eat in the week ahead. More importantly, I was genuinely doing it all in a very healthy way. I know, I even surprised myself! I made sure that I ate three healthy meals – breakfast, lunch and dinner – every day, and I was very much of the mindset that 'I need to eat a good diet to have the energy to love my time in London!'

As my mum had always told me, you need to eat well to do all of the things that you love – food is your fuel for achieving success and living your best life! I enjoyed heading off to Sainsbury's, Lidl and Waitrose (I know, living the high life) to do my shopping for the week ahead. Forever a creature of habit, I soon decided where I'd be getting different things from! I'd go to Sainsbury's for my milk and cereal, and I'd visit Lidl for my chicken nuggets and sandwich wraps. Meanwhile, I'd head to Waitrose for my mayonnaise and strawberry jam! I would always try to get as much fresh and healthy food as possible. For example, I made sure that I always had iceberg lettuce, tomatoes and a cucumber in the fridge. I would also become obsessed with the Hovis Granary Sensations bread (I was very specific – it had to be the blue one that cost 95p in Waitrose!)! There was never a day that my freezer was not stocked with those Lidl chicken nuggets and the M&S frozen fries!

So grocery shopping becomes my new go-to hobby. I also fall in love with homeware shopping and - don't ask me why - I discover that I also have a passion for toiletry shopping. Nothing makes me happier than buying M&S soaps and handwash! I find that there's something so satisfying about arranging your bathroom cabinet and positioning your hand wash by the sink (or is that just me?!)

I've lined my shelves with books, and I've got my Calvin Klein, and Ralph Lauren aftershaves lined up on the windowsill. My room is looking homely, but it needs a few finishing touches. I head off to Primark and buy out their homeware section, leaving with three giant paper bags filled with cushions, blankets and reed diffusers. I am living my very best interior design fantasy! I create a wall of colour co-ordinated cushions along my bed, and I get busy making my little room as cosy and homely as possible. I absolutely love it! It's my modern, cosy and safe space. It's my little home from home, where I feel completely at ease. When I'm not working at Heaven or catching up with Carl in the kitchen, I love nothing more than a cosy night in. Nothing makes me happier than lying in bed with my fairy lights on, a cup of tea in hand, and Real Housewives of Cheshire playing on my laptop. Well, there's no better way of ending a day than with a milky cup of tea and a dose of Dawn Ward!

I love all my little domestic duties, and it's so enjoyable to be doing everything for myself. I feel like my idol, Kris Jenner, only I'm designing an East London en-suite and not a Beverley Hills mansion! I love this opportunity to take responsibility for my life and create my own little 'home' here in Stratford.

***

I thoroughly enjoy cooking for myself, even if my culinary repertoire would not quite sweep Nigella off her feet. I am a big lover of routine, and I enjoy eating similar meals at similar times every day of the week. For example, I will always have my Sainsbury's cereal at 7 am every morning, and I will always make my dinner at 5.30 pm every evening. I felt very 'safe' in the food that I was eating – I knew what portion sizes I was comfortable with, and I knew which foods I enjoyed!

When it comes to the food that I am eating, I always like to be in control. I like to be the one deciding what I will be eating and how much I will be eating. I still have a compulsive need to check the nutritional information, which is something the government is increasingly encouraging every single person to do anyway. Is this need to check calories and always be in control of what I'm eating a remnant of anorexia? I'll be extremely honest with you – I think it is. However, here is the important thing: it does not control or take over my life. It is more than manageable, and it is not getting in the way of my happiness, health or success. I find it very difficult not to instinctively check calories when the nutritional information of everything is plastered over every piece of packaging and food menu! It's an ingrained habit and routine part of my behaviour! I will still always choose a 'lower calorie' option on the menu, and I always think twice before eating anything with more than 500 calories in it. It is something I just 'live with', and I very rarely have any conscious awareness of it. I don't feel that it restricts my life or harms my health. As I say, I am now the master of my own destiny – not the anorexia. I have taken back control, and I am in charge of my behaviours…I will never become a slave to anorexic thoughts and compulsions again!

There is still, as there was back in the height of my eating disorder, a national obsession with weight. Some people call it a 'diet culture', which refers to a social environment in which weight loss is worshipped as a way of gaining attractiveness and status. Everywhere we look, we are bombarded with 'low-fat alternatives' and 'beach body boot camps'. I think the average person can compartmentalise their relationship with their weight and body. They recognise that their weight and appearance is just one tiny part of who they are as a person. For somebody battling from an eating disorder, however, this diet culture and fixation on weight becomes an all-consuming 24/7 struggle. I'm fortunate that this all-consuming struggle is no longer my reality.

Instead, I realise that food and appearance is just one tiny part of your life. I am learning that your weight or appearance does not define your attractiveness as a human being. I realise that weight gain is not the worst thing in the whole world. We cannot change the 'diet culture', and the 'diet culture' itself is not necessarily the problem. As Epictetus says 'men are not disturbed by things, but by the views which they take of things'. We have to take full responsibility for our relationship with the media and advertisers. We have to become the master of our destiny, and we have to take control of our thoughts, feelings and behaviours. I see it like this: you cannot blame the diet culture for your fixation on weight. You cannot see yourself as a victim to the media, advertisers or even society as a whole. You need to take full responsibility for how you respond to the messages you are exposed to in the world. You need to ensure you are making your happiness and wellbeing your number one priority. Here's what I tell myself: if you have identified a 'trigger', you need to do something about it! Be proactive in protecting your mental health, and get smart about the information you soak up from the world around you! Think rationally, evaluate the things you are believing, and always keep things in perspective!

***

I'm enjoying being so busy, and I very quickly settle into London life. I establish new routines and daily rituals, which keep me feeling calm and fulfilled. One thing that keeps happening is that I keep getting ILL. I've lost track of the number of times that I have woken up with a sore throat, blocked nose, or high temperature! Now, back in the pre-Covid days, I didn't think twice before jumping out of bed and soldiering on with my day, even if I felt like I'd been hit by a double-decker London bus! I refused to be defeated by my constant colds! I stopped drinking the tap water (which I was convinced was causing me sickness and spots!), and I started stocking up on vitamin and flu tablets! I don't know about anyone else, but I just absolutely hate being ill! I hate feeling like death and lacking in the energy to even get out of bed! Nothing infuriates me more than having so much I want to do and not having the energy to do it! I don't know what's in that London air, but I do know that it's wiping me out! I dread to think about what I might be catching on the Central Line at rush hour, and I am convinced that the 5 am finishes at work do not exactly help! But I am determined to make the most of every single day I have in London, and so I refuse to be defeated by illness or tiredness! It's funny to think that, in these times before the Coronavirus, we were all shameless 'super spreaders' of countless coughs and colds! I find that a healthy diet – with lots of fresh fruit and water – helps to revive me, along with plenty of cups of tea and bottles of water! I power through and continue taking London by storm, refusing to be defeated by constantly recurring colds!

***

The days and weeks that follow fly by, as I settle into the new routines of London life. I make sense of the Tube, find my way around the shops of Stratford, and meet some of the loveliest people in the city. I start to realise that London might not be quite as big as I had imagined. I realise, for example, that I can easily walk from the Strand to Soho. And I realise that I can easily navigate my way from Trafalgar Square to Regents Street (albeit with a bit of help from Google maps). As with anything, practice does make perfect! The more time that I spend exploring Central London the more confident I become finding my way around the city. I love heading off for little walks along the Thames, taking in the iconic landmarks whilst also discovering places off the tourist trail.

I've paid for a month-long Oyster Travelcard, which means I can go anywhere I want within Zones 1 and 2. I make full use of it, heading off for walks in Hyde Park and exploring the area around Tower Bridge! I love having so much freedom and autonomy! I love walking over Waterloo Bridge and thinking 'I actually live here in this incredible city!' Whilst it still doesn't feel real, I do feel like I'm getting into a very positive London routine. I'm finding my way around, and I'm finding that the days are flying by. I keep missing poor Queen P's calls, but I do keep the family WhatsApp chat updated with pictures from around London! I very selfishly did not consider that my parents might be worried about how I might be getting on in London, but at least I did send them selfies of me finishing work at 5 am on a Sunday! Whenever I did speak to Queen P, I (truthfully) assured her that I was living my best life and having the best time. I emailed Gran and Grumpy with pictures of my new room, complete with my view of the Eurostar train line! They were delighted to hear that I was getting on so well, although Gran nearly had a heart attack when she heard I was working in a nightclub until 5 am in the morning!

I'm so happy that London feels like a home-from-home. I love that I can travel between my two little worlds – London and Cheshire – and I love that I feel so comfortable in both places. I can be walking around Alderley Edge woods one day, and racing across Waterloo bridge the next!

I am absolutely addicted to London life – I love the pace, the energy and the buzz. Wherever I go, I am surrounded by busy people and iconic landmarks. Every single morning, I wake up ahead of another busy day racing across the capital. I am genuinely living my dreams, and I could not feel more blessed. It just shows; when you dream big and work hard, absolutely anything is possible in life! Even after a couple of weeks, I know that London is my new favourite place on the planet. Every day here feels like a dream. Will this novelty ever wear off? Will walking over Waterloo bridge ever get boring? Will I ever end up taking using the tube for granted? I certainly hope not! Moving to London is the best thing that I have ever done. And the best thing about it? This is only just the beginning of my life in the capital…

26. MY LONDON LIBERATION

It's such a cliché, but I always describe arriving in London as like a caterpillar emerging from its chrysalis. Arriving in London felt like finding freedom. It was the most exciting, empowering and liberating experience in the world!

Moving to London meant having the opportunity for a brand new start. I could be whoever I wanted, do whatever I want (within reason!) and go wherever I wanted! I felt so free! London was the city of my dreams, and here I was turning that dream into my reality! I genuinely couldn't believe it.

As I started to find my way around the city, I began to become so much more confident in myself. It was like I was proving to myself just how much I was capable of! I was doing things that were totally outside of my comfort zone every single day…and I loved it! Every day in London brought new people, new places, and new opportunities. I loved how fast-paced and frantic things always seemed. I was racing around a city that never slept, and I loved every second!

London also presents with me an opportunity to broaden my horizons. After a lifetime spent in the Cheshire suburbs, London is edgy and exciting! What's more, after a lifetime of being in bed by 9.30 pm, I'm now in a job where I don't start work until 10 pm! Oh, I'm living on the edge! London gives me the space to express myself in new ways. I try wearing make up, for example, and I go on night's out in mesh tops paired with cycling shorts. I feel so much freedom, and I feel so liberated as a result. I've been given the space to find my feet and figure out who I am – it's the best opportunity in the world!

As I say, starting my job at Heaven gives me an enormous boost in confidence. I'm surrounded by people with so much self-confidence, and so much kindness as well. They wear what they want, and they own their identity. I feel genuinely inspired by their self-confidence.

So I do just that – I start allowing myself to have a bit of fun! I stop worrying about being brand an attention seeker, and I start just having fun! Soon, I hear that people at home have been commenting on my outfits (my mesh crop top has apparently gone down particularly well). I genuinely could not care less. Here's how I think about it: I'm having fun, and I'm not hurting anyone! So take your criticisms elsewhere, thank you very much! Go and wallow in your repression, my loves! I do not have time for these rude and repressed little people from school. Get over yourselves you sad little people, and get out of the house once in a while! It's not my fault that I can be intelligent by day and then sexy by night! I stop caring, and I start living my best life. I go out in mesh tops, the shortest of cycling shorts, cropped hoodies and a whole wardrobe of outrageously revealing ensembles. And I love it! I feel empowered, I feel confident, and I have a lot of fun!

People may well have had a problem with this; they obviously couldn't cope with the idea of seeing a boy in a crop top or size four cycling shorts! But I was having too much fun, and drinking too much Echo Falls Summer Berries rose, to care! I felt so liberated and so empowered – I loved my body, my outfits and my nights out! I do not regret a single outfit, and I do not regret a single second of my wild nights out in London. Here's why: by wearing a mesh crop top, I wasn't hurting anyone! I was just following my heart and having the best time! Here's how I think about it: if my heart told me that I wanted to wear nothing but a see-through mesh t-shirt and a barely-there pair of black shorts, then why would I not do it?! This is what life, I realised, is all about – following your heart, having fun, and being unashamedly confident in your skin! As long as you are not hurting anybody, you have absolutely nothing to apologise for! So stop worrying about what other people think and start letting your hair down! I can't wait to be telling my grandchildren about my wild nights out in Soho!

When I think about the amount of criticism people receive just for being themselves, I find it so heartbreaking. So many people – I would say the vast majority of people – are far too repressed. They can't fathom the idea of a boy stepping out in a mesh crop top, because they have been so strictly conditioned by society's gender norms, boundaries and expectations. But as RuPaul famously says, we're all born naked, and the rest is drag! Take clothing, for example, which is nothing more than a social construct that has got out of control. Clothes were once used to keep our ancestors warm in cold weather – clothes were a very practical invention designed to fight off hypothermia! Today, clothes are a weapon used to reinforce gender differentiation and ensure conformity to gender expectations. Women wear dresses whilst men wear suits. This is even though there is no reason whatsoever for your biological gender to influence the clothing that you wear (other than underwear, I suppose!) People seem to act as if gendered clothing is something Biblical and unchangeable. They fail to realise that fashion is always changing – the Tudor men loved their skirts, and would never say no to a bit of powder on their noses! People don't realise how repressed they are. The vast majority of the population are like sheep, blindly conforming to society's rules and expectations. They never, ever once stop to ask: 'but why' is this the way that things are?

The vast majority of people are quite happy to just blend in and follow the crowd. And there's absolutely nothing wrong with that! But people need to realise that not everybody is content with a quiet life of conformity. Some people find happiness outside of the 'mainstream', whatever the 'mainstream' maybe. I strongly believe that every single individual should do whatever makes them happy. They should do more of the things that bring them joy, whether that is playing football, studying fashion, or whatever else it is that turns them on! We need to stop trying to control people and mould them into gender-segregated clones. Every single individual should be free to express themselves in whatever way they choose!

Indeed, every single person has a different definition of 'happiness', and everybody gets their kicks and thrills in different places. We don't all have to be the same, and we don't have to feel threatened by difference and diversity! If a boy wants to wear makeup, so what? If a girl wants to play rugby, so what? This causes absolutely no harm to absolutely anybody – so why can't we just let people follow their hearts and be happy? If I want to go out in a mesh crop top, then what on earth is wrong with that? Just because you're repressed and scared to express yourself, surely that doesn't mean I'm not allowed to express myself either? Every single person needs to get empowered in their skin and get confident following their own heart! Every single person needs to unapologetically dress how they want, live how they want, and be who they want! As long as you are not causing harm, then you are free to do whatever makes you happy as a human being!

I've mentioned before that, as a child, I really admired strong and sexy women such as Cheryl and Nicole (Scherzinger). Looking back now, I can see exactly why; they were strong, empowered and sex-positive. They were not here to be quiet, conform, and try to blend into the background. They were unapologetically themselves, and they were (rightly) shameless about flaunting their sexuality. They were exactly who I wanted to be! They had the confidence that I so desperately craved! Their freedom from repression was exactly what I craved in my life. I wanted to be fierce and fiery, just like these strong women! And London was my opportunity to enjoy this liberation and find my freedom!

***

Getting a job on London's gay scene was the best catalyst for finding liberation after a lifetime of fear-fuelled repression! I felt free to do what I wanted, wear what I wanted, and be who I wanted to be. All my life, people had told me to tone myself down or 'stop being too much'. I had finally found a space to be fully 'myself' – I could wear my mesh, do my slut-drops and imagine that I was Cheryl performing on the X-Factor 2008 results show! I had found my freedom, and it felt fabulous! Whilst there were, of course, several rude and bitchy people inside the LGBT+ venues, I had the most positive opportunity to just be unashamedly myself. I was in a safe space. It was a space where I could feel sexy, sassy. When I was on that dance floor, I was on top of the world (and, in many cases, on top of a man's shoulders!). This experience completely transformed my attitude towards life. I was no longer feeling so intimidated and inferior to people who I met, and I was instead keen to put everyone I met at ease. I wanted everybody I met to feel as liberated and empowered as I did!

When I was working on Reception, I wanted to give every single person I served a boost in confidence as they walked into the venue. I wanted everybody to feel strong, sexy and welcome! I know how scary it can feel to walk into a nightclub, especially one as big as Heaven. So I wanted to make sure that everybody felt as welcome and confident as they possibly could! And everybody I was meeting was so kind and friendly to me! I was so happy to receive so much warmth and love in response – people were smiling at me, chatting to me and being so lovely. I realised that if you transmit goodness and friendliness – no matter how intimidated or anxious you feel about some of the people around you – then you will receive friendliness in return!

I absolutely loved every second of my year working at Heaven, even if it did leave me feeling permanently tired and with the G-A-Y playlist on loop in my head. I loved turning up for my Saturday night shifts - a McDonald's cup of tea and about ten sugars in hand – and working. These were the best nights of my life; I was being paid to chat with people in the very heart of London's thriving gay scene! I cannot put into words how amazing this experience was, and what an extraordinary boost it provided to my self-confidence and self-esteem! I know for a fact that I would not have enjoyed my first year in London without my job working at Heaven. It was completely outside of my comfort zone, and I loved every single second of it!

Even nights out in Manchester could not have prepared me for working at Heaven! The word 'club' does not do justice to the size of this 1,625 capacity venue, with a queue of people double this number hoping to get inside before 4.30 am each weekend. I felt that I was part of something, that I was accepted, and that I was part of the LGBT+ scene. All of the staff were friendly, and I especially loved the security team working both on the doors and inside the venue. Heaven is well-known for its tight security procedures, including metal detectors and searches of every individual on entry. No matter how cold it was or how late it was, security always greeted me with a smile and chat, which would make my night. I thrived off the buzz of being in this massive nightclub, and I was genuinely living my best life! These gay people around me actually liked me…this was something I had never experienced before at home!

Other than my best friend of many years, all of the other gay boys at home just did not seem to like me. I had put it down to their internalised homophobia and their wish to be 'the only gay in the village'. I just didn't understand it! These boys seemed to openly proud of the fact that they were gay, and yet at the same time, they didn't want to be friends with someone who was gay as well? I didn't get it! Arriving in London, I found that it was a completely different story. I found that I found it relatively easy making gay friends – and I couldn't have been happier about it! I was getting on with people, different people were chatting to me, and I was even getting some attention from men! On Saturday nights just 12 months earlier, I would have been tucked up in bed and asleep by 9.30 pm. I would have been scared to make eye contact with another openly gay guy, never mind chat away to them or even – wait for it – flirt with them! But here I was, in my first year at university, working from 10 pm until 5 am!

As I say, my Heaven job took me completely outside of my comfort zone – and I could not be more thankful for this! Every job that I have had has taught me invaluable life lessons and social skills, and Heaven was certainly no exception. I learned how to stay awake until 5 am (spoiler: cups of tea, sweets and lots of water when the caffeine crash is about to happen). And I also found myself becoming so confident in an environment that would have previously paralysed me with fear. When I walked around that club, with my orange lanyard around the neck (and yes, it did blend into my fake tan!), I cannot begin to tell you how invincible I felt! It was a power trip and a half, as you can imagine, even though I had absolutely no power whatsoever! I just loved the fact that I was here, in this most iconic venue at the heart of the London gay scene. I – 18-year-old Ben – had a job here! These were the best – if also most sleep-deprived – nights of my life. I thank my lucky stars that I was able to have this once-in-a-lifetime opportunity during my first year at university!

***

So the first month of living in London flies by in a whirlwind of mesh crop tops, glasses of rose, and 5 am finishes. After just one month, I am feeling so liberated and alive – I genuinely feel as if I am on top of the world! I am no longer so shy about my social media posting, and I am no longer so shy when I step into a nightclub. Wherever I go, I arrive to have fun and be unapologetically myself!

October soon arrives, and I plan to head home for my birthday. I have genuinely had the best start to my time in London, and I feel as if I am literally on cloud nine. As I head home to celebrate my 19th birthday with Freya, Becky and Kristina, I write this in my diary:

"So happy to say – London, you have been AMAZING! But let me tell you, I am ready to be on this train – can't wait to go home and show them all my new sparkling personality, go and have drinks with my besties, and flirt with all those Manchester men…then have a productive week, of course, at home! I am SO ready for my birthday with my loved ones and my home comforts!!

I have LOVED meeting everyone in London, I feel I'm really getting into my course and of course, being at Heaven, but whilst all of this independence is lovely, I am so ready for greenery and Handforth Dean [M&S where I regularly go to the Café with my mum and gran!] **and reading the papers, watching my Friends box set on TV and being IN MY OWN COMFY BED! And Flash** [the dog]**! And my besties!**

I LOVE London, I really do. I mean it when I say that it's MY city and I love my lob…I just need to get into more of a routine here! I need to start making salads, looking sexy and be confident with the men! And, let me tell you, I finally don't care about what comments people make – I really love and value myself now! Thank you for that, London!

I am so ready to debut the 'London Ben' to the people of Cheshire! I am no longer bothered about what a single soul might think or say – I have been living my best life in London, and nobody can take that away from me!!"

27. MEN, MESH TOPS & MENTAL HEALTH

It's now been several months since I moved down to London, and I am genuinely having the time of my life. I love Stratford, I love my new friends, and I love my new job. Oh, and theology course isn't too bad either! I love everything about being in London; the tube, the landmarks…and the late nights! I might not be getting much sleep, but I am certainly having plenty of fun. I have managed to establish a new routine, which I find is very good for my mental health and wellbeing. I am good at managing my time – I know what time to leave to get to lectures, how much time I need to be getting on with my essays, and I know how to factor in time for a lie-in on a Sunday!

However, I am not afraid to admit that I was – very mildly - struggling with three different things. The first was the fact that I was feeling so judged as I walked around London. This was not what I had expected – at all. The second was a newfound obsession with getting validation from social media and dating apps.

I want to talk about both of these things here in this chapter. Let me be very clear: I am not here to be a victim or a martyr. I am not here to rant about people's prejudices or judgements. In the same way that I am entitled to wear what I want and do what I want, people are more than allowed to form an opinion on me. I want to write about how I managed to improve my mindset and cultivate the resilience required to handle these issues I was facing. Ultimately, my message is this: whatever happens in life, you can handle it! Be confident in your capabilities! When the going gets tough, keep going! You grow through everything that you go through, and every single day is another opportunity to become an even better version of yourself! Life is tough – but you are tougher! So think stoically, know your worth, and keep working towards achieving your dreams! Most importantly, always remember to be kind and compassionate to yourself! Every single one of your feelings is valid!

So let's talk about feeling so judged as I walked around London. I'm going to self-title this the 'staring situation'. Let me quote from a diary entry from October 2018:

"Oh my f*cking God I am so done. I thought that London was the most diverse and liberal place on the planet? I thought that this was where anything goes, and anybody can do anything? Well, that's all a load of absolute F*CKING RUBBISH! I am actually so confused right now. Every day as I walk around, I notice so many people staring at me. Like they aren't even subtle about it…these people openly just STARE AT ME in the street. It happens in Stratford when I'm walking to the tube or going shopping, and it happens in Central when I'm just walking around. I thought Central London was literally the Capital of Liberalism – well, I have never felt so judged in my whole entire life.

Why are people doing this to me? It is SO horrible. Is the fake tan, the skinny jeans, the way I walk? I just do not get how you can be so RUDE! Am I just being too sensitive, or would anybody feel the same way as I do? This is the worst thing for my self-esteem; it really is. Today I was literally wearing black skinny jeans, a black t-shirt and smart black shoes. The number of people who stared at me was ridiculous. It makes my blood f*cking boil SO much. I genuinely want to storm over to these people and ask them what the hell their problem is. And why they have the right to be so f*cking rude! I'm not even joking now; I am 99.9% sure one woman was actually FILMING ME as I walked towards her. She was with a group of men; they were all nudging each other, laughing together, and POINTING AT ME. I was literally staring directly at her, and she just kept filming. She did not care ONE TINY BIT. They were clearly tourists, so maybe they're not used to people being openly gay or wearing skinny fit clothes in their culture? But surely they have one single brain cell, which would surely tell them that is SO F*CKING RUDE! I literally stopped and glared at them all, and went (OUT LOUD) 'WOW'. They all start sniggering, one of them has the audacity to WAVE at me, and one of the STUPID MEN has the nerve to MIMIC ME and go 'WOW' in his stupid little accent. I was genuinely so shaken. I just had to walk away; I didn't know what to do with myself.

The worst thing is, it wasn't an exceptional situation. This is happening ALL THE TIME. It's usually builders or tourists. In fact, whenever I walk towards builders or a group of tourists, I know exactly what is going to happen. I am paralysed by fear, and I know what is about to happen. And they never EVER let me down – I feel the eyes on me, I hear the sniggering and laughter. What the F*CK are they saying? What the F*CK IS THEIR PROBLEM? I would genuinely appreciate it if they would just say to me 'Hi, we don't like the fact your jeans are so tight'. Or 'Hi, we think the way you walk is really weird'. I am literally wasting so much time and energy feeling so angry about this. I am awake at night wondering why the HELL this is happening. Is it the fake tan? Is it because I'm slim? Is it because they can tell I'm gay? I am so angry, I feel so attacked, and I hate this so, so much. It literally makes me hate all people – I now just assume that everybody I walk past is judging me and hating on me. It is so bad for my confidence, and it makes me feel so attacked. Why are people so VILE!!!! All I'm saying is these people laughing at me in the street better watch out, because oh my GOD am I going to have the last life…how sad and pathetic can they actually be! I need to toughen up and stop caring so much because I cannot let these random people keep destroying my soul."

As you can see, I was not best pleased about all of this unsolicited staring! I cannot put into words how upset I was about the number of people staring at me. It left me feeling so paranoid and so insecure. I kept asking myself the same question: what is wrong with me? I couldn't work out why this was happening to me. I was wearing the same clothes as I had worn at home, and in Manchester. Back at home, nobody had batted an eyelid. So why did it feel like the whole of London was staring at me?

I very quickly realised that London was not as accepting as I had thought it was. I had to accept that people here were not always as tolerant or kind as I'd assumed they would be. There are, to put it frankly, some extremely rude people on this planet. And it appeared that a lot of them were staring at me as I walked around London! It was fascinating that it was always, without fail, the same types of people who would stare and snigger at me. It was always the builders, and it was always the European tourists. The fact that I knew what was coming whenever I walked towards these groups of people didn't make it any more comfortable. Still, it did make it feel less personal. I knew that the problem was with these bigoted and rude people, not with me. I started to wonder: if they are staring and sniggering at me, how many other people are they so openly judging? How dare they be so openly rude to me! How dare they make me feel so uncomfortable! And how dare they start f*cking filming me!

Thomas De Quincey famously wrote that in London "you become aware that you are no longer noticed: nobody sees you; nobody hears you; nobody regards you…" Well, Thomas, I've got some news for you, darling! I was very much being noticed – and not in a good way! I would rant on the phone to Queen P, and I would demand that Becky and Freya told me what was wrong with my appearance. They were all completely clueless. They thought I must have been paranoid. 'You need to be honest with me!' I practically screamed, 'I know I'm not good looking, and I know I look gay, but surely that can't be the reason f*cking builders are laughing about me in their f*cking high vis jackets?'

I never did get my answers. I'm writing this chapter two years after that diary entry was written, and the staring continues. Just today, a group of Spanish tourists genuinely took a picture of me and literally stood by Monument tube station laughing at me. I genuinely do not get it. What the f*ck are they going to do with that photo? It makes me think that there must genuinely be something very unusual about me – and my appearance – because so many people do shamelessly stare at me.

The staring continues, but my approach towards it has monumentally changed. I've realised that I have two options: I can either change my appearance, or I can change my attitude. I have to take full responsibility for my life! And, considering I quite like my skinny jeans and fake tan, I'm going to go with the latter! As Epictetus says, 'men are not disturbed by events but by the views which they take of them. If I was going to keep stepping out in London, I couldn't change the fact that people were staring at me. And so, I had to change my attitude towards it. In other words, I had to toughen up! Just because I had been raised in an accepting and non-judgmental household, that didn't mean that everybody else had. My parents may have taught me that it was rude to stare or mock people, but that didn't mean that everybody else's had! People were going to stare and judge, end of the story. It was in their DNA and nature to do so! And so, if I wanted to survive in the city, I had to stop being so sensitive!

I always strive to be a visionary, not a reactionary. I knew that I could not continue going through life, getting angry about things over which I had no control. I could not go through each day feeling hurt and victimised by random strangers in the street. After all, what other people think of you is none of your business! Instead, I had to become a visionary. I thought of it like this: how would a role model respond in this situation? How would a leader respond in this situation? Would they let the behaviours of random people in the street get them down? Would they throw their toys out of the pram and go through life feeling sorry for themselves? Absolutely not! A role model or leader is too busy doing positive and productive things to care one tiny bit about what random people in the street think of them! Their self-worth and validation do not depend on what random strangers in the street might be saying or doing! I needed to stop caring so much about the staring and pull myself together! Was I really that insecure that I was going to let a couple of rude and (let's be real) talentless strangers in the street make me feel uncomfortable in my skin? After making so much progress towards self-acceptance and self-confidence, was I going to let these people leave my self-esteem in tatters? No – I was not!

These days, I like to think 'what would Kris Jenner do?' (well of course I do!) I like to pretend that they recognise me because I'm the next Mariah Carey. Sometimes, I'll give the people staring at me a little wave. I like them to know that I appreciate all of their interest and attention! You never know, I might start carrying around copies of this book that I can sell to the builders and tourists staring at me! I might even give them a cheeky discount…or if they're really lucky, a signed copy! I am secure in my skin, and so the fact people are so openly staring and commenting on me doesn't bother me so much. But I'd be lying if I said it doesn't get to me at all. I'm only human. My insecurities are ignited every single time that it happens.

But I refuse to be a victim to other people's judgements, and I am adamant that people's intolerances will not defeat me.

If I look at it from another perspective, I'm glad that these people are noticing me. They come from very intolerant and narrow-minded backgrounds. So I hope that my visibility is an education and an eye-opener for them. By Christ, they need it! They need to see how confident I am in my skin and take a long hard look in the mirror. After seeing me in my skinny jeans, maybe they won't be so shocked by the next person they see in skinny jeans? I am determined to transform something so painful into something very positive. I am determined to stand up, speak out, and fly the flag for a more accepting society. Do not be defeated by intolerant, judgmental or rude strangers! Especially rude and bigoted builders in their bright orange high visibility jackets! Leave them to their scaffolding, and focus on radiating even more star quality! Make it your mission to give them something to stare at! Keep shining like the star you were born to be, and leave their negativity where it belongs – very far beneath you! Here's how I see it: let those random strangers laugh at you. Let them stare and let them mock. You're the one who is going to have the last laugh! So keep your head held high, and don't let anybody get you down!

***

Not only have I been getting a lot of (unexplained and unwanted) attention on the streets, but I am also getting a lot of attention online. The only difference is, the attention that I am getting online is attention that I want! Or at least I think I do! Grindr quickly becomes my primary source of validation. I did become addicted to receiving messages from men online. This attention was brand new, and it felt long overdue! I realised that the more provocative my profile pictures were, the more messages I would get. The quality of the messages – and men – might have been questionable, but this was irrelevant to me. In my mind, it was all about quantity over quality! As I went around London, I was compulsively checking my messages at every opportunity. After being made to feel so sh*t by these strangers mocking me in the street, I took comfort in being told I was 'sexy' and 'stunning' online! Getting all this attention, I will freely admit, felt amazing. I loved receiving all of these messages, and it was all good fun. It was also a very genuine boost to my self-esteem. And – sparing you any unwanted details – I made the most of my time on the app, with all safety precautions taken, of course! I honestly don't know what I would have done without dating apps in London! I was working in a massive gay nightclub, but that was only for one night a week! Most people I crossed paths with at work wouldn't have remembered me by the next morning! I think it is very difficult to meet people – in terms of both friendships and relationships – as a gay person.

Apps such as Tinder and Grindr are very good for connecting and introducing people (even if there is often a sexual undertone to the relationship that is formed!) I do acknowledge the criticisms of online dating apps. I do agree that these apps promote a culture of quantity over quality, and they do emphasise physical appearance over everything else. However, if I'm honest, I do think this is what human beings have always done anyway. Dating apps such as Tinder and Grindr just make this behaviour appear more socially acceptable…not to mention accessible! Gone are the days of 'until death do us part' – the new approach is 'until the next attractive person up for some fun comes along!'

On the one hand, this is quite sad, because it's almost as if 'relationships' are less about connection and more about convenience. But on the other hand, sex has always been at the core of human life and behaviour. I think that dating apps have just facilitated the liberation! They have played a positive role in making conversations about it more socially acceptable! Humans have been sleeping around since time began…there just wasn't an app to make doing so ten times easier and more socially acceptable!

So I do I think that this 'dating apps, 'hook up' society and 'convenience' culture is perfectly fine, as long as it's what you want. And as long you are engaging in it with your eyes wide open! In other words, don't 'hook up' with someone and then get upset when they don't want to marry you the next morning! We need to see every single kind of relationship we engage in for what it is. For example, if someone just wants you for sex, then don't emotionally invest in them!

When I arrived in London, I was naturally nervous and eager to make connections. As a sensitive soul worried about 'popularity', I was looking for reassurance. I found myself feeling extremely anxious to 'find a place' within London's gay community. I happened to have a body type and age that fitted the 'desirable' and 'in demand' category of the market – I was young, skinny and 'fresh meat'.

There were two things that I found difficult about the gay scene: the focus on physical appearance and the 'hook up' culture. It felt as if everything was about 'quantity over quality' – the idea of a 'long term relationship' was not in the dictionary! When I arrived in London, I was still very much living with a Disney-like understanding of the world. I thought that everybody fell in love with their soulmate and that they then had physical intimacy with just one person for the rest of their lives. I thought that every relationship was monogamous, loyal, and grounded in mutual respect. Arriving in London turned this world-view on its head. And this took a lot of getting used to!

For a start, I needed to quickly toughen up and wake up to life in the real world! To put it crudely, the gay scene was a world of happy endings rather than happy ever afters (if you are old enough to know what I mean!) It was a very sexual, promiscuous and – I hate to say it – at times predatory environment. And I needed to grow up, wise up and wake up fast!

When I arrived on the gay scene, it felt as if my 18-year-old body was in demand. And I was happy to take all of the attention, validation, and interest that I could get! It was very easy to get physical and sexual attention. There is absolutely nothing wrong with this, and I always say 'if you've got it, flaunt it!' But there are, of course, many problems that can arise because of this.

For a start, I was confusing 'physical lust' with 'romantic love'. This is especially the case for someone with a history of battling insecurities. I had been through a lot of issues regarding my self-esteem and dependency on external validation. I was not always the most emotionally intelligent, and so I took many situations far too personally. I was always a perfectionist who was always flawed by rejection. A lot of the time, I unconsciously saw everything as a competition (that I could never win). For example, I found it so hard to understand and accept that there is always going to be a younger and more attractive model ready to replace you! No matter how hard you try, you will never win the *'I'm the most attractive'* competition! Suppose you are prepared to base your worth and value on your looks. In that case, I do believe that you have got to have the thickest of skin and the highest levels of self-confidence imaginable. It is very shallow, and it is certainly not for sensitive types such as me! Relationships – inclusive of friendships, sexual liaisons and romantic relationships – that are based on physical attraction (and lust) are extraordinarily superficial and lack genuine empathy, care, or investment.

Suppose you are attracting attention based on your appearance. In that case, you need to be a very emotionally strong person. You have got to be very real with yourself: if someone likes you solely for the way that you look, your value to them goes no further than your body or your worth as a sexual vessel. You are therefore very disposable, very temporary and very much the fulfilment of their physical need. You might as well just give them a signed photograph of you! This kind of objectification is not – in itself – a bad thing. I get that people have a 'physical type', and that an enormous part of sexual attractiveness is your physical appearance. Suppose somebody is only interested in you because of your physical appearance. In that case, they are not going to be interested in you for a long time. They are only going to be interested until a younger, more attractive model comes along (which, I don't like to be rude, will not take very long!) They will probably not care about your feelings, and they will probably not care for you once they've got what they want (sex).

I'm talking about this because I felt very let down by guys in my first year at university. Week after week, I would get with a guy who I thought was interested in me as a human being. In their eyes, however, I was just 'another twink' (gay scene term for young, slim boy) that they could sleep with. These guys were getting through about five boys a week. I hated the fact that these guys were only interested in me because I was eighteen and skinny. Of course, I took full advantage of this, and I shamelessly played the game! Well, it meant I got a lot of free drinks, and I did enjoy getting the attention! But I found it all so frustrating - I wanted to find a secure and loving relationship! I did not want to be the fulfilment of their fetish for young and skinny boys! Working in a gay nightclub didn't help with my trust in men. I would see the same guys who had been messaging me going home with a different eighteen-year-old every single week without fail! It was like a factory farming approach to dating, with a constant conveyor belt of younger models being shipped in! I did not want to waste my time on anybody solely interested in me for how I looked. I needed to toughen up and stop getting so attached to my Tinder matches! I needed to stop feeling so hurt and upset when I realised that I wasn't the only boy a guy was messaging! I needed to improve my self-esteem so that I stopped feeling so insecure about finding a man!

I do think that it is important to monitor how much you base your worth as a human being on how physically attractive other people think you are. Over time, your physical appearance will, and I hate to break it to you, change. Suppose somebody is only interested in you because you're young and skinny. In that case, they are only going to be interested in you as long as you are young and skinny! If you want anything more meaningful than appearance-based lust, then your relationships needed to be grounded in a real connection. You need to find somebody interested in you as a whole human being. The most important thing – and I cannot stress this enough – is that you share core values. If you do not share core values with the people you are closest to, then your relationship is doomed to catastrophe! Suppose you value honesty and kindness, for example. In that case, things are not going to end well if you're dating someone known for being deceitful and rude! Suppose you believe in the Christian concepts of monogamy and faithfulness, for example. In that case, you're not exactly well suited to somebody who believes in open relationships and attending sex parties!

I struggled with the idea that people judged attractiveness solely based on physical appearance. There is nothing wrong, of course, with finding somebody physically attractive. But I had to get my head around the obvious distinction between 'lust' and 'love'. You can find somebody physically attractive, and you can even enjoy a very physical relationship with them, without wanting anything more than sex with them! I couldn't get my head around this. At all. In my Disney-like approach to life, physical intimacy was an extension of romantic love. I now realised this was not how the people I was surrounded by – both on apps and in nightclubs - saw things! On the one hand, this was quite liberating. It meant that I could just get out there and have some fun – it was, as they say, an opportunity to 'play the field'!

But I also found that this 'quantity over quality' culture came with, like anything, its negative side-effects. This was especially the case for me, a former anorexic. For example, I loved posting body photos on gay dating apps. I became aware that many of the people messaging me had a fetish for 'skinny' and 'young' boys. This was toxic – I started to think that I was only attractive as long as people thought I looked young and skinny! I took things too far and became very anxious about whether I appeared sexually desirable. I was looking for validation, and I wanted to feel sexually attractive. Objectively, I don't think there is absolutely anything wrong with whatsoever. But here's where the problems began: I wanted to 'measure' my worth in a numerical way. For example, I wanted to have a certain number of likes or a certain number of matches on tinder. This would allow me to compare my 'attractiveness' with that of other people – the most toxic mindset to ever have! I wanted to receive compliments, and I wanted to feel desirable. I thought that this attention and these compliments would fill the void of self-esteem within me. I did not believe I was physically attractive. So I was desperate to hear somebody else say that I was.

As a result, I was basing my worth as a human being on how many messages I received on Grindr, or how many guys checked me out in a nightclub! This is all fun and games when you are getting loads of messages! But what about when the messages stop? Where do you find your validation and worth from then? I couldn't find it in the street, where I was being mocked and stared at!

What's more, I was extremely jealous of this good looking and confident boys who were receiving thousands of likes on their Instagram pages. I – mistakenly – believed that I would be the happiest person in the world if only I could be like them. Imagine having so many likes, so much attention and being seen as so attractive by everyone! I was so obsessed with what they seemingly had in their lives that I was unable to appreciate all the good things in my own life. I was failing to realise that I was on my own unique and personal journey, and I was instead turning green with envy and becoming overcome with desperation.

But once the novelty wore off – which was within about 2 minutes, let's not sugar-coat things! – this deep void of emptiness would emerge within me. What I was doing never seemed to be enough. I always wanted more likes, more attention. And I was always incredibly jealous of these boys who seemingly 'had it all'. Of course, I know now that all they had was good lighting, a good quality phone camera and the money to buy themselves Instagram likes. But I had fallen for the Instagram fantasy – I believed that their online profiles and popularity correlated to real-world happiness and success. Here's what I've learnt. Suppose you're going to put all of your eggs into the 'social media validation' basket. In that case, it's very hard to pull yourself out of that very superficial place. It is so fake, so artificial and so far removed from reality. You end up comparing your raw and real self to the airbrushed and edited image other people are presenting. How ridiculous is this? I was sitting in my bedroom feeling frustrated and inferior. Why couldn't I get that kind online attention? Why couldn't I be so good looking and, so I assumed, have so many men chasing after me? My frustrations were compounded by the fact that I wanted my Disney-style romance, whilst the men I was attracting simply wanted me to be their fifth hook up of the week. And so, I might have been getting 'attention' – if that's what we call receiving unsolicited nudes and offers to jump into some random man's bed! – but it was not necessarily the kind of attention that I was looking for!

There is – if I can put it quite crudely – an obvious difference between lust for your body versus a genuine connection with you as a human being. It had fallen into the trap of believing that our worth is predominantly dependent on our physical attractiveness. The hook-up culture – based entirely on appearance and the provision of a transactional service – reduces romance to the fulfilment of a need. I read some great advice in The Times that changes my approach to dating apps: on a dating app, you should act like you would in a bar. Would you strip off and get naked after talking to someone for five seconds in a bar? No! So why are you allowing yourself to feel pressurised into sending nudes online? If they start the conversation by sending a picture of their genitalia, how on earth can you feel let down when it turns out that they (shock of the year) want nothing more than a quick 'hook-up'?

It makes me smile looking back to think I was so confused about why I was attracting the wrong kind of men as a result of posting my underwear pictures online. I was so confused why these people just wanted to have sex with me, rather than go out for dinner or get to know me as a human being. I genuinely could not see that I was the one setting a very sexual tone for all of my interactions. As always, I needed to start taking accountability and responsibility for my own life!

When I look back at my first few months of using dating apps in London, I do not regret a single thing. I genuinely loved it, and I would do it all over again in a heartbeat. But I also wish that I'd had a little bit more self-esteem because then I wouldn't have been trying to find so much validation and reassurance online. I think I was compensating for lack of real-world relationships by trying to attract attention from men I had never met before on the internet.

***

In the cases of strangers staring and using dating apps, I wish I'd had more confidence and genuine self-esteem. If I had been more confident and secure in myself, I would not have worried so much about all these people staring at me in the street! And if I had been more confident and secure in myself, I wouldn't have got so upset about not finding my Prince Charming within a week of moving to London! I could have enjoyed the 'quantity over quality' culture for what it was, rather than being so sensitive and taking everything to heart. But we can't change the past, all we can do is learn for the future. And so, going forwards, I am learning to become a lot more self-confident and self-assured. I finally know what I want, and I finally know my worth. I also finally know what worries and anxieties are not worth a single second of my time! As a result, I am so much less sensitive and so much more resilient. I no longer need reassurance or validation to feel attractive and, as a result, I can 'play the field' without getting so emotionally invested. I can also walk down the street without getting so upset about the number of people staring at me!

I have started to realise that self-confidence is key. You need to be secure in your skin. That means unconditionally accepting yourself and finding validation from within! It also means realising that life is not about transactions or gaining attention (unless that is what makes you genuinely happy). Ultimately, life is all about being authentic, confident, and forming meaningful connections! For me, that means looking to form as many meaningful, sincere and genuine connections as I possibly can! More than anything else, it is so important to just be confident in yourself and know your worth! Command the respect that you deserve! Know what you want! Take the pro-active steps that will enable you to get what you want! And get serious about connecting with the people that you meet, and always be defiantly confident in your skin!

28. WALKING IN A (HYDE PARK) WINTER WONDERLAND

The semester is flying by, and it's quickly approaching Christmas. I love walking around the Olympic Park on cold December mornings, and I love seeing the clear blue skies above Central London. There's something so enjoyable about a Winter's morning walk across Waterloo bridge; the cold air and blue sky is just so beautiful! My Instagram quickly becomes a daily barrage of Waterloo bridge pictures! I love the festive celebrations taking place across the capital.

As you know, I am the ultimate Christmas obsessive, and no city does Christmas quite as well as London! Gorgeous lights illuminate Regents Street, and an enormous tree is erected in Trafalgar Square. Everywhere you go, thousands of rosy-cheeked tourists bustle past you clutching red festive coffee cups! One night, at about 5.30 am, I am arriving back from work whilst they are erecting an enormous Christmas tree outside the Westfield Centre in Stratford. Christmas is here, I think to myself, struggling to contain my excitement about the festivities! The most wonderful time of the year is on its way!

We get Flat 105 a little Christmas tree from Wilko, which ends up staying in place at the end of the corridor until we all move out in June. The nights quickly get darker and the days soon get colder. I get started on the Christmas movies – Deck the Halls and Christmas with the Kranks are firm favourites – and I start wearing extra layers to work on a Saturday night! I try to keep looking sexy, whilst simultaneously fighting off 4 am hypothermia!

Hyde Park Winter Wonderland opens its doors, and my mum comes down for a festive day out in London. She arrives into Euston at about 9 am, looking the part in a little blazer and skinny jeans. She's in desperate need of a latte (of course she is), so we head off for a coffee in Café Nero. Once

Queen P is revived by caffeine, it's time to get busy shopping, eating and soaking up the festivities. We have the loveliest time wandering around Hyde Park Winter Wonderland before heading back into Central London for lunch. And, after a bottle of sparkling rose, we head off for cocktails in Soho! She is delighted to hear Take That 'Relight My Fire', and ends up getting more male attention than I ever have. That blazer and skinny jeans combination is going down a treat! With a 'Sex in Soho' cocktail in hand, Queen P is living her best life!

I love spending a day with my mum in London, a city that now really does feel like home. I have her jumping on tubes and racing around the capital, trying to give her just a little taste of the 'rush hour' Underground experience! I feel so proud to be able to show her around the city. We have been coming down to London for day trips as a family for years, and I remember London would always feel so big, exciting, and overwhelming! But now, I'm living here – and so we actually know our way around (well, to an extent…) We no longer need to rely on my dad's 'A-Z London pocketbook' (even though I'm sure that we all secretly loved getting lost trying to find our way from London Euston to Covent Garden). I take my mum past the Travelodge where we used to stay, and I point out the different theatres where we watched spectacular West End shows. I feel so proud to know my way around! I love reminiscing about those day trips from over a decade ago, and thinking about how far I have come in the intervening years! Look at me now, I tell her, I'm finally confident and taking responsibility for my life! I even take her down to see where Heaven is, just off the Strand and 30 seconds from Trafalgar Square, and I think she is suitably impressed by the club's central location! This is where I work! In the very centre of London! We then walk past King's College London, which is just another five minutes further down the Strand. I feel so proud to show her where I study, right here in the heart of the capital! And we even pay a cheeky visit to Buckingham Palace (well, it would be rude for us to be having a day out together and not to call in on the Queen!)

We have the loveliest day wandering around London and catching up on our lives. 'I couldn't have done any of this without you', I tell mum as we stand on Waterloo Bridge, 'I would not be here if it wasn't for all of your support!'. As I take in the skyline, I could not imagine myself living in absolutely any other city in the world. I still cannot quite believe that I am here. 'It still doesn't feel real!' I tell her. 'It's all down to YOU!', she tells me, but I disagree. I know with certainty that it is only thanks to the unconditional love, support and encouragement of my family that I am where I am today. Yes, I am the one who sat my A-Levels, set my ambitions, and made the decisions. But I was only able to find my feet and dream so big as a result of their unconditional love and support.

Knowing that I have a loving and caring family home to return to – at any time – is the most reassuring thing in the world. This is what Queen P has always said parenting is about; you want to give your children the space to live their lives, whilst always providing them with a loving 'base' they can always come back to. As we walk down Oxford Street, I feel so much happiness and joy. Queen P is not only my mum; she is my best friend as well. Being able to show her the places where I work, study and socialise in London gives me immeasurable amounts of pride. It's the best day, with the best mum I could ever ask for. Everyone needs a Queen P in their lives!

***

A couple of weeks later and Christmas is now right around the corner. It's my last weekend in London before heading home for the festive season. Alyce and Abby are coming down to stay with me for the weekend, and I am super excited to see these absolute angels. I've known Abby since our days performing in Pantomimes and Musicals at the local theatre group. I never let her forget our memories of marching down the stairs dressed as sailors singing 'In the Navy'! And I have got to know Alyce after striking up a conversation about the Sixth form café food in the common room (of course I have!) We've all been working together at Mottram Hall, with Alyce over in the Claret Jug golf bar and Abby and I ending up together on reception. Over the past year, we have been on countless Pizza Express dates, making the most of those two courses for £10.95 vouchers that you find online! These two girls radiate so much love and kindness, and I cannot wait to spend a weekend with them in London. They are arriving down in London late on Friday afternoon, and I've said I'll meet them at Euston station. They arrive – with enough suitcases to last them six months – and we head back to Stratford to drop off all their stuff. We then head into Westfield for some food, before getting on the Central Line into Soho, where I treat them both to a drink at G-A-Y (very generous of me, I know!) That evening, we get back to Stratford and all squeeze into my ¾ size bed – well, this is what friendship is all about!

The next morning we are up early for a day of shopping and sightseeing. We head to Harrods – of course – before wandering down the Mall to Buckingham Palace and doing a bit of shopping in Central London. Despite torrential rain, we soldier on with our day and head to Hyde Park Winter Wonderland. Despite the deluge of rain, we enjoy the most delicious hot waffles and pancakes, hiding from the weather under giant plastic ponchos. We try and soak up the atmosphere – whilst getting soaked by the weather – before admitting defeat and finding our way back to the tube station. To avoid congestion, Hyde Park Corner station is closed, so we cling onto our ponchos and walk down to Knightsbridge tube station. Back at Stratford, we dry ourselves off and order a takeaway, looking back through the pictures of our washout of a festive day out looking like – in my case at least – a drowned rat!

It is so lovely to have these two down here in London. Abby loves being in the city, whilst Alyce (always a Cheshire girl at heart) is not pleased about the number of people we are fighting against to squeeze onto the tube! Despite the rain - and very little legroom in bed - I have the best time, and I can't believe how quickly the weekend goes. I wave the dynamic duo off on their train home to Macclesfield, knowing that I'll be back at Euston to catch my own train home in just two days.

***

I lie in bed that evening feeling glad to have the whole thing back to myself for the first time in two nights. I actually cannot believe how quickly the first half of my year in London has gone! It genuinely feels like September was only yesterday, and yet here I am getting ready to head home for Christmas. It just shows – time flies when you're having fun…and you're sleep deprived! I have, without doubt, had the best four months of my life – and I love the fact that this is just the beginning of my three years studying in London! The city already feels like home! Yet I also know that there's so much more to do, see, and explore. I never, in a million years, imagined that I would be here in London, studying at this university and working in this iconic nightclub! I do feel so proud of what I have accomplished and achieved. I am amazed at how I have been able to put myself out there and just 'get on' with London life. I have been jumping on at least four different tube trains a day, working Saturday nights in one of London's biggest nightclubs, and keeping myself alive and fed for over ten weeks! Who would have thought that I could cook, clean and function all on my own!? Not Queen P, that's for sure!

I feel so blessed to have had the experiences I have already had, and I feel even more blessed to have met so many gorgeous people. Whilst not every friendship has worked out, I've learnt that this is perfectly okay – some people come into your life for ten minutes, others come into your life for ten decades. Life, the last few months have taught me, is all about taking risks, daring to put yourself out there, and learning from every single experience that you have. Whatever happens, you will be able to handle it. Whatever you do, make sure that you do it with confidence, enthusiasm, and an open mind. Seize every opportunity that life hands to you, and dare to believe in your potential and capabilities.

Most importantly, stop worrying so much about what other people might think or say. When you become a prisoner to public opinion, you never get anything done. When you become a slave to social media validation, you forget how to live life in the real world. When everything you do is about gaining other people's approval or attention, you lose sight of who you are. No matter what happens or what other people think, you are enough. With hard work and self-confidence, absolutely anything is possible.

I feel like my four months in London have proved to me that I am capable of achieving success in my life! They have shown me that I am capable of making friends, making my way through life, and making a (somewhat) nutritious dinner for myself! If I can stand on my own two feet in London, then I can stand on my own two feet anywhere! If I can survive in this city, then I can survive anywhere! Suppose I can keep up with this pace and find my way around this big city. In that case, I should be confident in my ability to cope with whatever challenges the future may bring! Sometimes, we need experiences or opportunities like this to show just what we are capable of achieving. We need that little 'boost' to our confidence that comes from realising just what hard work, confidence and ambition can achieve for us!

***

I return home for Christmas with a serious spring in my step. Not one to hold a grudge, I hope that I'll bump into people from my Primary school when I'm walking around town doing my Christmas shopping. I'm desperate to see them and think, 'yes, you did put me down, and you did make me feel inferior…well LOOK AT ME NOW!' Of course, you should never feel like you need to 'prove' yourself to anybody because, no matter what you do (or don't do), you have infinite value and worth. But, equally, I don't think there's anything wrong with feeling proud of what you have achieved in your life. It's so important to acknowledge and celebrate your successes! If you don't fly your flag and blow your own trumpet, then nobody else is going to come along and do it for you! I've returned to Macclesfield with more self-confidence than I have ever had before. Even after just four months in London, I genuinely feel like a brand new person. I cannot put into words how good London has been for me. It has given me so much self-confidence, and it has taught me how to stand on my own two feet. I've learned how to do things for myself and how to stand up for myself. I never really believed I capable of surviving in London…never mind thriving! I do feel on top of the world. I feel so proud of what I have achieved, and I feel so proud of the person I have become. Thank you, London! I never want this experience to end!

29. CHRISTMAS ON CANAL STREET

I'm back home for Christmas and thoroughly enjoying the festivities. The Christmas movies are on, the mince pies are out, and Queen P is decorating the tree. Whilst I love the cosy evenings in, I am also absolutely desperate for a night out in Manchester. I've seen on social media that there is a gay club night happening this weekend, which is titled – just brace yourself for this one, Gran look away now – 'Sugar Boys: The Christmas Special'. My Facebook newsfeed has been overloaded with promotions for this event, which is being billed as the most iconic and well attended gay club night in human history. After my four months working at Heaven, I've decided that I am now ready to take the gay nightlife scene by storm, and I am desperate to attend this event. In my head – for reasons genuinely unbeknown to me - this is my big opportunity to find myself a man. The idea that you would find yourself any kind of genuine or serious relationship at an event called 'Sugar Boys' really does take absurd to a whole new level, but this is how my 18-year-old brain was working! I had decided that, if all these boys on Instagram could parade around in their underwear, then so could I! I wanted to get myself to this event and get myself to the centre of the stage – I was determined to waltz into this club night and be the star at the top of the (Sugar Boy) Christmas Tree. Well, if nothing else, you've got to admire my extraordinary level of confidence, even if it is dangerously bordering on delusional!

I was desperate to attend this event and feel 'involved' with all of the promotion that I had seen across my social media. I remember feeling so angry that I had not been asked to be one of the 'Sugar Boys' paid to promote and attend the event. I remember feeling determined to storm in there and show them all what they were missing. Once a diva, always a diva! Looking back, I genuinely do find this hilarious. Still, it is slightly concerning how seriously I was taking this all at the time! Of course, I could not turn up at this club night on my own. I needed a sexy and stunning partner-in-crime, someone who could always be relied upon for the best night out. I needed someone who could always be guaranteed to match my level of outrageous fun and outgoing behaviour on a night out. I needed someone who would always have me in hysterics, who would always join me centre stage on the dance floor. But I needed someone who was also switched on enough to know when to drag me out of the club and tell me off for my prosecco-fuelled antics. There was only ever going to be one candidate for this job – it was, of course, the FM (also known as Freya).

Before we continue with the story, let me just confirm this: I have offered, multiple times, to pay for the FM to get therapy as a result of what I subjected her to on this night out. I'm only joking, although she does deserve an award for putting up with me over the years! This girl is nothing short of (a) an amazing and unconditionally accepting best friend (b) a genuine Saint who deserves a Knighthood for her services to keeping me under control. The FM – the Queen of the 'dignity and decorum' mantra – did not deserve to be dragged to the Manchester Gay Village on this freezing cold Saturday night and subjected to this 'Sugar Boy' club night. But here she was, looking as sexy as always, and ready for an eventful night ahead! When I asked her to describe this event with the benefit of hindsight, a short silence was followed by the diplomatic one-liner, 'oh…it was an **experience**'. I think you get the idea!

I rock up in a candy cane crop top, red hot pants and a Santa hat. Well, what else did you expect!? For clarification, my head is probably the most covered up part of my body. It is freezing, but I am determined to show off my head-to-toe fake tan and find a man. Freya, looking as sexy as always, is slightly more covered up than me. However, this wasn't hard based on my utterly scandalous outfit (or, should I say, lack of outfit). In my defence, I am wearing a massive coat over the top of my outfit, which is my one line of defence against hypothermia…and being hate crimed! We have a few drinks, of course, and jump onto the Virgin train into Manchester, before stopping at one of the bars in the station for a glass of prosecco or two.

As far as I'm concerned, we need all the alcohol we can get before facing the 'Sugar Boy' event. Poor Freya is going to need a constant supply of beverages if she is to make it through this ordeal. Our next stop on this freezing December's evening is, of course, G-A-Y, where I order far too many Sourz shots (and yes, I do know that they're only 5%!) Once we believe that we are suitably prepared (intoxicated) to face tonight's main event, we head outside to find the club night venue. Fortunately, we do not have far to walk, and we make it inside before the hypothermia kicks in. 'Oh my GOD it is FREEZING' I exclaim, dragging poor Freya along a frosty Canal Street. I pay our entry, and we head down the stairs, into what can only be described as a little camp winter wonderland.

I do emphasise the word little. This venue is about the size of my uni bedroom back in London. Don't get me wrong; I wasn't expecting them to have hired out Wembley Stadium. Still, it would be quite nice if they had at least the room to swing a cat (or a Sugar Boy dressed as a cat, as the event organisers would probably have preferred). 'Oh my god we need a drink' I tell Freya, grabbing her hand and rushing over to the bar. Another drink does the job, and we are ready to make the best of these circumstances and this situation, which in broad daylight would be nothing but soul-destroying. Here's the thing with Frey and I – no matter where we are on a night out, we always make sure it's one to remember. Even if it's just us on the dance floor – and quite often it is – we always make sure to bring the party. Once I've had a drink, that's it – I am not bothered, in the slightest, about what anybody else thinks, does, or says. And now that I've worked in a nightclub I seem to believe (after a jager bomb and Sourz shot or two) I have every right to be up on stage in every venue. And so, that is exactly where the FM and I soon find ourselves. How we have ended up on this little stage they have set up; we shall never know (a.k.a we will never remember). But we are up here, on this raised platform, with one of the Sugar Boys taking his angel wings off and putting them onto the FM. Oh my God, the poor girl! Freya puts on the wings, and I whip out my phone to capture the iconic moment on camera. Freya's facial expression – of both horror and hilarity – is one that you could not forget in a million years. This is the thing about the FM; she may be the Queen of dignity and decorum, but she is also an extremely good sport. Far too good of a sport, some would say, especially when you have got a topless man forcing you to wear his angel wings whilst standing on a raised platform in the middle of a Canal Street club.

My next memory is of me being filmed by a man who wanted content for the next 'Sugar Boy' event promotional material. I was, of course, more than happy to star in this footage (especially after another set of Sourz shots and another - yes another - glass of prosecco). FM very wisely got herself away from the lens and avoided the possibility of there being any footage of her sexy and dignified self in attendance of such an event! Whilst Freya was thinking about protecting her future career, I was thinking that I was the next Jennifer Lopez. I imagined that I was J Lo, dancing around for the camera in my Candy Cane ensemble.

Meanwhile, poor Freya held onto her drink and kept her face well away from the lens. 'Oh dear Lord', I could see her thinking, 'just when you thought it couldn't get any worse'. As the best – and wise – friend that she is, Freya let me have my moment before (thank God) discreetly intervening and dragging me away from the camera. I don't know what happened to the footage of my Superbowl-worthy performance. I hope, for the sake of the nation's sanity, that this footage is being kept under lock and key, with no chance whatsoever that it will ever see the light of day. If it ever does, I'm sure Strictly Come Dancing will be straight on the phone offering me a place of the Christmas special (although I don't know how the Candy Cane crop top will go down on BBC One).

As the alcohol wore off – and the bar prices increased – we gave ourselves a very knowing look. It's a look we both know far too well – it's the 'let's get out of here and let's get to McDonald's now' glance. We've both become experts at giving, and reading, this look. It's the green light for escaping the venue and heading straight for the nearest McDonalds, and so this was exactly what we did.

We abandoned our drinks, grabbed our belongings, and escaped out of the club. Within minutes, we were ordering our Chicken Nuggets and Mozzarella Dippers in the iconic Oxford Road McDonalds, where the whole of Manchester seemingly congregates after every night out. As I order us an Uber to get us straight back to Cheshire, we digest both our Chicken Nuggets and the evening that we have just experienced. I absolutely love making these memories with Freya, and I just know that we will remember our 'Sugar Boy' night out for many Christmases to come. I just love that we have this 'let's just have fun' attitude to life – life is all about making memories, and this is not a night that we are going to forget in a hurry! When I'm older and looking back on my youth, I don't want to think 'oh yes I was very careful about what I did and I stayed in every single night'. I want to be able to look back and think 'OH MY GOD, WHAT WERE WE LIKE!? Yes, we made the most of it, made some hilarious memories, and we had some good fun'. This is what life is all about! And I am so blessed to have friends who will humour me, come along with me, and always look out for me. In return, I hope to give them experiences and nights out that will give them a good laugh, a chance to not have a care in the world, and that will not be forgotten in a hurry! And, if I may say so myself, I do believe that the 'Sugar Boy' night ticked all of these boxes…even if it may have been traumatic for my blonde bombshell best friend!

****

I absolutely love being home for Christmas, which as you know is my absolute favourite time of the year. We have a gorgeous tree my parents have picked from the Forest in the Dining Room, which is decorated with multicoloured lights and an impressive variety of decorations. We have dozens of different baubles, including a Harrods bauble, a Greek turtles bauble, plus stars and snowflakes that Sam and I have made in Primary School. And, if I may say so myself, this year's tree is giving Kris Jenner's militantly colour co-ordinated trees a run for their money!

I don't know about you, but I always love the build-up to Christmas so much more than the actual day itself. Don't get me wrong; I love Christmas Day itself. Still, there's something about all the run-up (the last-minute shopping and preparation) that fills me with so much excitement and joy. I love heading off for some last-minute present shopping or going to see Granny as she sets up her dining room table ahead of the big day. I love buying the Christmas edition of the Radio Times and seeing all the lights, displays and Santa's Grottos in the Garden Centres! I love watching the Christmas specials of all the comedies on TV, and nothing makes me happier than a cosy night in watching one of my favourite Christmas movies. It is the most magical and wonderful time of the year, and it always seems to go far too quickly!

This Christmas, as we usually do, we are going down to Alderley for Christmas lunch with Granny and Grumpy. We all sit in their gorgeous big lounge, opening presents and enjoying a festive drink (Mum, Gran and I on the Asti). We then head into the dining room for the most delicious Christmas dinner, with the turkey 'expertly' carved by Grumpy and the homemade Christmas Pudding generously covered in brandy by Gran. The Waitrose crackers are pulled, drinks are poured, and paper hats are worn. It is the happiest of occasions, not just because of the good food and regular refills of Gran's Martini Asti. This, in my opinion, is what life is all about. I have been blessed with the most amazing family in the world, and nothing makes me happier than spending this day in their loving company.

After watching the Queen's Speech and the Strictly Christmas Special, we head home for the next instalment of our family festivities. This evening, as always, Grandad is coming over for some of my dad's famous Christmas night buffet, which has become quite the tradition in our home. In previous years, Grandad would come with Grandma. Grandma was always guaranteed to bring plenty of fun and entertainment to any evening. For the past few years, she has been living in a care home after being diagnosed with Alzheimer's. So we had visited her earlier this morning instead. It is always so lovely to see her, especially if you can get her to sit still for longer than 0.5 seconds! I can remember how hard the first visit to the care home was for Sam and I – Grandma's condition had rapidly deteriorated. She was unable to recognise us at all. It was, of course, wonderful to see her and hold her hand. But it was also heartbreaking to think that our Grandma – someone we loved so much and whom we had known for the entirety of our lives – no longer recognised who we were. In the UK alone, there are over 850,000 people currently living with Dementia, with someone in this country developing dementia every three minutes. It is a very cruel and heartbreaking condition, which is extraordinarily difficult not only for the individual but also for their family and friends. Grandma was once the life and soul of the family gathering, keeping everyone entertained and showering us grandchildren with attention and love. Whilst she was still here in this world – and keeping the care home staff on their toes twenty-four hours a day! – it was extremely difficult to see her without that sparkle in her eyes, and it was heartbreaking not to be able to have any eye contact or conversation.

It was, of course, so important to see Grandma and spend time with her, whether she knew that we were visiting her or not. Perhaps she sometimes did, or perhaps she could at least feel our presence and sense our love around her. And so, we took her gifts to unwrap on Christmas morning, and we spent an hour, or two sat with her in the care home lounge. Sometimes, I might try and talk to her about memories of what we used to get up to when Sam and I were younger. I might talk, for example, about those Saturday morning school 'lessons' I would subject her and Grandad to in their dining room! Or I might mention her favourite sweets – Percy Pigs and Happy Hippos – of which she would always have a constant supply. Sam and I would talk about our fond memories of day trips with Grandma and Grandad during summer holidays. We reminisced about days out to Chester Zoo, Manchester Airport Viewing Park, and the little train at Brookside Garden Centre. Even if Grandma might not be able to recognise us, it was a blessing that she was here and that we could spend time with someone so important to us. After all of the love and kindness she had shown us over the years, it was the least we could do to see her for a couple of hours on Christmas morning. After we had left, Grandad would spend the day with Grandma at the care home, enjoying Christmas Lunch and the Christmas television specials with the other residents.

And so, on Christmas night, Grandad drove over to our house with a generous number of gifts and – I'm sure – an excitement about enjoying all of those iconic buffet bits. Now, here's what you need to know about my dad; when he is cooking, he is the next Jamie Oliver. When he is in that kitchen, he takes it very seriously indeed! His Sunday Roasts are a masterpiece, his Summer night BBQs are legendary, and his Christmas night buffet is an art form. Every nibble, picnic item, mini vegetable spring roll and humous dip under the sun is included in this Christmas night buffet spread. It won't surprise you to learn that this buffet then keeps us all fed well into the New Year. This Christmas night masterpiece is no exception to the trend – Stuart, as always, well and truly delivers with his mini sausage rolls and crisp selection!

We sit down to enjoy the EastEnders Christmas special and exchange presents, bringing the happiest of days to the happiest of endings. It makes me so happy to know that, whilst I can go off and live my best life in London, I will always be able to come back to the most accepting and loving of family homes. With Flash at my feet and my amazing family around me, I realise that it is a very happy Christmas indeed. And I dare to dream about Christmas Days to come when I hope to have the whole family at my Kris Jenner-style home for a gorgeous Christmas Dinner. I dream of my future children leaving mince pies and mulled wine out for Santa. I imagine them waking up early on Christmas morning ready to open all of their freshly delivered presents. My parents and grandparents have been the perfect role models to both Sam and I. They have been experts at showcasing what it means to create a strong and loving family unit. I do feel so genuinely blessed to have had these exceptional role models and to have been brought up in this loving family unit. I know, with my whole heart, that family is everything to me. Nothing matters more than my family, and I include within that term my parents, grandparents, brother and – of course – best friends. I cannot wait to create that family unit for myself, and I cannot wait for so many family Christmas celebrations to come. I have visions of Becky, Freya, Kristina, Darragh, Morgan and Sam all turning up with their families for extravagant Christmas Eve parties. Our loved ones will surround us, all enjoying the canapes, before we are carried home by our partners. Oh, Freya's had one too many Why does Christmas leave me daydreaming like this?! What is it about this time of year that leaves me itching to become the next Kris Jenner and take the festive celebrations to the next level up?! All I know is that it is the most wonderful time of the year, and I am so blessed to be surrounded by the most wonderful family. Now, where's the rest of that Prosecco, I ask Queen P, as she drifts into an Asti-induced coma on the sofa beside me. Well, it would be rude for a theology student not to toast Jesus on his birthday, wouldn't it! Merry Christmas, one and all!

30. NEW YEAR, NEW ME?

It's New Year's Eve, and I'm sat in an empty Virgin Trains carriage on my way back down to London. The last few days have been a blur of buffets (thanks Dad), Christmas TV specials, and catching up with friends. Freya is just about recovering from the 'Sugar Boy' ordeal and is getting over the trauma of seeing me dressed in a candy cane crop top and little more than a Santa hat. I love being home, but I am also excited and itching to get back down to London. We're not back at university until the middle of January, but I've been asked to work New Year's Eve at Heaven, and this is not an offer than I can refuse!

New Year's Eve, I'm told, is the club's biggest and busiest night of the year. The doors open at 9 pm, and people will be partying right through until 5 am. At midnight, stars of RuPaul's drag race will lead the countdown, followed by a balloon drop and confetti cannons as the massive on-screen clock strikes twelve. I am super excited to be working this evening, and feel ready to start the new year in style. To be honest, I have never really enjoyed going to New Years Eve parties. If I stay in at home, I find watching the fireworks on the TV rather anti-climactic. And so I'm quite happy to be working this evening – I will, essentially, be getting paid to chat to people and party. And I'll be busy working, meaning there will be a purpose behind me staying up so late just because it is the start of a new year!

***

I arrive at work, a McDonald's cup of tea and about ten thousand sugar sachets in hand, ready for the busy night ahead. And it looks like busy is going to be an understatement – it's barely turned 8 pm, and the queue is already ridiculously long. Embankment is closed off ahead of the firework display, and I was supposed to have a special wristband showing that I worked in the area and could have access through the cordon. Unsurprisingly, I did not have the aforementioned wristband. So I found myself waving my lanyard around and trying to convince the security staff that I did, in fact, work at G-A-Y Heaven. I don't know what gave it away, but it turned out they didn't need much convincing to believe that I worked at a club named G-A-Y. And so, to my relief, they let me through the cordon and down towards Heaven. They joked – although I didn't realise it was a joke in the heat of the moment – that I had to enter via a set of ladders leaned against Charing Cross station. 'You need to go in through the roof' one of them said, before bursting into laughter as he realised I was genuinely about to find a way to scale the roof of the bloody station! There were helicopters ahead, police everywhere, and it was all very exciting. In that adrenaline-filled moment, I believed that anything – including having to climb onto the roof to get into the club – could have been possible.

The doors open and it's a non-stop three hours of serving hundreds of people on reception. We need to get as many people in before midnight as possible, and the club is very quickly at full capacity. Midnight approaches, Jeremy appears on stage with the RuPaul stars, and the crowds go crazy as 2019 arrives. This is one way to start the new year, I think to myself, before getting back to work on reception as a whole new wave of partygoers arrives through the doors.

The rest of the night flies by so quickly, and I make it through to 5 am. Happy New Year, I think, let's make this year my best year yet…and let's get some sleep! Just as I'm ready to head off to bed, Alfee appears and asks me if I want to go out with him and a couple of the other staff. 'Go out?!' I ask in disbelief… 'but it's 5 am?!' To my surprise, I do not take much persuading before walking from Heaven at Charing Cross back into Soho. To my utter shock, it turns out that the party is still going strong. It is now already daylight, but this is no reason for anybody to be even considering heading home.

By some modern miracle, I manage to stay out until 10 am – yes, 10 am – before I completely and utterly crash and sneak off to head back to Stratford on the tube. When I tell you I have never felt tiredness like it, oh my God, I mean it! But do you know what? I do not regret it…at ALL! I have genuinely had the best night and the best start to the new year, and making this kind of memory is exactly what life is all about! So I head back to Stratford feeling very tired, but also very happy. I'm putting myself out there, stepping outside of my comfort zone, and letting go of my strict sleep schedule! And I love my life as a result! You're only young once, and you only live once! So you've got to make some memories, have some fun...and remember that you can catch up on sleep at a later date!

****

Let's fast forward a few weeks now, and I'm back at University for Semester Two of First Year. I've (just about) recovered from my sleep-deprived New Years Eve, and I'm having the best start to the new year. I've had one exam this January, which took place at an enormous conference centre called Kensington Olympia. The exam 'hall' was just ridiculous. There were literally hundreds, if not thousands, of students, sat in rows, whilst exam invigilators with high visibility jackets patrolled the aisles. They had a full microphone system in place, and they somehow managed to get every single one of us in the right seat with the right exam paper in front of us. I felt like it was education meets factory farming – the sheer size of this exam was just baffling! But I think I did okay in the exam, even if I was slightly distracted by the fact hundreds of students were sitting exams around me. I felt relieved to be able to tick one module off as 'completed' so early in the year.

We're back at university with four new modules, all of which I find very interesting, and enjoyable to study. I'm getting to speak to a few new people on my course, which is always good. I'm finding that there are some genuinely lovely individuals who I hadn't had the pleasure of crossing paths with yet. Back in Flat 105, Carl and Maisie are still putting up with my fake tan fiascos and rants about boys. The three of us are quickly bonding over angry notes that the lovely cleaner, Ava Maria is leaving us. Poor Ava Maria, who comes into the kitchen every couple of weeks, does not seem happy about the state of our surfaces. We frequently get left memos – usually in block capitals – asking us 'TAKE OUT YOUR BINS!!!' or 'WIPE DOWN SURFACES!!!' We proudly pin each of these notes up on the noticeboard in our kitchen. I'm sure Ava Maria was delighted to see this the next time she came in to inspect our kitchen!

I'm still recovering from my sleep-deprived New Year's Eve, and I'm also back working Saturday nights at Heaven. During my time working at Heaven, I would cross paths with the club's owner, Jeremy Joseph. I would see Jeremy – and his dog, Jacob– running around setting up the club for 10 pm. He appeared to have an unending source of energy, meaning he could run club nights all night, every night of the week. I could not get through one night shift without feeling like I'd been hit by a sleep-deprivation-fuelled bus. So I wanted to know how on earth this amount of endurance and energy was humanly possible.

As you know, I am always in awe of people I perceive to be strong leaders, be it in education, business or politics. Jeremy was a strong leader and exceptional businessman – he was the owner of a nightclub empire named, very creatively if I may say so, G-A-Y. He owned Europe's biggest LGBT+ nightclub, two other venues in Central London, plus another venue in Manchester. And every weekend, he would appear on stage to introduce the A-List acts that he had flown in from across the globe. And we are not just talking stars of RuPaul's Drag Race, although they did make weekly appearances on Thursday nights at Heaven. We are talking serious global stars that even my mum would be able to name! Heaven has played host to megastars such as Miley Cyrus, One Direction, The Pussycat Dolls, Rita Ora, Lady Gaga and Troye Sivan. The list could go on and on.

How did he manage to book these massive names? How did he manage to singlehandedly run this LGBT+ club empire? I had all of these questions, but I was terrified of the man! He was, after all, the big boss, and he was the man in charge…and so, I did not want to put a single foot wrong! And so, whenever I saw him around the club, I would keep my head down. I would usually see Jacob, the gorgeous dog, before I saw Jeremy. So I had five seconds to make sure that I looked busy and as if I was working hard (which, may I just confirm, I was!)

However, as time went on, I was becoming more confident working in the nightclub environment. It was now January, and I had been working at Heaven for about four months. It was about 9.30 pm, and I'd arrived at work early, overestimating how long it would take me to fight through the crowds along the Strand and down towards Embankment tube station. I was stood backstage – down a brightly illuminated purple corridor – and sipping my McDonalds cup of tea. I was checking myself out in the massive mirror on the wall and about to take a selfie (as I – being the vain 18-year old I was – regularly liked to do). Suddenly the double doors at the end of the corridor flung open and in came Jacob. Oh no, I thought, instantly panicking about the fact I was just stood here taking selfies in a backstage mirror. However, this Saturday night, I was feeling unusually confident, not to mention conversational. And so I decided that I wanted to chat to Jeremy about his nightclub empire.

As you know, I like to think I'm the next Holly Willoughby! As we chatted, I got onto the topic of mental health and how passionate I was about raising awareness of eating disorders. Jeremy told me that also been suffering from an eating disorder – for many years – and said how keen he also was to raise awareness of this mental illness. It was a lightbulb moment in my little 'Huw Edwards mindset' brain. 'I have a YouTube channel', I told Jeremy, 'and I would love to interview you about your experiences with an eating disorder'. To my absolute – and very pleasant – surprise, Jeremy agreed. It's another one of those times when you look back and think 'thank God I found the confidence to ask that question!' Imagine, I often think, if you had just kept your head down and allowed your nerves about starting conversations hold you back! Instead, I had secured my first opportunity to interview a high-profile figure on a topic I was so passionate about – mental health.

Several weeks later and I was still pestering Jeremy for a sit-down interview. One Saturday night, he finally agreed, and I spent the rest of my shift thinking about the best questions I could ask. Later that week, in daylight hours, we sat down backstage at Heaven, and I started to record. Whilst my lighting and sound were not going to put Phil and Holly out of a job anytime soon, I thoroughly enjoyed our 40-minute sit-down chat (and, if you're interested, you can see it for yourself over on YouTube right now!) I felt like this interview could achieve a lot of good – here was a prominent LGBT+ business leader speaking openly and honestly about mental health. Whenever you get a high profile figure speaking about mental health in this way, you are guaranteed to see a lot of good being done. This is especially the case for minority social groups, such as the LGBT+ demographic, where mental health struggles are often more prevalent. Men, in particular, encounter a lot of stigma when it comes to mental illness, especially eating disorders. I believed that, by doing this interview, I might be able to make a genuine difference.

Without trying to sound like Mother Teresa, making such a positive difference was exactly what I wanted to be doing with my life. Going out and feeling confident was one thing, but going through life feeling that you are making a genuine difference in other people's lives is quite another. You might get a buzz from a good night out with lots of attention from attractive people, but the buzz that you get from knowing you've genuinely helped someone is on a different level. After the interview, I was on an absolute high. I remember squeezing onto the rush-hour packed Jubilee line on my way back to Stratford and feeling absolutely on top of the world. Previously, I had been trying to create an online 'identity' – if that's the right word – by posting provocative pictures and seeking the attention of men. There's nothing wrong with doing this, but I realised this was not making me genuinely happy. Instead, I felt so empowered and so positive about becoming – I hoped – a positive role model who could give people a little bit of hope, motivation and, perhaps, inspiration. That weekend, I uploaded my YouTube video with Jeremy to an extremely positive response. I am extraordinarily grateful for Jeremy's kindness and support. His business had given me the parttime job of my dreams, and he had agreed to answer my questions about mental health on YouTube. I feel very blessed, fortunate and inspired. It's yet another amazing thing London has done for me that I could not be more thankful for!

***

As I say, I wanted to make my new year a brand new start. I saw the new year as an opportunity to establish myself as a voice known for discussing mental health and wellbeing. My first few months in London had given me so much confidence, and I had enjoyed this fantastic opportunity to work at the heart of the gay scene. But these months had also had their challenging moments in terms of my mental health and wellbeing. As I have mentioned, I struggled somewhat with my social media fixation and with that general anxiety that affects us all when we move away from home. I was in a place in my life where I wanted to make a positive difference in the world. I had wanted to make my mark – on Instagram and in the gay clubs – in a very shallow and appearance-based way. I had realised just how deeply unfulfilling this had ended up becoming for me.

So I was determined to make my mark in a very different, and much more positive, way. I wanted to make a positive change in the world and people's lives. I thought the best way to do this would be by speaking out on mental health. If I had been struggling with these insecurities, fears, thoughts and feelings, then so were other people as well! And I wanted to use my newfound voice – which I'd found as a result of moving to London and enjoying all these new opportunities – to make a genuinely positive difference in the world. Here's what I believe: It is so important to share our own stories and allow people to share their own stories as well. Every single person has a story to tell, and every single story can inspire others. It is my passionate belief that, in life, should 'aspire to inspire'. I wonder what 12-year-old Ben – anorexic, lonely and lost – would have thought of 19-year-old Ben interviewing one of the most famous LGBT+ figures in the UK about the importance of eating disorder awareness? It sounds very Mother Teresa, but I strive to become the role model I wish I had when I was younger. That way, I hope to give some confidence and support to any young people who might be struggling in the same way that I once did. That's why I am so proud of my interview with Jeremy. I believe that it sent a strong message to both my younger self and to anyone struggling with their own identity or mental health. Look at my journey, I think, and look at what you can achieve with your life when you work hard at becoming the best version of yourself and turning things around.

As a result of this interview, I felt like I'd found a new calling in life. I was having visions of joining Sussanah Read on Good Morning Britain, interviewing top public figures and starting important conversations on stigma-surrounded topics. I had found a new sense of place, direction and purpose in the world. This had begun in the months after leaving hospital. And it had developed in my role as Head Boy at All Hallows. But now I was here, in Central London, starting the conversation on mental health. I felt that this is what I wanted to be doing, and it was exactly who I wanted to be. Never mind if you think I'm attractive or not, I thought; anyone can become the next attractive model! My new focus was now on empowering people, spreading kindness in the world, and tackling the stigma that continues to surround mental health. If I can make a difference in just one person's life, then my work here is done!

I started speaking more openly about mental health on my YouTube channel. In the past, my content had focused on Othello, English Language and Philosophy revision videos! Today, I was sat down in my university bedroom filming a video titled 'life after an eating disorder'. At first, I found this genuinely difficult – I did not want people to think I was weak, insecure, or unwell. There is so much stigma around mental health, and I feel that many people still do not fully understand what we mean by 'mental illness'. The problem, I believe, is that mental illness is often invisible. You cannot see the thoughts that are shaping someone's mood or driving their seemingly irrational behaviour. Consequently, many people who have not battled with mental illness think that you should just 'pull yourself together' or 'get over yourself'. People do not take conditions such as anorexia or anxiety seriously – they see it as attention-seeking or as a 'phase' that someone just needs to grow out of.

Here's how I see it: you wouldn't tell someone with a broken leg or a heart condition that they are attention-seeking and just need to get over it. And so, in the same way, you cannot tell someone suffering from mental illness that they are just attention-seeking or being stupid. Would someone really choose to be so unhappy? Would someone really choose to have these irrational thoughts and compulsive behaviours? At the end of the day, we all want to be happy, and we all deserve to experience this genuine happiness and fulfilment in our lives. Consequently, we need to invest in understanding mental illness and learning how best to support the millions of people suffering from conditions such as depression, anorexia and anxiety. Somebody going through mental illness deserves love, support and compassion – not judgment, misunderstanding or stigma!

I had spoken about my mental health, as I have mentioned, in my role as Head Boy. But I felt this was different. Back then, I was talking about mental health to a group of students at my school in Macclesfield, and it was all in the context of education. This time, I was sitting down and sharing this with the world. My biggest fear is being perceived as an 'attention seeker'. I was terrified that people would think I am too full of myself or that I loved the sound of my own voice too much. I was not sharing my story because I wanted sympathy and attention. However, the process of speaking through my experiences *was* incredibly cathartic and healing. I was sharing my story because I genuinely wanted to help others. I genuinely believed that talking about my mental health on YouTube could make a positive difference in the world.

This is one of the benefits of social media – it gets homemade and heartfelt content directly into homes across the country. Social media platforms such as YouTube give people direct and unfiltered access to inspiring and organic content that they can watch from the comfort of their bedroom. I have personally been so inspired by social media personalities whose videos and content that I have *just so happened* to stumble across online. Social media has an extraordinary ability to empower, inspire and connect people across the globe. I wanted to play my part in starting difficult conversations, sharing difficult stories and – hopefully – making a very positive difference. A couple of years ago, I couldn't bear to hear the word 'anorexia' being mentioned anywhere around me. Today, I was using the word about five-times-a-second in a YouTube video being posted on a public platform. I found that, once I'd got into it, I actually thoroughly enjoyed filming this kind of video. I got over my worry about coming across as self-obsessed or sympathy-seeking. I wanted to share my story in order to inspire others, not to blow my own trumpet.

Once I was clear about my motivation for producing these videos, I started investing all of my time and effort into sharing my story and talking about taboo topics! Over the next few months, I write blog posts, film YouTube conversations, and really make an effort to 'start the conversation' on Mental Health. It feels so good to be making what I hope is a very positive difference in this issue, whilst also getting to live this amazing life in London. It really does show how you can succeed at turning your life around – I had gone from being hospitalised with an eating disorder to, some seven years later, being confident enough to speak out about this experience and feeling seriously motivated to tackle the stigma surrounding mental health in modern British society.

Of course, I still had a lot of things to work through myself. I really do think that being in London did me a world of good, and it also highlighted a few of the self-limiting beliefs and defensive-behaviours that continued to be a barrier to my happiness and fulfilment in life. Don't get me wrong, I was loving my time in London, but I don't think it's bad to admit that you are still struggling with a few irrational beliefs and fears. My 'respond to people staring with a smile' approach is working well. But I am still extremely defensive and anxious in many different social situations (not that anybody around me would ever know!) I am terrified of being lonely, for example. I still feel this sense of inadequacy and unattractiveness compared to other guys, But, after working at Heaven – and just being in London – I have noticed an increase in my self-confidence and self-esteem. It has done me a world of good!

***

The rest of Semester Two flies by in a blur of studying, cocktails, and Saturday's spent working at Heaven. As exam season approaches, I get serious about revising and spend most of my time revising in one of the ten-million Prets that you find in Central London. I head back to Cheshire to revise at home for a couple of weeks, figuring out that I'll be much more productive and focused if I am studying in my room or the dining room at home. I feel like I'm back in the A-levels headspace, which I can confirm I had not missed in the slightest! I head back to London, to Kensington Olympia, for my end of year exams, which seem to have gone. We all celebrate finishing our last exam with a trip to Wetherspoons – of course – for a glass of prosecco, or two. First-year, I think, it has been a pleasure! I now have about one month left in London, and that means that one single thing is on the agenda… PARTY!

31. ONE SUMMER IN SOHO...

It's now the middle of May 2019, and I've got a month left in London with absolutely nothing to do. University has finished for the year, but I still have a month left on my student accommodation contract. I want to make the most of every single day I have got living in London, and so I fully intend to stay in London until the very last day of that contract! Oh, they're going to have to drag me out of Flat 105, let me tell you that now!

I have been having lunch – at the Montagu Pyke Wetherspoons, Tottenham Court Road – with Darragh every Saturday since September. We would meet at lunchtime and order the same food every single week. I always, without fail, ordered the Skinny Chicken Burger, with an enormous serving of the Mango Chutney on the side. I had met Darragh, you may remember, on my first night working in Heaven, when he had been doing a shift dropping the balloons every hour throughout the night. It turned out that dropping the balloons was just one part of Darragh's nightshifts at G-A-Y and Heaven.

Before arriving at Heaven, he would do a three-hour shift outside G-A-Y Bar giving out wristbands guaranteeing people discounted entry to Heaven. He would work on the 'Flyer Team', as they are known, several nights a week. I loved the sound of this job, and I had visions of all the sexy men I would be able to meet whilst giving out wristbands. I knew that they were looking for new members of the Flyer Team, and so I sent my application and CV through to Jeremy. I was offered an interview and then a trial shift, before starting work that weekend. I would work Monday, Thursday, Friday and Saturday nights from 8.20 pm in Soho. I would then head down to Heaven for a shift working until either 2 am (Thursday), 4 am (Friday), or 5 am (Saturday). Jobs at Heaven included running the charity tuck shop, giving out flyers to people leaving the venue, or signing people up to take part in events.

Words cannot even describe how much I loved every second of this job. My summer spent working on the Flyer Team was the best summer of my life. I was living what seriously felt like the absolute dream. I was getting to spend my summer's nights working in the very heart of Soho, handing out flyers and signing people up for club night competitions. And, to top it all off, I was flirting with the many sexy men walking along Old Compton Street! If only younger Ben could have seen me now! I was so proud of how far I had come and what I was managing to do with my life! I was here in the heart of Soho, working at these iconic venues and having genuinely the time of my life! I was full of confidence and having a fabulous, care-free time. What more could you ask for?

As I spend my summer's nights working in Soho, I meet some of the loveliest people I could ever have hoped to meet. Of course, I already knew Darragh and Alfee, but I also met Nathan and Nana. They would later come and visit me in Manchester for Pride in September. I also met countless other genuinely lovely humans, including Ivy, Charlie, Harley, Will, David, Jacob, and James. I loved every single second of my evenings working in Soho with these wonderful people. I felt confident, and like I belonged. We worked hard, and we played hard! These were the best summer nights! As you can imagine, sleep wasn't at the top of my priorities list during my time working on the Flyer Team. However, I was quite happy to ignore my constant tiredness if it meant getting to work, flirt and party in Soho all night long!

There is absolutely nothing that can compare to the buzz of working at these venues. I will forever be thankful for this amazing opportunity to make memories, find self-confidence and party the night away. I could not be more grateful for this amazing opportunity to just 'be myself' and have fun. I loved giving out the wristbands and signing people up for strip contests, and I loved being back in Heaven every week as well! I remember first walking into Heaven and feeling so terrified of this enormous nightclub. These days, I was strutting around like I owned the place. Looking back, it is a miracle that I was not arrested for some of the outfits that I was wearing to work. My go-to "uniform" typically consisted of a very tight mesh top and some very short cycling shorts. I paired this with a little black coat that I hoped would keep me warm when walking between venues or getting the tube home in the morning! This Summer working in Soho was one of the most amazing and entertaining life experiences that I will forever treasure and never forget. I got to flirt, dance, and laugh my way through the evenings. And, by the end of my time working on the team, I was *almost* capable of actually putting a wristband on somebody's wrist (oh it was a struggle!)

I was genuinely heartbroken when my last night in London arrived, and it was time for my last shift at G-A-Y. After finishing my shift in Soho, I made sure to go out in style with one last night out at Heaven with Nana and Nathan. At around 4 am, I headed back to Stratford One for one last time this year.

What a Summer it had been! What a year it had been! I was feeling so sad to be leaving, but I was also very ready for a couple of months at home! After all of these 5 am finishes, I felt as if I could hibernate for at least 12 months! The fact that I had arranged to stay at Stratford One for Second Year – this time moving into a gorgeous big flat with Morgan in the room next door – meant that I had September to look forwards to. I knew that I would be going home for the best summer with Freya, Kristina and Becky, before moving back down to London in no time at all. I got back to Flat 105, where our Christmas tree was still standing in the hallway, and headed straight to bed. Mum and Dad were driving down the next morning to help me move out, and I had already planned a night out on Canal Street with Freya and Becky for the very next evening. It meant I would get home and have about four hours to sort out my things, before getting back into my mesh-and-shorts ensemble for a night out with my girls.

This has been, without question, the best year of my life so far. It is ridiculous to think how much has happened, and how much I have grown, in the past 12 months. I do feel like a brand new person – and I could not be happier! I have been living my very best life. I have made amazing friends and amazing memories that will last a lifetime. As that Royal Navy advert says; I was born in Cheshire, but I was made in London! After just one year in the 'big smoke', I was now one confident, self-assured, and fiery individual! I was finding my feet, finding my voice, and – most importantly

– feeling so happy and fulfilled in life. Thank you London…I'll see you in September!

32. BACK TO REALITY IN CHESHIRE

I'm back home for summer after an incredible ten months living in London. It genuinely has been the best year of my life. London has been everything that I'd dreamed it would be – and more! I still cannot believe that I have been living in the capital city – it's insane that my commute to university was on the Central Line. It's ridiculous that I spent my Saturday evenings working at a world-famous LGBT+ nightclub in Trafalgar Square! I have come home for the summer feeling absolutely on cloud nine – I can't wait for September and to be back down in London doing it all over again!

I'm excited to be back at Mottram Hall for the summer, and I love seeing Ella and the team once again. This job made me who I am so proud to be today, and these corridors are filled with so many happy memories. This was the place that I found my feet, found my confidence for working with the public, and I will forever treasure my Mottram Hall family!

We head off for our annual family holiday to Kefalonia, before I head off to Manchester Pride weekend with Emma. Nathan and Nana get the coach up from London and join us on Canal Street for the Sunday evening, which is nothing but iconic. I love this celebration of authenticity, not to mention this fabulous excuse for the biggest rainbow-themed party. After just a couple of drinks, Nathan and I are living our best lives dancing on every raised platform we can find. I love being able to just have fun and go a little bit wild, surrounded by genuinely the most loving and kind friends that I could ask for. Poor Emma, I think, who has been stuck with me since Secondary School. We used to go to Year 11 parties with me wearing a little blazer and refusing to drink alcohol. Now, she is seeing me in a tiny mesh top and cycling shorts, consuming prosecco like it's tap-water. God help the poor girl!

***

I was excited to get back down to London, and I wanted to go back with more self-confidence and self-assurance than ever before. That meant confronting the insecurities I had faced over the past year, and working out how I could learn from them. My main problems had been my sensitive skin, insecure mindset, and my defensive nature.

What was driving all of this defensiveness? Why did I keep taking every single thing that happened to me so personally? I know that I was always quite sensitive as a child, and I made a really bad habit of taking everything to heart. After a lifetime of feeling so – for want of a better word – victimised, I finally realised that being so sensitive was not serving me in any way, shape, or form. I was far too emotional and far too dependent on external validation. I had this unsatisfiable and untameable desperation to be liked. I could not cope with even the slightest bit of criticism or questioning. In the past, the slightest little thing would leave me feeling deeply upset. These days, the slightest thing would leave me feeling extraordinarily angry. It was almost as if I was at war with the world; I felt like I was always on the defensive and I was always endlessly chasing approval. Why was I so desperate to be universally liked, and why was I so seriously devastated when I was not? What void was I trying to fill, what insecurity was I trying to heal?

As always, it was reading and education that saved me. I read a book entitled 'A Model For Living', written by the psychiatrist Julian Short. In this book, Short wrote about the importance of living your life with 'kindness and dignity', at all times. He wrote that to be liked by other people; you must act like somebody who likes themselves. That means being able to admit when you are wrong, being able to apologise, and knowing that rejection is not the end of the world. It means living in accordance with your core values, which go to the very core of who you are as an individual. It means striving to be someone who is 'respected' rather than desperately wanting to be 'liked'. As I read these wise words, everything started making sense. I realised the root of my problems – I did not, deep down, like myself. All of that homonegativity was still having an impact. I still believed that people only ever saw me as this stereotypically gay, attention-seeking and 'over-the-top' schoolboy. They thought I could be funny, but they didn't think I was attractive. Again, everything was coming back down to the question of whether I would find a boyfriend. I was so desperate for a relationship, and yet I couldn't quite understand why. Was I trying to prove that I was loveable? Was I trying to prove that someone could be committed to me? Was I scared of letting them in behind the external confidence and flamboyant façade?

I genuinely had not realised that I had been doing this, but I started to become aware of how much of a closed-book I actually was. I was all about preaching authenticity, confidence, and connection, and yet I was unable to open up to people myself. I loved listening to people's stories and asking them one million and one questions about their own lives. Still, I hated it when the tables were turned, and the questions were about me. I had it in my head that everyone thought I was this annoying attention-seeker and so, to be liked, I needed to prove them wrong. I could not talk about myself, and I could not open up about my feelings – I didn't want to be a burden, and I didn't want to be seen as this annoying and dramatic boy. I didn't mind opening up, as you know, to a therapist, who was paid to listen to my problems. But I didn't want to start pouring out my soul to anybody else. I was terrified of showing 'weakness' because I was terrified of losing people's friendship, time or attention. I didn't want to become a burden, and I didn't want to scare them away!

But now I realised that my approach was extremely counter-productive! By being such a defensive and closed-book, I was pre-empting attacks and refusing to explain myself. I would become very defensive very quickly, meaning that people could find me to be hostile, confrontational and angry. This would drive people away because nobody wants to be around someone who is overly sensitive or defensive!

What I needed to do, instead of getting so defensive, was either snap myself out of my little mood or explain to whoever I was angry with *why* I felt so upset. I was even irrationally defensive with my mum, who I would argue with over the smallest of things. I would shut down, shut her out, and tell her to shut up! This would, inevitably, push her buttons, which would escalate into a blazing row. All of this could have been avoided if I'd simply sat her down and explained how I was feeling or why I didn't like something that she had said. My default response was never to stay calm and explain; it was to launch straight into defending myself via angry outbursts and ridiculous mood swings. I'd march around the house, refusing to speak and glaring at my whole family. In my head, I was being treated so badly and unfairly. In the real world, I had taken someone's throwaway comment to heart and made a complete mountain out of a molehill.

In life, I pride myself on my ability to articulate and explain in my essay writing and lessons. Despite this, I was completely incapable of articulating how I was feeling, even to my closest family members and friends. It's ridiculous! Perhaps it's because I knew how irrational or ludicrous some of my insecurities were. So I felt embarrassed by how sensitive I was being. I've realised that, whenever I feel insecure, my defence mechanism is to become very angry, very quickly. I try to protect myself and defend myself by throwing grenades at everybody around me, lashing out and shutting people out before they have a chance to hurt me. It is extraordinarily counterproductive – lashing out like this pushes people away, scares people off, and presents me as a very insecure individual.

I knew, thanks to reading Short's book, that I needed to take back control of my life and my self-esteem. I needed to start acting like somebody who actually liked themselves, which meant much less defensiveness and much more calm. I needed to stop caring about being liked and start learning to like myself. I needed to stop being so sensitive and angry. Instead, I needed to start becoming much stronger and stoical. I could not go through adult life with the emotional intelligence of a two-year-old! I could not continue riding this rollercoaster of emotions, reactions, and

This is the perfect segway to the second book that has helped me to get over my defensiveness and put to bed my heightened sensitivities. 'The Daily Stoic', written by Ryan Holiday and Stephen Hanselman. The book promises to provide '366 meditations on wisdom, perseverance, and the art of living' – and it most certainly delivers! Holiday and Hanselman offer a short Stoic quote, from a philosopher such as Marcus Aurelius, Epictetus or Seneca, along with a short paragraph explaining what the quote means and how it can be applied to the world today. Typical titles included 'Cultivating Indifference Where Others Grow Passion', 'Wherever You

Go, There Your Choice Is', 'One Day It Will All Make Sense', 'Revenge Is A Dish Best Not Served', and 'Train To Let Go Of What's Not Yours'. These daily reflections were the perfect tonic for my defensive, sensitive and emotional soul. They whipped my sensitivities into shape and effectively dealt with my defensiveness. I soon started learning how to take a step back from my feelings, see the bigger picture, and start taking ownership of my life.

Stoicism did save me. It is an incredible philosophy that is extraordinarily practical. Despite being over 2,000 years old, the wisdom at the core of this school of thought could not be more relevant or important in the world today. One of my favourite Stoic quotes – and I have quite literally hundreds! - is this golden nugget from Epictetus: "Men are disturbed not by events but by the views they take of them". I think this goes to the very core of what I'm starting to learn about my life – to be happy, you must become the master of your destiny, mindset and emotions. You do not have to be a victim to other people's opinions or your emotions. Instead, you can take back full ownership and control of your life! As a result, you can become responsible for curating a happy and fulfilling life for yourself!

One of the most powerful lessons from Marcus Aurelius is this: stop getting so frustrated. Being angry is not attractive or appropriate – it's not a good look! There was one particular Daily Stoic blog that spoke to me on this issue: It's wonderful that you have high standards. It's wonderful that you are demanding of yourself. It's wonderful that you do your job. But you have to be willing to be flexible and tolerant with other people. You have to be patient. You have to keep your frustrations in check."

One of my favourite takeaways from Short's book is this: even if you know that somebody does not like you, always act as if they do. I think this is something the Stoic philosophers would have undoubtedly endorsed; your choice of behaviour should never be dictated by somebody else! You should focus on living in accordance with your core values and principles, for example, that you will always conduct yourself with kindness and dignity. Instead of impulsively reacting to circumstances, we must choose to intelligently respond.

This is something I have struggled with. Whenever I see someone who I know has been rude about me or actively tried to cause trouble for me, I am overwhelmed by uncontrollable fury! I want this person to know how angry I am about what they have done to me, and I have this serious need to have the 'last laugh'. I will always stand up for myself, and I will always stand up for those I think are being bullied, picked on, or exploited. This is unquestionably a good thing, and I am so glad to have finally found my voice. But it's also an insecurity thing – I am so sensitive that people's actions have the power to dent my self-esteem and self-confidence. As a result, I go through life constantly on the defensive. And so I regularly cause conflicts and 'call people out' over the most trivial and irrelevant issues. I need to learn to start picking my battles wisely, and know when it's best to just walk away from a situation! I don't always need to put every single person in their place! Sometimes, it's best to let karma do the work for you. Instead of becoming overwhelmed by rage, I need to learn to become the bigger person! This is only possible once you learn to actually like yourself as an individual, and once you stop depending so much on external validation. I'll know that I've got there once I start to see people who have hurt me or been rude about me, and I can treat them as if we were friends. If I can be kind, pleasant and friendly to people who have upset or hurt me in the past, then I'll know that I've sorted my self-esteem issues out! I want to choose inner peace over proving points or settling scores that are utterly irrelevant to my life! It's important to stand up for yourself, but it's also vital to protect your inner peace! And so it's time to learn the art of letting it go and letting karma do the work for you!

I am so thankful to have discovered Julian Short's book, as well as Stoicism. As a result of these brilliant books, I have started learning how to more intelligently manage my emotions and actively become the master of my own destiny. Life is all about learning, growing, and making small steps of positive progress. It's about turning every obstacle into an opportunity and realising that every setback brings you one step closer to success. I don't beat myself up for being so sensitive and defensive – I just strive to learn from it! I don't expect that the defensiveness will disappear overnight, but I do think that progress makes perfect. And I hope that I'll be able to avoid countless unnecessary confrontations in the future by learning to explain myself, rather than getting so defensive!

***

Here's another thing that I've noticed: when I look in the mirror, I have to look skinny. It is an instinctive and impulsive question that I ask without thinking: do I look skinny? LI am obsessive about it and fixated upon it. As long as I look skinny, I'm happy. The fact that I fit into women's size 2 or 4 jeans isn't enough to satisfy or placate my mind – I need to look in that mirror and believe that I look skinny. This has become my source of self-esteem and reassurance. It's irrational, and it's totally without foundation. It's also - if we are honest - pretty toxic! So how do I learn to shake this off? I've found that the best way to challenge such irrational beliefs and thoughts is through presenting yourself with empirical evidence that cannot be disputed. For example, I make myself consider empirical facts, such as the fact I fit into size four women's jeans or the fact that even 'XXS' t-shirts in the men's section are sometimes too big for me. If you can fit into size four jeans of XXS t-shirts, I ask myself; then surely you realise that you are obviously very skinny? The thing is, I actually don't. Denial of things continues to be my modus operandi, in so many areas of my life. I deny that I am really skinny, I doubt that people actually like me, and I debate whether I will ever find someone who wants to date me. In my head, I'm just being modest and trying to avoid being seen as egotistical or arrogant. In the real world, I think I am genuinely sometimes seriously delusional.

The anorexic thoughts – and some undoubtedly remain, hiding away in the very back of my brain – are the great orchestrators of my denial. They refuse to consider the empirical evidence, and they refuse to listen to my rational counter-arguments. Fortunately, the rational voices in my brain far outweigh any remnants of the anorexic beliefs. So any irrational beliefs do end up getting drowned out pretty quickly. It's taken a very long time to get here, but I am now mentally stronger – not to mention so much more rational in my thinking – than ever before. But that fear of putting on weight – and someone ending up overweight overnight – remains lodged in my mind. I am forever vigilant against eating 'too much' of the 'wrong' type of foods.

On the one hand, that's good – it means I will never end up becoming overweight! But on the other hand, it's so restrictive. I can't just shake off those chains and stop worrying about food –

I always do a thought experiment. If you could eat absolutely anything in the world (safe in the knowledge that you would never put on weight) would you still order the same items on the menu? I can tell you with confidence that I absolutely would not! Which is how I know that I'm still a prisoner, even to just a small extent, to anorexic thoughts. As much as I love having the Caesar Salad or 'skinny' chicken burger, I know that I am ordering them because they are the lowest calorie options. And suppose (as many restaurants now do) the calories are written down on the menu next to each item. In that case, this will always influence my decision about what to eat. In other words, I will always – without exception – 'choose' to the lowest calorie item on the menu.

And I use the word 'choose' very carefully. There is very little active or free 'choice' in my decision to pick the lowest calorie option available! There is, of course, nothing wrong with consciously picking to eat the lowest calorie item on the menu. This is – I'm assuming – the whole point of putting the nutritional information on the menu in the first place! After my experience with anorexia (which included months of obsessively counting every calorie I consumed), it is hard to break free from an obsession with nutritional information. Whilst I do genuinely believe I have recovered from my eating disorder, I believe that I remain a prisoner to an irrational fear of putting on weight. I still have it in my head that any weight gain will result in people making comments such as 'oh he's let himself go' or 'oh he's not so skinny anymore!' Why do I care so much about what other people think? Why am I so worried about their opinions on my waistline? Because I still have a long way to go in terms of achieving a much healthier relationship with validation and self-confidence. I need to work harder to detach myself from other people's opinions. I need to realise that my worth is not dependent on whether I can impress, please, or gain the approval of other people. I'm not going to beat myself up for this – life, as I always say, is about progress and not perfection. As long as I am slowly learning to challenge those thoughts, tackle those beliefs, and become much more secure in my skin, then I can feel happy that I am heading in the right direction.

My new 'obsession' is my belief that certain foods are giving me spots, and so I avoid certain things – such as fizzy drinks or chocolate – like the plague. We all want clear skin, but I do think we all become so obsessive and controlling about it! And I think 'control' really does go to the heart of what I'm dealing with. Everything in my life has to be controlled… at all times. Whether that's my daily routine or my dietary intake, I always feel the need to be in complete control! I cannot cope when I am not micro-managing my life. I need to know what I'm doing, and when I'm doing it; otherwise, I feel out of my depth and vulnerable. Why is this the case? What has caused this irrational need for control? What is fuelling my fixation on organisation? It's always important to keep your growth mindset in mind – you can change absolutely anything you want to change about your life! And so this need for control is another thing I'm working on hard – I'm daring myself to be vulnerable and be a little bit more spontaneous! I am learning to 'let go' a little bit and realise that it's okay not actually to know what you're doing! It's okay to just go with the flow, and it's okay to admit if you're scared or anxious. Letting down your guard is a sign of strength, not weakness! So I'm practising what I preach when I tell people that 'whatever happens in life, you can handle it!' I'm forcing myself to step outside of my comfort zone and to let go – even if just for one evening – of my need to be in control! It's small steps, but every time that you do something, you break through one more of your insecurities and fears. Remember, it's all about progress, not perfection! And it's all about unconditionally accepting yourself, irrespective of what mistakes you might make or what other people might say!

33. GETTING SERIOUS ABOUT SECOND YEAR

One of my favourite things about the drive down to Stratford is the moment that the London skyline comes into view from the M1. One minute, you're driving down what could be a standard motorway anywhere in the UK, the next minute you're driving directly towards the skyscrapers of the City. I always find this to be a beautiful moment – it's a reminder that you're heading towards London, the busiest and most amazing city on Earth.

It's September 2019, and mum and dad are driving me back down to London for my second year of university. This year, there is a lot more space left in the car – I've learnt which kitchen utensils I actually need, and which ones I can get through a year at university without (which, it turns out, is the vast majority of appliances that I came down with last year). I'm so excited to get back to London and to be heading back to Stratford One. Morgan and I have booked rooms in the same flat, and I am super excited that she will be living in the room next to me. Pray for our new flatmates, I think, they're not ready for the dynamic duo who are about to arrive in that kitchen, prosecco in hand and chicken nuggets in the oven!

We had thought about getting a house to live in for second year, but in the end, we decided we'd much rather stay together at Stratford One. We love the place, and it feels stupid to move out when we've found somewhere that really does feel like home. Stratford One is safe, secure and in the perfect position. We have the Olympic Park on our doorstep, Westfield is twenty seconds away, and it's just 16 minutes to Holborn on the Central Line. The accommodation is extremely modern and absolutely gorgeous, and our second year is twice the size as last years! I cannot wait to get back to Stratford and throw myself straight back into London life.

Even though I know Morgan is already checked in and waiting for me at Stratford One, I am feeling absolutely terrified. I'm nervous about our new flatmates and what they'll think of me – are they going to think I'm too much? Are they going to find me too annoying? Are they going to get my sense of humour? I reach for the bottle of Sparkling Rose that I've brought with me in the car, and pour myself a glass (I've come prepared with my Poundland Prosecco flutes). I feel like Mariah Carey, sat in the back of dad's car, the London skyline coming into view in front of me, and a glass of sparkling rose in my hand. The things that my poor parents have to put up with! Although I do think that this is much less of a 'diva' moment, and much more of an 'I need some Dutch Courage!' moment!

Several miles and several glasses of bubbly later, and the Olympic Stadium has come into view. We pull around the corner, and there it is – it's Stratford One! By this stage, I am feeling excited, terrified, and slightly tipsy. We pull into the car loading bay, where our car is surrounded by men ready to help with all of the luggage. Now I really *do* feel like Mariah Carey! I abandon my bottle of sparkling rose and quickly call Morgan, tipsily demanding her to come outside as quickly as she possibly can! Poor Morgan soon appears, and I head into the building, feeling ten million times more confident now that I've got my partner-in-crime back by my side. My parents and the luggage-carrying men follow, Queen P very excited to have these men helping her to carry the duvet. I head over to the registration desk and check-in, before heading straight up to our new flat.

I walk into our new kitchen and nearly pass out with excitement (or maybe that's the prosecco?) The kitchen is – as promised – twice the size of our kitchens from last year, and includes a wall-to-wall panoramic window offering views across the Olympic Park and skyline. We have several fridges, ovens, and a gorgeous long sofa. It is so spacious, modern, and clean…I AM IN LOVE!! Morgan has brought a Zac Efron cardboard cutout that was 'just collecting dust in my car boot' (of course it was). So Zac now takes pride of place in the centre of our beautiful new kitchen. Queen P and dad arrive, both suitably impressed with the kitchen and gorgeous view of London, and both demanding a cup of tea. I put the kettle on whilst Morgan reaches for the bottle of prosecco she has chilling in the fridge, and I head off to see my new room. Morgan and I are both at the end of the – very long – corridor, and our rooms have amazing views over the Olympic Park and London skyline. We may only be on the second floor, but this view towards the City centre beats last year's view of the Eurostar and building site cranes! Morgan starts helping me unpack my clothes –

which consists mainly of mesh tops, shorts, a couple of t-shirts and too many black spray-on skinny jeans. I get a phone call from Darragh, who is outside the main entrance and demanding to be let in. Oh my God, I think, he's here already! I'd forgotten that I'd demanded Darragh come over and see me once I'd checked in. All of the bubbles had meant I'd lost all track of time...now if that's not the story of my life, I really don't know what is!

I run down and let Darragh into the building, before bringing him up to show off the new kitchen views and pour him a glass of prosecco. Queen P is delighted to see both Morgan and Darragh, and whilst she chats away to them, I get dad to help me set up my new printer. Oh my god, this was a saga and a half. It's a miracle I didn't throw the thing out of the window! After what feels like three hours of trying to set this bloody printer up, I admit defeat and leave the poor man to it. I head back to the kitchen, where I interrogate Darragh on everything he's been up to over the summer. As I quiz him on everything that he's been up to, whilst enjoying what must be my 10th glass of prosecco of the day, the kitchen door opens and in walks an unfamiliar face. It's a new flatmate, I think, praying that this tall and youthful-looking guy is going to bring some charisma and appreciate my sense of humour. 'Hello! How are you!?' I begin, slightly over-enthusiastically introducing myself as Ben, his new flatmate…and, judging by his facial expression, new worst nightmare!

The guy introduces himself as Jamie, a first-year film student who has also just moved in. Fuelled by prosecco, I begin to interrogate poor Jamie. I demanded to know everything from his choice in A-levels to his relationship status (he had a girlfriend, Lucy, who he had met back home). I then proceeded to grill Jamie on his choice of degree – which he had yet to start – and wanted to know his career ambitions after his three-year course. Jamie reminded me of Sam, which was a very good thing, and I instantly knew that he would be an iconic addition to the Flat 201 kitchen. When I asked Jamie to describe this first encounter in the Flat 201 kitchen, he diplomatically put it like this:

"The first conversation we had I was very struck by your persona".

This is a diplomatic answer. In other words, he was seriously traumatised by this prosecco-wielding second-year student wearing far too much fake tan! Jamie, bless his soul, made his excuses and escaped the kitchen as quickly as he could. I finished catching up with Darragh and Morgan, said goodbye to Queen P and Dad, before suddenly remembering that I had to get ready for work that night. That's right, it was my first day back in London…and I was back at work! Well, you know what they say – the devil works hard, but Kris Jenner works harder! After three months off, I was genuinely concerned whether I would still be awake by the end of my shift at 5 am, but I could not have been more excited to be heading back to the nightclub life! I had missed my Saturday nights on reception, and getting back to Heaven was the real reason I was back in London! Never mind the degree, I just want to be back on that dance floor!

And so, after a quick outfit change, I head off to the Central Line. I'm soon back in the Strand McDonalds and ordering my obligatory large PG Tips tea (complete with their entire supply of sugar sachets). I headed down to Heaven, and within minutes of the doors opening, it's like I have never been away. I'm serving hundreds of people on reception, and I'm living my very best life! It was so good to be back – even if I was utterly exhausted by the time 5 am came around, and I was heading off to catch the night tube home!

Just like that, I was back! Did you miss London?! I certainly didn't miss rush hour on the Central Line! Well, actually, I really did! Walking through the Cheshire countryside wasn't quite as exciting as fighting for your life on the Central Line! After a much-needed lie-in on Sunday morning, I was straight back into the swing of Stratford life. It was as if I had never been away! I was back, and this time things were better than ever! I had Morgan next door, we had a gorgeous big kitchen down the hallway, and we now actually knew what we were doing and where we were going (well, most of the time…)

On Monday morning, I was back at university on the Strand. Second-year brought a new set of eight modules for the year ahead:

- **An introduction to the Doctrine of the Person of Christ**
- **Paul In Context**
- **Religious Differences – Jewish, Christian, and Other Perspectives**

- **Lived Religion: Making Sense of Religious Practices**
- **The Bible in the Artistic Imagination**
- **Faith and Enlightenment: Philosophy of Religion from Anselm to Kant**
- **Religion in International Relations**
- **Buddhist Ethics**

I was excited to be back at university, and I was hoping that this would be the year I made more friends and felt a little bit more like I belonged. As I have mentioned, I knew that London had the potential to become quite a lonely and isolating place. London is, of course, a very busy and anonymous place – nobody is going to start chatting to you whilst you wait for the tube. The chances of bumping into a familiar face whilst walking down Oxford Street are very rare! So I was determined that I would make an extra effort! I would motivate myself to attend social events, get to know new people, and really 'put myself out there' socially. I didn't just want to commute in and out of university – I wanted to make connections and form friendships with the potential to last for life!

***

As part of my effort to build more of these 'meaningful connections', I applied to join the committee of 'National Student Pride'. I had originally heard about Student Pride when working at Heaven last February when I had worked on reception on 'Student Pride' night. Prior to this, I didn't know a single thing about 'National Student Pride', but I absolutely loved all the hype and excitement as students from across the UK arrived for what I learnt was an annual event. When I saw that Student Pride were recruiting new committee members, I knew that I needed to get involved. I thought it would be a great opportunity to make a positive difference in the lives of countless LGBT+ students. I also thought that it would be a great opportunity to meet likeminded people, which I was absolutely desperate to do! I imagined that the committee would be a fun, intelligent, and very accepting group of young people, who had the potential to become firm friends for life. So I had applied, and I had an interview with Max, the co-chair, for the role of 'Outreach Officer', over Skype. Max offered me the role, and I excitedly looked forward to rolling my sleeves and getting involved. Fast forward several weeks and I've arrived at Canary Wharf tube station. I'm here for our first Student Pride committee meeting, which is taking place at one of the Student Pride sponsor's skyscraper offices. I step out of the tube station and instantly fall in love with this busy, modern, and glamorous new world that I have just walked into.

Canary Wharf is this little world of its own. There is nowhere quite like it in London, with its modern skyscrapers and riverside developments. I am absolutely in love with the place. Oh, how I'd love to be one of these busy and important businessmen and women, working in such glamorous offices and hurrying from the tube station with such a sense of purpose and importance. It's about 15 minutes until the meeting is scheduled to begin, and I realise that I don't have a single clue where on earth I am meant to be going. I look up at all these skyscrapers, and I don't have an absolute clue where to start. I quickly pull up Google maps and type in the address, discovering that I'm apparently just 5 minutes from my destination. Brilliant, I think, I've got plenty of time. So I set off in what I believed to be the right direction, and start thinking about how I'm going to introduce myself and how I can make the best first impression possible. I keep walking, but it doesn't look like I'm getting any closer. Google Maps, as always, is starting to confuse me more than help me! I end up arriving at an M&S, which is never a bad thing, and it dawns on me that I may not be heading in the right direction.

I run off to the M&S toilets before running back down the road I have just spent 5 minutes walking up, desperate not to arrive at the meeting late. Several minutes later and I have finally found the skyscraper I am meant to be at, which turns out to be literally five seconds around the corner from where I'd set off from 15 minutes previously. At least I got a chance to see some of Canary Wharf, I console myself, and at least I now know where the nearest M&S can be found! I stand outside the entrance for a minute and try to compose myself. To say that I feel terrified would be the understatement of the century! I am almost shaking with nerves! What is wrong with me, I ask myself, why on earth am I so bloody nervous?! I have never met any of these people before, and I really do not have any idea what to expect. All of my self-conscious worries and self-limiting beliefs are back at the forefront of my brain. Will these people like me? Am I going to be 'too much' for them? Will I fit in? What if nobody gets me or wants to talk to me?

After so many years of encountering these anxieties and self-limiting beliefs, you'd think that I would be better at identifying them and managing them! But even now, at the grand old age of 19, I am still unable to take back control and sort out these irrational fears and concerns! Well, enough is enough, I think to myself – I cannot continue being such a victim to these self-limiting beliefs any longer! And so, as I stand outside on the Canary Wharf pavement, I give myself an internal pep-talk. 'What is the worst that can actually happen?' I ask myself, 'What have you actually got to fear about this situation?'. I tell myself to 'fake it till you make it' and 'just do it' – 'you need to stop thinking about it and just bloody walk in there, I tell myself, because you really are making such a ridiculous mountain out of the tiniest molehill'. How do I expect to be a successful teacher or leader in life if I keep allowing my fears about what people think of me hold me back and drag me down? I need to get into my Mottram Hall 'meet & greet' mindset, and refuse to give my fears another single second of airtime! If you don't get decisive now, I tell myself, you will never overcome these self-limiting beliefs! And so, I remember Susan Jeffers mantra – 'feel the feel…and do it anyway'. With her words in mind, I march straight into the reception area, ready to make small talk with the first person I see…

As I walk into the lobby area, I see a very friendly looking girl who has also just arrived for the meeting. 'Come on Ben', I psyche myself up, 'she looks super lovely and friendly'. So, I head over and introduce myself, glad to have found someone I can cling onto for dear life so soon! I find out that her name is Bex, and then ask whereabouts she is originally from. It turns out that Bex is not only also from Cheshire, but that her high school was a three-minute walk from my house. 'Stop it!', I shriek, forgetting I'm standing in a swanky business lobby, 'Oh my GOD it's a small world!' Well, that was it for Bex; I grabbed onto the girl and informed her that she was now stuck with me indefinitely.

Well, a year later and I think she's not realised that I wasn't joking! We went into the meeting and met the rest of the team, who were all lovely. Bex and I found out that we were both doing Outreach, which meant we would be contacting universities and giving them information about the event. I was assigned 'Central & Wales', whilst Bex was put in charge of London. After a presentation and short meeting, we all headed off to a gorgeous cocktail bar in Canary Wharf. Over a glass of rose, Bex and I befriended a gorgeous girl called Lauren, who had been recruited to work on social media. The three of us sipped our drinks and made small talk with some of the other new committee members, excited about the year ahead.

Joining National Student Pride did me an absolute world of good. It got me out and about, meeting new people and feeling as if I was making a positive difference in the world. Student Pride introduced me to some of the loveliest people in London. And it also gave me a sense of purpose and brought some very-welcome routine into my week. I looked forward to our weekly Wednesday night meetings at the University of Westminster, which would always be followed with a group trip to the Baker Street Wetherspoons across the road! Everyone was so social and supportive, and we all soon felt like a little family.

This is, for me, what life is all about – we are at our happiest when fulfilling our potential and making a positive contribution to the common good of society! When we commit to causes and campaigns that we feel passionately about, we have an amazing opportunity to make a difference and leave a powerful legacy. We all have our own unique set of skills and talents, and it is so rewarding to bring these to the table and use them to make a meaningful difference in society. As Gandhi once famously said, 'be the change you wish to see in the world'. Joining Student Pride gave me that opportunity to 'be the change' and to feel as if I was able to make a positive and productive difference. So I got to work emailing the LGBT+ societies of universities in Central England Wales and really threw myself into the role. I loved firing off emails from my Student Pride account, and I really felt as if I belonged to a cause and community that was doing a lot of good in the world. This is what I had always been looking for. I finally had the chance to make a positive difference for LGBT+ young people, with the opportunity to meet some amazing – and very wholesome - new friends along the way!

With Student Pride meetings on a Wednesday and my Saturday night shifts at Heaven keeping me busy, the first term of Second Year flew by. I was living my absolute best life. I had the best flatmates, Morgan and Jamie, keeping me entertained in the kitchen. And I loved my daily commutes into Central London for lectures. I knew that my best friends and family were only ever a phone call or train journey away, and I genuinely felt like London was now home. I felt 100% settled and secure in Stratford – I felt on top of the world. It was the best and most fulfilling feeling…I felt like I was living my best life, and I loved every single second of it.

The course content was interesting, and I started to think more seriously about pursuing a career in teaching. I loved the passion some of my lecturers had for their subject. They had written books about philosophers, for example, or had appeared on the news talking about religious ethics. You could tell that they lived and breathed their subject, and you could tell that they loved sharing this passion with others. These lecturers were just like Mrs Garvey, Mrs Stewart, Mrs Williams and Mrs Connor back at school – they were strong, well-dressed and immaculately put together professionals…and I wanted to be like them! I dreamed of my future in the classroom, delivering assemblies and celebrating with my students on their Results Days. Imagine the difference you can make in people's lives, I think to myself, when you are responsible for helping them to fulfil their potential and thrive through life! Imagine the amount of good that you can do through educating, empowering and inspiring young people as your full-time career! I was itching to be standing in that classroom, inspiring young people to be fearlessly authentic and pursue their ambitions! I couldn't wait to tell my classes of the future about my experiences at university in London (the PG version, of course!). I might even bring them down to London for a day trip, teaching them that if I could turn my dream into reality, then so could they!

I felt so proud of my journey, and I felt so proud that it was my hard work, effort and determination that had got me to where I was today. I couldn't imagine myself in any other city or living any other life – it was as if this was exactly where I was meant to be in life. I wanted to inspire others to do the same with their own lives. I wanted to show people that they were more than capable of fulfilling their potential and living their best life. If I can turn my life around and take full responsibility for creating my dream life in London, then so could anybody else! It broke my heart to think about the amount of unmet and unfulfilled potential in the world – everybody deserves to live a truly happy, enriching and fulfilling existence! I never wanted my time in London to come to an end; could we just keep going like this indefinitely, I wondered?! But at the same time, I knew that the experience was so amazing precisely because it was finite. I had always known that my time at university in London wouldn't last forever.

But I also now knew that the lessons I had learned, and the confidence I had cultivated would remain with me for many years to come! This is my favourite thing about London – it has forced me to take full responsibility for my own life! Moving to London gave me no option other than to dive headfirst into life in the real world. During school and sixth form, I did live in a little bubble. My London life was still very much a bubble; I was living in gorgeous student accommodation and only had lectures 8 hours a week. But moving to London was still a very sharp learning curve. I'd had to get a job to fund my food shopping, and I'd had to do absolutely everything for myself. I had to work hard, keep putting myself out there, and keep stepping outside of my comfort zone. I'd had to take on the rush-hour commuters, work through the night, and even buy my own cleaning products! What a thought! As a result, I had grown so much in self-awareness and self-confidence, and I had cultivated social skills that would serve me well for the rest of my life.

***

One of my all-time favourite things to do is take a walk through the Olympic Park and along the East London canal towards Stepney Green. I loved going off for my daily walks through the parkland and alongside the barges, soaking up all of the Autumnal sunshine. I would always come off the Canal path at Victoria Park, which was a gorgeous cacophony of Autumnal colours. I loved walking through the leaves and around the parkland, with the London skyline visible in the distance. These walks gave me the perfect opportunity to pause, reflect, and just breathe. Even in the busy and bustling city that never sleeps, there are these wonderful pockets of parkland and greenery. My walks around the Olympic Park gave me so much time to think and just be at peace with nature, which was very important before a busy day in the centre of the city!

I am somebody who enjoys their own company, and I enjoy having time to get on with doing things for myself. I think that is one of my favourite things about London – there is so much that you just have to do on your own! You can't be trying to get on the tube at rush hour in a group of five! If you want to do something or go somewhere, you've got to just do it! Having my best friend Morgan next door was, of course, a blessing. But it was also nice to have so much independence and autonomy. I am fiercely independent, and London was the perfect place to enjoy this independence to the full!

34. NEW YEAR, NEW CAREER

It's Sunday 20 October, exactly one week before my 20th birthday and just over one year into my time working at Heaven. I'm exhausted after another busy Saturday night working on reception from 10 pm until 5 am. I get in at around 5.30 am – the night tube has been on my side tonight! – and jump straight into the shower. I grab a cup of tea and jump straight into bed, making sure the 6.30 am alarm that wakes me up for university during the week is switched off! Instead, I set the alarm for 11.30 am, which means that I'll get about five hours of sleep. This is nowhere near enough, but it is better than lying in bed until 4 pm and then not being able to sleep on Sunday night! After a year of working Saturday nights until 5 am, I've finally cracked the technique for getting your sleep cycle back to normal as quickly as possible! As I drift off to sleep, I try not to think about how tired I will be tomorrow. Instead, I think about how much I am absolutely loving my job, which is continuing to give me the biggest boost in confidence, not to mention the best Saturday nights I could ever have imagined! I know how lucky I am to be working at Heaven as my part-time job, and I know that I'll be looking back on this incredible experience for the many years to come.

Feeling so tired on a Sunday is a price that I'm happy to keep paying to keep experiencing the high that I get from working at Heaven! I still can't get over the fact that I am here working in this iconic nightclub. As you know, I am an absolute workaholic, and I love to be busy hosting, meeting, and greeting at every opportunity! It's in my DNA, and I would be doing it whether someone was paying me to do so or not! The fact that I get to work here in this nightclub – where I would have wanted to be every Saturday night anyway – was genuinely a dream come true. I don't enjoy nights out that much, but working in a nightclub was a different story. It was genuinely the best of both worlds – I was in the nightclub, but I didn't have to have a 'night out'. My purpose for being there was working, and it just so happened that I was able to get some boy attention and have a good time as well! In this job, I have met the most amazing people (including friends that I know I'll keep in touch with for life). I have loved having this opportunity to spend my Saturday nights at the heart of London's gay scene. The job has made me feel so confident, connected and empowered.

For so long, I had worried that I wouldn't fit in on the 'gay scene' because I wasn't as attractive, outgoing or well-connected as the other guys. I'd always felt so judged, out-of-place and, to be frank, ugly. Getting this job meant that I was working in the UK's biggest and most iconic gay nightclub. Every night genuinely left me feeling as if I was worth a million dollars! I genuinely appreciated this opportunity so much, and I genuinely felt so blessed to have been given this most amazing boost to my self-confidence. I get into bed at around 6 am, and I drift off to sleep, utterly exhausted and yet still slightly buzzing from all of the Red Bull and caffeine I have been consuming since 10 pm!

My alarm goes off at 11 am, when I drag myself out of bed and glance at my phone. I see that I have received a WhatsApp message from the bars manager, which was sent at 6.30 am that morning, just an hour or so after I left the club. As I wipe the sleep out of my eyes, I read the paragraph I have been sent:

"Hey Ben we have been talking about it, and we definitely need people full time (Friday/Saturday), and people who can be bartending and cloakroom aswell and I know you don't like [sic] so I think is better if we finish now…How you understand our point…If you can commit Friday & Saturday & you are happy to help in the bars we would love to keep u…But you told you can't commit to it"

I knew at this moment that I had two choices. I could get back into bed and feel sorry for myself. I could spend the rest of my day feeling frustrated, upset, and angry about what had happened. I could very easily let that anger and 'victim mindset' consume me. I haven't done anything wrong, I thought to myself, and all I ever wanted to do was work one day a week bringing some 5* customer service to the reception desk! However, it was not my decision to make. It is one of my firm beliefs that **"life is 10% what happens to you and 90% how you choose to respond"**. And so, I sat up, and I snapped myself out of my sulking. I was not, I told myself, going to let this break my heart. I was not, I insisted, going to let this drag me down. Honestly, it was like I was going through a bloody breakup! I genuinely had such a strong attachment to this place and to this job that I had got on my very first weekend in London. This job, as I have said about one hundred times, made me the confident person I am today! Working here has given me the biggest boost and the best experiences!

I got myself up, jumped in the shower and got dressed. I needed to fully accept this decision and, frankly, toughen up! I needed to be more stoical about it – if you can't change the situation, then you need to change your mindset towards it! So, I started to think like this. Everything happens for a reason, and the fact my time working here has ended doesn't mean that all of those memories, confidence and friendships have been lost. Indeed, I was not prepared to let this end to my time in this job taint my amazing memories of the past few months. I was not a victim to anybody else's decision making – I was the master of my destiny! So I resolved to make peace with the situation and, instead of getting bitter, use this as an opportunity to get better!

I was so thankful to have enjoyed this job for as long as I did. During my year at Heaven, I did have the best time. I felt so lucky to have made so many memories and to have grown so much in self-confidence. I would be reminiscing about my Saturday nights, and 5 am finishes for many years to come!

With that, I headed out for a quick walk around the Olympic Park. Well, nothing wakes you up in the morning – especially after working all night – like a bracing walk around the Olympic stadium… followed, of course, by a strong cup of tea! I just needed a minute to get my head clear. I needed to see the positives here; an even better opportunity might now come along because I do believe that 'as one door closes, another door opens!' I was also excited to no longer spend my Sundays feeling so tired – I wouldn't be spending so much on caffeine throughout the week now that I had my sleep cycle back! And I also knew that I would have to leave the nightclub one day, especially with third year and all my exams coming up. It's good to go out on a high, I thought to myself, and to leave whilst you're still having an amazing time. Whilst it is always okay to be sad, I was not okay with feeling sorry for myself. You're living in the real world Ben, I told myself, and unfortunately, shit happens!

I logged onto my laptop and, just hours after realising that I no longer had a job, I found myself another job! I had been on Indeed searching for 'reception', 'hotels' and 'nightclubs' when one advert caught my eye. The website was looking for a 'VIP HOST – PARTTIME, CENTRAL LONDON'. I instantly clicked on the link, excited to find out more. As I read through the job description, it was like I'd been sent some kind of divine intervention! It was a weekend-only role working as a host at Be At One Regent's Street, welcoming guests on the front door and taking group bookings to their tables. Within minutes, I was filling in the application forms and uploading a copy of my CV. This job looked perfect – if I had asked someone to create me any part-time job in the world, this would have been my exact specifications! To top it all off, I would be working on Regents Street, home to the gorgeous flagship stores of the world's biggest designer brands. I fired off my application and hoped for the best, before heading off to make some lunch.

***

A couple of days later, I received an email inviting me to interview. I was over-the-moon! By now, I had fully accepted I wasn't going back to work at Heaven, but I was adamant that I would leave on good terms and with my head held high. After all, I hadn't done anything wrong, and I was certainly not going to think of myself as a victim to somebody else's decisions! So I sent this reply to the bar manager on WhatsApp: **"Thank you for informing me [bar manager's name] – may I take this opportunity to thank you for the opportunities you have given me over the past year & wish you every success for the future!"** He left my message on read and never replied. Meanwhile, I was too busy preparing for my job interview to have even one single second for looking back.

Luckily, I had brought one of my black blazers down with me from home, and I had a white shirt, black trousers and skinny black tie all in my Stratford One wardrobe. Ever since my sixth form days, I have loved nothing more than heading out in a suit. It felt so sophisticated, powerful and important. And, let me tell you, I have never felt more important than walking off the tube at Oxford Circus wearing my full suit and tie combination! As I headed down Oxford Street and onto Regent's Street, I felt ready to give the best interview of my life. I was nervous, of course, but I was clutching a freshly printed copy of my CV, and I was ready to go! I headed into the venue and sat down with Laura, the absolutely lovely Sales Manager, who asked me a few questions and listened to me going on about my time working at Mottram Hall. Laura suggested I do a trial shift that Saturday evening, and I left feeling very confident about the future. Just days after losing a job, I was walking straight into another one – one with better pay and better hours! But I didn't want to get too confident about it all – I needed to 'wow' on this trial shift first.

And so, that Saturday night, I arrived back at the venue to be greeted by Sophia, a stunning girl who was the Head Host. For a second, I felt extremely intimidated – here was this tall, stunning girl strutting around the venue with a headpiece, clipboard and the attention of everyone in the venue. What was I doing here in this…*gasp*…**_straight_** bar and nightclub?! How was I supposed to flirt and charm my way through each shift now?! I needed to exude confidence and charisma – I needed to impress Sophia so that it would be impossible for her to say no to me! And so I snapped straight into my Mottram Hall 'Meet & Greet Mindset', plastered on my biggest smile, and exuded as much confidence as I could muster. I chatted away to guests, just like I would back at Mottram Hall, and I kept myself looking engaged and busy throughout the whole four-hours of the trial. By 10 pm, Sophia grabbed me to let me know I could now go home…and that I had got the job!

As I walked back down Regent's Street that evening, I was over-the-moon. It was exactly one week since I had done my last shift at Heaven, and now here I was with a brand-new job in Central London! The next day was my 20th birthday, and so I had a train home booked for early in the morning. I practically skipped onto the tube at Oxford Circus, feeling as if I was on Cloud 9. My new job would mean working from 7 pm – 2 am on Fridays and Saturdays, meaning no more getting home at 5.30 am…and considerably more money! I would no longer be working at the heart of the gay scene (so I would no longer be receiving a stream of attention from guys). But I would still be working in Central London, which means that there were still going to be lots of attractive guys nearby! I'd just have to track them down on Tinder! So as I walked down Regent's Street, I felt good about life. And I was determined to make my 20s the best decade of my life so far…

35. CHRISTMAS NIGHTS ON REGENTS STREET

It's reading week, and I head home for a flying visit. I celebrate my 20th birthday with Freya, Kristina and Becky at the Alchemist in Manchester, my all-time favourite place for a Pornstar Martini and a Chicken burger! I also go out for food with Mum, Dad and Sam, filling them in on what I've been up to in London (well, the parent-friendly highlights, anyway). We head off for our annual family day trip to – wait for it – Blackpool, always a highlight of my year!

Blackpool is just brilliant and will forever hold a very special place in my heart. I fully intend to be taking my children for day trips to see the donkeys, illuminations and enjoy a few doughnuts on the piers! It's so British and so nostalgic – who needs Disneyland when you've got Blackpool's Central Pier is what I want to know?! I really do love our annual day trips to Blackpool – it's good fun, nostalgic, and, let's be honest, nothing beats walking down the seafront battling against gale-force winds! We wander down the promenade, Dad and Sam play the 'Camel Derby' in the Coral Island arcade. Then – of course - we all enjoy some traditional fish and chips in a friendly seafront restaurant. It's all good fun – the illuminations turn on, the trams drive past, and families head off for the Pleasure Beach, piers and arcades. This is what it's all about, I think to myself, some light-hearted family fun! Our trip to Blackpool is always my – very welcome – reminder that Christmas is just around the corner. Driving through the illuminations always marks the start of my excitement for the festive season. A trip to Blackpool also always blows away any cobwebs, with that sea breeze taking absolutely no prisoners whatsoever!

I feel so refreshed and recharged by the Irish sea breeze! I head back down to London as the Christmas lights are switched on and Hyde Park Winter Wonderland once again opens its doors (well, gates…)! I'm now getting into the swing of things at Be At One. I love welcoming guests at the door, seating them at their tables, and ensuring that they have a fabulous night enjoying good cocktails and good company. We have two floors, with the downstairs area transforming into a nightclub – complete with DJ and lighting – after 9 pm. I feel very important in my smart all-black hosting ensemble, complete with a clipboard, Sharpie marker pen, table reservation signs and walkie-talkie with an earpiece! As you can imagine, I get excited every time I use the radio (even if it takes me a few attempts to get my head around the "copy copy" and "go ahead" linguistics of communicating on Channel 1)! Everybody at the bar is lovely, and I love every second of strutting around the venue with my clipboard! As Christmas approaches, the nights get noticeably busier, and the shifts rapidly increase in frequency.

One of my jobs is to run off to Pizza Express in Chinatown and collect orders of up to 50 pizzas, which are included in some of our Christmas party packages. I can remember turning up at Pizza Express to do my first collection, anticipating perhaps six pizzas at most. When I walked in and saw four towers of pizzas boxes – plus giant see-through bags filled with boxes of dough balls and slices of garlic bread – I nearly passed out! How on earth was I supposed to work out the logistics of transporting what appears to be one hundred pizzas, plus approximately one million dough balls?! You should have seen me, staggering down Shaftesbury Avenue with 50 pizza boxes and endless amounts of dough balls squeezed into giant bin bags! There I was, trying not to collide with the theatregoers or collapse under the weight of so much pizza dough and mozzarella! It was the longest ten-minute walk of my life, I can tell you, not to mention the most strenuous workout I have ever done in my life. I arrived back at Regents Street, with the pizzas fortunately still warm and intact, and vowing never to look at dough balls in the same way again.

It's now December, and work is non-stop. We are fully booked every evening, with drinks packages to prepare and bottles of Champagne – complete with sparklers on top – to be taken to tables. I love being so busy, and I love the buzz of hosting in a vibrant cocktail bar in Central London! Everyone is excited for Christmas and, as guests enjoy a selection of the Christmas cocktails, you can feel that festive spirit in the air! There are plenty of Christmas party bookings, which means plenty more trips to Pizza Express. I'm now getting to know the lovely Pizza Express staff now, and

I'm keeping entertained with my stories of couriering margarita pizzas across the West End. To be honest, I enjoy doing my pizza runs through Soho and down Shaftesbury Avenue! I've discovered that there's a real technique to weaving your way around the tourists taking pictures of the Christmas lights! I love being so busy and having a job where I get to rush across Central London and chat with so many different people. And I love strutting down Regents Street in my skinny jeans and little blazer, dashing past Hamleys and peaking at their festive window display! Whilst being confronted with so many Christmas shoppers is not ideal if I happen to be running late. I love seeing the twinkling Christmas lights and soaking up the festive atmosphere. There is nothing like Christmas on Regent's Street! It truly is magical! I also love the increasing size of my paychecks, and I so treat myself with a trip to the Tommy Hilfiger flagship store on Regent's Street. Well, if I'm going to be working so hard, I think that I deserve a little bit of luxury in my wardrobe, don't you!?

***

One of my favourite things to do is walking down Regent's street after finishing work at 2 am. With the Christmas lights twinkling and the Christmas, window displays fully illuminated, it truly does feel magical…even in the middle of the night! Nicola and I love walking through Central London without any of the tourists or Christmas shoppers. It's so surreal to think that we're working here, in Central London, and that right now we have the whole of Regent's Street to ourselves! It's funny to think about how London has started to feel like home for me. I can remember when I first arrived and feeling so overwhelmed by the size of the city; I would jump on the tube and hope for the best! I can remember thinking 'how on earth does anybody know where they are or where they are going?' Well, how times had changed! I think the secret to feeling at home in London is finding out where 'your' bits of London are. For example, I feel most at home around the Strand, Tower Bridge, Oxford Street, Regents Street, Charing Cross, and Stratford. But put me anywhere South of the Thames and the chances of me getting lost within five minutes are no less than 10/10!

I rely so much on the London Underground to get around, and I have fallen in love with tube travel! Whenever we came down to London when Sam and I were little, we would never use the tube. And so I was quite apprehensive about it all when I first got down to the Big City. But by now, I am jumping on and off the tube all day, every day! I challenge you to name a more convenient way of getting around! It's impossible to do so! The tube gets you exactly where you need to be, in very little time at all! There is always another train no more than 3 minutes away, and the Central Line can get me from Stratford straight into Central London in 16 minutes. Compare that to having to spend at least an hour on the bus! There is nothing like the London Underground for getting you where you need to be, when you need to be there! I mean it when I say that my Oyster card is like the third arm I never knew that I needed!

With all of our shifts at work, Nicola and I seem to spend half our lives waiting for the Central Line night tube at Oxford Circus. At least, I always joke as we wait for the tube, the platform is always nice and warm! As we wait for the next Eastbound service, we chat away about the customers we have looked after that evening. We chat away about what we're going to snack on when we get in and catch up on our love life dramas. Life on the Night Tube is a whole different world, and there's little Nicola, and I haven't seen – or talked about - whilst waiting on that Oxford Circus platform in the early hours of the morning! Waiting for that Night Tube is one of the best bonding experiences you could ever wish to have in this world!

***

On my nights off from work, I head off for drinks with Morgan or snuggle up in bed to watch Christmas movies. I love cosy nights in a hot drink in hand, watching endless episodes of Friends or one of my favourite Christmas films. Wednesday nights continue to be Student Pride meetings on Baker Street, always followed by a trip to Wetherspoons for a glass of rose (or two!). One weekend in December, Morgan and I head off for some Christmas shopping at Harrods, one of my absolute favourite places on earth. We soak up the seasonal displays and fall in love with the atmosphere of festive magic, treating ourselves to some (discounted)

Harrods water bottles from the gift shop…well, I'm easily pleased! As long as it's got that gorgeous Harrods logo on the front of it – and it costs less than £20 – then I'm the first in line to be buying it!

The festive season flies by, and I'm soon on a train home for Christmas. As I sit on the train watching the English countryside go by, I realise that I'm now exactly halfway through my degree. That means I'm also halfway through my time in London, and I genuinely can't believe how quickly that time has flown by! If there's one thing that I've learned about life, I think as I sit in Coach E watching fields and bollins whiz past me, it's this – you've got to seize every single day and make the most of every single moment! Time goes by so quickly. You've got to seize every opportunity with both hands. You've got to live every single second of your life to the full! Say 'yes' to more opportunities, and always keep fearlessly putting yourself out there! Nothing lasts forever, and things will never stay the same – so make those memories, seize those opportunities, and live every single day to the absolute full!

I enjoy another lovely Christmas at home, before heading back down to London for a New Years Eve shift at Be At One. We have a fabulous evening welcoming in 2020 in style, and I am thoroughly excited to make the most of the year ahead.

The first few days of January are spent sales shopping in Westfield. I also squeeze in some time to do some studying! I know that I've got essays to submit before the end of January, so I enjoy taking myself off to Café Nero in Westfield for some distraction-free writing. I feel so excited for the year ahead – I've got a lot of dreams and ambitions for the years ahead, and I am determined to make 2020 my 'best year yet'. I want to go on some dates, work harder on my degree, and do more of the things that scare me most. I want this to be the year that I step outside of my comfort zone, face more of my fears, and start genuinely living my best life. After half of my degree has gone by so quickly, I've realised that time is precious, and I've woken up to the fact that my time in London will not last forever! I, therefore, know that I need to get serious about seizing every single day in this city, and I am determined to start doing so today!

Come on 2020, let's make this the best – and most iconic – year yet…

36. ONE VIRAL VIDEO LATER...

It's mid-January, and it's another weekday evening in the Stratford One kitchen. It's been a long day, and I'm busy making myself some dinner. I always eat quite early – around 5.30 pm – which means I usually have the kitchen to myself. I've just put some food in the oven when Jamie bursts into the kitchen, having just got back from a full day at university. He wants to know whether I have downloaded 'TikTok' yet, an app he keeps mentioning to me and I keep insisting that I don't know anything about. Jamie has been talking to me about TikTok for weeks, and his girlfriend Lucy agrees that I need to create an account and start posting. The one word that Jamie keeps repeating to me – every time I see him - is 'TikTok'. I keep insisting that I do not understand what TikTok is; isn't it just teenagers dancing, I ask? What would I post if I had it?

I can't sing, I can't dance, I can't do stunts or even challenges! In other words, I have absolutely nothing to bring to the table! 'Just post the kind of things you put on your private Snapchat story', Jamie suggests. He's referring to the cringe-worthy videos that I regularly post on my private Snapchat story. These usually consist of me dramatically complaining about daily life (e.g. getting fake tan on my wall and trying to scrub it off with Lidl multi-surface wipes). I do quite like his idea. However, I am still not convinced, mainly because I am still confused about what on earth TikTok is.

Jamie is insistent that I need to get myself on TikTok, and I start to think that he might have a good point! What have I got to lose from giving it a go, I start to wonder. Isn't this the year of putting myself out there, trying new things, and living my best life? I'm not getting any younger, so I need to just seize every opportunity that I get and see what ends up happening! And as far as I can see, there is nothing to lose from giving TikTok a shot. Jamie asks Morgan to back him up. She is also convinced that I would go down well on the app (or at least she says she is; Morgan is far too kind to say anything but complimentary things!) And so, after several weeks of Jamie's persuasive efforts, I download TikTok and see what it's all about. At first, I can't work out the app, which makes me feel very old and ancient indeed! I'm struggling to understand the difference between the 'following' and 'for you page' feeds, never mind work out how to post a video myself.

After a quick bit of teaching from Jamie and Morgan, I think that I know what I am doing…almost. I look through my Snapchat memories and pick a couple of my favourite 'vlogs' from the last couple of weeks. One is a video of me walking through Trafalgar Square talking about 'going to get some bargains' (I was clearly enjoying my day of Christmas sales shopping). Another is a video of Morgan and I soaking wet in the middle of a foam party. This footage is just meant to be a meme, I think to myself. I pick a couple of others, and I start uploading them to TikTok. I don't know what is supposed to happen next, and I genuinely don't have any expectations whatsoever. Let's just enjoy doing it, I think; let's have some fun, and see what happens!

I post these videos, and then I forget all about TikTok for a week. They've got a couple of views, which I'm very excited about, but I don't give the app another moments thought. Until a week later, when I find empty 'frozen Donner Kebab meat' packaging on the top of our flat recycling bin. I am genuinely horrified at the prospect of eating defrosted Doner Kebab meat. So I whip out my phone and film a 30-second video ranting about how I'm 'going to be sick…get that away from me right now!' I upload the video to TikTok and get on with my day. Again, I forget all about the app and keep busy with my studying and work. Another week later and I am in the kitchen making some Sainsbury's Carrot and Coriander soup for lunch. This £1.60 soup – which promises to provide me with two of my five a day – has become a staple of my weekly diet. I take the soup out of the microwave, ready to enjoy with a slice of bread. Suddenly I am hit by the unmistakable scent of popcorn. Someone has clearly – and why not! – been making popcorn the night before. Now I love popcorn (both sweet and salted!) but, as the dramatic soul I am, I am not okay with the fact that my carrot and coriander now smells like a cinema. Forever channelling my inner Kris Jenner, I suddenly realise that this moment could be TikTok gold. So I pull out my phone and record a 30-second video of me ranting about the 'sweet and salted scents' and asking 'does this look like a cinema? No!' I do not feel that strongly about the smell of popcorn. Still, I do sense an opportunity to produce some entertaining TikTok content! Just call me Kris Jenner! I upload my video and get on with eating my soup, which is delicious as always...even though it is served with an unrequested cinematic aroma!

****

The next day, I am back in the kitchen, making some lunch. Jamie comes running into the kitchen, asking if I have seen my TikTok. I think he's trying to be funny, so I laugh and brush him off with a 'yeah yeah sure'. He insists that he's being serious, and tells me to guess how many views my latest video has had. 'Oh I don't know', I reply, '500?' He tells me to guess higher, before realising that I genuinely have not checked my TikTok and so do not have a clue what he is talking about. 'It's had 30K!' he informs me, which makes my jaw drop and leaves me running off to find my phone. Back in the kitchen, I tell Jamie that I can't believe it – and I sincerely mean it! Thirty THOUSAND people have been my video, I keep repeating, WHAT!? At that moment, I feel like Kim Kardashian. At that moment, I am living my J-Lo and Cheryl fantasy! Jamie goes off to university, and I take myself off for a walk around the Olympic Park. I'm in shock, but I'm on Cloud nine...how on earth has this happened, I wonder, nobody even knows who I am!

Every day, the viewing figures increase. Eventually, this video ends up with half a million views. Other videos I post will soon attract 2 million views each! I seriously cannot believe it! This is the funny thing with TikTok – any video, produced by absolutely anybody, can go 'viral' in a matter of days...sometimes even in just minutes! I don't understand how the algorithm works. Still, I do know that it means someone with 100 followers can upload a video that ends up getting 1 million views. As a result of my Soup Saga, I was riding on a little TikTok wave. I absolutely loved it, but I was determined not to get too caught up in views, likes, and followers. I was very aware of how toxic social media and external validation can become for me. So I was keen to be vigilant about how I used the app. I wanted to enjoy TikTok as a little bit of a hobby, not become consumed by it as a source of validation.

I loved the idea of being able to entertain people and showcase my personality online. Unlike Instagram, which is all about your physical appearance, TikTok allowed people to showcase their personality. It was a platform on which you could entertain, as opposed to just posing for a picture! For someone who has not been blessed with physical attractiveness, but at least has a sharp sense of humour, this was the answer to my prayers! I have always had this little 'entertainer' within me, and I love knowing that I've put a smile on somebody's face. I got busy 'vlogging' the little dramas I encountered as a went about my life in London. For example, I film myself being surrounded by a flock of pigeons in Elephant & Castle ("Oh they're all flocking like the boys on my Grindr"). And I film myself taking refuge from Storm Ciara in a fake phone box ("It is cold, it is wet, and I am being blown like I have never been blown before…and not in a good way!").

Within two weeks, I have 10,000 followers and 100,000 likes. Sam messages our family WhatsApp chat with a screenshot of these statistics from my account, to which Dad replies: "Modesty prevents me disclosing how many followers I have". And people wonder where I get my comedic genius from?!

I am genuinely stunned to have gained what seems like so many followers in such a short amount of time. I have absolutely no frame of reference when it comes to using TikTok. For example, I do not know any of these 'TikTok famous' people who have millions of fans. So I am quite happy just doing my little thing, without getting caught up in a 'how many followers have they got' competition. As I say, I don't want to start taking it too seriously – I just want to enjoy doing my little thing and enjoy having some fun creating content!

I know that the perfectionist within me could very quickly ruin my enjoyment of TikTok. I knew that the moment I start getting obsessed with the statistics is the moment I would need to walk away. For now, I love filming these vlogs and videos. It's my chance to channel my comedy idols and favourite TV icons. I adore classic British comedy, complete with double entendre and innuendo. I also love a good TV 'icon', spending my spare time watching 'Celebrity Big Brother' compilations and endless reality TV shows. I am obsessed with any celebrity with a strong, sassy, and outrageously flamboyant personality. I find these figures genuinely empowering and seriously entertaining, and I am seriously inspired by how much self-confidence and flamboyance they exude. Think Kris Jenner, Gemma Collins and - the most hilarious of them all - Kim Woodburn. They are larger-than-life and not afraid to own it – and if that's not me, then I genuinely don't know who I am anymore!

***

There's nothing I love more a good British sitcom. I am obsessed with classics such as as 'My Family' and 'Keeping Up Appearances', and nothing makes me laugh-out-loud more than the online series 'Charity Shop Sue'. I adore – and regularly watch on repeat - the 'Carry On' film series, especially any starring the late Kenneth Williams. And it is these classic British sitcoms that inspired the TikTok videos I was creating. I wanted to emulate a 'golden age' of camp, innuendo-filled, and feel-good British comedy. It felt like I spent half of my life living in a 'Carry On' film anyway! So it felt very natural to be channelling Kim Woodburn and Kenneth Williams in my videos! Over the next few weeks, I had a lot of good luck – and I do think TikTok comes down to having a lot of good luck – in terms of the exposure my videos were receiving. Highlights included:

> Tasting Hot Cross Bun tea that I'd found in Sainsbury's ("Oh I'm getting carrot…")
- My trip to JD Sports ("Yes I did get out alive…the XXS was a double duvet with extra legroom…so I went off to the kid's section and bought a jumper from the 10-11-year-olds section")
- Being obsessed with Mozzarella Dippers from McDonald's ("Why does it take so long for them to turn up…Jenny got her Big Mac in half the time it took me to get three little dippers…It's not right dear")
- Tasting Pineapple Jaffa Cakes that I'd found in Waitrose ("Someone has decided to put Pineapple in a jaffa cake…what next, a broccoli infused bourbon? Oh it smells like sick in a box dear…")

- The decreasing size of Crème Eggs ("what's this all about…I thought someone had shrunk it in the wash…I've never handled such a small package dear…Oh good heavens")
- Using a teeth whitening kit for the first time ("Apparently you're meant to keep it all in your mouth for 10 minutes my love, well it's bigger than it looks dear…I can't fit it all in")

As you can see, everything was very British, and everything was very camp. I was certainly ramping up the camp and playing up to the stereotypes, creating a – quite literally – larger than life online persona. I loved it; it was good fun, and my content was getting a very good response. I also uploaded a couple of 'life coaching' videos. This consisted of me talking directly into the camera about the importance of 'feeling the fear and doing it anyway', or sharing my mantra of 'don't get bitter get better'. I had always dreamed of being a life coach or TV therapist, and I had visions of me sitting on the This Morning sofa giving people life advice! I started to think that TikTok could be my opportunity to become the nation's next 'Agony Aunt'. I found sharing these little 'life coaching' so fulfilling and rewarding. It felt like I was doing something meaningful and that I was making a genuine difference in the world. Watch out 'Dear Deidre' and The Speakmans, I thought… I'll be on that sofa with Phil and Holly very soon!

***

I absolutely love posting on TikTok, and I am seriously stunned to have received such a positive reaction. To have 450,000 followers, 15 million likes, and an average of over 12 million video views per month is just ridiculous. I may not be anywhere close to any of the real TikTok celebrities, but I think that this is a pretty good achievement for me! I find it so surreal when people come up to me in Westfield, the Arndale Centre, or even on nights out, asking the same question each time: "Oh my god are you the guy from TikTok?!" The idea that people had watched a video of me on Tiktok, and then actually bumped into me in the street, was seriously baffling! I was on an absolute high, and it felt as if my dreams of following in the footsteps of Kris Jenner and Gemma Collins were finally coming true!

However, one thing that is getting my attention is the amount of hateful and critical comments I am receiving on every video I post. Every day there are hundreds of messages attacking me with every label under the sun. These range from the classic 'gay' (really?!?! I hadn't noticed!) to the more offensive language such as 'fag', 'it needs to be put down', 'act like your gender', 'and 'f*cking freak'. Oh, let me tell you, the anonymous trolls were *not* holding back when it came to criticising everything from the way I looked, to the way I talked, and the way I carried myself. To be honest, I had expected nothing less! Well, I had heard it all before! Don't get me wrong; at first, I was a little bit upset that I was on the receiving end of this barrage of hate. But I very quickly pulled myself together and, with a little bit of time, got over it. As I say, I had heard all of these insults ten million times before. The words 'fag' or 'freak' couldn't hurt me anymore. I already knew that people thought I 'acted like a girl', 'needed to act like a boy' and that they thought I wasn't 'normal', whatever their definition of normal was.

After years of hearing these comments, nothing anybody was saying was new. The important thing was this: I was now secure in my identity and my purpose in life. And so, these pathetic comments did not have any power over me, whatsoever!

One thing that broke my heart was this; I knew that I wasn't the only person on the receiving end of such nasty comments and language. It broke my heart to think that people who hadn't been on my journey to self-acceptance might be receiving this kind of horrible comment. These comments could destroy their self-esteem and self-confidence. Imagine how crushing and harmful this kind of comment would have been for my younger self! How could people be so thoughtlessly cruel in their attacks on innocent people they'd never even met?

It is no exaggeration to say that every single person with a social media platform or in the public eye receives vile, vitriolic comments every single day! You could be the most perfect, gender-conforming and likeable person on the planet, and you would still have an army of anonymous online haters coming for you! There is no pleasing the whole population…and, more importantly, there should be no desire to do so either! As long as you feel happy in your skin, you are surrounded by people who truly love you, and you are living in accordance with your own values… then do not worry about what other people think! There's a quote that I love – **'what other people think about you is none of your business'.** Of course, it is never just as easy as ignoring what people say or think. And I do think that we should always listen to constructive criticism that people give us. Indeed, we can only grow and develop when we take constructive feedback on board! But here's what I strong believe: if you wouldn't turn to somebody for advice, then don't listen to their criticism! Would you really ask an anonymous online troll for their advice or support? If you don't admire and respect somebody, why on earth are you paying attention to their opinions? People, of course, have a right to hold an opinion on you and your life – but you have an equal right not to care! Just because somebody has an opinion of you, that doesn't mean it is accurate or true! You cannot please everybody, so **stop trying** to please everybody. Instead of craving to be liked, strive to become somebody who genuinely likes themselves instead!

So many people limit and restrict themselves because of the nasty and rude comments made by other people. This breaks my heart! We are on this planet for such a short and precious amount of time – we must live every single second of our lives to the full! And that means doing more of the things that make you genuinely happy, irrespective of what the haters might think or say! Don't waste a single drop of your precious energy, worrying about what people might think or say! Instead, invest that energy into living a fearlessly authentic and deeply fulfilling life!

I wrote a chapter about 'How to Handle the Haters' in my debut life-coaching book, 'Live Your Best Life'. I wanted to share an extract from this chapter with you here:

How To Handle The Haters (from 'Live Your Best Life: A Guide to Authenticity, Confidence and Resilience')

"Haters only hate things they can't have and the people they can't be. It's just a little thing called jealousy" (Lil Wayne)

When I first started posting on TikTok, I was shocked at the kind of things people would comment on my videos. Whilst 99.9% of the comments I was receiving were overwhelmingly positive, there was still a 0.1% who would comment things like 'wish it would go kill itself' or 'this creature deserves to be put down...this is the reason I would never let my son be gay'.

Despite all those wonderfully kind and positive comments, it was always these horrible and hateful ones that would catch my attention and stay in my mind. At first, I was hurt – how could someone say that about me? Did they not realise I was just a human being like them? How would they feel if someone spoke about them or their loved ones in that way? But then that hurt turned to anger – how DARE they say these things to me! How DARE they be so rude, horrible and cruel from behind their keyboard! I was absolutely furious – these people had the nerve to tell me to kill myself or tell me that I was 'disgusting'...simply for posting a video of myself walking through a field or reacting to an Instagram filter. If they were so cruel to me, then they were surely cruel to thousands of others – and other people are not able to shake it off as well as me. What if someone receives one of these comments on their videos and never uses this app again? What if they completely take these hateful and vile comments to heart?

It is so easy to tell someone to 'just ignore' what people say or think about them. Even in this very book, I have a chapter titled 'what other people think of you is none of your business'! But just blocking out these nasty and hateful comments is a lot harder than it looks. I really don't believe you can just become immune or desensitised to such vile comments being made about you – and actually, how appalling is it that someone could become used to being spoken to in this manner!

I began feeling that I had to apologise for my personality to everybody I met, assuming that every single person would find me "too much" or "too gay". I always expected people to roll their eyes and make a passive-aggressive remark about my flamboyant personality and – of course – assumed sexuality because of it. I'd start conversations with comments like "I know I'm too full on and too much most of the time..." or "I promise I am intelligent and that I am actually a good person"! I felt I had to explain myself to everyone and be constantly apologising for my personality, putting myself down before they had the chance to.

This is completely and utterly wrong. You should never, ever apologise for being who you authentically are. **Here is something you need to know: anybody trying to put you down is already beneath you.** *As I always say, the only thing you should ever apologise for in life is causing harm. Why should me being a little bit flamboyant and walking with a little bit of sass something to apologise for? Why on earth am I apologising for my positive and friendly personality which has actually lifted the mood and kept everybody entertained? How dare you say I am 'too much' for you – it's not like I'm here making rude comments about your lack of charisma and personality am I, my love!*

What I soon realised was that anybody who was 'hating' on me was actually jealous of me. They were intimidated by my ability to be totally comfortable in my own skin and my confidence to be unashamedly myself. Perhaps, I thought, they were bullied for not conforming to stereotypes at school. Hence, they now lived a life of repression and couldn't stand to see someone actually being themselves. If anyone feels the need to attack you for your personality or appearance, you are triggering them in some way. You should actually feel flattered – they want what you've got, and they're angry that they're never going to get it.

So it becomes very apparent that people trolling you says more about them than it says about you. **Someone who is happy, secure and genuinely fulfilled in their lives would never behave in this manner.**

Now I have to tell you something – I do not care what someone who is trolling might be going through in their lives. I do not give an absolute toss if they are struggling to accept their sexuality or have been bullied by others in the past. What matters is that they are trying to cause you harm – and what matters is that this is not allowed to happen!

What matters is that you do not let other people's opinions and nasty comments stop you from being your authentic self. You are allowed to be upset, of course, because anybody would be upset by this kind of comment. But what you are not allowed to do is apologise for being who you are or change a single thing about your self-expression because of the comments sad and pathetic trolls online make.

I think everyone with a social media platform has a different approach to dealing with trolls. In the same way, every person has a different approach to dealing with nasty comments or discrimination they face in everyday life. You need to kind the strategy that works best for you – it needs to keep you safe, from both physical and psychological harm.

Here are a few pieces of advice that I want to share with you when it comes to dealing with what we society likes to call 'the haters' –

- ***Do NOT take it personally.*** *This point goes without saying. Do not take any trolling, negativity or rude comments personally. They are 100% about the person behind the keyboard and say 0% about you as a person. Trolling is someone projecting their insecurities and jealousy onto someone else – it is an expression of self-hatred and a shameless exercise in attention-seeking. Really, you should feel sorry for the trolls! Do not take what they say to heart – you are absolutely perfect, whole and fabulous exactly as you are. You must be relentlessly authentic and know that you are a role model to the rest of the world in showcasing what it means to be a confident and authentic human being.*
- ***Do not get addicted to reading it.*** *It is too easy to get addicted to reading people's negative comments about you. No matter how much you have this desire to find out what they're all saying, DON'T DO IT! It is an act of self-sabotage and will achieve nothing but lower your mood and leave you feeling angry and attacked. Remember that the trolls do not speak for the world but only their sad, lonely and insecure selves. Remember that your time is precious and that you don't have time to be reading these pathetic so-called 'opinions'. What other people think of you is none of your business – especially when they don't really think it but are just saying it for attention!*
- ***You can choose the 'report, block & ignore' approach.*** *You can choose to completely ignore what someone says – but you can also choose to respond and, as I like to say, put them back in their little boxes! Most people do choose to just completely ignore: 'report them, block them but don't engage with them!' The idea behind this is that trolls are simply bored and lonely attention-seeking keyboard warriors who feed off getting a reaction out of people online. If you*

take the bait and bite back, you're giving them exactly what they want! Don't give them the satisfaction of a response – as Michelle Obama says, 'when they go low, we go high'.
- **You can choose the 'kill them with comedy' approach.** *If you are feeling strong enough, take my very own 'kill them with comedy' approach. This is where you can turn people's negative you find a cure pal" on a recent video, I replied to his comment with a video stating "Yes dear, you're right - I hope we find a cure for your stupidity and ignorance soon! Go and find a brain cell my love...good luck because you'll need it". My response video gained me 140K views, thousands of likes and hundreds of comments within hours – not to mention thousands of new followers on both TikTok and Instagram! I had totally shut down this rude and pathetic comment, entertained thousands of viewers and sent a very clear message to people watching about LGBT+ rights all in one go. Suppose you're going to post rude comments on my content. In that case, I'm going to turn them to my advantage by using them to entertain and educate as many people as I can!* **If you can take any rude comment someone makes about you and turn it into a joke, you instantly disarm and undermine them.** *Humour is a very powerful weapon in undermining bullies, trolls and haters in that it allows you to take full control of the situation.*
- **Never engage in conversation with a troll.** *Whilst you can bite back with a humorous punchline to any comment left on your public profiles, make sure you always leave it at that. Never, ever under ANY circumstances, engage in any kind of conversation with an internet troll. If they message you on private messaging, they must be blocked instantly. They do not deserve your dialogue, and they do not deserve any kind of discussion. One humorous or sassy reply is fine and maybe funny – but replying to any replies after that is a NO GO ZONE! It's all about taking control of the situation – the second you start entertaining conversation, you are handing power back to the trolls. They do not deserve one second of dialogue with you – you can publicly shame them but do not otherwise entertain them.*
- **Always choose the 'don't get bitter, get better' approach.** *Whatever you do in response to trolling or hate, make sure it is not about getting bitter but getting better. I actually thank the trolls for their*

negative comments because it gives me a chance to make a put them down with a sassy one line response! It's nice to get that sass out of my system once in a while! Never let the toxic and pathetic comments of online trolls lower your vibration as a human being – remember we are on a journey to becoming the best versions of ourselves. That means rising above it, perhaps making a joke out of it and being even more emboldened and confident in ourselves because of it. Don't you dare get bitter and join the trolls in their cesspit of negativity – you owe it to yourself to keep growing and keep glowing through life!

Perhaps one of the best pieces of advice on this comes from the incredible Michelle Obama. She says: **"You don't have to say anything to the haters. You don't have to acknowledge them at all. You just wake up every morning and be the best you can be. And that tends to shut them up".** *At the end of the day, haters deserve absolutely nothing from you. If you can use their nasty comments to your advantage, then go for it! But make sure you give the haters themselves no air time and no attention – trust me when I say they are absolutely not worth it. Leave them to their negativity and focus on being unashamedly your fabulous self. And make it your mission to keep getting on their nerves – if they are not getting triggered by what you're doing, then you need to up your game!*

(Extract from 'Live Your Best Life: A Guide to Authenticity, Confidence & Resilience. Available to buy at www.benwardle.org today).

***

It's important to say that the positives of using TikTok far outweigh any negativity that I might have encountered online. As Epictetus teaches us, 'it's not what happens to you, but how you react that matters'. Life is 10% what happens to you and 90% how you choose to respond! I choose to use my TikTok to spread a bit of positivity, hopefully, make people laugh, and hopefully inspire people to be more confident in their skin. And so I am not going to let some anonymous and miserable online troll stop me from doing something that I enjoy! I am not going to let the 1% negativity cloud the 99% positivity that the app provides!

TikTok may just be a social media app. Still, it has ended up having the most incredible impact on my life. It has given me opportunities that I could never have dreamed of – more on those a little later! – and it has allowed me to just be myself…and make people's day by doing so! I have always been a little performer and comedian, and TikTok has been the perfect platform on which to let my inner 'Carry On' and 'Kim Woodburn' to shine! It truly has been the most positive experience and the most wonderful opportunity – you wouldn't be reading this little book, for example, if it wasn't for TikTok! Without that platform, nobody would know who I was…and so my three readers would be Queen P, Dad, and my Gran!

Let me just give you a little bit of advice, if you perhaps do want to 'put yourself out there' on a social media platform such as TikTok. I have two words: DO IT! What have you got to lose? What is actually the worst thing that could happen? If things don't work out, that's okay – you are more than capable of brushing yourself off and getting on with your life! Don't worry about the likes, the followers, or the haters – if you enjoy putting yourself out there and sharing your talents, then make sure that you do it! Life is too short not to be doing the things that you love! So dare to put yourself out there and just have a bit of fun! Don't take it too seriously, but also don't sell yourself short! You never know what video could go viral, and you never know what doors your social media presence could open! Seize those opportunities and enjoy the success that you deserve! As I hope my story shows, all that it takes is just a little bit of encouragement (in my case from Jamie!) and a little bit of self-confidence! Once you've got that ball rolling, there can be no stopping you! So have a bit of fun, do more of what makes you genuinely happy, and just enjoy the journey!

37. THE STUDENT PRIDE SPECTACULAR

I start February 2020 feeling busier than ever; I have my university work to do, and of course, I am busy making TikToks! I am also working on the planning and preparation for National Student Pride. The 'big weekend', taking place at the University of Westminster and G-A-Y Heaven is now just days away. I am so excited to finally see everything come into fruition. Tom has asked me about my plans for next year and has asked me whether I would be interested in applying for the position of co-Chair. I am flattered, humbled, and absolutely stunned – little me as co-chair of National Student Pride! Of course, I responded, I would be honoured to have such an incredible opportunity!

After my journey over the past few years, the opportunity to become co-chair of this organisation seemed incredible. It was my opportunity to make a difference and give something back. It was my opportunity to make a meaningful contribution and, I hoped, inspire and support LGBT+ students across the UK. It was an opportunity to be the role model I wish I'd had growing up, and it was an opportunity to become the change I dreamed of seeing in the world. It was the 'icing on the cake' of my time in London. It felt like everything I'd been doing had been building up to this moment. Life is all about learning, growing, and becoming the very best version of yourself. Well, I had certainly done a lot of that learning and growing! And then, when you have become that best version of yourself, you can fulfil your potential by making a positive difference in the world. This was my opportunity to inspire, empower and – I hoped – leave a positive legacy. It felt so right, and it felt like the perfect culmination to my journey of finding self-awareness, self-love, and self-confidence.

But before I could get too distracted thinking about next year's co-chair duties, we had this year's Student Pride spectacular to pull off! We had up to 2,000 students from across the UK attending the event, including a daytime festival at the University of Westminster and then a performance by the Pussycat Dolls at G-A-Y Heaven on Saturday evening. I hadn't been back to Heaven since leaving back in October, and I felt nervous and excited about being back. Our tickets were practically sold out, and everything was arranged for the big weekend. As the event got closer, the news bulletins and newspapers had started talking more about this so-called coronavirus that had been spreading in the Wuhan region of China. The news coverage had begun back at the start of January when news programmes had talked about Wuhan being sealed off and placed into lockdown in order to stop the spread of a deadly disease. Whilst I had felt bad for the people of Wuhan, I had not been worried about the coronavirus in the slightest. As far as I was aware, this was something happening on the other side of the world. It didn't – for one single second – cross my mind that this coronavirus could end up causing any bother or disruption to my own life whatsoever. It's like the Ebola crisis, I thought. People will talk about, and it will be desperately sad and heartbreaking to see on the news. But it will not personally affect or disrupt my life in any way whatsoever.

However, the news coverage seemed to be changing in tone, and some people seemed to be getting worried. I listened to the Radio 4 six o clock news every evening, and the Coronavirus was climbing higher up the running order day-by-day. The incumbent National Student Pride co-chair Max asks whether we need to order in some hand sanitiser use at the event. Oh, he's dramatic now, I thought to myself, why on earth would you need to use hand sanitiser at a university in London?! The Student Pride weekend arrived, launching with a night at G-A-Y Late on Friday 21 February 2020. David and I looked after RuPaul's Drag Race star Cheryl Hole. She performed a couple of numbers for the students before we jumped in an Uber and took her to the University of Westminster. Once she got here, she was set to perform at our Student Pride Sponsors Dinner, which was being hosted on the same night. After grabbing some sleep, we were back at the University of Westminster bright and early for the main Saturday event.

Saturday was the most amazing day, and the entire event was a resounding success. It was lovely to finally meet the students I had been emailing about coming to the event. And a couple of people even came up to me saying they had recognised me from TikTok! All around me, there were beaming faces, bright colours, and brilliant role models. We had fantastic A-list speakers, dazzling live performances, and the UK's largest LGBT+ graduate job fair. And that evening, we all headed off to G-A-Y Heaven for a fabulous night partying and seeing the Pussycat Dolls perform live. I had about 1000 tokens for free Double Vodka-Redbulls, which I was liberally handing out to anybody and everybody I saw. Morgan, Nat (her gorgeous girlfriend) and I ended up about three rows from the front of the stage as Nicole Scherzinger finally arrived onto the stage at about 1 am. We stayed for a few more hours before arriving back in Stratford at about 4 am, glad to finally have some chicken nuggets in the oven and our beds calling our names!

A couple of hours later, I was back at the University of Westminster for our last event of the weekend, a 'Drag Olympics brunch'. With sleep-deprivation sending us delirious, we all laughed our way through the day, thoroughly making the most of the enormous Greggs delivery and Sainsbury's sandwich platters. It was the loveliest end to the best weekend – I knew we had pulled off something amazing, and I knew that I had made genuine friends for life. And I also knew that I needed to sleep for at least a week – I couldn't hack the sleepless Saturday nights in the same way that I could back in first year!

***

Working on Student Pride was another one of those 'only in London' university experiences that I will treasure for the rest of my life. It was, as I say, a fabulous chance to meet new people and a wonderful opportunity to make a positive difference.

The rest of February was spent catching up on sleep and working hard on university assignments. The seasons are starting to change, although the Winter Wardrobe is still very much required! I'm looking forward to becoming co-Chair of National Student Pride next year, and I feel so privileged to have such a positive opportunity. This will be my chance to make a positive difference and do a lot of good in the world. It will be a chance to 'give something back' and help to support and inspire the next generation of LGBT+ students. I cannot wait! But first, we've got the rest of Second Year to enjoy…

***

It was around this time that I read a book called 'Emotional Agility: Get Unstuck, Embrace Change, and Thrive in Work and Life', written by Susan David. I had purchased this book completely by chance. I had set myself the challenge of reading '52 books in 52 weeks' throughout 2020, and this one had just so happened to come up as a recommended purchase on Amazon! I'd heard a bit about 'emotional intelligence' before, and I was interested to learn more. After reading just a couple of pages, I instantly knew that this was a book that was going to change my life. The concepts being developed were very similar to those I'd read about in Dr Russ Harris' book 'The Happiness Trap', another book which transformed my life! As I read about 'emotional agility', every single page spoke to me; these were words t hatI never knew I needed to hear!

David wrote about the importance of 'emotional agility', which she described as a process of navigating life with self-acceptance, clear-sightedness, and an open mind. She urges us to confront all of our emotions 'courageously and compassionately'. She introduces four key-concepts for living with emotional agility. 8They are:

Showing Up: Acknowledging all of your emotions with kindness and curiosity

Stepping Out: Detaching from your feelings and learning to observe them instead. Seeing yourself as a chessboard with lots of possibilities/options.

Walking Your Why: Choosing to live your life in accordance with your core values. These values give you purpose and direction in life. These values anchor and inspire you. They are the true path to willpower, resilience, and effectiveness.

Moving On: Making small, deliberate tweaks to your mindset, motivation, and habits. Make these changes in accordance with your core values. Find the balance between challenge and competence.

I instantly fell in love with the whole concept of 'emotional agility'. It provided me with the resources to make sense of my emotions, and with the inspiration to make positive improvements in my life. For example, I could take some time to work on overcoming my defensiveness and perfectionism. I could learn how to stop worrying so much about what other people thought of me and focus instead on living in accordance with my own values. And, most importantly, I could learn to manage all of my emotions in a much more mature and intelligent way. It is so important for us to realise that life – including your emotions and mindset – is a very flexible and agile thing! If you want to change something about your life, you have the power to do it! Suppose you are going through a difficult time or experiencing an uncomfortable emotion right now. In that case, I can guarantee that it will pass! When we learn to embrace and celebrate change – rather than fearing and resisting it – life becomes a much more positive and enjoyable experience. Embrace every obstacle, make friends with your feelings. And, as my favourite psychologist of all time Susan Jeffers wrote, know that 'whatever happens in life, you can handle it'.

38. THE ONE WHERE LONDON GOES INTO LOCKDOWN...

"FIRST UK DEATH FROM CORONAVIRUS AS TOLL RISES" declares the front page of the Times, which I have just bought in Sainsbury's. It's Friday 6 March, and the coronavirus is now starting to dominate the news agenda more and more. I still don't think it sounds like anything that might affect my life, and so I get on with business as usual. I'm working from 8 pm until 2 am this evening, which means I've got plenty of time to read the newspapers and catch up with university reading before I've got to head off to work. We haven't been in lectures for the past couple of weeks because of strike action, but I'm quite happy doing the work at my own pace at Stratford One. Some days, I head off to a coffee shop and get on with my reading. I love people watching whilst I do my reading, a cup of tea in one hand and a highlighter in the other. Other days, I'm quite happy to sit in our kitchen in Flat 201, with our gorgeous views over London, Zac Efron cardboard cut-out, and regular appearances from Morgan and Jamie. There are only two weeks left of Second Year, which feels genuinely ridiculous. Where on earth has the time gone?!

Over the next few days, I'm kept busy doing university reading and hosting at the bar. The coronavirus appears to be just another item on the news agenda until the coverage suddenly starts to significantly shift in tone. By Friday 13 March, The Times is quoting Boris Johnson as announcing that 'Many more families are going to lose loved ones before their time'. The Telegraph is declaring that 'MASS GATHERINGS TO BE BANNED', and it starts to dawn on me that this whole coronavirus thing is actually a pretty big deal. I am supposed to be in London until the end of June. Morgan and I had been looking forward to a summer of going out, partying and living our best London lives. But the papers were now talking about the country going into some kind of 'lockdown', with large gatherings banned and talk of restrictions being placed on people's movements. What was going to happen to our second-year exams, which normally took place in a giant conference centre in West London? Surely these exams couldn't go ahead if concerts and sports events were being banned? Whilst I was secretly delighted by the prospect of not having to sit these exams, I was seriously now concerned about what was going on with this virus. The news bulletins were now talking about a global health pandemic which was going to be causing unprecedented amounts of disruption for months.

Jamie had already gone home for a couple of weeks, but we were expecting him to be back by the end of the month. Morgan and I both said that we wanted to stay in Stratford and see what happened – we both still had our heads completely in the sand about the scale and magnitude of what was actually going on. One evening, we came back from drinks at Wetherspoons to find our Spanish flatmate, Jacob, hurriedly speaking on the phone. When he had finished his call, he told us that he was packing everything he could and heading to Spain the very next day. 'Don't be silly!', we had told him, 'don't worry about it, everything is going to be okay!' Morgan pointed out of the window, 'look! The world's still turning out there!', she said.

The very next day, we realised the extent to which we had spoken too soon. Hour by hour, the world started shutting down. I was on my way into work - and had even got into Central London - when I found out the news that all restaurants, bars, and nightclubs were being ordered to shut their doors. Stunned and shocked, I didn't know what to do with myself. You mean to say, I thought to myself, that I have just spent 20 minutes on the Central Line to go back to Stratford again?! I decided to go off for a walk around Central, wandering through Soho and following the route that I used to take from G-A-Y Bar to Heaven. It was dawning on me how deserted everywhere was; where I had once had to fight past tourists, the only company I now had was pigeons. I arrived at Trafalgar Square to find the most extraordinary scenes – there was not another soul in sight. I stood there, genuinely shocked, to see an empty Trafalgar Square. I suddenly had this feeling and awareness that I needed to savour this memory and just be fully present in this moment. I had this overwhelming feeling that I would not be back here – in this Square, or London – for a very long time indeed. I wanted to fully embrace this moment, and just be thankful for all the amazing memories I'd made over the previous year and a half. What the hell is going on, I wondered out loud; this is history in the making.

After walking down the deserted Strand and past the King's campus for one last time, I jumped on the District line at Embankment and headed back towards East London. It was such a funny feeling, knowing that this was the last time I'd be racing around London for a long time. I hadn't expected it to all be coming to an end so soon. In my head, I just needed to get to the end of the term in March, and then it would be three months of going out, meeting guys and enjoying a summer of fun in London! None of this made sense; Morgan and I had got so much planned – this was going to be our summer of having fun and going wild in London! How on earth had this small news story from page 44 of The Times ended up becoming an international news story that would end up defining an entire generation?

This situation, I now realised, was not just big – it was massive. Everything was going to change; there would not be 'business as usual'. 'But I haven't found a boyfriend yet!', I complained to Morgan, 'how on earth do I find a man if I'm locked in my house in Macclesfield?!' We were both still desperate to stay in London, still trying to convince ourselves that this situation wasn't happening. But as news of an imminent nationwide lockdown continued to pour in, we soon realised that our hopes of staying in Stratford were a serious case of wishful thinking. We decided that we needed to fully accept reality. We needed to appreciate the fact we were both healthy and safe, and make peace with our time in London coming to an end early. The next day was Mother's Day, and I thought it would be a nice surprise for Queen P if I came back on the train to see her…and move back home for as long as this 'lockdown' was going to last! Queen P and Dad **had** – as always – been extremely liberal and understanding when it came to what I wanted to do after news of the lockdown broke. 'You do what makes you happy', Queen P had told me over the phone, 'Stay as long as you want, but if you want to come home we will come straight down to get you!'

That Saturday night, I called Dad and told him of my plan to make a 'surprise' return home. I swore him to secrecy and arranged that we'd both come down at some point before June to collect all of my belongings.

Morgan and I enjoyed once the last dinner in our Stratford One kitchen, with plenty of Prosecco, Chicken Nuggets, and tears. We did not want to leave – the past five months had been the happiest five months of our lives, and we'd only just been getting started! But we knew it was all for the best, and we knew that – one day – we'd be back, prosecco in hand, to make some more iconic memories on nights out in London! That evening, I sat in the window and took in the view of the London skyline for one last time. I have been so lucky, I think to myself, and I must treasure these memories for a lifetime. Who would have thought it, I say to myself, little Ben Wardle from Macclesfield having the time of my life here in London? I've had a good run, I tell myself, and these are memories to treasure for a lifetime! I get tucked up in bed and think back to the day I first arrived at Stratford One. How much I have grown, how much I have learned, and how many amazing memories I have made! Moving to London was, I know with more certainty than ever before, the best decision that I ever made. These have been the best years of my life, and London has made me the individual I am so proud to be today. I have been living my dreams, and no global pandemic is going to take those fabulous memories away from me!

The next day there are more tears, more chicken nuggets (well, we needed to eat our freezer section up!) and plenty more prosecco. Morgan and I head up to the Stratford One roof terrace, where we take in the skyline views and reminisce about our time together in London. 'You are the biggest blessing and the best friend I could ask for' I tell her, and I truly do mean it. Since day one, we have been having the best time and making the best memories. Morgan has unconditionally accepted me for who I am. And we have given each other immeasurable amounts of love and support. She has been my dream partner-in-crime, and I know that I would not have survived in this city without her. Who else would put up with my scandalous antics on nights out, and who else would answer all of my philosophical and inquisitive questions, every single day of the week? We have a big hug goodbye, and I rush off across London to catch the Avanti west coast train home.

I've told Dad I'll be back for about 8 pm, and he says he'll pick me – and the ten bags I'm dragging along behind me – up from Macclesfield station. I make it to Euston in one piece – and with all my bags – and get comfortable on the train. I feel heartbroken, but I am genuinely happy to know I'll be back at home with the best family I could ever ask for. The train driver than announces – of course, he does – that this train has actually broken down, and so we all need to get off and run across to a platform on the other side of the station. Well, at least there's never a dull moment when I'm around, even if it's on an emotional journey home because of a global pandemic and national lockdown! I finally arrive back in Macclesfield at about 11 pm, where Dad meets me on the platform and rescues me from the ten bags I am drowning under. He tells me he's had to persuade Queen P to stay up late, but that she still has no idea I'm going to be back home that evening. Perfect, I say, as we drive through town and back home. Queen P is genuinely shocked – in a good way! – to see me, which puts a positive gloss on my reasons for coming home. I collapse on the sofa, grab a glass of rose, and force the entire family to watch a 'Charity Shop Sue' montage on YouTube. Let's see how long this happiness lasts, I laugh, after we've spent potentially months under the same roof in lockdown together! Who is going to go insane first? What petty issue will our first lockdown row be about? I'm placing bets on it being about who secretly finished the last bottle of rose wine…

39. STAY AT HOME, FILM TIKTOKS...AND WRITE A BOOK

The very next day, Boris Johnson appears on national TV to announce the aforementioned national lockdown. It all suddenly starts to feel very real, and denial or aversion of the subject is no longer a possibility! I realise very quickly that complaining about what's happening is not going to help anybody. So I make it my mission to make the most of the months ahead at home.

It very quickly starts to feel like I'm back in Sixth Form. I very quickly slip back into my old Year 13 routines, which is very comforting and enjoyable! It turns out that I'd missed going for the newspaper at 7 am every morning, and I'd missed being tucked up in bed by 9.30 pm every evening! I think everybody had a very different experience of 'life in lockdown', and for some people, it will have been a lot harder to adjust and adapt than for others. I did find it weird to suddenly lose all of the freedom and independence I had enjoyed in London. Just a week ago, I was doing my weekly shop, jumping on and off tubes, going to work and doing everything for myself. Today, I was back in the family home and feeling like I was back in Sixth Form. Fortunately, mum and dad got that I wouldn't take kindly to being treated as though I was in year seven again, and they made sure to give me lots of space, even if we were all now under one roof! Lockdown was just as difficult for them; we are all people who like to be out and about keeping busy every day! There isn't a day that Queen P isn't either working, attending a fitness class, walking the dog or going out for brunch! The idea of sitting around watching daytime TV and twiddling her thumbs was alien to Queen P. So we had a mutual agreement to give each other the space to do our own things! Sam, of course, was living his best life; he would surface at around 4 pm, ask Queen P 'what is there to eat', and then could be heard shouting on the Xbox until the early hours of the morning. It wasn't uncommon for Sam to be going to bed at the same time I was getting up and heading off to buy the newspaper!

This is what I love about my family. It's why I feel so incredibly blessed to have them – everything is about liberty, freedom, and individuality. We are all so different, and never once have mum or dad tried to mould me, shape me, or tell me what to do with my life. As long as Sam and I are living with good manners and morals, we are given the freedom to do whatever makes us individually happy. This is the kind of parenting I hope to give to my future children. However, I can't promise that those poor children won't be subjected to a Kris Jenner moment – or two – over the years!

The first few weeks of Lockdown are – for everyone – very strange. I walk Flash with my Mum, wave at Granny across the driveway, have daily FaceTime calls with Freya, and find myself little jobs that will keep me busy. My dad isn't able to go and visit Grandma in her care home, and then Grandad, who is supposed to be shielding, becomes unwell at home. The doctors can't work out what is wrong with him, and he is unable to see the GP because of all the Coronavirus precautions. My dad visits him daily, and my Auntie Sue moves in to look after him,

A couple of weeks later and, with a very slight easing of restrictions, Dad and I drive down to London to collect the rest of my things from Stratford. It is the strangest experience driving down deserted motorways and arriving in a practically abandoned East London, with barely a car on the road and not a person insight. It feels genuinely dystopian and seriously surreal. We head up to Flat 201 for the last time, taking in the view of carless roads and a deserted city. We pack up my bedding, books and cutlery, before emptying my freezer section (filled with, unsurprisingly, a lifetime's supply of Lidl Chicken nuggets and Quorn burgers). With everything packed, we head back down to the car. I don't like seeing the usually bustling Westfield shopping centre looking like a ghost town, and I wonder how on earth life could change so much in just a matter of months. I say goodbye to Stratford – the place where I've found confidence, a love for London, and made the most amazing friends for life – and we head back home to Macclesfield.

***

A few weeks in and I find that I'm quite enjoying lockdown in our laid-back and loving household. I keep myself busy with my TikToks, filming vlogs of me being chased by cows as I walk Flash. To my genuine surprise, I discovered that videos of me thinking I'm Kim Woodburn and reacting to Instagram filters end up going down very well. After my first 'Guess the Gibberish' filter video gets a million views, I decide that I'm going to absolutely milk the concept dry. So I start filming no less than ten reaction videos a day! Well, what content can you create during a national lockdown other than reacting to 'What plane are you?' and 'What is your future career?' Instagram filters?! On Wednesday nights, I would always treat myself to a glass of my all-time favourite drink – the Sainsbury's White Zinfandel Rose (it's the best £4.50 you've ever spent). After a couple of glasses, I would film literally dozens of TikTok videos. My poor neighbours! After just one glass of rose, I genuinely seemed to believe that I was Kim Woodburn! And after two glasses of rose, whatever I was saying in response to the Instagram filter was bordering on incomprehensible! I would sit there swaying in my seat and shouting 'oh my GOD my loves' louder with every sip of my drink! Whoever was scrolling through TikTok on a Wednesday night during Lockdown was in for a treat (or should I say trauma?!) The number of videos that I would post – and then have to delete by 9 am on Thursday– was a serious concern! By some miracle, people do not start unfollowing me in their thousands (clearly they were never on TikTok on a Wednesday night), and my follower count actually ends up tripling instead. How on earth people were people putting up with my daily barrage of Instagram filter videos I will never know. Still, I felt so seriously blessed to have such lovely comments from the loveliest followers.

My favourite thing – in the world – was hearing from people who said my videos had brought a smile to their face or brightened up their day in lockdown. Whilst my level of public service was not quite on the same level of Joe Wicks, it did feel good to think I might have brightened someone's day, especially during such an uncertain and unprecedented time in all of our lives. I knew that people must have been struggling and finding everything quite scary, and I wanted to provide a little bit of comic relief in people's day.

Despite my Wednesday nights filming reaction videos on TikTok, I still had a lot of spare time on my hands. I love a day with nothing to do, I do, but only now and then – not every single day for weeks or even months on end! I needed to keep myself busy, and I needed to keep myself active! At first, I did struggle with my eating, as I think many people with a history of eating disorders may also have done. Mealtimes because main events in the day, because there was absolutely nothing else for me to think about. I will often mistake boredom for hunger, and I became paranoid that all I was doing each day was eating! I became very conscious that I was not burning any of the calories I was consuming off. We were, of course, not allowed out for more than one hour of exercise a day. And so I started to feel bad for eating as much as I was. I was eating the same amount as I used to eat whilst at university in London. But I wasn't doing half as many of the things I was doing down in Stratford. I wasn't on my feet working at the bar for over 12 hours a week, for example, and I wasn't running around London all morning, afternoon and evening! I started to become paranoid and obsessive about whether I was going to end up putting on weight. I still, I realised now, saw weight gain as this terrible and toxic thing. I had a deep-rooted fear of gaining weight. It didn't matter that everybody else in the country was in the same situation. It didn't matter that I might have looked a lot better if I put on a bit of weight. Remnants of those anorexic beliefs were still floating around in the cracks and crevices of my mind. And lockdown appeared to be a catalyst for their resurfacing.

I was certain that I would not allow anorexia to return – under *any* circumstances, including during a national lockdown! I had – after so many years in recovery – learned the best ways of keeping myself happy, healthy and eating disorder free. I knew, for example, that I felt happiest when I had something meaningful to work on and something purposeful to keep me busy. Ideally, this would have meant hosting at a hotel, restaurant or nightclub, but, of course, the lockdown meant that this was a non-starter! I had my university work to keep me busy, and of course, I had TikTok videos to film! I also made sure that I went for a long walk every morning, following the route that I used to walk with Becky down to school, just so that I could get some fresh air and feel alive! These daily walks were the essential weapon I needed for fighting off Cabin Fever, and just getting out of the house every morning did me a world of good! But I wanted – I needed – something else! I needed a project to work on; I needed something that would challenge me and keep me on my toes all day!

***

Step forward my brainwave idea to start writing a self-help book! I don't know what in the universe allowed me to decide that I was (a) qualified or (b) capable of writing a self-help book. But, never one to do things by halves, I decided that I was going to write a book and give JK Rowling a run for her money! I had dreamed of being some kind of life coach or psychotherapist for many years, and I had always been passionate about speaking out on mental health. After reading so many self-help books myself over the years, I had a lot of soundbites and pearls of wisdom that I was eager and keen to share. 'Write books' had always been on my bucket list, and I thought, well, what better time is there than now to sit down and churn out my debut title? I seemed to have this belief that writing a book would be a total breeze and walk in the park. Well, I've written so many blog posts and diary entries, I thought to myself, I'll be able to write a book in no time at all! I then went full Kris Jenner and started dreaming of a book writing empire. I ended up planning the next five books that I would write before I had even written a single word of the first one! This is absolutely typical behaviour from me!

I knew that I wanted my book to be a real source of inspiration and empowerment. I wanted to write a book that would motivate and energise every single person who picked it up. Every single page had to be a motivational call to action and a catalyst for personal transformation! Nothing made me happier than knowing I had made a difference in someone's day or, in a more dramatic sense, someone's life! And what better – or easier – way to make a positive difference than write a book that could give somebody the inspiration and motivation that they needed in their day?! I knew that self-help books, such as Susan Jeffers' 'Feel the fear...and do it anyway' and Vex King's 'Good Vibes, Good Life', had completely and utterly transformed my life. I know that many people remain unconvinced by the power of self-help books. Still, I genuinely believe they have the power – like any good book - to be genuinely life-changing. I have read countless books that have genuinely changed my life. Now that I don't have counselling appointments, 'self-help' books have become my new primary source of personal growth and healing. Authors such as Susan Jeffers and Vex King have given me so much confidence, inspiration and empowerment. They are changing lives, and even the whole world, through their writing! Considering the number of motivational quotes that I have read over the years, it feels like a natural next step to get all my ideas down in a book!

The timing also feels so right – I have all the time in the world, with nowhere to go and nothing to do! And, most importantly when it comes to self-publishing a book, I had a platform which I could use to actually sell my book; I now had 300,000 followers on TikTok, which meant I had the chance of selling at least a couple of copies! I was slightly worried about how I would market this book on TikTok. People followed me because of my 'guess the gibberish' and 'I'm being chased around a field by cows' style of content! They were not interested in my content because of my reputation as an author! Would they get confused when I started waving a book around? However, at least I had *some* potential readers, which meant I could finally fulfil my ambition of becoming an author!

***

Whenever anybody asks me about writing my book, one of the first questions is always – how did you get it published? I decided I wanted to self-publish my book, which is a very easy and straightforward process! The hard bit was – as I soon found out – writing 80,000 words to fill the 300+ pages I wanted to write! I had heard about this service from Amazon called 'KDP', or 'Kindle Direct Publishing', which enabled absolutely anybody to self-publish their book for free. All that you needed to do was submit your manuscript and your cover design, and Amazon would do the rest! Your book could then be sold on the Kindle store, where you would profit approximately 70% of the cover price. You were then also able to see your publication as a Paperback book on Amazon, where you would profit around 30% of the cover price. This meant that you had no upfront costs – other than the use of your time to actually write the book! – and you could become a published author with a book available on Amazon! It seemed perfect, and I started dreaming of the day when people would be holding my paperback book in their hands!

Before that day could come, however, I had to write the bloody thing! It turned out that writing 80,000 words took a lot more effort than composing a 500-word blog post (who would have thought it?!). I got about ten pages in and quickly realised that repeating mantras such as 'you grow through what you go through!' and 'you are the master of your own destiny!' might get quite tiresome 300 pages in! I decided that I wanted to write 50 short essays – much easier than trying to write an entire book! – and that I would centre them around three core themes; authenticity, confidence and resilience. I wanted to share my own story (of overcoming anorexia and accepting my sexuality). But I did not want to make the book all about me (that's what this one you're reading right now is for!!) I wanted to share all of the life lessons I have learned over the years, bringing in all of my favourite life coaching messages and philosophers along the way.

Of course, the key ingredient to any good book is a good cover. I strongly believe that the cover of a book will make or break the sales figures –– without a good cover, your book will not sell! They may say that you should 'never judge a book by its cover'. Still, anybody with the slightest interest in business or marketing will tell you that everybody in the world does! I needed an amazing book cover that would both make it look like a 'real book', and also provide a much-needed boost to the sales figures! The cover sets the tone for the entire book, and so it does need to be perfect. Obviously, the content inside the book is also pretty important. Still, I really believe that nothing matters more than a stand-out cover! Fortunately, I knew just the man – or, more specifically, former flyer boy – for the job. It just so very, fortunately, happened that Darragh had just graduated from his degree in Graphic Design. He was, therefore, a literal professional at design – designing posters, adverts, and BOOK COVERS was his career! He'd seen a prototype book cover I had hurriedly made on paint. Oh, it was genuinely diabolical, consisting of white Times New Roman font on the most sickly light pink background. Darragh knew that he had to intervene. After all those months of Wetherspoons lunches – not to mention those Summer's nights watching me trying to flirt on the street of Soho – he couldn't let me embarrass myself like this! Oh, he's a saint!

He messaged offering to design me a book cover, gently informing me that my efforts on Paint made a three-year-old look better than Picasso. He wondered if I wanted him to design a quick cover for the book, considering that he had a degree in graphic design (unlike me, in case you didn't know). I have never been more delighted or excited in my entire life. 'This is the answer to my prayers!' I tell Darragh on FaceTime, 'THANK YOU so much my love…this is a divine intervention!' I promise him that I'll treat him to a Wetherspoons date once they re-open; 'prosecco on me!' I excitedly scream down the phone. Oh, the poor boy! So Darragh got to work designing a cover for my book, whilst I finally got serious about writing it. By this stage, I've decided that I'll call it 'LIVE YOUR BEST LIFE'. These were, as I've mentioned, the final words that Dana had typed to me in my last Kooth online counselling session, and 'live your best life' had become my new go-to mantra. It was the perfect title, and Darragh had soon designed the perfect book cover. 'Oh my GOD it looks AMAZING' I exclaim in our next weekly FaceTime, 'like it actually looks like a real book you'd find in Waterstones!!'

I am more excited than a 6-year-old on Christmas morning, imagining bookstore shelves lined with copies of AN ACTUALLY BOOK WRITTEN BY ME! In my excitement, I demand Darragh's PayPal details and transfer him some money. I don't know what I was thinking – he's never done a single poster, Instagram layout or book cover for free since! What started as a favour designed to save me from my pink background disaster has now become a Kardashian-style business deal. Watch out, Kris Jenner! All I can say is thank God, my best friend turned out to be a graphic designer!

***

I'm now too busy getting excited about the cover to focus on writing the book. We're about halfway through, and I'm finding the whole writing process to be both enjoyable and infuriating. I've got myself into a little routine, which brings a sense of purpose to each day. I'll wake up at 6.30, go for a walk to buy the newspapers, have breakfast, write for two hours from 8 until 10, go for a walk into town and back, and then write through lunchtime from 11 until about 2. I find that writing in the mornings is so much easier and productive for me – I love just getting up and getting on with it whilst the rest of the world is still just waking up! One thing that I don't lose during lockdown is my work ethic, something for which I am very grateful and glad! I really think that strong self-motivation and a willingness to work hard are the real secrets to achieving success in this world. It's that self-motivation that keeps me going when I'm totally fed up of writing and just want to watch Keeping Up with the Kardashians all day (I try to save that for my Sunday evenings, which were just made for watching Kris Jenner).

It's this work ethic that results in me sitting back down and continuing to write after dinner, which is usually some kind of Quorn with a side of Sainsbury's fries and loads of salad. I desperately try and get as much writing done in one sitting as possible. Still, my phone ends up becoming an endless source of distraction! One 'oh I'll just check my Tinder messages' moment quickly becomes thirty-minutes of mindlessly scrolling through Instagram, Twitter and TikTok, a habit that it both mind-numbing and zombifying. I decided to ban myself from my phone other than for 30 minutes every day. However, most days, this ended up being 30 minutes of every hour!

I am desperately impatient to just get this book ***done***, especially now that I've got a book cover and I'm promoting the book online! Why can't I wave a magic wand and have a fully completed 300-page publication?! The whole writing process is a love-hate situation that transpires to be both infuriating and enlightening in equal measure. I find that writing is the best therapy in the world. I firmly believe that you learn so much when you put your thoughts and ideas down onto paper. Never mind publishing the book; just the process of writing does me a world of good (even if it is also sending me slightly insane!)

40. GOODBYE GRANDAD

One afternoon I'm busy, as usual, typing away at one of the essays for my book, when my mum comes to me with a heartbroken and troubled look on her face. I can read her like a book, and I know straight away that she has come bearing bad news. Oh God, I think, preparing myself for whatever is about to come. Queen P has tears before she even starts talking, 'I'm so sorry Ben' she manages, 'Your dad's just been on the phone…he's on his way to the hospital…they think that your Grandad is dying'. My blood runs cold and the most enormous lump forms in my throat. What? He's what?

'Oh my God', I reply, genuinely taken aback by what I'm hearing. I knew that he'd had been ill, and I knew that he'd been taken into hospital. But I never had, for one single second imagined that he might not make it through whatever this illness was. I felt terrible – I had not seen him for months, and I had not, in a million years, anticipated receiving this news. It just did not make sense, at all. What do you say in this kind of situation? What even is there to say? I ask mum about what was happening – she said Dad was on his way to the hospital – and then tried to take a minute to process this information. He's dying? Am I never going to speak to him again? He's not going to be coming over for Christmas day night?

I had never experienced the death of a family member before, and I did not know what to do with myself. As I always do in a situation where I feel helpless, I got out my Bible and started to pray. I needed to feel as if I was doing something to make sure that he was okay, and I needed to express how I was feeling about what was going on. It is at times of crisis, pain and helplessness that I always seem to suddenly believe in God. I try to make sense of the situation and find some comfort through praying to the Lord.

Once I have finished asking God to look after Grandad and make sure that he is not in any pain, I sit down and handwrite a four-page letter to Grandad. I write about how much I love him and how thankful I am for everything that he has done. I write about the Saturday's I used to spend giving him and Grandma my bossy lessons in their dining room. And I reminisce about our days out to Chester Zoo, Brookside Garden Centre, and

Blue Planet Aquarium. I write about trips to Blackpool and Christmas night buffets, and I thank him for being the kindest and most generous gentleman in the world. It's my way of being able to express how I am feeling. I hope that he will be able to hear these words, even in some kind of divine or eschatological way.

My dad returns home from hospital later that night, absolutely devastated and heartbroken. He has seen Grandad, and the doctors have said there is nothing more that they can do. Their focus now is making sure that he is comfortable and not in pain. He is drifting in and out of consciousness, unable to move, eat, drink, or talk. Despite the Coronavirus precautions, there is a chance that Sam and I might be able to go and see him for one last time tomorrow. This will depend on whether he makes it through the night. I feel heartbroken and devastated – but I know that I *have* to go and say goodbye in person. The deep spiritual conviction is back, and I have this overwhelming sense that I have to see Grandad, no matter how hard it may be. Dad is planning to go back the next morning, and I ask him to take my letter – along with a little crucifix I have cello taped to the paper – down to the hospital for me. It is the most desperately sad and heartbreaking situation, and I cannot bear to see Dad so devastated.

The next day, Dad is back at the hospital and has read Grandad my letter. He calls home and says that, if we would like to, Sam and I can go to the hospital and see Grandad. We both say yes, and so that evening we all spend time with Grandad for one final evening. I walk into the room, and I am completely flawed. It is devastating and heartbreaking – how on earth did we get to this stage? How on earth has this happened? What on earth are you supposed to do in the face of such sadness?

This moment provides me with a major wake-up call. It instantly puts everything in life into perspective, and it makes me realise how much I need to get real about life. Life is too short to be worrying about someone staring at you in the street, petty dramas and social media statistics. Nothing matters more than showing love to the people who you care about most Death is so final and declarative – there is no coming back. Having studied death so much as part of my theology degree, I found that I was quite good at putting a philosophical spin on the situation. Still, on a personal level, it was the most devastating and heartbreaking news. Even more devastating was to see my Dad. I couldn't even begin to imagine the day that I would receive a call telling me either of my parents were dying. It is the worst, most devastating and horrific news you could ever hear, and it broke my heart. Again, it was another wake-up call – when it came to my anxieties, worries and fears about life, I needed to – frankly - get a bloody grip. Why was I so obsessed with what people thought of me? Why did I care whether someone made a comment about me or embarrassed me in a social situation? These were the most trivial, irrelevant and pathetic issues – was I twenty-years-old, or was I two?

Having this kind of experience with death shakes us up, wakes us up, and disrupts our world views. It is a very real reminder of the fragility of human life and the preciousness of every single existence. It reminds us that we need to stop taking the most important people in our lives for granted. And it forces us to confront the temporality of all human life. It's a massive reminder that the clock of life ticking, and so we you must tell people how much we love them – and do things that show that love – whilst we still can.

The next day, Grandad passes away. The medics had attempted to bring him back to Macclesfield in an ambulance so that he could spend his final hours in his own home. This was where so many happy memories and so much love remained. Grandad had sadly died just as the ambulance arrived in Macclesfield, which meant that he was at least back in his hometown for one last time. Although I'd had a couple of days to process what was happening, it was still the most difficult situation to face. The hardest part was seeing Sam, Dad and the whole family so heartbroken, knowing that there is nothing you can do to alleviate the grief or pain. Words seem so empty and shallow – there is nothing you can say that will make the loss of your dad or grandad anymore bearable.

Death is something every single human being is so familiar with. We all lose our loved ones – some who are lost before their time – and we must all go through the grieving processes. Every single day, people lose their parents, grandparents, cousins, husbands, and even children. In the western world, we have lost sight of the fact that such suffering and grief is universal. We shy away from conversations about death and suffering, taking comfort in distractions such as Reality TV or petty everyday disputes. Perhaps – I think – it would be easier for everybody if we started talking more openly and honestly about death and grief? What if we started having more conversations with our loved ones about our fears of dying, our fears of them dying, and how we are supposed to cope when someone close to us dies. Refusing to talk about death will not make it go away! Burying our head in the sand will not make grieving or mourning anymore bearable! If only we could talk more about our fears and our feelings concerning death, grief, and the end of life. If only we could sit down and speak much more frankly about this thing called 'death', which seems to scare and shock us all so much.

There is a Buddhist parable on making sense of the pain caused by bereavement that goes like this:

"In the time of the Buddha, a woman named Kisagotami suffered the death of her only child. Unable to accept it, she ran from person to person, seeking a medicine to restore her child to life. The Buddha was said to have such a medicine. Kisagotaami went to the Buddha, paid homage, and asked, 'Can you make a medicine that will restore my child?' 'I know of such a medicine', the Buddha replied. 'But to make it, I must have certain ingredients'. Relieved, the woman asked, 'What ingredients do you require?' 'Bring me a handful of mustard seed', said the Buddha. The woman promised to procure it for him, but as she was leaving, he added, 'I require that the mustard seed be taken from a household where no child, no spouse, parent or servant has died'. The woman agreed and began going from house to house in search of the mustard seed. At each house the people agreed to give her the seed, but when she asked them if anyone had died in that household, she could find no home where death had not visited – in one house a daughter, in another a servant, in others a husband or parent had died. Kisagotami was not able to find a home free from the suffering of death. Seeing that she was not alone in her grief, the mother let go of her child's lifeless body and returned to the Buddha, who said with great compassion, 'You thought that you alone had lost a son; the law of death is that among all living creatures there is no permanence'.

The knowledge that death is a natural part of the human experience doesn't make grieving, loss or bereavement any easier. But it does remind us that we are not alone in our suffering. It reminds us that it's natural to feel sad, and it's normal to feel heartbroken, but it also reminds us that we will survive this feeling that we are going through. Every single person has been through a bereavement, and every single person has been able to adjust to the new normal of a world without their loved one. It's not easy, and it will at times feel impossible... but you will get there. And you will never forget that person or the essential life lessons that they have taught you.

***

Living a good life, I believe, includes having a 'good death'. We cannot fear death, and we should not be afraid of other people dying. I try and look at it philosophically, and I try to consider it within the bigger context of the 'circle of life'. The only thing we should be scared of is not feeling brave enough to talk about death. We need to talk more about how to help someone who is faced with the prospect of their death. And we need to talk more about how to help someone grieving the loss of a loved one. What should I say to them...if anything at all? How can I support them through this impossibly sad time? How can I be there for them without causing more harm than good?

I found that the best way for me to work through the grieving process was to actively talk about it and to focus on doing what I could to support those around me. The important thing to remember is that the process and experience are so different for everyone. We all cope with death, grief, and bereavement in different ways, and there is no one particular right answer. As I say, my approach has been relatively philosophical – I try to look for the lesson behind whatever is happening in life. I try to work out why the universe might be sending me this particular challenge at this particular time. That's not to say that there is any 'purpose' or 'reason' by what has happened. Or, at least, there's not a reason beyond the fact that 'life is sometimes cruel' and filled with suffering.

But I think you certainly have the option to find some meaning or purpose in whatever is happening in your life. I do not believe that death is the end. Whilst I do not believe in physical heaven or bodily resurrection, I have complete conviction that the person's legacy, love, and wisdom will live on. Every single person we meet touches us and leaves an imprint on us in some way. And just because a loved one is no longer physically with us, that does not mean we cannot still feel their love, hear their words of wisdom, or feel close to their spirit. I move forwards in my life determined to remember Grandad, his kindness, generosity and spirit, and determined to look after Dad, Sam and all of the family for him. I have always wanted to make my Grandparents – and parents – proud. I would have loved nothing more than to have shown him my book or to have talked to him more about life in London. I would do anything for one last Saturday morning sitting in Grandma and Grandad's lounge, a cup of tea in hand. But, at the same time, I am comforted by my firm conviction that I carry his spirit with me in everything that I do, and I know that he's aware of how much I thank and love him. Death may be the physical end of human life, but it does not extinguish any of the love or memories that you hold onto. They will remain with you forever. And that is the important thing to remember.

Rest in peace, Grandad, I cannot thank you enough for everything.

41. A WHOLE NEW PERSPECTIVE

Losing Grandad is yet another one of those 'wake up' call moments that forces me to recognise the futility of my self-obsessed anxieties and confront the fragility of human life. It is another one of those moments when I am forced to reflect on my priorities and confront the bigger purpose behind my existence. I'm starting to realise that I spend far too much time worrying away about petty, pathetic, and irrelevant issues that have no importance in the real world. People are dying in a global health pandemic, and people are living in literal war zones. Yet I spend my time worrying about the fact I've "only" gained 50K followers in a month on TikTok, or that a boy I've been speaking to on Tinder hasn't replied to me yet. Get a grip, I think to myself, pull yourself together!

And so, I get serious about getting myself together. I resolve that this time, I *really* will stop worrying about what people think. I really will stop being so sensitive, and I really will stop worrying about who is doing better than me on social media. And so, I throw myself into completing my book – at long bloody last! – and I resolve to get serious about my teaching career. I know now that I want to be a teacher – ideally a headteacher! – by day, and then I want to be writing my books and appearing in the media by night! I'm going to stop dreaming about appearing on Sky News to talk about the day's newspaper front pages. Instead, I'm going to work harder now than ever before to make it happen! I'm going to stop dreaming about being a headteacher and becoming the next Mrs Garvey and Mrs Connor, and actually, work hard to turn that dream into my reality! Let's get serious about making things happen! Let's stop wasting energy, thinking about issues that just could not be more irrelevant!

I decide that I need a new relationship with TikTok. I'm now on 400K followers, which is insane, and I genuinely feel both shocked and delighted about it all. However, I worry that I'm starting to take it too seriously, and wonder if – like I often do – I'm getting too invested in this one particular thing. If the app disappeared overnight, I know that I'd be fine – I've got my books to be writing, my life to be living, and my teaching career to be working towards! I know that it won't last forever, and so I just want to have fun, make memories, and enjoy it whilst I can! As long as it's bringing some fun into my life – rather than taking my happiness or peace of mind away – then I am free to enjoy the app and have some fun! It's like a little hobby I can enjoy, preferably on a Wednesday evening after a glass of my favourite White Zinfandel rose wine!

I genuinely am so incredibly thankful for TikTok. It has given me a platform to express my inner Kim Woodburn and have five minutes of thinking that I am Kris Jenner! It is a fabulous, fun and feel-good creative outlet, which has given me more opportunities and exposure than I could otherwise have dreamed of ever having. TikTok is amazing because absolutely anybody can go viral overnight. All that you need is a bit of good luck, and you could wake up one day with 2 million views on a video (it is the most surreal thing in the world!) In this sense, I think it's a very egalitarian innovation. However, I think success on this app does often come down more to luck and chance rather than raw talent and hard work. You'll see someone with – and I'm not being rude – really poor content who has got over a million followers.

Meanwhile, you'll see someone who posts amazing videos ten times a day who has barely got a thousand followers. Of course, it's not about the number of followers or your level of 'fame'. Still, I do often find the TikTok algorithms very baffling! And the end of the day, it all comes down to luck!

Being on TikTok – which is, of course, all thanks to Jamie – has given me the most incredible opportunities. I would never have sold copies of my first book, for example, because the only people who would have been interested in reading it would have been my mum, dad and Gran! I would never have met some of the kindest and genuine people in the world if we hadn't connected on TikTok! TikTok has opened doors, inspired me, and given me the most amazing platform. I always wonder what my lockdown would have been like if I hadn't ended up in a flat with Jamie, or if he had never brought up TikTok in conversation! It's so weird to say it about a social media app. Still, I can't imagine my life today without TikTok...which is slightly worrying when I've only had the app for eight months! My only concern is how my old TikTok videos might end up going down in the classroom if the app hasn't disappeared before my teaching debut! Will my videos of being 'blown like I've never been blown before' by Storm Ciara in the Olympic Park cause trouble during my Year 7 Religious Studies lessons!? Will footage of latest 'fake tan shower fiasco' undermine my authority as an expert on New Testament ethics? I imagine that the TikTok videos will – at some stage – have to be archived and locked away, which I am fully expecting and understand. I would not change a single thing about the 'Carry On' inspired content that I have posted online. Life is too short to worry about the consequences of your online content! Whilst it's important to be aware of your online footprint and trail, it's equally as important to live your life to the full! You need to know that everything is, in the words of the fabulous Marie Forleo, ***figureoutable***!

I spend the rest of the summer catching up – at last! – with Becky, Freya, Kristina, Erin (both of them!), Emma, Alyce and Abby. It's nice to finally be out and about again! I enjoy day trips into Manchester and a cocktail (or two) at the Alchemist! Well, we were doing our bit for the nation by eating out to help out...and drinking the venues out of rose and prosecco! Freya and I go for a drink – or five – at the newly reopened Popworld, where we are the only people in the club-turned-bar, and I get told off by security for getting out of my seat. We leave clutching complimentary fake glasses, flower lanyards and photo props. However, not even these freebies could change how we felt about the impact Covid-19 was having on nightclubs!

Mum, Dad, Sam and I head off for our annual two weeks in Kefalonia. Did you think that a global health pandemic was going to stop Queen P from enjoying her 14 days of drinking Greek rose in the Mediterranean sun? After flying back into Manchester, I take part in an exciting media opportunity, which I am unfortunately banned from telling you absolutely anything about! All I will say (to avoid being taken to court!) is that it was an eye-opener, a lot of fun, and an incredible life experience! And, after months in lockdown, this bit of fun was exactly what I needed! As you know, I believe very strongly that life is all about stepping outside of your comfort zone, taking risks and trying something new. And it's all about making memories (even if you are banned from talking about those memories with anybody!)

Here's what I've learned in life: whatever you are doing in life, never say 'no' to an exciting opportunity. Never turn something down because you're not sure how it's going to turn out. Never decide to 'play it safe' or 'stick to what I know'. Life is too short to stay hidden away in your comfort zone! You've got to follow your heart, seize every opportunity, and live your best life! Just remember that, whatever happens, you can handle it! Everything that we do teaches us an important lesson for life – you grow through everything that you go through! So keep taking those risks, keep daring to dream big, and never say 'no' to an exciting opportunity! Things might not work out, but you're never going to know – and you're never going to grow – until you try!

So get yourself out there, give it a go, and grow through everything you go through! All I will say is this: never undersell yourself, never underestimate yourself, and never lose sight of yourself.

As long as you stay true to your principles and remember your life's purpose, you can't go far wrong! Remember your worth, stand up for what you believe in, and don't you dare put up with anyone trying to put you down! Never be afraid to speak up when you think that something isn't right, and never feel afraid to walk away.

At all times, remember that you are the master of your destiny and the author of your whole future. Only do what makes you feel good and helps you to grow – never forget that, more than anything else in the world, you deserve to be happy!

42. THIRD TIME LUCKY IN LONDON?

It's September – once again – and the sun is shining as my Dad and I jump into the car. After six months at home for lockdown, it's time to get back down to London. It's finally the start of my third (and final) year studying Religion, Philosophy & Ethics in London. I'm seriously concerned about where on earth the past two years have gone. It genuinely feels like yesterday that I was first arriving in Stratford. I can vividly remember feeling both terrified and excited at the prospect of spending the next three years living, studying and working in Central London. It makes me smile to think about the nervous, innocent and enthusiastic 18-year-old Ben. If only I could go back and tell myself – stop worrying so much, everything is going to be okay! Stop doubting your social skills or your ability to survive, I'd tell myself - you're going to do just fine! I wouldn't change a single thing about the past two years. Everything that has happened has strengthened me and shaped me into the confident and self-aware 20-year-old I am extraordinarily proud to be today. I can say, hand on my heart, that I am genuinely proud of the person I am today. And so I appreciate every single part of my journey – all of those nerves, setbacks, lost jobs and lost friends. Life is all about learning on the job. And what better place for me to have learned than in London?!

London had proven to be a city where I have been challenged and changed for the better. It would provide me with the most incredible self-confidence and resilience, and it has taught me how to adapt, adjust and assert myself. It has been the most liberating and empowering experience of my life. I have loved every single second of my life living in this fast-paced and never-quiet city. I would not change a single thing about my experience, and I would do it all over again in a heartbeat. Every single day I thank my lucky stars that, all the way back in Year 12, I set my heart on London. I made that decision, and I have never once looked back. I will treasure my London experiences, memories, friends and life lessons for the rest of my years on this planet!

Arriving back in London for third year had a very different feel to the years before. Perhaps it was the fact that I was now almost 21 and felt more wise, mature and self-aware than ever before. Perhaps it was the fact that I knew this was now my final year, and I was no longer worried about finding my way around or finding people who I could spend my time with. I felt secure in my identity, secure in my friendships and secure in my plans for the future. I knew that this time next year, I hoped to be beginning my career as a Religious Studies teacher. I didn't expect to be doing this in London – I had my heart set on doing this teacher training up in Manchester. And so I was simply looking forward to enjoying one final year living as a student in the capital.

I had decided early on in Second Year that I wanted to continue living at Stratford One until the end of my degree. I loved the building, the bedrooms, the staff and the location. It was so modern, convenient, and familiar to me – Stratford felt like a genuine home. Whilst half of me would have loved to live in an actual house somewhere in the city; the other half was very aware that Stratford One was the perfect place for me to remain. Morgan decided to live at home for third year, which was just 30 minutes away - on the High-Speed Line - down in Kent. I felt like Stratford One provided me with the best of both worlds; I would get my room with en-suite, whilst I would also get the social benefits of a shared kitchen as well. For someone who would describe themselves as probably a 50:50 introvert/extrovert, this was the perfect set-up!

***

So I arrived back down in London unsure what, several months into a global pandemic, I would find! It felt good – but also strange – to be back. I was back in Block A, in a ground floor flat directly beneath Flat 105, the gorgeous flat where I had lived with Maisie and Carl throughout first year. Like first year, my view was of the Eurostar train line and the cranes building swanky new apartments in the Olympic Village. I missed my stadium and skyline view from last year, but I was genuinely excited to have my hourly train announcements back in full swing! It was nice to know that 'the train now approaching platform one does not stop here' about ten times an hour!

I quickly got settled into my new – but very familiar – room, and I excitedly headed off for my favourite thing in the world…grocery shopping! With my face mask on and hand sanitiser ready to go, I was far too excited to be heading back to Sainsbury's, Lidl and Waitrose! There's something that I just love about grocery shopping! And yes, I do genuinely question whether I am 20 or 65 years old! I also had a lot of work to be getting on with. I was filming GCSE Religious Studies revision videos, getting started in my role as co-chair of National Student Pride and I had lots of dissertation reading to be doing! As you know, I love being busy and having lots of things-to-do in my diary. Well, the diary was certainly full, and I was very well stocked up on green tea, post-it notes and ring binders. In other words, I was ready to go!

One of the things keeping me busy through the third year is my dissertation, the pinnacle – some would say – of the undergraduate experience! The thought of doing a dissertation had been, I must admit, filling me with dread. It had been a thought bubbling away in the back of my mind since the start of First Year. Still, I had never expected the day when I had to write one to actually come! And so, when we receive an email asking us to submit our dissertation proposals, I nearly choke on my green tea and go spiralling into full-on panic mode! I have to be honest. I have never understood the weighting and marking of my degree course (probably because it had never actually been explained to me). But I did understand that the dissertation was a pretty big deal and would have a pretty big influence on my final degree classification! The thought of writing 10,000 words on one topic genuinely blew my mind – I knew that I needed to find a topic that I could read, talk and write about for literally hours!

As you well know, I love working away on little projects, hence the existence of this book! I love any excuse to get organised, write information in my diary and go shopping for brand new stationery! And writing a dissertation was the perfect opportunity to indulge my love for planning! At first, I decided that I wanted to write about the decline in religious belief in the United Kingdom. I had this vision of me appearing on Sky News to talk about the 'post-religious void' that had opened up in Britain. I had dreams of writing books about why the decline of religion had left people looking for new sources of meaning, purpose and morality in their lives!

And then, just like Saul on the Road to Damascus, I am struck by a bright light and flash of inspiration. Well, in reality, I woke up one morning and have a very good idea whilst eating my Special K cereal! I realise that I want to make my dissertation – of course, I do – about attitudes towards LGBT+ people within Christianity. I want to find out why the Catholic Church has a reputation for being so anti-gay, I and want to work out whether this genuinely has a solid Biblical basis. Does the Bible really provide a credible criticism of homosexuality? Can the Bible really be used to justify homophobia and discrimination? The Catechism of the Catholic Church declares that homosexual acts are 'of grave depravity', 'intrinsically disordered' and 'contrary to the natural law'. The Church claims that sacred scripture – in other words, the Bible – provides the 'solid foundation' for this condemnation of homosexuality. I wanted to explore this claim and work out on what grounds. Biblical writing about homosexuality could justify the Church's continued discrimination against LGBT+ people.

The only New Testament discussion of homosexuality is found in three verses written by St Paul. For thousands of years, the Catholic Church has argued that these verses provide a 'solid foundation' for its condemnation of homosexuality. I loved the idea of being able to really investigate and evaluate this claim by completing an exegetical study into these letters. I felt so excited about the prospect of working out precisely why the Church is so opposed to homosexuality, before reviewing the influence of Paul's writing on Catholic social teaching today.

My wonderful dissertation supervisor – who taught me 'New Testament: Origins, meanings and contexts' in the first year - approves my title 'Paul on Sexuality: Then and Now'. I decided that I will break the dissertation down into two parts:

- **Part One – Paul's position on homosexuality as outlined in his New Testament letters**.
- Part Two – **The impact of these letters on the attitudes of the Roman Catholic Church today**.

The central question of my dissertation will ask whether Paul's letters do indeed provide a 'solid foundation' for the Catholic Church's condemnation of homosexuality.

Over the summer, I had read a fascinating book entitled 'Unclobber: Rethinking our Misuse of the Bible on Homosexuality'. It was written by Colby Martin, a former evangelical pastor who had become a Progressive Christian and outspoken advocate for LGBT+ inclusion within the Church. Colby, who was heterosexual, believed that the Church has 'misunderstood and misused' Paul's letters. He called for a new approach to understanding homosexuality from a Christian perspective, which included taking a much more loving and inclusive approach. I was fascinated by his research and writing, and I knew that this was a topic I had to explore. So I got to work studying St Paul's letters, researching Catholic teaching on homosexuality, and reading up on religious attitudes to homosexuality! It was fascinating, and I absolutely loved it!

Alongside my dissertation, I have six other modules to study in my third and final year at University in London:

- **Philosophy of Religious Life**
- **New Religious Movements in Global Perspectives**
- **The Principles of Systematic Theology**
- **Jesus in Context**
- **Religion, Politics and Global Media**
- **Special Questions in Social Ethics**

I am so excited to get stuck into these modules! I genuinely feel so passionate and excited about my subject. That is, I think to myself, probably a good thing considering I want to teach it in secondary schools once I graduate! And I know one key piece of advice that I'll be giving to all of my students: pursue your passions! Make sure you are excited to wake up every morning! Make sure you are unapologetic about doing more of the things that bring you genuine happiness and fulfilment in life! Turn your passion into your career and turn your dreams into your actual reality! Be excited and energised by the things that you do in your life…life is far too short not to enjoy it!

***

In the first few days back in London, I caught up with Morgan, Carl, Shadi, Farah, Darragh, Bex, Kaine and Hannah. It was so good to see everyone again after so long back home – it almost felt like I had never left London for a solid six months of the past year!

On my first Saturday back in the city, I headed off on the High-Speed train to stay with Morgan for a weekend in Kent. We went off to the Bluewater Shopping Centre, where I was beyond excited to discover the shelves were already lined with Christmas trees, baubles and decorations. After Coronavirus had hijacked 2020, I thought that an extended season of Christmas festivities was exactly what the nation needed!

After heading around the shops and spending far too much money, we sat outside in the glorious September sunshine with a much needed McDonalds order in hand. As we ate, a group of young boys – perhaps aged seven - came over to our table. They wanted to know if I was 'that boy from TikTok', and they wanted to know whether I was actually 'a boy or a girl'. One of these boys had his iPhone out and was pointing the lens directly at Morgan and I, hoping to capture some entertaining footage of our reactions. As I sat there in the September sunshine, I was not in the mood to get worked up about these young boys. Their questions about whether I wanted to be a girl and if I was gay were going straight over my head. These young children were not phasing me – in the slightest.

It was at this moment – as I sat there feeling genuinely unfazed by what these children were saying to me – that I realised just how far I had come over the past couple of years. Here's the thing: if this kind of incident had happened even a year or two earlier, I would have been left feeling incredibly angry and anxious. I would have felt attacked, frustrated, and angered by the fact that these children – as young as six or seven – were judging and mocking me in this way. It reminded me of when I did work experience in a Primary School, and a year one student asked me 'are you a boy because you sound like a girl?' I used to be so shaken and upset by these children – without, I believe, malicious intent – making comments about my gender or sexuality. I knew that I was different, but I hated young children without filters instantly picking up on it and 'calling me out' for it.

It had made me feel embarrassed, ashamed, and desperate just to be 'normal'. But as I sat there, basking in the sunshine, I did not sense that all-too-familiar feeling of horror and hurt rushing through my veins. Instead, I felt very in control of both my feelings and the situation. Years of meditation, introspection and reading about emotional intelligence had paid off! 'Yes, I am gay' I replied to these boys, 'and I'm very proud of that fact'. They giggled away and continued filming, so I added, with the brightest smile I could manage, 'have a great day guys!'

With that, I turned back to Morgan. I continued our conversation (about Tarot cards and whether mysticism, in case you were wondering!) I had remained completely calm, collected and in control of this interaction, which was just as well considering that these boys were 15 years younger than me! I felt extremely proud that I was now able to calmly manage my emotions and confidently control my reactions. These boys were not saying anything I hadn't heard before. They were not telling me anything I didn't know. Because I now understand and accept who I authentically am, this kind of comment no longer phases me. I feel so secure in my own identity that I do not need to fear the judgements, critiques or remarks of anybody, whether they are aged 6 or 60!

I have realised, at the age of 20, that I want to be a role model and become a positive advocate and ambassador for change. I want to inspire people to become more authentic, confident, and resilient in their daily lives. I want to empower individuals to become the 'masters of their own destiny' and to take full responsibility for their lives. After so many years of suffering from my insecurities and 'victim mindset', I want to help people 'take back control' of their lives. I want to help others to become genuinely confident and deeply fulfilled individuals! The is what every single person deserves to be! I care deeply about creating a world where every single individual is treated with kindness, dignity and respect. And I am extremely passionate about the fact that every single human being has a fundamental right to be happy.

What is it that sustains and inspires me in my mission to 'be the change' and make a difference? It is – as it always has been – my love for philosophy and ethics! This subject saved me, and this discipline has truly transformed my life! Philosophy has provided me with the principles and foundations for living a secure, fearless and genuinely confident life. No matter what other people say or what is happening in the world around me, philosophy gives me the most robust principles and foundations for living.

I am anchored in life by a belief in John Stuart Mill's 'non-harm principle'. I could not agree more with the belief that 'over his own body and mind, the individual is sovereign'. As long as you are not causing harm to anybody, then you should be free to do whatever brings you genuine happiness and fulfilment in life. This principle reassures me that my fight against homophobia is right. It gives me the confidence to keep speaking up and keep being myself, irrespective of what people may think or say. Aristotle's theory of 'eudaimonia' – and his argument that the purpose of human life is flourishing – has empowered me to become the very best version of myself. It has inspired me to dream of making the best contribution to the common good I possibly can. This ancient philosophical wisdom invigorates, sustains and inspires me in my 21st-century life today! And my study of Jesus, Christianity and religious ethics reminds me of the sanctity of all human life and the preciousness of human existence. Christ's teachings leave me feeling emboldened and empowered to speak out against intolerance and to be fearless about becoming an advocate for authenticity, acceptance and diversity. The central Christian principle of 'love' has infused every single area of my life with meaning, joy and connection. It has instilled in me this insatiable love for meeting new people, making a difference in society, and striving to empower every individual I meet! I pray for a world in which every single individual has the freedom to pursue their flourishing and take responsibility for their own life. And I don't just want to be praying for it or talking about it. Instead, I want to actively play my part in creating that accepting, compassionate and kind world in which we all deserve to live! It is only when we accept everybody for who they authentically are and acknowledge that diversity strengthens us that we will truly thrive as one humanity!

***

I'm have enjoyed popping back down to London, and I'm still busy making TikToks. I'm now on 460,000 followers – which is ridiculous – and I cannot believe this many people find me entertaining. I still just enjoy TikTok as a bit of a 'hobby'. My filming schedule still consists of me having a glass of White Zinfandel Rose on a Wednesday evening! The lockdown traditions are still going strong! As I say, I am so thankful for the opportunities that TikTok has brought into my life, even the ones that didn't end up working out! TikTok has opened so many doors, and it has introduced me to so many talented, iconic, and hilarious human beings.

One such person was Max Balegde (also known as Max Trobe), a fellow Northerner living down in London. Max's videos – usually entertaining updates on his mattress based legal dispute with landlord Natascha – were always on my 'For You Page'. I was invested in the mattress saga and thought Max was an absolute icon. He also happened to be following me on TikTok. He had first stumbled across my 'Hot Cross Bun Flavour Tea' tasting video ("oooh I'm getting carrot" has to be the standout moment of that video) several months earlier. Surely you would need therapy after that, I thought, not decide to follow me? In September, Max had launched his podcast, which was proving to be a massive success. He tells me that he had seen one of my TikTok Lives, in which I was speaking about studying religion. It had given him the idea of doing a podcast discussing religion, and he asked me if I wanted to feature. OF COURSE, I DO!, was my response, delighted to have a chance to talk about theology on this icon's podcast! We finally found a date that we were both free (very hard considering Max was at Heaven seven nights a week), and I told Max to come over to Stratford One.

He made it to Stratford, and we sat down for some pizza and prosecco (well of course we did!) One hour later, and I genuinely felt as if I had known this icon for life. 'Well I suppose we'd better actually record the podcast' says Max, as I track down a bottle of rose. 'Oh, yes, the podcast!' I reply, slightly concerned about how I am going to discuss the eschatological and soteriological doctrines of Christianity after three glasses of prosecco. A podcasting-professional, Max is busy setting up one million and one pieces of equipment that are far too technical (and expensive) for my little brain. I have my notes on God, everything is set up, and we have a new glass of prosecco in hand.

However, there is a problem. 'I've forgotten my charger', says Max, 'and I'm losing 5% charge every 5 seconds'. Max decides (yes, I'm blaming him here) that he needs to go to the Apple shop in Westfield to buy a new charger. It sounds like a very simple solution to the problem! So we head across the road to Westfield, leaving all of his equipment – and the prosecco – in my room. Despite the fact it is 8 pm on a weekday night, there is a queue at the Apple store. 'I'm sorry I can't get you inside tonight' says one of the staff, gesturing to the long queue of people in front of us. We are in an absolutely deserted Westfield, but of course, there has to be a queue outside the Apple store! 'But I just want a charger', Max protests, but the man is not moving. We run down to Argos and, to Max's absolute joy, they have a charger in stock. Relieved and ready to record, we race back to Stratford One. It's getting late, and we have got a lot to discuss!

We walk into Stratford One, and I instantly realise we have a major problem. The night reception staff have set up a little table in the doorway – something they have never done before – and they are checking people's ID cards. On the table is a sign 'NO GUESTS ALLOWED'. You have got to be joking. 'Hello!' I beam, flashing my key card and walking straight past the man. 'Can I see your key card?', the security guy asks Max, who obviously does not have a bloody key card. 'Oh, he left it in his room!', I try to tell the man, 'do you not recognise him - we literally just walked out of here five minutes ago!' To say he does not believe me would be an understatement. We are sent over to the main reception desk, where the man on the desk demands to know who we both are. We try absolutely every trick in the book to get Max back in the building. Every single trick in the book fails miserably. 'He's my cousin!', I say, 'he's literally got nowhere else to stay!' The man on the desk does not give a toss. 'Well that's your problem, isn't it?' he replies, before asking me 'do you not understand English?'

Well, that's it. The Prosecco has now gone straight to my head, and I have launched into full 'Charity Shop Sue' mode. 'I need to speak to the manager', I demand over the desk, deciding that I'll just glare at this man until he gives in. I am informed that I will not be able to speak to the manager which, as you can imagine, riles me up even more. There is now practically steam coming out of my ears, as I try and decide whether to get Max to just run up the stairs and hope for the best!

I ask if Max can come up and get his stuff, and the answer is a definitive no. I, therefore, leave Max in the reception area, whilst I storm back to flat 007 to pack up his podcast equipment. On my way up to my flat, I try and open the fire exit door. In my mind, this means Max will be able to sneak in from outside. This does not quite go to plan, however, because opening the door has activated an alarm. For the love of God! The man from reception runs outside to defend his door, leaving Max on the streets of Stratford, with not even a podcast episode to show for it!

I get outside with Max's bags and a newfound determination to get this podcast episode filmed. I am adamant that we will not be defeated. There has to be a way, I say! Suddenly, I see the bright lights of the Premier Inn glistening just down the road. Oh my god, I say, let's go to the Premier Inn! At first, I am joking, but the more that I think about it, this could be an absolutely genius idea. The hotel is literally 30 seconds away! Surely it won't be too expensive on a weekday night during a global pandemic? Max looks online, and the Premier Inn is £100. Are they serious? Do you get a three-course dinner and swimming pool included in that pricing? 'Oooh hang on', says Max, 'where's the Travelodge? The Travelodge is £40!'

'I know where that is!' I excitedly replied, 'let's do it – just book it!' Fast forwards fifteen minutes, and we have arrived at the Stratford Travelodge. It turned out that the Travelodge was on the other side of Stratford. So we enjoyed a lovely walk across the bridge and along Stratford High Street. We finally make it to the Travelodge, and head inside to check-in. 'Hi guys!' says the lovely lady on reception, 'what brings you to Stratford this evening?' Oh, what a good question, my love! We update this lovely lady on the night's events, and the security guard standing beside her cannot believe they have practically thrown Max out on the street. 'Don't get us started', we say, and wish them a good night! We head up in the lift and track down our room. The situation is both ridiculous and hilarious in equal measure. We have a lovely little room, complete with miniature kettle and milk pods. You can practically see Stratford One from the window. You really couldn't make this up, I say, as Max sets up his podcast equipment once again. The lighting is not ideal, but I have brought my ring light (of course I have), and so yet another disaster is averted! 'Right come on, let's do this', says Max, and we sit down to – at long last – record the podcast! Now I've got to be very honest with you: I could not tell you what comes out of my mouth in the next 90 minutes. The Prosecco, the drama, and the new bottle of rose I have now started pouring into plastic cups have all well and truly gone to my head. As you'll see in the YouTube footage of the recording, I end up shouting at Max about the hypocrisy of the Catholic Church and even grabbing onto the poor boy on more than one occasion. I enthusiastically answer his listener's questions and attempt to sound like an expert on theology (not easy when drinking rose from a plastic cup in a Travelodge). We make it to the end of the podcast, Max is still alive, and I have to say I have thoroughly enjoyed it. It's literally now about midnight, and we just have to take a minute to digest the events of the past few hours. 'The things you do for this podcast!', I tell Max, 'I hope this episode leads to a sponsorship deal from Travelodge!'

I leave Max to enjoy a night's sleep in Stratford's finest hotel, still not quite believing the events of this evening. It's not every Tuesday that you're practically thrown out of your £200 a week accommodation and end up filming a podcast on religion in a Travelodge bedroom! I have actually loved it, and I know I have found a friend for life. It really does feel like I have known Max for years, not just a couple of – albeit very eventful! - hours. I arrive back at Stratford One, where our friends are still guarding the doors as if they were defending the Tower of London. In a final act of defiance, I refuse to flash my key card as I strut past the little desk and head up the stairs. I glare back down at the little man sat at his desk, who then gestures that I need to be wearing a face mask. Oh, he's spoiling for World War Three tonight! In the words of my favourite icon Kim Woodburn, don't start with me, my love! By Christ, don't do it!

***

As you know, I believe that we can find meaning in everything that happens in our lives. I'm not saying that 'everything happens for a reason' because there are many things that happen in life that clearly don't have any positive purpose (e.g. a mass killing or natural disaster). But I do believe that we can choose and decide to find a purpose behind every single that happens in our lives. We have to realise that the universe will never present us with a challenge that we cannot overcome! We have to trust that we can survive every single setback that we face (because we can!) In this spirit of 'everything happens for a reason', I believe that lockdown was – in some ways – the best thing that ever happened to me! It was an awful and heartbreaking time for millions of people. And I wish, like everyone, that the global pandemic never happened! But (and I'm talking specifically about the abrupt end to my second year at university) I do think that I gained a lot and grew a lot, as a result of it all. For example, I was able to write my first book and spend quality time with my family! However, I think that we have to acknowledge the catastrophic consequences this whole situation has had on young people. For some reason, the government does not appear to care about the psychological implications of banning students from socialising or leaving their rooms for months on end. It was hard being back in London without being able actually to do anything. I had gone from being so busy in my first two years – I'd been working, going out and dating – to having absolutely nothing to do in my third. My only option was to spend all day in my room studying. Whilst I certainly had a lot of studying to be doing, this just wasn't good for my sanity or my soul! I do enjoy my own company, but not all day, every day, for weeks on end! I just didn't feel like I was bad in London. It felt like I was living in some dystopian horror movie! I love seeing Shadi in Pret and I love heading to Tower Bridge Wetherspoons for drinks with Morgan (before stricter Tier 2 rules were imposed). But London just doesn't feel the same in lockdown!

I cannot imagine how it has felt for the poor first-year university students! Their entire university experience has been ruined. It is utterly appalling. I cannot imagine spending my first few months living away from home living in lockdown with flatmates I had never met before! Socialising, going out, getting a job and living in the real world is an essential part of the university experience! I cannot help thinking that this government has led down millions of students across the country. Millions of students have had their university experiences ruined because of poor leadership and planning. I am so thankful I got to enjoy London as long as I did. Thank

God I went out, had fun and worked in a nightclub before lockdowns were imposed across the country! After a month back in London, I became utterly fed up with being confined to my student accommodation twenty-four hours a day, seven days a week. So I was glad to be heading back home for some Cheshire air! I've never been more thankful for technology and electronics! Thanks to the internet, we can work and talk to people, irrespective of whether we are actually allowed outside of our homes or not!

I wonder what future historians will make of this government's response to the coronavirus crisis? I wonder how future generations will reflect on the concept of 'locking down' millions of people for months on end. It is extraordinary that, in a liberal democracy, you will be fined for leaving your home or meeting up with your friends. Considering that 99.9% of young people who contract the coronavirus recover without any complications whatsoever, it is extraordinary that 100% of young people have been banned from socialising by the state. Whatever happened to individual autonomy and responsibility? Whatever happened to mental health and psychological wellbeing? Whatever happened to having a student experience?

43. ASPIRING TO INSPIRE

Despite the continuing fallout of the global health pandemic, I start my third and final year of university in a very positive headspace. As I say, I think that the lockdown has, in many ways, been very good for me. I've certainly been so blessed to have such a wonderful family around me. The lockdown has given me quality time at home with my family and allowed me to build a platform on TikTok. It has given me the time to write a 'self-help' style book, and it has also given me a chance to think ahead to the future. Whilst a global health pandemic was never going to be ideal, the lockdown has not been without its opportunities. I had fun drinking my White Zinfandel Rose and filming for TikTok! I went through the casting process for a TV series which sadly did not end up on the screen! And I even kept myself busy writing an 80,000-word book!

Most importantly, I genuinely learned so much about myself. The whole situation made me – and I'm sure so many of others – re-evaluate my priorities, principles and purpose in life. I woke up to the fact that life is too short. I woke up to the fact that our greatest sense of meaning and happiness in this world comes from pursuing our passions, connecting with others, and contributing to the common good. I realised that I am at my happiest when I'm working hard, keeping busy, and surrounded by the people I love. I had a fantastic opportunity to think and reflect on where I'm at in life, and what I'd like my future to look like.

Obviously, not seeing my friends, not being able to hug my grandparents, and not seeing Grandad before he so sadly died was hard – but I was also so blessed to be spending lockdown in the loveliest home with the most loving family. As Epictetus says, 'men are disturbed not by events but by the views they take of them'. By accepting a situation and resolving to make the best of it - rather than futilely struggling against it - we can thrive through life, irrespective of the conditions that we find ourselves in!

Returning to London whilst social distancing is still being heavily enforced means spending a lot of time talking into a webcam and socialising via FaceTime.

***

In terms of my personal 'road to recovery', I think that there's still some work to do. But that's fine – life, as I always say, is all about progress and not perfection! I've finally realised how often I self-sabotage my happiness and reputation because of my defensive responses to the slightest sign that someone may reject or belittle me. I've been able to acknowledge that I am fiercely defensive. And I have been able to identify my self-limiting doubts about whether I am genuinely loveable as a romantic partner. Despite my external confidence, I do still struggle to believe anyone would be genuinely interested in me. Ultimately, it's about learning to internalise the mantra that 'I am enough'. It's about that learning that putting yourself down in comparison to other 'better looking' or 'more attractive' people is the most counter-productive waste of your energy! And it's about learning that you will never be happy or feel secure in a relationship unless you can unconditionally accept who you are. You must confidently know your worth as a human being! Realise that there is only one of you in the entire universe. So you must celebrate, embrace and genuinely treasure who you authentically are!

I am becoming stronger and wiser with every year that passes. I'm learning to manage my emotions, challenge my irrational thoughts, and focus on doing things that make me genuinely happy. I have taken responsibility for my life. I am working harder than ever before to turn my dreams into my reality. And I am thoroughly enjoying every single step of the journey! I write this in the notes section of my phone:

"YOU ARE THE MASTER OF YOUR OWN DESTINY! You have nothing to prove, and there is nobody you have to impress. Just do what makes YOU feel happy and fulfilled! So if you want to wear mesh on a Monday and then wear a suit on Tuesday, do it! If you want to read a book on Wednesday and then go to a party on Thursday, do it! As long as you are happy and not causing harm to anybody else, never apologise for following your heart. Never apologise for making the

most of every single day that you have on this planet! Make a difference! Try to inspire everybody you meet! Make as many connections as you possibly can…make people feel amazing! Stop feeling the need to people-please and just get confident being you! AND MOST IMPORTANTLY…ENJOY YOUR JOURNEY!!!"

I think this little 'note to self' really encapsulates my new attitude and approach to life. I really do appreciate every single second of my existence. I really do cherish every single opportunity that I am so fortunate to get here on this planet. More than anything, I am thankful for the lessons I have learned on my journey through life. I could not appreciate adversity more! I know with complete conviction that I wouldn't be half the person I am proud to be today without going through everything that I've experienced so far in life! I am so grateful for the journey…and I am so excited about its future direction!

***

All of the Stratford One en-suite rooms have the same full-length mirror on the wall next to the desk. For the past three years, I have been staring into this rectangular mirror and scrutinising my appearance. Every morning and night, I would see myself in this mirror. I would look at my face, my waist, and my legs. These mirrors have seen some scandalous outfits and some shocking fake tan disasters, I can tell you! As I look in this mirror today, I notice a very significant shift in the way that I see myself. The mirror hasn't changed, and I haven't changed. But the lens through which I see myself has. The mindset through which I interpret the world could not be more different than it was the very first time I looked at myself in one of these rectangular mirrors.

I finally realise that, for at least eight years, I have had absolutely no concept of how skinny and slim I am. Even during my time in London, I have not realised just how skinny I am. It is shocking to think of how distorted my thinking has been…for SO many years! However, I am so happy to finally see things as they really are. The clouds are clearing, and a new dawn is breaking. I am so relieved to finally see myself as I really am. I am finally in a position to see just irrational my thoughts have been. I am now, at long last, determined to learn and determined to grow. I am determined to see myself, and the world, with real clarity and accuracy. I cannot believe how delusional I have been for so long! I am absolutely determined to look forwards to the future with more clarity and insight than ever before!

Who is this wise and emotionally intelligent individual staring back at me in the mirror? Who is this confident, self-assured, and ambitious young man who I can see in front of me? The last couple of years have taught me so much. I have learned so much about who I am and what makes me happy in life. I have become so much more confident, resilient and self-aware. I have faced so many fears, done so many new things, and consequently grown so much as a person. Perhaps most importantly, I believe that I see myself – and my body – in a more rational way than I ever have before. It's like I can see my body as it really is, not through the distorting filter of my irrational thoughts. It's like I can finally accept myself as I authentically am.

After years of therapy, reading, and meditation, I have learned how to healthily manage my emotions and intelligently communicate how I feel. And, whilst I still have moments of insecurity and defensiveness, I know with confidence that I am making progress. For a start, I have more self-awareness than I have ever had before. I am finally capable of seeing myself as I really am, and I am finally beginning to work out where I really want to be in life. I'm older, I'm wiser – and I have never been happier!

Perhaps most importantly, I have realised that life is about progress, not perfectionism. I don't need to get everything right or have everybody on side tobe a good person. As long as I am heading in the right direction and striving to grow through every experience that I go through, then I can feel satisfied and secure in my own skin. When we make our family, friends, core values, passions, and growth mindset our priority, we can't go far wrong! When we live with a desire to make a positive difference in the world, we discover the most amazing sense of purpose in our lives.

I'm learning to be self-confident, and I am daring to keep stepping outside of my comfort zone. I am daring to be authentic. I am daring to be confident. And I am learning to be resilient. And I hope that, after reading my story, you might just dare to do the same. Because if I can find authenticity, confidence, and resilience, then so can you. So I urge you: Be proud of who you authentically are. Do more of the things that scare you. Dream bigger than you have ever dreamed of before. Take risks, seize opportunities, and make memories…every single day of your life! Remember: if you can dream it, you can achieve it! Things will not necessarily be plain-sailing, but always remember that you can handle whatever challenges life sends your way! You are an amazing and incredible human being. You have infinite worth, and you have limitless potential. Whatever you are going through, you've got this. Whatever you dream of achieving in life, you can achieve it! Be authentic, be confident, and believe in yourself! Learn from every single thing that you go through, and be proud of every single thing that you have overcome.

Most importantly, enjoy the journey! You only live once, so live every single day to the absolute full. You deserve it.

AFTERWORD

This book has, I hope both you and Debbie the Café Nero psychic would agree, quite a journey! As I write this, I am looking out of my bedroom over the Olympic Park. I can see the stadium, the Orbit landmark and, in the distance, the iconic London skyline. I think back to the time when I was last here in the Olympic Park, a whole eight years earlier. Back then, I was in the middle of my battle with anorexia, unable to break free from my irrational thoughts and an obsession with calories. If only anorexic young Ben could have seen me now! If only anorexic young Ben could have glanced over at the Stratford One student accommodation and have realised – don't worry, everything is going to be okay! You are going to get through this, and you are going to be back here, in London, absolutely thriving and living your very best life! I would never have believed – not in a million years – that this is how my life would turn out. It feels too good to be true. In my head, I'm still the ambitious but secretly insecure young sixth former dreaming of moving to the bright lights of the big city. I have to pinch myself and remind myself that this isn't a dream anymore – I have managed to turn my dreams into my reality! I'm actually here, living in London and studying the course of my dreams!

Even in these Covid-19 times, being in London is a dream come true. I cannot believe this is my third and final year of studying in London. When I think back to the first day that I arrived here, I genuinely get emotional thinking about how much I have grown and how much more confident I have become. My time working at Heaven, my amazing flatmates and friends, and just the fact that I have been…LIVING IN LONDON! I remember being 17 and timidly walking past the gay clubs on Canal Street in Manchester, trying to imagine what it must be like to go inside and have a night out on the gay scene. Never did I imagine I'd spend over a year working at the heart of the London gay scene,

Every time I walk down to the university, down Holborn and onto the Strand, I have to pinch myself to confirm it is real. Yes, I have just got the

Central Line into university. Yes, I *have* just walked over Waterloo Bridge as part of my daily commute!

Never in a million years did I genuinely believe that this would be my reality. Never in a million years did I imagine that I would be here, in London, living what I genuinely believe to be my very best life. I feel blessed beyond words and incredibly proud of what my ambition and hard work has achieved.

I wonder how it will feel when, in years to come, I tell my children and grandchildren about my adventures in London? I wonder if any of them will want to follow in my footsteps, or whether my stories will put them off going anywhere near London for life?! I can't wait to bring them down to London for day trips and show them the sights. I'll point out every single Wetherspoons I have been to for a glass of rose or two (that excursion could end up taking some time)!

Here's what I want to say: if I can overcome a life-threatening mental illness, turn my life around, and achieve my dreams, then so can you. Let me just repeat that for you: If I can do it, then so can you. Dream big, work hard and believe in yourself. Make connections, spread love, and remember how important the people in your life are. Never tire of telling them how much you love them, and never let your fears and anxieties stop you from reaching out to people and making new friends. Life is far too short to be anything but fearlessly authentic and unapologetically fabulous!

Life is so precious, and our time on this planet is so short. You do not know when your time – or a loved one's time – is going to come to an end. We, therefore, have no option but to seize every day, embrace every opportunity, and live every single second of our lives to the absolute full. Never say 'no' to an opportunity you are interested in! Never let fear hold you back from living your life to the full! There is no guarantee that you will get to enjoy tomorrow, and so you must live a fearless and truly fabulous life today!

Stop holding back and stop worrying about what other people think! Stop putting yourself down and stop selling yourself short! Start saying 'yes' to more opportunities, and start believing in your limitless potential as a human being! Dare to put yourself out there, dare to make a positive difference in the world, and dare to live your very best life. Dare to take on new challenges, dare to be fearlessly authentic, and dare to enjoy your journey.

There's only one of you, and this is your one lifetime. So be proud of yourself, be kind to yourself, and make this journey one to remember. Dare to live your best life. You deserve it. You've got this. X

#ShareYourStory

Don't forget to tag me on social media!

Instagram: benwardle_

Twitter: benwardle_

TikTok: benwardle_

Get 10% off my self-help books 'Live Your Best Life' and '101 Mantras For Life'

Apply the code 'SAVE10' when you checkout online at www.benwardle.org/shop

Printed in Poland
by Amazon Fulfillment
Poland Sp. z o.o., Wrocław